Stories from *Pioneer Post*

Stories from *Pioneer Post*

compiled by

Thelma Batchelor

George Ronald
Oxford

George Ronald, *Publisher*
Oxford
www.grbooks.com

*A catalogue record for this book is available
from the British Library*

ISBN 978-0-85398-544-0

Pioneering is the greatest bounty that can come to one – one steps into a new arena of service . . . one stands on the threshold of this arena and knows that there is only one weapon that will permit victory. There is only one weapon that we have that will absolutely guarantee victory, and that weapon is complete reliance on Bahá'u'lláh. One prays every step of the way. One feels within oneself a new connection with God, a sense of nearness is born because one soon becomes aware of answers – the path being marked for one; the needs of self that seemed so important at home, that took up so much time and energy fall away or find a new level. One knows, eventually, that one is never alone, one feels a new dimension, one walks the mystical way with practical feet. There are tests – one cannot step into the arena and have focused on one the spiritual spotlight of service without exposing weakness. This, too, is part of the bounty. One begins to know himself. So I would say to anyone – grab the chance before it's too late. Embrace this bounty. Have no fear. Step into the arena. Above all things, pray that one will succeed, will not falter halfway across the arena. What a great bounty to have been born now, in the early days, when pioneering is possible . . . when you offer to pioneer you don't need to know where you're going, you don't need to care where you're going. Because you're going out you will be guided by Bahá'u'lláh. We are blessed that God will assist all those who will arise to serve Him. We know that we are accompanied by a band of chosen angels who will open the doors and prepare the way for us . . .

John Robarts[1]

To my husband and pioneering partner Ron

with whom I shared eleven years in the international pioneering field

in the Solomon Islands and Nepal

and to our pioneering children

Simon, who was born in Honiara,

and Suzanne,

who spent their childhood growing up in Kathmandu.

And, of course,

to all the wonderful pioneers and travel teachers around the world,

without whose stories this book would not have been possible.

THANK YOU for writing!

Contents

Foreword

The newsletter *Pioneer Post UK* was initiated in 1988. Through it, Bahá'í pioneers from the United Kingdom have, over the years, enjoyed the stories of other pioneers and I have had the pleasure of editing them. These stories have become a captivating record of what pioneering life overseas is like and they are now part of our Bahá'í history. After reading and editing these stories for more than two decades, I felt it was time that other Bahá'ís, in the UK and around the world, should know of the pioneers' exploits, their sacrifices and their achievements.

Here are the stories of Bahá'ís young and old who heeded Shoghi Effendi's advice to 'plumb greater depths of consecration',[2] who answered the call of the Universal House of Justice to take the Faith of Bahá'u'lláh to remote parts and who arose with verve and passion to teach the Faith in Africa, the Americas, the cold north, the far south and 'in the islands of the North Sea and of the Mediterranean, as well as in the remote territories situated in the Pacific'.[3]

Their stories are those of modern heroes and heroines. Poignant, touching, insightful, some of the stories will make you cry, others will make you shake with laughter. If you have ever been pioneering, you will recognize yourself here. If you haven't, these stories will motivate you to go. They will inspire all who fondly dream of following in the footsteps of earlier pioneers and, indeed, of standing on the shoulders of giants.

Also included here are the stories of travel teachers and the youth who answered the call of the House of Justice to dedicate a year of their lives to the service of the Faith. Their stories are variously heartwarming, funny, poignant and uplifting.

In the more than two decades that this collection of pioneer stories spans, significant events have taken place in the Bahá'í world. Times change. Countries that were closed to the Faith at the beginning of the narrative opened to it after a few years; countries developed and became easier to travel to and conditions improved. At the same time, the challenges of teaching the Faith sometimes increased. New Plans were initiated by the Universal House of Justice, with different goals and new ways of teaching and consolidating believers. These stories reflect these changes. The stories also sometimes reveal the naivety of the Bahá'ís, as well as their enthusiasm, their initial shock at how different things are from the way they are in Britain, and their gradual appreciation of the country to which they have pioneered and the people they have gone to serve.

Some of the pioneers tell stories of difficult periods, of hardships and the tests and trials of pioneering. There can be times when no one appears to be interested in hearing about the Faith and others when pioneers are joyfully able to relate how their teaching efforts have resulted in their friends becoming Bahá'ís. All pioneers face culture change and in time learn to adapt to it. Sometimes they find themselves living in inhospitable climes and are lonesome for Bahá'í companionship and activity. But isolated pioneers are like lamps – representing a force for good, like a lighthouse of Bahá'u'lláh shining at a strategic point and casting its beam out into the darkness.

These stories are about pioneering experiences the world over. Included are contributions from long-term pioneers, short-term pioneers and travelling teachers. They have written about a multitude of subjects – their travels, their friends, their services to the Faith as pioneers. Sometimes their travels have involved very long journeys over great distances, such as the seven-day train ride in Russia for delegates attending National Convention. Teaching trips have often involved riding in run-down buses or in the back of trucks. One intrepid traveller paddled his kayak 'Bahá'í Viking' from Sweden through Europe in an effort to reach Istanbul but, sadly, weather conditions made him give up the trip in Odessa. The same traveller, a few years later, walked and hitched lifts from his homeland in Scotland across Europe as far as Cyprus – travel teaching on the way – before finally taking a flight to Israel in order to arrive on time for his pilgrimage. Pioneers have written about their services as schoolteachers in Bahá'í-inspired schools, about life in places as remote from each other as Botswana, Venezuela, Guyana and Greenland. The trials of the world have not passed them by and they have written about tribal war in Ghana, and the devastation of a category 4 hurricane on the Caribbean island of Grenada. Travel teachers have visited Krakow, Tirana, Dar es Salaam, Kampala, Ulaanbaatar, Fiji and a host of other places.

Pioneers have dangled their feet in the bright blue seas surrounding the Marshall Islands in the Pacific Ocean, have travelled north to the Copperbelt in Zambia, have won prestigious awards for services to their adopted countries. Many have become involved in drama and the arts. They have raised families in their pioneering posts and, in turn, often the children of these families have themselves become international pioneers. Several families have been in their pioneer posts for over 40 years, a remarkable record of perseverance, love and a sense of duty. Some pioneers have pioneered to more than one country and have written more than once of their experiences. Many British pioneers have served on National Spiritual Assemblies around the world, others have served as Counsellors and Auxiliary Board members.

Recent years have seen the emergence of the institute process around the globe. The core activities have become the new focus of the Bahá'í world and this has resulted in study circles, devotional meetings, children's classes and junior youth activities being given high priority attention on the part of pioneers.

UK pioneers were present at the UN Conference on Environment and Development in Rio, Brazil in 1992, and at the Bahá'í World Congress in New York later the same year. They have experienced the joy of living through the Holy Year in Mongolia, the tragedy of war in Belgrade. They have experienced the extremes of heat and cold by living close to the Arctic in Alaska or Greenland or near the Equator in Central Africa or in some of the tropical islands of the South Pacific. Others have recalled earlier days of teaching in Ireland, in the Solomon Islands, in Nepal. Pioneers have memories of some of the Hands of the Cause of God and of earlier pioneering servants of Bahá'u'lláh – such sweet memories.

These pioneers have, in the course of their travels, made pilgrimages to the Bahá'í World Centre in Haifa and to Edirne in Turkey and, of course, visited the Bahá'í Houses of Worship on each continent. They have provided us with glimpses of the sacred and the glorious. They have attended summer schools, National and International Conventions, and they have met with kings and presidents and princesses. They have made short-term visits to remote islands such as Malaita in the Solomon Islands, to St Helena in the South Atlantic, have settled as lone pioneers in Corfu, and served the Faith long and diligently in the Faroe Islands in the North Atlantic. They have become increasingly aware of environmental and educational issues facing the world at large, they have taken part in women's forums, been concerned about ageing parents back home, worried about sending their children away to be educated.

There were pioneers who attended the funeral in Haifa of Hand of the Cause Rúḥíyyih Khánum in January 2000. Other pioneers were present at the gathering of Counsellors and Auxiliary Board members in Haifa in January 2001 when a new epoch of the Formative Age was announced to the Bahá'í world. And then there were the fortunate pioneers who had the privilege of attending the inaugural ceremony of the opening of the Terraces on Mount Carmel in May 2001. As a result of the Knights of Bahá'u'lláh going out in the Ten Year Crusade, 50-year anniversaries of the establishment of the Faith were celebrated in a number of countries around the globe and their achievements marvelled at by present-day visitors and pioneers. The final story records the spirit of the 41 Regional Conferences called by the Universal House of Justice for 2008 and 2009.

Pioneers have written about feeling happy, about feeling sad, about the challenges all too often facing them in their pioneer posts, of tragic happenings and of happy ones; from sadness about being air-lifted out of their surroundings because of approaching danger, to the happiness of being able to adopt African children. Last, but not least, there are those pioneers who, having left their pioneer posts and returned to the United Kingdom, have felt moved to write about their feelings on returning 'home'. Life is full of 'hellos' and 'goodbyes' and the pioneer is acutely aware of the number of times these occur.

Not all stories can be told. At present there are regions of the world classed as 'sensitive teaching areas' and, for reasons of prudence, no mention can be made of them in this book. And to use every story written for *Pioneer Post* over the years would have made this book an impossible length. Permission has been received from everyone whose stories are published in this book – some 180 stories representing in total some 70 countries.

The voices of the authors have not been changed in the editing of this book. They write with their colloquialisms and colour, and we all wanted to keep it this way.

***

There was a great desire to go pioneering overseas during the 1960s and 1970s. Most of my Bahá'í friends travelled overseas to serve the Faith during this period (more often than not to those countries coloured pink on the map of the world at the time).

My own urge to go pioneering began at Teaching Conference in Manchester in January 1970 when there was a call for overseas pioneers. I desperately wanted to pioneer – but I couldn't at that time because I was going to be married the following month and it wasn't convenient! I sat there with tears pouring down my face! A lovely Bahá'í friend, Ronald Bates, said to me that I shouldn't worry about not volunteering at the time because if the urge was there, I would be given the chance to go pioneering at a later date.

I was married in February 1970 and just a month or two later my husband, Ron, was given at work a list of countries to which he could be posted by the British Government and where he could carry out his professional work as a structural engineer. Amongst these countries was the Solomon Islands in the South Pacific, a country then requiring pioneers. At the time Ron was not a Bahá'í but he applied for the post and was successful. However, on the way out to our pioneering post, we stopped in Haifa for a three day visit and Ron declared his faith as a Bahá'í in the Shrine of the Báb! So, in the end, there were two of us going out as pioneers, not one!

The second time we had the priceless privilege of international pioneering was to Kathmandu, Nepal, with our two small children. If anyone had told us before we left the UK just how much ill health we would suffer, we would most likely not have gone. Thankfully we knew nothing of the times ahead, and in retrospect we are eternally grateful, for we would not have wished to miss those most precious nine years in Nepal for all the tea in China! The Solomon Islands and Nepal were very different from one another (one was of the ocean and the other landlocked for a start) but in both countries we learned valuable lessons whilst sharing our years with the remarkable indigenous believers of those beautiful countries and with other international pioneers.

We have to admit that often we missed our fellow Bahá'ís back home and it was as a result of having pioneered and returning to live in the United Kingdom that the need was felt to launch some sort of newsletter to communicate and share news amongst the British pioneers around the world. While living in Nepal we had felt quite envious of the American pioneers who were regularly kept in touch with each other by means of their pioneer newsletters and so the idea became reality and crystallized into *Pioneer Post UK*. Rapid advances in technology have meant that over the years my job as Editor has become easier. For instance, when I started *Pioneer Post* I was using an electric typewriter. Kind friends used to offer to photocopy as many as 200 copies so that these could be airmailed by post to each UK pioneer. With the advent of computers, and then email, life took on a new meaning when it came to the much more rapid distribution of *Pioneer Post* through cyberspace. Now the *Post* is distributed far and wide to UK pioneers at the press of a button – and also to many hundreds of other friends interested in reading the stories contributed by our UK pioneers.

For the present generation of Bahá'ís the call to pioneering is as urgent as it always has been. The Universal House of Justice has underlined the importance of pioneering, saying:

> The desire to pioneer arises naturally from deep within the heart of the individual believer as a response to the Divine summons. Whosoever forsakes his or her home for the purpose of teaching the Cause joins the ranks of those noble souls whose achievements down the decades have illumined the annals of Bahá'í pioneering. We cherish the hope that many will be moved to render this meritorious service during the next Plan, whether on the home front or in the international field - an act that, in itself, attracts untold blessings.[4]

The call for a 'concerted effort' to produce an 'outflow of pioneers' to 'areas destined to become the theatre of future conquests'[5] is for each one of the followers of Bahá'u'lláh to respond to as best we may. We cannot all be like

Martha Root or Marion Jack but we can at least try to follow in their footsteps.

O that I could travel, even though on foot and in the utmost poverty, to these regions, and, raising the call of 'Yá Bahá'u'l-Abhá' in cities, villages, mountains, deserts and oceans, promote the divine teachings! This, alas, I cannot do. How intensely I deplore it! Please God, ye may achieve it.

'Abdu'l-Bahá[6]

Thelma Batchelor
Leatherhead, Surrey
January 2010

Introduction

The annals of the British Bahá'í community, small in numbers, yet unconquerable in spirit, tenacious in belief, undeviating in purpose, alert and vigilant in the discharge of its manifold duties and responsibilities, have in consequence of its epoch-making achievements been vastly enriched.

Shoghi Effendi[7]

They that have forsaken their country for the purpose of teaching Our Cause – these shall the Faithful Spirit strengthen through its power. A company of Our chosen angels shall go forth with them, as bidden by Him Who is the Almighty, the All-Wise. How great the blessedness that awaiteth him that hath attained the honour of serving the Almighty! By My life! No act, however great, can compare with it, except such deeds as have been ordained by God, the All-Powerful, the Most Mighty. Such a service is, indeed, the prince of all goodly deeds, and the ornament of every goodly act.

Bahá'u'lláh[8]

'Pioneer' is a hard-worked word in Bahá'í parlance, and it means, according to *Webster's Dictionary*, 'One who goes before into that which is unknown or untried, to remove obstructions or to prepare the way for others.'

In one way or another we can all be pioneers – pioneering the Faith in our own lives, with our families, at work, at school, in our communities and amongst our friends. It is as if we are cutting a pathway through the jungles of uncertainty and mistrust to enable others either to follow that path or make their way towards their own thrilling encounter with Bahá'u'lláh. Pioneering, then, may not necessarily be a question of place but of attitude: when Bahá'u'lláh refers to 'forsaking their country', He may also be thinking of forsaking things familiar – patterns of behaviour, approaches to problem-solving and constraints to thinking and imagination.

From the point of view of the purpose of this book, however, the following two descriptions may best fit the definition of a pioneer:

Any believer who arises and leaves his home to journey to another country for the purpose of teaching the Cause is a pioneer.

The Universal House of Justice[9]

[Pioneering] is basically and clearly intended to establish the Faith of God securely and firmly in the hearts of people of the area and to ensure that its divinely-ordained institutions are understood, adopted and operated by them. *The Universal House of Justice*[10]

'The first great travelling teachers and settlers in foreign lands – who later became known as "pioneers" – were the Persian believers in the nineteenth century, followed, during the first decades of the twentieth century by Bahá'ís primarily of North American origin' in response to 'Abdu'l-Bahá's 'Tablets of the Divine Plan'[11] revealed in the middle years of the First World War. Since then, as the Bahá'í Faith has encircled the planet and plans have been laid before the Bahá'ís, first by the Guardian of the Bahá'í Faith and then by the Universal House of Justice, believers from many and various countries have left their own native lands to settle in other areas of the globe in order to establish the Faith's teachings.

There is no such profession as pioneer or teacher in the Bahá'í Faith as there are professional missionaries or clergymen in other religions.

A pioneer or a travelling teacher does not go out to another country to make people over in his own image and to teach them his personal opinions and the customs of his nation, he goes out to tell them Bahá'u'lláh has come and that they too are welcome to drink from the life-giving waters of His Revelation and be recreated by them as we hope we ourselves have been . . . there is not yet a Bahá'í world order or Bahá'í culture or civilization; the tiny embryo of these is developing in the Faith through the spread of its teachings and the establishment of its Administrative Order all over the world. No one knows how much or how little of any one race's, nation's or tribal group's customs and outlook may eventually become part of the glorious future World Order.[12]

'The threshold of a new and glorious epoch'[13] emerged when the Africa Campaign was launched (1950–3) following the successful conclusion of the Six Year Plan in Britain. In 1950 the British Bahá'í community was called upon by Shoghi Effendi to spearhead and coordinate four national Bahá'í communities in a Two Year Plan to spread the Bahá'í Faith in Africa.

So magnificent an achievement has, no doubt, endowed the entire community, now representative of the peoples of England, Wales, Scotland and Ireland, with tremendous potentialities, empowering it to launch on the first stage of its historic overseas mission destined to bring that community into closer and more concrete association with its sister communities in North America and Egypt, for the purpose of promoting the Faith in the vast virgin territories where its banner is still unraised and which constitute an integral part of the territories of the British Crown beyond the confines of that community's homeland.

... How great the honour with which the Bahá'í pioneers of the present generation of the subjects of the British Crown will be invested in the eyes of posterity within their island home and abroad! How great the debt of gratitude of those who will labour after them and garner the fruit of their present day assiduous exertions to those whose privilege is to blaze the trail and break the soil in the virgin territories destined, as prophesied by 'Abdu'l-Bahá, to acclaim the Faith of Bahá'u'lláh and establish the institutions of His embryonic World Order![14]

Claire Gung, a German-born nurse who had become a Bahá'í in Torquay, left Britain in 1950 for Tanganyika; Philip Hainsworth pioneered to Uganda in June 1951: Hasan and Isobel Sabri left for Tanganyika in July 1951, and Ted Cardell for Kenya in October 1951. 'The Plan was successfully concluded in April 1953, being the first plan involving international cooperation in the Bahá'í world and thus laying the groundwork for subsequent international teaching plans.'[15]

In 1953 the Ten Year Crusade was launched by Shoghi Effendi. During the Crusade Bahá'ís dispersed far and wide over the face of the globe to plant the banner of Bahá'u'lláh in no less than 131 new countries and territories. This was the period of the Knights of Bahá'u'lláh – Bahá'ís who pioneered to places where no Bahá'í had previously lived – a number of whom left for their pioneering posts from the British Isles. The Guardian eagerly awaited cables informing him 'whenever a pioneer entered a new territory', 'giving the name, place, and any pertinent information'.[16] In the Crusade the British National Assembly collaborated with the other 11 National Spiritual Assemblies then existing, sharing the burden and responsibility for ensuring the settlement of pioneers in the 'virgin' territories and islands specified by Shoghi Effendi. He constantly encouraged the British National Assembly not only to send out pioneers into the virgin areas but also to translate Bahá'í literature into a number of languages. So important did he consider this that he himself would from time to time arrange for a gift of money to be sent to assist the National Assembly to accomplish it.[17]

In a letter written on 25 June 1953, the Guardian praised the accomplishments of the British Bahá'ís:

The successive victories won, in recent years, by the British Bahá'í community, proclaiming, on the one hand, the triumphant conclusion of the first collective enterprise undertaken in British Bahá'í history on the morrow of the centenary celebrations of the Founding of the Faith of Bahá'u'lláh, and on the other, the successful termination of the Two Year Plan, marking the inauguration of the community's historic Mission beyond the confines of its homeland, have immensely enhanced its prestige throughout the entire Bahá'í world, have won for it the abiding gratitude and profound admiration of all who labour for our beloved Faith, and entitled it to assume a prominent share in the conduct of the world spiritual Crusade launched amidst the festivities signalizing the climax of the celebrations of this Holy Year commemorating the centenary of the birth of the Mission of the Author of the Bahá'í Dispensation.

Much has been achieved in the course of the past nine years, both within the borders of this community's island home, and throughout the widely scattered Dependencies of the British Crown, on the shores as well as within the heart of the vast and far-off African Continent, to merit the pride that fills the hearts of its staunch and stalwart members, to deserve the applause of the Concourse on High, to evoke the fondest hopes for the steady unfoldment and ultimate consummation of the historic Mission entrusted to the care of the British followers of the Cause of Bahá'u'lláh, and to befittingly usher in a new Era in British Bahá'í history – an Era that will for ever remain associated with the systematic introduction of God's triumphant Faith, through the concerted efforts of the heroic band of Bahá'í pioneers, dwelling within the British Isles, into the Chief Dependencies of the British Crown scattered throughout the European and Asiatic continents and the islands and archipelagos of the Seven Seas.[18]

In a letter written on 11 July 1956 Shoghi Effendi again praised the British Bahá'í community for its achievements in the field of international pioneering:

Its sister communities in both the East and the West, and particularly its daughter communities, now blossoming into new life, and marching forth, unitedly and resolutely, along the path traced for them in the Ten Year Plan, cannot but feel proud of the tremendous work first initiated in the heart of Africa by British Bahá'í pioneers, and of the organizing ability, the sound judgement, the unquestioning fidelity, and the dogged determination that have characterized every stage in the rise, the development and fruition of the first collective enterprise embarked upon beyond the confines of the British Isles by the British adherents of the Faith of Bahá'u'lláh.[19]

Over the years British pioneers have settled in tens of countries around the world: 'It is estimated that between 1951 and 1993, Bahá'ís from the United Kingdom settled in 138 countries. It is probable that only Iran and the United States have sent out more pioneers than the United Kingdom, and they have much larger Bahá'í communities.'[20] There can be few countries where British pioneers are not found today. As well as to Africa, they pioneered to the Pacific islands, to the Mediterranean islands and, in particular, to the Republic of Ireland in order to help establish its first National Spiritual Assembly in 1972. When it was possible to travel freely to Eastern Europe in the early 1990s British pioneers moved in numbers to help establish communities in what were once the 'iron curtain' countries.

Youth especially have been at the forefront of taking the Bahá'í Faith to Eastern Europe and the former Soviet Union. A Youth Year of Service Desk was set up in the United Kingdom in 1994 to encourage young people to volunteer a year of service and facilitate their efforts to provide help and assistance to blossoming Bahá'í communities around the world.

Stories from Pioneer Post gives us a glimpse of the lives of pioneers from the UK in the closing decades of the 20th century and the opening decade of the 21st.

Acknowledgements

Many years ago in Kathmandu, Zena Sorabjee (then a Counsellor for the Indian sub-continent) gave me the idea of initiating a newsletter by which UK pioneers could keep in touch with each other. The idea was brought to fruition a few years later after we had returned to live in the UK when the International Goals Committee asked me if I would be interested in starting up such a newsletter.

Over the years I have been extremely grateful to the international pioneers and travel teachers who have provided me with constant support and encouragement, especially, during the past few months, those pioneers whose stories are included in this book. They have answered my questions and provided me with biographical information almost at the drop of a hat. Thank God for email!

I wish to thank my husband, Ron, for his continual support during the past years and months while, immersed in *Stories from Pioneer Post*, I have spent more time facing my computer than facing him.

Also, I greatly appreciate the assistance which Wendi Momen has provided me in reviewing and editing the text and to Erica Leith for all her hard work in turning the manuscript into a book. Also I am grateful for the enthusiasm and encouragement given me through the years by Rita Bartlett; also to Ged King who has helped me with the intricacies of the *Pioneer Post* website. Lastly, but not least, to our Baha'i friends in Nepal for it was there that I first got the urge to be of some service to other pioneers in the pioneering field.

October 1988*
Gayle and David Rutstein
Caroline Islands, Micronesia

Gayle grew up in Henley-on-Thames. She married David from the USA and they pioneered to Ponape in 1987. David writes:

We feel so lucky, so honoured to be here. The small hardships we've faced and will face are well worth the privilege of being on this lovely island among such a fascinating people. Work at the hospital is really interesting. The physical structure of the hospital is less than ideal but it serves its function of providing usually dry shelter for the incredible numbers of inpatients and their families, outpatients and their families that fill the halls, large open wards, outpatient clinic and semi-attached Public Health Department.

The practice of medicine in this setting is very different from that of home. It is not uncommon to have literally hundreds of patients waiting, quite patiently and quietly, to be seen in the out-patient department by one or two physicians. The examining rooms are usually in disarray and poorly stocked. The pharmacy, the only source and supply of prescription medicines on the island, is understaffed and under-supplied. It frequently runs out of critical medicines with little or no recourse for obtaining them until the next shipment arrives from Maryland or Sydney or Tokyo. The lights even go out in the operating room with the back-up generator not generating. Surgeries have been completed with flashlights, kerosene lamps, even candles. But, despite these and many other 'idiosyncrasies' of Pohnpeian medical practice, there is a great deal that can be accomplished. The patients, as a whole, are very compliant; much more compliant than western populations. The standard of health is so far below average western standards that even small improvements have far-reaching effects. And, for the most part, with a little patience and lowering of one's expectations, one can practise medicine in a rewarding fashion with results that are tangible and without many of the complications of western practice such as malpractice worries, insurance paperwork, numerous committee meetings and burdensome 'on-call' schedules.

For the most part my daily responsibilities centre around the busy outpatient clinic. When someone wants to see a physician he either takes his

---

*   The dates in the headings refer to the section of *Pioneer Post* in which the original story appeared.

chances in the emergency room or he comes through the out-patient clinic. This holds for everyone on the island, from the ordinary villager to the president of the country. Consequently, I have got to know lots of people in Pohnpei. It's interesting because I see my patients (which is basically everyone on the island) everywhere I go. I'm on 'general call' three times a month, which consists of seeing all the patients that come through the emergency room in a 24 hour period as well as caring for all the in-patients from 4:30 in the afternoon until 8:00 the next morning. In addition, I am on OB (Obstetrics) call every third night and every third weekend. Midwives do nearly all the normal (and some-times not so normal) deliveries. I am only called to attend to the complicated ones. There are no foetal monitors, no IV pumps. We do have an ultrasound machine donated by some missionaries. It's an equestrian ultrasound machine that's meant for horses but it's very useful in the labour room. We have no radiologist so all x-rays and ultra-sounds are interpreted by the physician who orders them. There is no pathologist. Necessary specimens are sent either to Honolulu or to Manila with, generally, a three week turn around time. We have a physical therapy department but no crutches or braces. There is a psychiatric ward but no psychiatrist. In addition to hospital-based medicine, physicians on Pohnpei are periodically sent to the outer islands of Pohnpei State, some of which are reached by plane (one to two hours) and others by ship (five to ten days). These outer islands are atolls and are the places people have heard about, where scores of wreath-bearing canoes come paddling out to greet the visiting ship. A general clinic is held when the doctor makes a visit and is often fol-lowed (or preceded) by some sort of feast with lots of smiling, staring, waving and, of course, eating. The people are very gracious, very generous.

How difficult it is to describe the spirit of the Pohnpeians, a spirit that has survived domination and local rule by four different nations (Spain, Germany, Japan and America) while retaining so much of what is truly Pohnpeian. Although the superficial influences of other cultures are obvious everywhere in and around Kolonia (cement and tin houses, cars, western dress) the customs, beliefs and practices of a rather isolated and simple people have remained pretty much intact. A man may have served in the state or federal legislature or may have received an education in Guam or Hawaii and may own a size-able piece of land on an island where land is precious, yet his standing in the community is nonexistent if he does not own pigs and if he cannot or does not grow yams. A woman may own property, employ several people in her own small business and be related to the Nahnmwarki (roughly, this is the 'king' of the municipality), yet if she has not born children by her early twenties or does not know how to (or care to) cook any of a variety of yams in a multitude of ways, she is treated with suspicion and, occasionally, mockery.

2
January 1989
Conrad Lambert and Michael Hainsworth
A musical research and documentation trip in Southern Africa

Conrad writes:

We spent a lovely five days here in Malawi, the people being very poor but beautiful. We had a successful recording session at a teaching institute miles off the main road in the tea-farming region. The Bahá'í Centre building and land were of an exemplary standard as far as cleanliness, simple taste and beauty (physical and spiritual) were concerned. It was here that I felt the first regrets about being on a whistle-stop tour of these touching African regions. As the Bahá'í villagers danced up the road singing songs expressing their happiness at having spent the day with us and having sung to and with us, and the sun went down on the Bahá'í-owned woodland and the mothers started cooking the evening meal over the fire, I thought of the reverence that the choirs showed when singing for the recording. While singing songs about the suffering of Bahá'u'lláh, which they themselves had written, some gazed into the sky, others held their hands over their faces, even the small children had a stance like a prince. Though dressed in what we might call rags, their spirits shone: an example worthy of humbling a king. It most certainly had an effect upon me.

3
July 1989
Susan and Shidan Kouchek-zadeh
Guinea-Conakry, West Africa

Susan and Shidan pioneered from Manchester in 1966 to Sierra Leone and since 1975 have been pioneers in Conakry.

This is our fourteenth year in Guinea (our twenty-third in Africa). It's very easy for us to remember how long we've been here because, after 12 years of childlessness, our eldest daughter Vadiay was conceived soon after we pioneered on from Sierra Leone to Guinea.

The National Spiritual Assembly of Guinea has come to the end of its first year of life. It has not been easy for all the Assembly members to get together. Five of us live in the capital but three live in an area 300 or so km to the west.

The journey can take as little as five hours or as long as two days, depending on the state of the roads, the vehicles and the ferry that has to be used to cross the river. The ninth member is from the forest region in the northeast where we have our largest and main concentration of Bahá'ís and it's a minimum of two tough days' journey away.

At Christmas the National Assembly held its meeting in the forest region: the five Conakry members made the arduous trek and were amply rewarded by the cries of Alláh-u-Abhá that greeted us as we entered some of the villages that have a large proportion of Bahá'ís and by the Bahá'í songs they had composed and sung and the dancing of the communities. One village we entered after dark. We were met and escorted, stumbling in the obscurity, to some seats where we sat wondering for about 15 minutes, hearing only the occasional clang of steel hammer on wheel rim that summons people. Then we heard a soft distant singing which gradually swelled until a great throng of people with two or three lanterns between then surrounded us dancing and singing their greetings. It was overwhelming. The village Bahá'ís here in this predominantly animist region have really taken the Faith into their lives and made it part of themselves. They really USE the expression Alláh-u-Abhá, with many different meanings from 'Welcome' and 'How wonderful' through 'Order!' 'Hush now and listen' to 'Hear! Hear!' One village has built its own beautiful Bahá'í Centre out of bamboo with no material help and very little encouragement from anyone else (communications between them and the Assembly are very difficult and are really confined to actual visits). I hope the village Bahá'ís enjoyed our visit. It certainly did the NSA members a power of good.

In February we held the meeting in our other area where the few friends we saw are having the same long, hard struggle that we in Conakry experience. People can see the verities and goodness in the Faith but cannot bear or care to change from the religion of their grandfathers and families and tribe, that is Islam. And now the Muslims here have formed a League in which their only point of agreement is against the Bahá'í Faith and the clergy everywhere are warning the youth against 'a new and very attractive sect'.

Truly, to become a Bahá'í here, one has to be something of a hero . . . and we appreciate the small band of heroes that we have. We persevere and remember with joy our singing and dancing Bahá'ís of the forest.

4
July 1989
Marie and Eddie Whiteside
Falkland Islands

Marie and Eddie, from Northern Ireland, pioneered to Stanley in 1988. Previously they were pioneers in Ghana.

During Ayyam-i-Há we organized a treasure hunt for the children, which took them all over Stanley – the 'treasure' being buried in the sand – real pirate stuff! This was followed by a party in the town hall, to which the children could invite their friends. Both events were a huge success. The friends from Camp, the Humphreys and the O'Sheas, had come into town for a few days during Ayyam-i-Há, which gave us a wonderful opportunity to have the whole Bahá'í population of the Falklands together for a very useful consultation on the teaching work in the islands.

At Naw-Rúz we had a buffet dinner and party at our house with 35 adults and children attending. It was wonderful to have so many islanders present. They really made themselves at home and thoroughly enjoyed the occasion. It was a mild and warm evening so the children were able to spill over outside to play in our daughter Kerry's 'hut', known by the local children as the 'Bahá'í hut'! There were many opportunities to answer questions on the Faith. We also had the local media present and the following day a detailed report on the event was given on the Falkland Islands Broadcasting Service News Programme. We had more media coverage when at Riḍván there was an announcement on the radio about the election of the Assembly of Stanley and how at this time Bahá'ís all over the world were taking part in a unique worldwide election, mentioning some of the indigenous peoples of the world who are Bahá'ís.

Our monthly 15 minute broadcast 'Bahá'í Viewpoint' continues to go out. Eddie is now responsible for the formulating of this broadcast, which is a wonderful opportunity to reach everyone on the islands, since the radio is listened to widely and the broadcast goes out on prime time. Last month's broadcast was entitled 'Some Common Misconceptions about the Bahá'í Faith' and the next one will be 'What's New about the Bahá'í Faith?'

The first weekend school for nine years was held on 24 to 26 March at Goose Green, about 60 miles from Stanley. Now 60 miles might not sound far by UK standards but driving over the Camp on a rugged track took three hours (the *Camp* is the term used in the Falkland Islands to refer to any part of the islands outside of the islands' only significant town).

However, we were blessed with a beautiful sunny and mild morning as three Land Rovers full of adults and children set off from Stanley to make the trip, which took us over hills and valley, across wide sandy beaches and even through rivers – talk about the Wild West and covered wagons! On the way we passed Swan Inlet, where over 60 Black-Necked swans were swimming in the water. At last, rounding a bend there was Goose Green, nestling in the valley beside the sea, its little coloured roofs glistening in the morning sunlight. Goose Green is where Des and Cynthia O'Shea run the local school. The children of the settlement came running out to greet us and soon made friends with our lot.

One old lady whom Eddie and I went to visit lives in a beautiful two-storey stone cottage built in 1881 by her grandfather. The sea was lapping the bottom of her garden and she was fascinating to talk to as we sat by her peat fire munching the lovely scones and cakes she had just baked. The rest of the world seemed a million miles away – come to think of it, it very nearly is!

Des O'Shea told us there have been many repercussions following the weekend school and he has been asked questions about the Faith from many people in Goose Green who have known him for years and known he is a Bahá'í but who, up to now, have not shown any real interest. A few months ago we presented the new Governor to the islands with a copy of the peace message, the book *A Crown of Beauty* and a welcome letter on behalf of the Bahá'í community. It turned out he had already come across the Faith and was pleased to be able to renew his study of it.

I work for the Falkland Islands Development Corporation, which I like very much. Eddie is very busy with school. He is the only Spanish teacher and Spanish is taught throughout. He also takes an adult evening class, which has 30 people attending. The link we now have with Chile is a strong incentive for people to learn Spanish.

5

July 1989
Wendy Ayoub Lind
Greenland

Wendy, originally from London, pioneered to Sisimiut, Greenland, after spending three years in Denmark.

Greenland is an incredibly beautiful country. Everything is either very big or very small. Nothing in between! Nature is breathtaking but one must look up or down. There are hundreds of varieties of plants and flowers but all below our knees. There are no trees as we know them – only a few bush-like specimens in the far south. There are approximately 55,000 people in the whole of Greenland. Fifteen thousand are in Nuuk, the capital. Sisimiut is the second largest town, with a population of five thousand. We have two schools and I teach English, part-time, at one. We have a small hospital – seriously ill people are sent to Denmark. Our shopping facilities are limited. We have two banks, a post office, a city hall and a police station, two hotels (small), a heliport (you can travel only by boat or helicopter in Greenland). There are no roads between towns, no trains, no buses, except a school bus. Almost everyone has a boat, as we do. We fish a lot. The sea cod is delicious, as are the halibuts. Trout from the mountain lakes and streams is sweet and delectable and shrimp is readily available. We hunt caribou and the meat is lovely. We have very little in the way of vegetables, salad and fruit, as these are very expensive and all have to be imported. We have eight months of snow and about four to six months of below 0 degrees and often 20 to 30 degrees below. We have more sunshine than England but it's coupled with snow.

The Greenlanders are anxious to learn English so they love to talk to me and I have several private students. Many I teach just for the love of it and also to help in my Bahá'í teaching efforts. Life for the Greenlanders is hard and many non-Greenlanders who work here just don't care – when you do care, it is really appreciated and we are beginning to be asked about the Faith. I think the greatest gift I've learned from being here and not speaking the language is that teaching the Faith is an attitude. It has nothing to do with how much you know. You must really learn to love the people. Everywhere we go, anywhere in the world, if we are loving, kind, helpful and considerate of others, people will respond and then we can share the little we know. They may not become Bahá'ís but they will respect the Faith and who knows when the precious seed we plant will blossom and flower? The end result is not in our hands, we are just signposts pointing the way!

6

July 1989

Kathy and Hamid Farabi

Trinidad

Kathy and Hamid pioneered to Trinidad from Birmingham in 1978.

We would need to write a book to give an account of all the wonderful, sometimes incredible, experiences we have had in our almost 11 years of pioneering here.

We arrived in Trinidad in August 1978. We were much better off than most pioneers who go through real hardships. Hamid had a good job with the university, which he obtained from England. So the university paid our fare and provided us with accommodation as soon as we arrived. Members of our beautiful Trinidadian Bahá'í family welcomed us at the airport and gave us all sorts of help and support, so that within a month we had bought a car and were taking part in all sorts of community activities.

We had only been married a year so there were just the two of us and we really didn't have any material problems. Hamid was well-travelled so he settled easily but I had real problems with homesickness. I had never left England before and I had never heard of culture shock, so I struggled a bit at first, but the experience we shared together really consolidated our marriage. Then at the end of the first year I was lucky enough to go home and was amazed to find how much I had developed and how difficult it was to relate to my non-Bahá'í relatives. It was like living in two different worlds at the same time. Now, 11 years and three children later (Ruhiyyih [9], Anisa [7], Samandar [16months]), and after buying our own home in 1987, we are both well-established. Hamid has even become a Trinidadian citizen and all the children were born here so I now have a real Trinidadian family and we have really taken root.

The people of Trinidad and Tobago are very special. Owing to historical circumstances over the centuries – colonialism, slavery, indenture, labourers, etc. – the people of Trinidad and Tobago are a mixture of many nationalities and races, for instance, people of African descent and East Indian descent, Chinese, Spanish, English, Irish, Lebanese – you name it! Along with this variety, there are four main religions – Hinduism, Christianity, Islam and the Bahá'í Faith. Yet, amid all this diversity people live peacefully alongside each other with amity and tolerance and mix and intermarry freely. These islands have often been called the embryo of the New World Order and surely this is how it will come about, through generations of different peoples living and being educated together. Prejudice is not innate – it has to be taught. Here they don't teach it because no one regards themselves as African, Indian or Chinese – they are all simply Trinidadians and Tobagians.

People respond well to the Bahá'í teachings because they can see it happening. After only half an hour of teaching, they declare as Bahá'ís. For many years Trinidad was very affluent and the teaching was slow but recently, owing to a recession, we have been astounded by the successes, with over a thousand new Bahá'ís in the past year, and the numbers growing daily. They also have a unique, official organization here called the Inter-Religious Organization which actually seeks to promote unity between the different religions. It is far more than an ecumenical movement. Its members are Hindus, Christians, Muslims and Bahá'ís and it hosts numerous interreligious services for all sorts of events and is quite influential.

There are many exciting things going on here at the moment, such as plans for mass teaching and the inclusion of the Bahá'í Faith in the official syllabus for the CXE Caribbean examination (equivalent to 'O' level). The opportunities for teaching are many and the response is good.

7
January 1990
Bill Brown
Ghana

Bill, originally from Liverpool, is living and working in Tamale in the Northern Region of Ghana.

My wife Paulina is from Ghana and we have three boys. Currently I am in charge of the building unit for the Catholic Diocese of Tamale. It involves the design, building and repair not only of churches but also of schools, offices and workshops, as the church is heavily involved in the development efforts of the country. My employers know of the Faith and one or two of the priests have shown some curiosity. A Dutch priest is quite impressed by the Faith and was very happy to receive some photos of the Indian Temple from his sister when she visited it in Delhi. I simply have to be careful that when I express views on matters of religion my hearers realize that I am not speaking as a Catholic.

We are situated in what is called the Northern Region of Ghana which is more of an historical anomaly than a strict geographical fact. The Upper East and Upper West Regions are 'above' us. Tamale is the largest town (population of at least 120,000) for over two hundred miles and we are in a savannah area about five hundred miles from the coast.

With such a large and rapidly expanding population it is impossible for the local services to keep up. The water company can pump at most 1.3 million gallons of water a day and there are many days that it does not pump at all for lack of one spare part or another. It sounds a lot but that simply means about three buckets of water per day per person for bathing, cooking, washing, etc. Obviously inadequate. People rely either on saving rainwater during the rainy season or collecting it from dug-out dams during the dry season. These also are inadequate and the result is that most people end up walking for miles simply to get a bucket of water.

9

The rainy season is just ending (mid-October) and we expect no rain now until next April or May. This year the rains have been particularly heavy. We have experienced floods here for the first time in over 20 years. And the floods were not as bad then as they were this year. A dam in the centre of town burst, thankfully at midday when most people were out or at least awake. If it had happened at night so many would have drowned; as it was, the death toll was probably less than 20. It is hard to get an accurate figure. The other tragedy associated with this is that so many houses were destroyed – so much property, saved up for for years, was washed away and destroyed. Irreplaceable items. When a simple bicycle costs two months' salary and has to be saved hard for as there are other priorities on a family budget such as food and clothing, the loss of even that is major, how much sadder it is then to lose everything. The government is trying to help, so are the aid agencies, but the need is so great, the resources stretched already to their limits, that most of these losses can never be made good.

After that disaster the rains continued and continued. Crops have been washed away, more lives lost, more houses collapsed. The local houses are made of dried sun-baked mud. They can withstand a normal rain but not what has happened this year. Often it rained at night. Occupants of threat-ened houses then had no choice but to leave their rooms and stand in the rain, praying that their house was spared. Two young boys were killed when their room collapsed on them. After a while people took to sleeping in the schools which the government opened for them at night, returning in the mornings to see if their houses were still there. The electricity generating station was flooded twice, resulting in no town power for two months now. Even before that electricity was at best sporadic, normally three or four hours a day. I have a small generator which I run in the evenings so we can manage all right. Soon we will have hydroelectric power sent from the south.

The real miracle is that although I have seen people standing looking at their collapsed houses in shock or weeping for a life lost, the people's faith in God has not been shaken. Their basic optimism for life remains intact. 'God is there' is an often heard expression, meaning He will look after us. In situations where everything seems against you, small victories mean a lot. Tomorrow will be better simply because there is nothing left to lose; it can't get worse. There is more to life than material possessions, there is life itself, and with that there is always hope.

8
January 1990
Heather Lansing
Treasures Found in Botswana in the Summer of 1989

Heather grew up in Kendal, Cumbria. In 1989 she travelled to Botswana as a youth to participate in one of the summer Star Projects just before completing her degree in education.

I once knew a young girl whose heart had a longing to be in Africa. By the age of 21 she took her heart to Botswana – her dream had turned into a reality. Prior to this point in her life she had wondered where her once 'smiling' and radiant heart had gone. She felt that she was losing something that had been enkindled within her soul at the age of 15 when she sat on the floor of her bedroom and quietly prayed . . . that 'something' was the Spirit of Bahá'u'lláh – a covenant between herself and God. This concerned her greatly and so she set out to do something about it. This young girl didn't quite know what she was looking for and she would ponder upon this for hours on end when she had time to herself. Was it a maturity of spirit or was it simply what one could describe as happiness that she wanted? But, then, what exactly was that?

Her days and nights passed by in Africa – days of tests and sorrows at times – indeed at one point she wondered if she was ever gong to discover what it was that her heart yearned for.

At last she truly turned her face towards God and literally wept for her Beloved to reveal what it was that her heart desired. It was from here that the tide changed and she witnessed the true power of prayer. Slowly the veil was lifted from her sight – indeed, it took a period of some weeks for the treasures of her heart to be found.

It all began with a short journey where she caught a very small part of the hearts of the African people – but that small part developed into something close to her soul, and she didn't stay away for long. The young girl then went on another journey but this time it was not one in the physical sense. It was a journey that allowed her to discover something about herself and about her capabilities. She found that she was able to share with others the Faith that she had always so dearly believed in. She found that she could communicate from her heart something that she had longed to share with her fellow youth. She spoke of the power of faith and at the same time experienced such a power within. It was as though nothing could ever shake her faith now that she had discovered this power.

From here she went on her final journey of discovery connected with this chapter of her life. She travelled to discover yet greater treasures that had been hidden from her eyes – these were the treasures of what living was about. The young girl was attracted back to the hearts of the African people. As the sun would gently fall upon the horizon like a bubble does to the ground, the wind would wear itself out and darkness would take over. A fire would be enkindled and voices in the distance would come closer – people would be attracted to the fire like a moth is to light. It was this atmosphere that moved the young girl's heart. She felt safe within the heart of the desert and its people – there was security from all the ills of the world. Thoughts of any problems were absent from her mind. When she sat between the sands and the stars, nothing could come between herself and God – her soul had experienced what true peace and tranquillity were. They could almost be likened to a rainbow manifesting itself as the heavens open up and the sun spreads its rays.

Adding to this the young girl witnessed something else, something very special. Beside that fire that had been enkindled, through the smoke and flames, she saw a vision of ebony faces that were filled with radiance. Materially these people had nothing but spiritually they had everything. Their eyes would reflect a joyousness that ceased to exist in the eyes of the people back home. Emanating from their mouths were smiles of truthfulness, sincerity – what a smile should offer another person. And when all these qualities were merged into one, the young girl realized what she was looking for . . . it was her True Lover, Bahá'u'lláh – she had found Him at last. To her this was the purpose of living, the whole meaning of life. She had always believed in Him but to love Him like a lover gave a whole new concept to the shaping of her life. What had lain dormant deep within the ocean of the young girl's heart had finally come to the surface. She had found a new spirit – she had found her inner strength.

And now the young girl sits in quiet places from time to time in order to ponder upon what she has found. She thinks about the next chapter in her life and feels that her heart shall weep for the simplicity of life that she had discovered – for the radiant faces – indeed the joyous and happy faces that enraptured her soul. She wonders what she will be returning to when her physical self has to depart from this land. She knows that tests will surround her but with that inner strength that has been unveiled she can withstand anything – this is what will make her grow. Her task now will be to convey the Spirit that she has found to a society that has forgotten how to live, that has forgotten the foundations of true happiness. She knows that whenever an emotion of unhappiness wafts in her direction, all she has to do is rekindle the spirit that she found within her soul so that the experiences never leave her side and always stay close to her heart. But perhaps the most important thing is that she feels her love for

Bahá'u'lláh is a gift that she will hold and treasure for eternity – nothing will ever be able to shake her faith and love for Him now.

I once knew a young girl whose heart had a longing to be in Africa. By the age of 21 she took her heart to Botswana – her dream had turned into a reality. She was searching for something, she found it and vows never to lose hold of it – she will be totally dedicated to it. Her heart will never leave Africa and her people – it will rest there happy and content.

9
July 1990
Brian and Pamela O'Toole
Guyana

Brian and Pamela have been pioneers in Guyana since 1978.

In October of last year the International Teaching Centre initiated a major pilot programme in Guyana. Fifteen short-term pioneers from the Americas were to be selected to spend a period of from one to three years in Guyana with the two-fold focus of 'enrolling an appreciable percentage' of the population and raising up new manpower. The progress to date with the project has been tremendous. Five per cent of the population has now enrolled in the Faith. The Faith is now emerging as one of the religions of the country alongside Hinduism, Islam and Christianity. We now have several villages with a Bahá'í population in excess of one thousand. The Faith constitutes up to 20 per cent of the population of these villages. A handful of people are working full time on consolidation. There are now 20 Guyanese Bahá'ís who are working full time teaching the Faith, the great majority living in very modest conditions. A series of institutes have been held over the past months – one day, three days, five days on a variety of topics. Over five hundred persons have now attended a minimum of a one-day deepening. Regular classes are being held in schools.

The USA has decided to greatly increase its radio time from one monthly programme and one weekly programme to two weekly programmes and devotionals every day. In one community on the border with Suriname the Bahá'ís are beginning to respond to the question 'What impact does the Faith have on our society?' The Bahá'ís invited the people of the community, Bahá'ís and others, to meet together to discuss what improvements could be made to the environment. The outcome of the consultation was more than 50 people from the village working together to build a bridge and a playground. Apart from the obvious material improvements they bring, they also provide a crucial sign that the community has within itself the capacity to bring about change. In one rural area, within a 15 mile radius, over three hundred people gathered at 11 different meetings to analyse the Riḍván message.

A medical project spearheaded by Drs Rahmani and Beheshti of Swindon and Broadstairs, has had a tremendous effect, with excellent relations now being established at the highest level within the country. The doctors have managed to provide a very considerable amount of medical equipment to the government hospitals. A beautiful Bahá'í Centre is being built in the capital to reflect the growth of the community. A number of the Guyanese youth will be on projects throughout the Caribbean over the summer.

The community has produced a literary magazine in collaboration with a major local publisher that is being distributed throughout the country and overseas. The same publishers have now requested an article for another magazine on the history of the Faith in Guyana.

Pam and I and the boys are all well. We have recently bought a farm in a beautiful rural area of the country and plan to move soon. My work with disabled children in the rural areas has gone very well and I'm hoping to work full time on some other project over the next three years. The three British pioneers here – Andrew Mancey and ourselves – are all on the National Assembly. We send our love.

10
January 1991
Susan and Shidan Kouchek-zadeh
Guinea-Conakry, West Africa

An extract from a quite hair-raising account of a journey from Guinea to the Monrovia Music Festival, Liberia, in December 1989 – the kind of journey familiar to many pioneers in third world countries:

It was nightfall when we arrived at camp and we were enormously glad of lovely warm baths to get rid of all the dust of the road. The kids and I were entertained by Shidan's engineer colleague, who had arranged for the car to be looked at in the garage the next morning, for which I was thankful at first; but when time went on and it still was not back I began to get very anxious because of all the stories we'd heard about broken bridges, etc. on the road to N'zérékoré and we didn't want to be doing it in the dark. At 2 p.m. we got the car and assurance that it was only four hours to N'zérékoré, with nothing worse than what we had experienced the day before.

At the first broken bridge we forded the river with little problem. We crossed the big Diané river on the government ferry, a large metal barge which can take about three vehicles and is hand-pulled across on a chain. By now it was getting on and when we hit the second broken bridge I was horrified. The local villagers had made a raft out of oil drums and planks of wood and were charging money to get you across. But the road down to and up out of the river was just thick churned up mud. Fortunately passengers could cross a little wooden walkway. I crossed and tried not to look. The river was just a bit too wide and deep for us to ford as large lorries did but our jeep was just a bit too heavy for this little raft.

I didn't see the Toyota get onto the raft, having averted my eyes, but once it was on it bogged the craft down in the mud so there was a lot of heaving and pulling and shouting and the thing kept swinging to and fro and Cellou (the driver) was sort of spread-eagled against his vehicle, hanging on for dear life. It took an age and by the time Cellou gunned the Toyota up the slope through the thick yellow mud it was beginning to get dark.

There were a lot of people stranded there without transport but we couldn't help them all. I was really alarmed when I heard one of them say that there was another broken bridge ahead but we decided he had just said that to make us give him a lift. But, horrors, it was true and we met this one in the pitch dark (we would probably not have noticed that it was broken had there not been some other vehicles parked there) and had to ford this stream by feel almost . . . again more mud made it very tricky but at least we had a four wheel drive.

We reached N'zérékoré at 8:00 p.m. and had to look for lodgings in the dark. Dark is an understatement: it was pitch black. We found the Bakoli hotel and restaurant – just a dim kerosene lamp inside – and they told us they had good rooms just a little up the road.

Returning to the car I walked straight into a cement drain. It was about two foot deep and two foot wide with sharp cement sides and I just fell head-long! I got up completely unhurt except for a small scrape. I felt it was an absolute miracle – people are always breaking arms and legs and goodness knows what falling into these drains. And there I was alone with the kids with no way of communicating with anyone in the outside world. What enormous good fortune that I broke nothing.

Just along the road was a small square building tucked in between all the other huts and houses with four bedrooms, each with its own bathroom (toilet, sink and shower) and tiled too. Real luxury except for the fact that there was no water and no electricity. But there was someone to bring buckets of water so I took a room (which I shared with the kids) and we threw mugs of water over our dirty selves and went to bed exhausted but satisfied that we'd made it.

Next morning the kids refused to move – they'd had enough of bumping around in the car – so Souanon Doré (NSA member) and I went off to go round some of the Bahá'í villages. First, in N'zao (just ten minutes from N'zérékoré) where the Bahá'í musical group was living and practising, we found Kanté (the Conakry Bahá'í who had gone up to help organize them) grey of face and shaking with malaria but quite cheerful. He invited us to a rehearsal that evening. Souanon Doré and I continued our drive to other Bahá'í villages but the road was BAD. We reached Gamma Koni Koni where they have built their own Bahá'í Centre, which I was thrilled to see. It is a pretty little bamboo building with a large enclosed yard and a tyre rim hanging from a tree to summon the people and a large notice with UNIVERSAL PEACE written on it. We met only a few Bahá'ís because everybody was out in the fields.

That evening we all went off to N'zao to see the rehearsal of our group and it was a very pleasant evening in the dark in the village listening to all the songs they composed. I thought our team was wonderful – they made lovely music that night and had me up dancing before the evening was over.

Many checkpoints further on along the road to Liberia . . . and on reaching Monrovia, we found Shidan waiting for us and able to share further responsibility . . .

We had been booked into a Methodist hostel and our place was great, with bathrooms and hot and cold water. The only problem was saggy beds but I solved that by putting my mattress on the floor the second night and thus discovered a new species of mouse, which we baptised the 'frouse' because of it being a pale froggy colour with a froggy way of leaping into the air as well as a mousy way of scooting along the floor – it also ate half a packet of biscuits in the children's room!

There were buses to take the Bahá'ís to the Festival and we met lots of old friends from different parts of West Africa and the kids were thrilled to find Conrad Lambert there, as part of the El Viente Canta group which had been at the other two African musical festivals in Botswana and Kenya earlier in December. Other special guests were Doc Holladay, jazz musician from the US, a wonderful flautist from Bermuda and the Liberian National Drumming group.

We now discovered that the Sierra Leonean group and the Ivoirian groups, both coming by land, although from opposite directions, were overdue and we realized we had been lucky to get through at all. The Sierra Leoneans finally arrived at 1 a.m. It had taken them 18 hours to do a two hour taxi journey because of the hassle they suffered from police and immigration officials. The group of Bahá'ís about 50 strong coming from the Ivory Coast never were allowed in.

Anyway, on the first day we had some wonderful drumming from the Liberian cultural group and were introduced to all the Bahá'í groups. In the evening there was a special concert to which the president was invited – he didn't turn up and didn't send anyone and we started late. The concert was marvellous. The Counsellors performed too – there were eight Counsellors present, who had come straight on from their annual meeting in Abidjan and seven of them were African and they gave a great performance of a Xhosa Bahá'í song . . . so great they were asked to repeat it the next day. Doc Holladay was meant to be the star but his plane was late and he finally arrived without any luggage and had to borrow some instruments to play to us. On the Friday all the Bahá'í groups performed and it was a feast of a day. Each group had something completely different to offer. I was amazed at the variety and some were absolutely superb.

We finally left Monrovia with Ghana Airways and were whisked back to Conakry with very little delay. It was strange to be sailing effortlessly along in an airliner after four arduous land journeys. And I relived the Monrovia/Freetown flight that I used to do every month in the early 1970s. Reflecting on changes in travelling since those days I can see that by and large roads have improved. The Sanniquellie/Monrovia highway, although still unpaved, has been broadened and straightened and is no longer the winding, bumpy little track it was in 1970. But the formalities have increased a hundredfold and the hassle and bullying one receives from officials of all sorts is now the problem and takes up all the time gained from the improvements in the road.

11

April 1991
Debbie Conkerton
Swaziland

Debbie left Liverpool in April 1990 in response to a pioneering call to run the first Bahá'í primary school in Mbabane, Swaziland.

The Bahá'í Primary School has just begun its second year. We now have two classes: Grade 2 (seven to eight years old) and Grade 1 (five to six years old).* There are 35 kids altogether – and we still have new ones registering. The school is small but our reputation has grown quickly and I think next year we will see a big growth in the size of the classes. We are still in temporary accommodation as building costs have rocketed recently but we hope to have a proper school built this year.

It's so nice to be able to tell children openly about Bahá'u'lláh, 'Abdu'l-Bahá and the Manifestations of God, knowing that their parents are supporting the school and its methods even though none of the children nor their parents are Bahá'ís themselves. The Grade 2s (who have been in the school for a little over a year) now know by heart four or five prayers, many Bahá'í songs in English and Siswati, and stories from the lives of the Manifestations and 'Abdu'l-Bahá. Of course their general education is (we hope!) of a high standard. Many of the parents have said how pleased they are at the standard of reading and writing we have set.

My fellow teachers are Gabriella Torstenssen (Sweden/Botswana) who organized STAR in Botswana and came to Swaziland in January 1991 to take the Grade 1 class, and Funekilo Malaza (not a Bahá'í) who turned up one day to teach after the Ministry of Education decided they would provide us with a paid teacher! This is quite handy as I can now divide my time between teaching the Grade 2s and doing all the admin. It still feels a bit weird being Head Teacher of a school as it is only three years since I left teacher training at university but I suppose Bahá'u'lláh decided I was ready for it!

Outside of school there is lots to do. National Youth Committee and Local Spiritual Assembly duties mean lots of meetings and commitments but at least the NYC tends to hold its meetings somewhere close to a hot spring, or up a mountain, or at a picnic spot! (and we DO get the work done!) We're having an International Youth Conference here in April on Creativity and the Environment to be held at Malolotje Nature Reserve. To anyone who says I can't still possibly be a youth – our limit here is 30 and so I've got three years to go! I'm living in a rondavel (traditional round house) with Mrs Val ('Gogo') Allen, the Knight of Bahá'u'lláh for Swaziland. She tells me stories of life in Swaziland over 30 years ago when she and her late husband John first pioneered here. I really am happy to be here in Swaziland – I feel I am where I should be!

*Note: The school now caters for 5 to 15 year olds, having built up by one grade each year since it began.

12

July 1991
Adrian Davis
New Era School, Panchgani, India

Adrian left Ealing, London, for India in August 1990, shortly after becoming a Bahá'í.

Life here in India continues to be an unforgettable experience, for apart from one's professional duties of teaching in the school and managing two classes of 45 children each in English, Social Studies and Morals, there are certain physical factors that add depth to the memories. For example, daily temperatures are 90 degrees F plus, with high humidity and an increasing population of mosquitoes and mango flies! Power sharing on the limited local electricity grid makes power cuts a not uncommon occurrence. The beautiful sights and aromas of local fauna and flora are interlaced with the attack of strong smells from open sewers. The water supply is cut daily from 9 a.m. to 3 p.m. in order to deal with the annual water shortage, thus making early-morning bucket-filling the first order of the day, and the scenes of poverty and begging are a reminder that India is still trying to emerge from third world status. The local panoramic views are breathtaking and there is a local beauty spot replete with camel and horse riding, and a fun fair with ice cream galore – a most welcome sight on these hot and humid days. The ensuing sunset is also a glory to behold as it sets in the west and heralds a dawn for friends elsewhere. And on top of all this is the 150+ strong Bahá'í community with all its diversity and wonderful and inspiring individuals, as well as the visitors attracted from all over the Bahá'í world.

13

July 1991
David Smith
Travel Teaching Trip to Albania

With teaching opportunities opening up in eastern Europe, David (from Leatherhead, Surrey) made this short trip to Albania in April.

In April I travelled with a group of 45 people on a 'Classical Tour of Albania'. I was the only Bahá'í . . . Yá Bahá'u'l-Abhá! A sweet fragrance of flowers and pine trees greeted us as we stood in no man's land between two Balkan countries. All eyes craned into the darkness as we tried to make sense of the dark shadows that lay before us. Albania, mystery of Europe. Albania, blessed by a visit from Hand of the Cause of God Martha Root in 1929.

We were met by a hardline Party official who informed our English guide that we would not be allowed to bring any books into the country. One by one we filed past and watched as our bags were emptied onto an old wooden table and the contents examined. No one spoke. As I did not wish to cause a problem for the rest of the group I told our guide that I had a suitcase and a shoulder bag full of books, pamphlets and tapes and that, if asked, I would have to disclose this. She said that was up to me but that she could not help. As I stood in line waiting the moment my turn would come, I whispered the Greatest Name and called out in my heart to the Concourse on High to help me in my endeavours to take the Word of God to this country. I looked into the guard's eyes as he asked 'Any books?'

'Yes,' I replied.

'OK. Go through.'

I held his eye for a moment longer, then walked on. I was first confused, then shocked and finally elated. It seemed that there was a guiding hand helping me. Throughout my stay this guiding influence was never to leave me.

Days were spent visiting different places of interest in Albania. As I alighted from the coach I recalled a talk by Professor Bushrui in which he said that we should look at the values, practices and ambitions of the society around us and, whatever they do, we must do the exact opposite! So I decided to adopt this as my decision-making process on the trip. I spoke to many people about the Bahá'í Faith and many people were interested. On one occasion a short, blonde-haired man, covered from head to foot in white factory dust, held me in my tracks, gripping me with a very strong hand. He led me to a cafe where we had coffee. I stumbled through my few Albanian phrases and somehow we managed to communicate. He told me that he loved his country, that he hoped I loved it too and that he hoped his people had shown me love and friendship and he wanted me to visit his family. Four generations of Muslims and myself a Bahá'í! I fell in love with this family – I gave them *The Hidden Words*, which my friend, the blonde young man, held close to his heart. My friend, I was informed, was liked by everyone and had a pure heart!

Another day I was interviewed on the radio in Tirana and spoke for 20 minutes about my travels and impressions of Albania. I said that my strongest impression was of the unity and fellowship of the diverse peoples of Albania: the Christians, Muslims, atheists, Greeks, Turks, all living and harmonizing together and that, as a Bahá'í, this made me very happy. We then talked for 30 minutes or so about the Bahá'í Faith. Later my interviewer expressed great personal attraction to the teachings of Bahá'u'lláh and she took the 'Perspective' booklet and the Hidden Words. I was also interviewed by a reporter for the Radio Tirane Foreign Service – another 30 minutes on the Faith.

14
October 1991
Cymbeline Smith
'Vision' in Poland

Cymbeline is from Wisborough Green, Sussex.

'Vision' is a youth group of nine Bahá'í musicians, singers, dancers and three enthusiastic coordinators from the UK. Armed with literature generously subsidized by the German and British National Spiritual Assemblies, 'Vision' intrepidly embarked on 9th August on their tour, leaving from Wisborough Green, Sussex, in the 'Big Red Minibus' which they hired and which was soon to become well known to the Polish people and a well-worn friend to the group. Before we arrived in Poland we stopped at the Bahá'í House of Worship in Frankfurt, Germany. It was an ideal opportunity to say some prayers for the success of the tour in Poland.

Poznan was the first city we arrived at in Poland. We were met with a warm welcome from Bahá'í pioneers and travel teachers and taken to our accommodation. Our first concert in the town square at Poznan was a great success. Approximately 300 local Polish people danced and sang with us in the streets. We had TV coverage during the afternoon performance and were on the TV station's news broadcast that evening. The following day the newspapers stated that the Bahá'ís had brought life to the Old Square.

As well as performing in Poznan, we made personal contact with the people there, who continued to attend firesides and concerts later that week. While we were in Poland we found a great spirituality amongst the Polish people. This showed particularly in the types of questions that were asked at the firesides. There seemed to be a special 'rapport' between the people from the UK and the Polish people (very much, we were told, as a result of the last world war). This removed barriers more easily and presented undreamed of possibilities, especially where media coverage was concerned.

In Warsaw we performed in the City Square, where we were filmed for national TV. That evening we were to perform in a theatre in 'nightclub' surroundings, which reminded us once again always to keep our productions as adaptable as possible! Two TV stations attended our concert that evening and filmed different items. One of the TV stations returned the following evening and asked if it was possible to film us for a documentary. They interviewed us before the performance, asking probing questions about the Faith. Towards the end of the performance enthusiastic members of the audience jumped up and joined us on stage, dancing, singing and clapping. The TV cameras were glad to record this, as apparently it is a very rare occurrence. We were surprised and delighted when, at the end during the encores, a man jumped up, intoxicated with the spirit, and shouted, 'Bahá'u'lláh, Bahá'u'lláh, please sing Bahá'u'lláh again!' As it is unusual for the audience to remember the very first song of a concert right through to the end of the performance, thoughts drifted into our heads that maybe this man had been 'planted' in the audience by local Bahá'ís! However, we were soon to discover that he was a local Polish man who had been inspired and moved by the name of Bahá'u'lláh.

The Russian coup occurred while we were in Krakow, enhancing the importance of our message of peace. We were repeatedly delighted during street performances when people in the audience responded by giving us bouquets of flowers and showing interest in our beliefs, thus leading to large, interesting and successful firesides. Again we were supported by interest from local radio stations. At this stage of 'Vision's' tour we were so united that comments and remarks were made about the unified appearance and spirit of the group, and particularly that there was no one main member of the group always coming to the fore, that we all had equal and important parts to play. This we feel was largely due to praying, reading the writings and consulting before and after each performance.

When we arrived at Novy Sancz we were all exhausted from the early morning start and long journey in our Big Red Minibus that day. However, we were revitalized when we discovered the effort that the local Bahá'í youth had gone to in order to arrange our concert and felt very honoured at the sacrifices people had made so that they could attend.

In Wroclaw we joined forces with the summer school at Hajdany nearby. We attended a dignified press conference at an impressive hotel, along with other Bahá'ís. Afterwards we were filmed in the streets of Wroclaw for a TV company that wanted to do a short film about us. Later in Wroclaw we were joined by a group of new Bahá'ís from eastern Europe performing pop music. More TV coverage followed as we walked through the streets of Wroclaw singing, 'All the Peoples of the World', written and composed by two members of the group.

We ended the tour on a high note with a live TV interview. 'Vision' was presented with a video copy of the programme. We sang original compositions by the group, including one proclaiming Bahá'u'lláh, as we made our entrance and exit. During the interview the camera focused on Bahá'í leaflets and pamphlets for a few moments – this too was helpful proclamation for the Faith!

By the end of the tour we had also finally discovered how to order properly in the Polish restaurants but, alas for Susannah, the vegetarian member of our group, it had been cheese sandwiches nearly the whole time!

One of our most memorable incidents was with a dynamic young Bahá'í, Thomasz, who not only helped us teach in the streets, but also had a skill we'd never seen anywhere before! As it was hot while we were there, wasps sometimes bothered us and he would come along and get rid of them, catching a wasp by clapping his hands around it! We were amazed that he never got stung and always got rid of the wasps, much to our amusement. He had us all clapping – though none of us dared to try to kill a wasp in the palm of our hands like he did!

We returned to England via the Bahá'í Temple in Frankfurt and again we were able to spend some time in prayer and meditation. We had the bounty of meeting briefly with the German NSA (quite coincidentally, in session on our arrival), sharing with them some of the highlights of our tour. Now back in the UK, we are all excited about further events and sharing a great 'vision' of the future.

15
January 1992
Brian and Pamela O'Toole
Guyana

Dr Brian O'Toole with his wife Pamela (whom he met whilst studying at Strathclyde University in Glasgow) have been UK pioneers in Guyana since 1978.

The National Assembly has made a goal of enrolling ten per cent of the population of Guyana by the centenary of Bahá'u'lláh's ascension. At present the figure is about six to seven per cent. For the past two years Guyana has hosted a pilot project inspired by the International Teaching Centre whereby a number of short-term pioneers come to Guyana for a two to three year period with the major goals of enrolling a significant percentage of the population as Bahá'ís and developing an institute programme from which significant numbers of Bahá'ís would rise to a high level of service in the Faith. A number of dedicated Bahá'ís in the Americas were invited by the Board of Counsellors to give one to two years to the project. Bahá'ís from Peru, Brazil, Uruguay, USA, Canada, Trinidad, Venezuela, Bolivia and Malaysia have given their services to great effect. They have been complemented by 45 Guyanese Bahá'ís who have given six months to two years to the project.

As we look back over the course of the project we are inspired to realize that so many have arisen to such levels of service. Significant efforts have been made towards achieving the second major goal and now hundreds of Bahá'ís have attended intensive institutes. As one reflects over the achievements of the past few years there is much to appreciate. There are now 23 literacy/reading classes; well thought-out children's classes are conducted regularly across the country; grassroots development in one region has brought the Bahá'í community together to bring water to the regional hospital; pioneers are now leaving Guyana for sister communities in the Caribbean; a beautiful National Centre is to be opened next month . . .

However, there is far more to ponder on the challenges that lie ahead.

We have now moved to a farm in a beautiful area of the country. We are 'pretend' farmers – our neighbours are much amused to see the four of us – myself and my wife Pam, Liam (10) and Cairan (7) – venture into the back dam with our boots and rusty cutlass. We've started a small coffee business that has shown some promise – called New Era – demand it in all your supermarkets – which has been exported within the Caribbean. I now work full time on a community development project funded by the EEC working with disabled children and their families. The work is tremendously satisfying and challenging. Much is being done for the Bahá'í children of Guyana to develop a real identity of what it means to be a Bahá'í today. I'm sure in years to come our children will look back with deep appreciation for the experience Guyana has offered them.

16
January 1992
Barbara Smith
Travel Teaching in Romania

Barbara lives in St Austell, Cornwall.

Having recently retired, I said 'yes' immediately when my friend Homa Khalilian asked me to accompany her on a travel teaching trip to Romania. We left on 7th November and took with us enough food to last two weeks. I had not been to eastern Europe before and it was an incredible experience. The opportunities for teaching and talking about Bahá'u'lláh were unbelievable.

On our second day, on a five-hour train journey to Tirgu Jiu, we taught the

Faith the whole time. As people got out of the train so others, who were listening from the corridor, would ask to join us to have their questions answered. The entire visit would have been worthwhile for that one train journey alone!

In the city of Tirgu Jiu we went to schools where teachers were happy to accept Bahá'í literature. We made many friends of these English teachers, who asked us to talk to (and teach) their classes and of course they also wanted to listen to, and practise, their English. We were entertained in their homes in spite of the difficulties under which they were living.

It is hard, physically, to visit Romania but perhaps easier for someone younger. The whole country appears to be so gloomy. No lights anywhere. Empty shops. Queues for bread. All night queues for petrol for their cars. In their homes they have water for only two hours each day. We existed on the food we had taken with us. There was no milk at all and I felt that, in spite of the exhilaration of the teaching work, that two weeks was about my limit.

The local Bahá'ís are so helpful and so in love with the teachings but so new to the Faith – they need contact with older Bahá'ís. The situation is changing rapidly. The eagerness of people to learn of the Faith will not last. We learned that already in the capital, Bucharest, it is noticeable that not so large a crowd gathers to listen as did, say, a year ago. Students are the ones to talk to – you can go into the colleges and universities – they want to talk in English about anything, so why not the Bahá'í Faith?

17

January 1992
Adrian Davis
Soviet Teaching Trip

Adrian is a teacher at the New Era School in Panchgani, India. Here he writes about his recent Soviet travel teaching trip.

Eight Bahá'ís and one other charming new-found friend left Glasgow for Kiev, where we met up with our young Soviet Bahá'í translators, all of whom were a blessing to us with their enthusiasm, dedication and sacrifice. We toured Kiev for two days, marvelling at the golden domes of the Orthodox churches. On 11th August we arrived in Moscow after a very comfortable overnight train journey, being welcomed to this famous capital with early morning tea poured from a samovar and served in exquisite glass cups in decorated metal holders. We later toured Red Square and also took a stroll in Gorky Park.

In the Ukraine and Russia we saw queues for food but the longest queue by far was for the new McDonald's! Anything western in origin, viz. food, clothes, music, language, etc., was in demand. One of the saddest sights for me was in Kiev where a store the size of Harrods had so little in the way of choice when it came to buying clothes.

On 12th August we took off on Aeroflot with a fiery sunset behind us and, seven hours later, landed in southern Siberia to a sparkling sunrise! In this vast nation Siberia was to be the focus of our proclamation and teaching efforts. After a day in the city of Ulan-Ude (where we visited the Bahá'í Centre and crossed paths with some other visiting European Bahá'ís, including Wendi and Moojan Momen!), we all took a local flight across the deepest lake in the world, Lake Baikal, to the town of Severobaikalsk.

With our friendly and essential interpreters we soon found our chalet situated on Lake Baikal's picturesque northern shore and spent the next eight days proclaiming in the town square with visual aids such as posters plus lots of Bahá'í literature in Russian, which is also essential. This information was consumed ravenously by a robust and hardy people wondering why we had come so far to visit them in a remote Siberian town. Although we were consolidating a visit made a year earlier by an American Bahá'í band, we explained that the Bahá'í teachings were for everybody in the world. With the help of some wonderful local Bahá'ís we held a public meeting in the local TV station where one of the managers allowed us to show, as part of our programme, a video presented to them a year earlier on the construction of the Arc.

Bahá'u'lláh gave us so many opportunities, including a newspaper and radio interview. In addition, local non-Bahá'ís helped us distribute leaflets in the town square, and in our public meeting another local non-Bahá'í came to the stage personally to state that although Marx had frightened a lot of people away from religion, Bahá'u'lláh's teachings were clearly obvious and self-evident! We thus found people very cooperative and kind.

Amongst our activities we also enjoyed swimming in Lake Baikal's waters, visiting local beauty spots, having dawn prayers on the lakeshore, swimming in a local hot mineral spring, and making friends with the Russians, who impressed me with the strength of their constitution and character. Unfortunately the attempted *coup d'état* against Mikhail Gorbachev prevented a trip to St Petersburg – but that is my reason for returning as soon as possible! With tears and sorrow we left our Soviet Bahá'í 'brothers' and 'sisters' in Kiev when we departed on 26th August.

18
April 1992
Helen Smith
Lithuania

Helen, from Guernsey, Channel Islands, pioneered to Vilnius, Lithuania, in January 1989.

My maternal grandparents left Lithuania at the end of the 19th century, during Czarist times, so I was brought up in a Lithuanian flavoured community. I didn't speak Lithuanian but I remember some of the tunes of the songs I used to hear sung at celebrations although I don't think I ever knew the words. When I became a Bahá'í (I think rather egotistically and because at that time it seemed an impossibility), I thought I would like to be a Bahá'í pioneer to Lithuania. At that time pioneering to Lithuania was about as possible as taking a bus to the moon.

My first travelling teaching trip was to East Germany in the spring of 1983, my first time into the Soviet bloc. In 1984 I had a letter from an elderly schoolteacher pen pal in Lithuania asking me for some books on Esperanto. At this point I wondered if this was a way of introducing the Faith into Lithuania through telling my friend about Lydia Zamenhof.

I wrote to the National Assembly of Sweden for advice. The Assembly advised me to do nothing except try to go there on holiday, which I did but was refused a visa. In 1987 I went to Poland to attend the Esperanto Congress. This was the nearest I could get to Lithuania. Towards the end of 1987 I contacted Mr Grossmann, a member of the Continental Board of Counsellors, who, at the request of the Universal House of Justice, was raising the call for pioneers to open those countries not yet open to the Faith, one of which was Lithuania. Encouraged by a friend, I contacted Mr Grossmann, who suggested that since opportunities were becoming available for pioneers to go to eastern Europe, I should go to Lithuania to try to find a job that would give me the necessary visa to stay in the country for a fairly long period of time.

It took many months to get a visa, each application being turned down.

Eventually, in January 1989, I was granted a five-day visa and during that five-day period I had to find a job. It was the middle of January and my first port of call in the Soviet Union was Moscow.

When I arrived in Moscow the magnitude of what I was trying to do suddenly hit me and, as the plane was coming in to land, I became very emotional. My thoughts focused on Bahá'u'lláh and I found myself thinking, 'OK Bahá'u'lláh, you got me in, you get me out' and it was at this point that I realized what it really means to put all your trust in Bahá'u'lláh.

In Lithuania I met my distant relatives but having only three days (two days in transit through Moscow) in which to find a job I hadn't the foggiest idea where to start. My relatives thought I was quite mad when I told them I wished to stay a few years in Lithuania and that I wanted to find a job.

On my last day in Vilnius, when I really thought that all was lost and the possibility of finding a job was zero, my translator took me to some office where a woman interviewed me, saying she would call me later. When she called back I was told to go to the Social Bank and at 5 p.m. that day I was offered a job. At 7 p.m. I was on the train back to Moscow for my flight back to the UK.

The woman who interviewed me was elected the first prime minister in independent Lithuania. Eventually I got my visa to return and in July I was back in Lithuania with a visa for two weeks. During the next year I seemed to spend most of my time getting my visa renewed. There was no immigration department – nobody immigrated! I was given accommodation with an English teacher who was highly delighted to have me live with her because she would be able to practise her English. It didn't do much for my Lithuanian!

We shared one very small room and my share of the room was behind the wardrobe.

My bed was my only domain. My suitcases were piled on the bed and I had to remove them each night when I wanted to get into bed. I had never shared a room with anyone before, except my husband, and here I was in a situation where I couldn't even say my prayers because there was no privacy. When my roommate's family came to stay things became even worse as there was her father, mother and brother to accommodate. This affected my health and I was ill for several months but I got over it.

Those first few months were very difficult but, like everyone else, you make the best of it and keep in mind why you are where you are. I was busy at my job and after about a month I was able more or less to teach the Faith, not openly but with caution, and that made me feel better.

I was told there was a Bahá'í in Vilnius but I didn't know who and I was not allowed to contact her. Saying prayers was a problem because there was no privacy so I used to get up at 5 a.m. and say my prayers in the kitchen. My roommate did not approve of my inviting people to her flat so firesides were out. By 12th November I was able to hold the holy day celebration with my roommate because by this time I think she understood that I was not to be feared, that I wasn't a spy! Strange though this may sound today, at that time it was a very real issue. To get around the problem of not being able to talk to interested folks about the Faith I used to invite people to cafes or to the central post office where there were big easy chairs and where, in winter, it was always warm.

Friends sent me Bahá'í literature in Russian, 'The Promise of World Peace' and the letter to August Forel. It was very difficult to teach the Faith with my very limited knowledge of Lithuanian and no literature in that language. In March 1990 a student of English became interested in my ideas and wanted to know where they came from. I gave her a copy of 'The Promise of World Peace' and after reading and discussing this she read the letter to August Forel. Shortly after this she registered as a Bahá'í. Thereafter two more people came into the Faith through reading the same literature in Russian – it was all I had to offer them at the time.

Another young lady became a Bahá'í quite by accident. I had passed on to her the same two pieces of literature and after reading them she decided against becoming a Bahá'í but when she told me I misunderstood and warmly welcomed her into the Faith. (She is still a Bahá'í at the time of writing in 2008.)

During this time in Lithuania there was a great surge in the movement to secede from the Soviet Union. There were what seemed to be weekly demonstrations with many thousands of people attending, singing national songs and carrying the national flag. I was not at these demonstrations. I was on an empty bus exploring the opposite side of the city. During 1989 there had been quite a significant increase in the number of foreigners with Lithuanian roots who had come to Lithuania to help in the drive for independence and were involved politically in the freedom movements. Towards the end of February and into March foreigners were being expelled and were given 24 hours to leave the country. I wasn't expelled.

On 11 March 1990 Lithuania declared itself as the Independent Republic of Lithuania. This did not please Moscow. A blockade was placed around the country; no foreigner could cross the border into Lithuania. The streets were crawling with weapon-carrying Soviet militia who stopped anyone at random to check their papers. I was never stopped. I went about my daily business of going to and from work. It was a far from pleasant time; in fact, it was scary. I went to East Berlin to celebrate Naw-Rúz with friends who were visiting relatives there and it was at that time that we heard that absolutely no foreigners were being allowed into Lithuania. I boarded the train for Lithuania and had no trouble crossing the border. I don't know how many foreigners were on that train but I was certainly the only person in the carriage. I had the place to myself.

Lithuania is a very Catholic country and for many local people the idea of not being Catholic means you are betraying your country, especially so at that time. The few Bahá'ís in Vilnius were almost afraid to teach the Faith; afraid to tell their parents, families and friends that they had become Bahá'ís; and many of them didn't for several years. It was a very difficult time for the local community. There were some interested youth but they were forbidden to have anything to do with us. In September 1990 we were nine believers and we built the first Local Spiritual Assembly of the Bahá'ís of Vilnius. Later that year a Tatar family from Ufa in Russia moved to Vilnius, bringing the number of believers to 12 adults and one child. This meant that at Riḍván 1991 we had to have our first election.

A short time after the fall of the Soviet Union a youth conference was held in Estonia; about 138 Bahá'ís were present. A few came from Denmark, Norway and Finland but the rest came from Lithuania, Estonia, Latvia, Ukraine, Siberia, Azerbaijan, Murmansk, Moscow and from many other parts of what used to be the USSR. It was absolutely wonderful to see all these young people with so many cultural differences learning to leave their prejudices behind. Much consultation and deepening took place. My group consisted of a mixture of Russians and Estonians who could not at first come to terms with the dignity of consultation, so we had quite a difficult time. However, things progressed from the first group session where there was a lot of shouting and nobody listening, to the next session where there was more explanation and prayers and not so much shouting and more listening, to the third session where we had an extraordinarily dignified group meeting. The discussion was about the Local Assembly and consultation. There was a great depth of understanding from the participants, especially, it seemed to me, from the Russians who appeared to have a real sense of spiritual matters. Of course there was some tension between the Russians and the Balts. It was to be expected but, even so, it was difficult for us from the West to understand: we had never lived in a Soviet-occupied country. Amazingly, some of the Russians and the Balts formed strong ties during that conference and visited each other over the years.

We from the 'free West' cannot understand what it must be like to be denied freedom of speech, of worship, etc., always being careful about what one says and to whom. I remember in 1989 when teaching at an institute the students asked me to teach them Christmas songs. No problem. I did – and found myself being reprimanded by the Dean.

It took a great deal of patience to try to deepen the friends with a minimum of literature. Nineteen day feasts and holy days were always celebrated, perhaps not always as they should be. For a long time we had to have prayers while the TV was on; eventually I managed to persuade the friends to turn the sound down! The Fast was quite a challenge for the friends and for me, as they would call me at odd times during the day to tell me if they had been able to fast after midday or if they managed to fast until 3 p.m., etc. Some of the friends who could read English became very deepened and strong in the Faith. One young man after hearing Mr Grossmann give a talk on the Covenant was very indignant because I had not told him about it. I explained there were a great many things I had not told him and a great many things I did not know. To date, of those first eight local believers, one is deceased, three are still active and two are still registered and call themselves Bahá'ís but their circumstances hinder them from being active.

Reflecting later [2008] on what she had written above, Helen added a little more in order to bring things up to date –

As the years passed and we had more and more literature translated into Lithuanian and freedom of speech, worship, etc. became the norm, so many more people heard about the Faith. In 1999 the first National Spiritual Assembly of the Bahá'ís of Lithuania was elected.

As the doors to the West opened, so travelling teachers visited and helped with the proclamation work. I remember very clearly in 1995 the young woman from the US who had just qualified as a doctor and wanted to spend some weeks in Lithuania. She managed to get the money together – she sold her car in order to do this – and she spent just over three weeks with me in Kaunas. What a joy it was. She was a heaven-sent angel. We travelled around on old Soviet buses, slept on floors and not once did she complain or compare Lithuania to the US or try to promote the American way of life.

After some time we had Bahá'ís in Vilnius, Kaunas, Klaipeda, Visaginis, Plunge and Ukmerge. Of course, some of these communities collapsed but with such a young community coming from the depths of communism, I think it was to be expected, however much it saddened us. We have been blessed with long and short-term pioneers who have all contributed to the growth of the Faith in this country. It has not been easy for them but they have carried out their God-given tasks with radiance, joy, humour and courage. At this time [2008] there are many towns open to the Faith, not with large numbers of believers, but they are open and proclamation and teaching work goes on in them.

This year the Auxiliary Board member spearheaded a major teaching project in Klaipeda. We were fortunate to have several Bahá'í youth from Canada who worked like Trojans to teach the Faith. There were some registrations in Klaipeda and a few still continue to be classed as Bahá'ís. There followed another project in Vilnius with even greater results. There are youth groups and children's classes, study circles and devotional meetings. A new surge in teaching has taken place.

The attitude to different religions has really not changed. To be Lithuanian means to be Roman Catholic and this makes it difficult to get folks interested. The fear of being different is still an issue, as it was in the early days. However, with our few stalwart believers we continue to teach and be involved in the core activities, knowing that the numbers will increase and the Faith will go from strength to strength.

19

July 1992

Bill Brown

Ghana

Bill, from Liverpool, has been living and working in Tamale in the Northern Region of Ghana since 1979.

Recently there has been a tribal war going on about 80 miles from here. There was a flare-up about some land dispute with its roots going back a century or two. Last year about 10 to 20 people were killed and a large village burnt down about 120 miles away in the bush. I was there a couple of weeks ago and they still had not rebuilt it. It is too late now for this year, as the dry season, which is the time for building, has passed.

I went to look at the mission station which was not attacked but is old and needs repair. The attacking tribe threatened to cut off the priest's head when they suspected him of smuggling out refugees. He is a very nice man from Chile and he *was* smuggling them out. Anyway, the Nawuris counter-attacked and then the army went in and since then it has been quiet but obviously uneasy. The army left a few months ago and a couple of weeks back the Nawuris were attacked again by the Gonjas. This time they made the mistake of also killing some Konkombas and Basaris as well as Nawuris. The other tribes then ambushed the Gonjas in the village where the fighting took place last year - probably 60 people were massacred there. At least another one hundred people died, ten villages burned to the ground and ten thousand people were made homeless, by official count – many coming to Tamale.

Over the years tribes have migrated and built villages in each other's territories, paid a form of tribute to the local chiefs and settled. Now the Konkombas in strongly-held Gonja areas are very scared of reprisals and they have already started packing up and moving back to more secure areas. The main immediate problem is that these are all farmers and they have recently planted their fields; now, after abandoning them, where will the food come from? There will be greater strain on the crops produced in more peaceful areas. The other problem is to contain the fighting just in the area where it flared up, as there are many other tribes here, all with overlapping, ill-defined boundaries, all with long histories of fighting each other, and all with long memories. As Bahá'ís we are too few in number to be able to help the refugees but we are praying and talking privately to those who may have some influence to try to find a peaceful way to live. The simple suppression of armed conflict is not enough and land ownership is everywhere a most sensitive topic. 'No land for peace,' the Gonjas say. Then I tell my Gonja friends that in that case they will need their land for cemeteries. We pray God will open up more hearts, as there will be no other lasting solution.

We, the Bahá'ís in Tamale, are planning to hold a study group to study the scriptures from the African cultural and historical perspective. We will choose topics such as children, illness, the elderly and see what the scriptures have to say on these subjects and how we can move from where we are now to the ideal described there. I think we from the 'developed' North can learn a lot from such exercises. In the Bahá'í writings Africans have been described as the 'black pupil of the eye' through which 'the light of the spirit shineth forth'. In Tamale we have discussed this and feel that since the pupil of the eye is the area where the light passes through before it can be understood by the mind, so there should be something in our culture and history here which can contribute to an understanding of the Faith. We must study each other's cultures if we are to live together without confusion and misunderstanding. As Bahá'ís we meet a great number of people from different parts of the world and such contacts will increase and enrich our lives as we learn from each other's experiences.

20
October 1992
Hooman Momen
Brazil

A personal report based on information from a participant (not an official record of the event) regarding Bahá'í activities at the UN Conference on the Environment and Development, Rio, Brazil, 1–14 June 1992.

Prelude

On 28 May the Chamber of Deputies of the National Congress of Brazil held a special session to pay homage on the centenary of the ascension of

Bahá'u'lláh. The session was held in the plenary of the congress building and was presided over by the President of the Chamber of Deputies, the third highest ranking public official (after the President and Vice-President) of Brazil. The other members at the podium were six deputies, each representing one of the main political parties. The President, in a break with protocol, also invited the chairman of the National Spiritual Assembly to the podium. Each of the six deputies spoke with dignity and respect on different aspects of the 'Life of Bahá'u'lláh'. The session was closed by the President, who read with emotion a special message from the Universal House of Justice addressed to him and containing a prayer revealed for representatives of legislative assemblies. After the session a commemorative postmark of the event was inaugurated by the Post Office.

Global Forum

About 100 to 150 Bahá'ís participated in the Forum as members of official Bahá'í delegations, as members of other official delegations or NGOs, or as volunteers from all parts of Brazil and other countries, as well as local Bahá'í residents. The numerous Bahá'í contingent was characterized by the diversity of the nationalities, races and ages of its members. Many wore a Bahá'í T-shirt with a distinctive logo which soon became a common sight in nearly all Forum activities.

The Bahá'í Stand

The Bahá'ís occupied a triple stand with an exhibition of Bahá'í development projects; free literature and books were available. This stand had a very favourable central location and was continuously manned by volunteers during the entire two weeks. From the very beginning it attracted the attention of the participants and public and received a continuous stream of visitors. At peak periods the stand would become completely surrounded by enquirers, several people deep. A minimum of a thousand people a day took literature from the stand and approximately 17,000 requests for literature were recorded. Those taking literature from the stand included people from over 50 different countries, many of whom were journalists, who received a special press kit. One of the highlights was the visit by the President of Iceland, who specifically asked to visit the Bahá'í stand.

Tree of Life

This was a centrepiece of the Global Forum and was the idea of a non-Bahá'í British environmentalist. The tree received pledges in the form of leaves from people and children all over the world. The Bahá'ís were involved as volunteers in sorting out the pledges by countries which were then taken to the tree for hanging. The exit of the Bahá'í youth from their tent all dressed in their distinctive T-shirts, pushing the wheelbarrow of pledges always attracted the attention of the public and press. In fact, the continuous energy and movement of the youth served to multiply the public perception of the numbers and omnipresence of the Bahá'í participation. The tree was also the stage for the opening and closing sessions of the Forum as well as the visits of dignitaries and authorities. On all these occasions the Bahá'í participation was guaranteed either as speakers, by the reading of a prayer, by providing entertainment, by being publicly thanked for their support of the Forum or by the simple presence of the Bahá'ís in their T-shirts on the stage. On some occasions the Bahá'ís had the opportunity to present literature to the dignitary, such as on the visits of Prime Minister John Major of the UK and former governor Jerry Brown of California.

Evening Series in the Park

A selection of musical and dance performances took place every evening at an amphitheatre in the Flamengo Park. The coordination and programming of the whole series was given by the Forum to the Bahá'ís. This information was featured in the official programme of the Forum and obviously increased the awareness and prestige of the Faith in artistic circles. During the whole period performers would come to the Bahá'í stand or office looking for information. The last evening of the series was a unity show performed by Bahá'í artists. The show lasted about four hours and was assisted in full or in part by about five thousand people. The acts included modern dance, jazz, a Bahá'í school children's choir, an Indian hoop dance and flute music, traditional Latin American music and Brazilian folk music. Between each act selections from Bahá'í writings on unity were read.

Peace Monument

This monument was the initiative of the Bahá'ís and probably had the greatest repercussion in terms of publicity for the Faith. The monument was designed by a famous Brazilian sculptor in the form of two hollow concrete pyramids, one inverted above the other with a glass collar where the pyramids meet, the whole forming a kind of gigantic egg-timer five metres high. The Bahá'ís invited each national delegation to bring one kilo of soil from their country to be placed in the monument. The construction of the monument captured the interest of both the press and the public and its construction was followed by articles and pictures in all the principal newspapers and TV networks. Inscribed on the bottom pyramid are the words 'World Peace' in many languages and

on the top pyramid 'The earth is but one country, and mankind its citizens –
Bahá'u'lláh' in four languages, one on each outer face. On the top facing the
sky is the symbol of the Greatest Name.

Other Global Forum Activities

On World Environment Day an official gala ceremony was held in the opera
house of Rio de Janeiro to present the last of the Global 500 awards, a distinction given to persons and institutions by the UN Environment Programme
which have markedly contributed to its aims. The fact that one of the awar-
dees was the Bahá'í Institute for Rural Women in India increased the prestige
of the Faith and stimulated interest in it among a very select audience.

General Comments

Never before had the Faith been proclaimed to so many prominent people
and leaders of thought at the same time. It is safe to assume that at least 90
per cent of those attending the Global Forum became aware of the Bahá'í
Faith. Those who already knew of the Faith were amazed at the breadth of its
involvement and the seriousness of its purpose, while the prestige of the Faith
was greatly increased in the eyes of its friends and admirers.

21
October 1992
Janak McGilligan
India

Being a Bahá'í Representative at Rio.

The supreme body, the Universal House of Justice, the Bahá'í International
Community and the National Spiritual Assembly of India bestowed on me
the honour of going to Rio to receive the Global 500 Roll of Honour by
UNEP on behalf of the Bahá'í Vocational Institute for Rural Women [now the
Barli Development Institute for Rural Women]. Receiving the award was one
of the most important opportunities to participate in the process of establishing the new World Order of Bahá'u'lláh.

This was my first experience of being one of the 140 Bahá'ís from many
different parts of the world who were working together in perfect harmony as
one team in the biggest non-Bahá'í historical, global event. All of us realized
our feeling of achievement was not just from making our presence felt but also
because we presented the Bahá'í point of view to the world, which might go a

long way to help mankind. It was very enlightening and a practical experience of being a Bahá'í in action.

I would like to mention that one of the fascinating experiences was meeting Bahá'ís without there being any formal or informal introductions. The Bahá'ís with T-shirts reading 'Bahá'í – Rio – 92' just came across each other and we met our folks by just greeting each other with 'Alláh-u-Abhá'! Every Bahá'í there was a worker (no matter whether an old or new Bahá'í, learned or unlearned!) and this was one of the most touching experiences of being a Bahá'í, for which we felt distinguished from the whole world.

22
October 1992
Cymbeline Smith
Czechoslovakian Teacher-Training Institute '92
Youth Service

Cymbeline lives with her family in Wisborough Green, Sussex, and has been involved in a number of Bahá'í youth activities.

At the start of 1992 the European Bahá'í Youth Council called upon believers to offer an extended period of service from a minimum of three months to a whole year during the Holy Year. It was in August that I attended the large scale teacher-training conference in Brno, Czechoslovakia, and it was from this conference that the volunteers were divided into the 14 set routes which went out all across Europe from the Atlantic to the Urals.

It was with great anticipation and excitement that I left England to travel to Brno. I was fully aware that we were nearly half way through the Holy Year and that I, personally, had not felt close enough to Bahá'u'lláh, nor was I, as a result, very inspired to teach the Faith regularly. So with great hope I awaited this intensive teacher-training institute, as a child anticipates its medicine when ill, for it may be painful and hard to take at first but will as a result benefit and heal the child.

We arrived late one night and were welcomed warmly by about 80 Bahá'ís from all over Europe, as well as from America and Africa. It was encouraging also to have the chance to meet and deepen with the new local Czechoslovakian youth who had recently declared their faith and were already participating in the routes. For the first few days of the institute everyone took their time settling into the intensive sessions and format each day; starting with prayers at 7 a.m. – or 6 a.m. on two other mornings on top of a hill!

The sessions were on just the right subjects for what I personally needed, as well as preparing the volunteers for nine months of service. The subjects covered included 'The Power of Divine Assistance', which inspired and comforted us all, as well as 'Welcoming New Believers' and 'The Power of the Word of God'. Much of this was a build-up to introducing us all to a new way of direct teaching; direct as well as sensitive in its approach and always appealing to people's hearts rather than to their intellect! For Bahá'u'lláh says, 'That which He hath reserved for Himself are the cities of men's hearts; and of these the loved ones . . . are in this Day, as the keys.' The teaching method also aimed to bring 'champions' into the Cause, who would be able to teach their own people with even greater understanding than the volunteers on the routes.

We were lucky to have Counsellor Patrick O'Mara and Auxiliary Board members from England and Spain to introduce us to this new method which has been so successful when used. It was not only the teaching method that was direct; we were told clearly that the short obligatory prayer was out and the long obligatory prayer was in!! And from then on, the 14 routes were also to say the Fire Tablet at 10 a.m. (GMT) every day.

Every afternoon we had practical sessions on using music and drama in our teaching, as well as dealing with the media and making exhibitions and slide shows with the resources people already had with them. People with musical talents got together and helped those who weren't born with a violin in their right hand or ballet shoes on both feet! The use of the performing arts in the 14 routes' teaching was really important because, as we are told in the writings of 'Abdu'l-Bahá, 'Whatever is in the heart of man, melody moves and awakens.' This is in keeping with the method of direct teaching and the 'performing' was seen as a welcoming mat for the new believers, as well as comforting the volunteers, for in Brno we created a song that we all learned and took with us on the different routes.

It was in the evenings, when mostly we celebrated Bahá'u'lláh's life, that I really felt moved. People individually told stories about Bahá'u'lláh that had touched them and together we shared with each other how excited we felt at the prospect of nine months' teaching.

We had two large sessions every day where all the routes were together, and then afterwards we all split up into our individual routes to discuss the subjects further. This helped the 14 routes to feel united with each other as well as beginning to have bonds with the individuals on their own routes.

On one of the final mornings, with music in the background, there was a long session on 'martyrdom', which I felt really made us all feel so honoured to be free to spread the Cause of Bahá'u'lláh as well as to remind us of the pure, high standards we can all aspire to. The session on 'The Power of Divine Assistance' helped all the volunteers to rely on Bahá'u'lláh and the Abhá Kingdom, as well as to really use intense prayer to get through and feel connected; and it was in the 'martyrdom' session that we all felt we could also turn to the martyrs. How blessed with assistance and encouragement we are as Bahá'ís.

As the week continued, my heavy heart and occasionally (western-influenced) cynical mind was not only healed but inspired. I so much admired the Bahá'í youth who were going for nine months, for I am only going for a month on a route to the Shetland Islands and then on down to Southern Africa for six months. All the Auxiliary Board members were so encouraging but for me it wasn't simply these people that made this institute so good, it was the atmosphere there. It was a spiritual atmosphere – like the Abhá Kingdom was there to really assist us – and this is why it was so good, because when I left the conference it was only the start and not the finish!

I left there with a new way of teaching, some more knowledge of the Bahá'í writings and a more personal connection with the Abhá Kingdom. With each day in my everyday life this institute has helped me to know where my priorities lie. I realize now, more than ever, for the institute clearly showed this to me, that spiritually I have so far to go but at least I feel like I am actually trying now. I don't want to be a half-hearted Bahá'í anymore. I want to jump in head first and to aim to be a lover, not just a believer. The institute by no means removed all my faults and limitations but instead of always looking at my reflection in the mirror, and at the floor and others around me, the institute gave me the courage to face the sun of Bahá'u'lláh, to see its brilliance and to try to get closer day by day, so that by facing this sun I can forget about the limitations in my reflection.

For me, the Brno institute had a large impact on my life, for it pointed my feet in the right direction.

23
January 1993
Janak McGilligan
India

Janak McGilligan sent the following report concerning the Guinea worm-affected villages of Dhar district in Madhya Pradesh (for which the Global 500 Award was given in Rio earlier in the year).

As soon as we read in the newspaper about the 62 Guinea worm-affected cases in the villages of Umerban blok in Dhar district (150 km from Indore), we contacted the Superintending Engineer of Public Health, who encouraged us to visit the villages to organize the awareness programme for the eradication of Guinea worms. We were introduced to the Government Medical Officer in the area and on 13 July 1992 the Institute's team stayed two days in the Guinea worm-affected area. The team gave slide shows showing how the voluntary associations and the government, with the help of women and youth, freed Jhabua from Guinea worms. Various methods were demonstrated to show how to get rid of the worms. These shows were put on at night to ensure the villagers' maximum participation.

After the slide show Mrs Janak McGilligan was able to motivate the villagers, especially the women and youth, to participate. They showed lots of interest and enthusiasm. Next day the team made door to door contact with Guinea worm-affected patients and their families to inform them about the causes of the disease and the simple ways of prevention, such as sieving the water, treating the infected source with the prescribed chemical, taking out the buried drinking water pots for cleaning and using a mug with a handle to take water out of the mud-pot (normally they use a glass and the hand goes with it) and using a hand pump to pump water for drinking whenever it is available. How to nurse the patients was also demonstrated. All this information was given to them in a very practical and careful way. With the help of the representative of the Public Health Department, the village youths were trained to clean their wells so that when the time comes, they will be able to take care of the safety of the water and its resources.

During the door to door contact in Mandlawda village Janak identified two women having a thyroid problem and two children with swollen bellies. Both cases were referred to the doctor for medical treatment and examination. The total number of patients in this area is 68 and out of them 51 are in Mandlawda. The team stayed there for two days. One of the very active local youth, Mr Bandu Singh, said, 'Till now many persons came but the Bahá'í Institute is the first to make an effort to encourage the villagers to participate in this programme.'

Service to the Institute inspired a Bahá'í to come with tree saplings for planting.

The Institute is becoming very pleasing for all the visitors. One recent story concerns a dormant Bahá'í from Indore who visited the Institute after many years and became very impressed by the beauty and growth of the Institute. Recently he came over on his scooter carrying three saplings that he had bought from a commercial nursery in the town. He handed these to Jimmy McGilligan, the manager, saying that he had felt inspired to come with these plants. Jimmy dug the holes in which to plant these trees and our friend planted them. Now this same friend is going to bring mango trees for planting in the Institute grounds. This has been an inspiration to village Bahá'í men and women who were with us in the Institute for nine days attending a family training programme for couples.

24
January 1993
Lois and David Lambert
Mongolia

Lois and David (originally from Kirklees in Yorkshire) arrived in Ulaanbaatar, Mongolia, in September 1992.

When we emerged from the airport on our arrival in Mongolia in October 1992 we were greeted by the lady who was to be our Head of Department from the Institute of Foreign Languages. We had never met each other before but she opened up her arms and hugged us. From that first moment, we have been absolutely overwhelmed by the love and generosity we received from the Mongolian people. They immediately befriended us, offering us hospitality, help and much of their time.

Ulaanbaatar is a long, thin city bounded by mountains changing colours with the seasons – they are now a dazzling white. Skies are always blue with plenty of sunshine even though it is 30 or 40 degrees below zero at the moment. After living for three years in China, the fact that there are so few people and so much open space is amazing to us. Many people wear the traditional Del – a double breasted garment with a high neck and a wide sash, worn with high boots with curled up toes. Dels are really warm and look very colourful and dignified, especially on the men. David is much too tall for any he has tried on so far – there's a big, draughty gap between the hem and his boots!

Mongolia is currently suffering a severe economic collapse – after the abrupt transition in 1990 from a socialist system to a free market economy. Few shops are open and those are almost empty. You can buy meat and potatoes but little else. Sometimes carrots arrive from China and Russia, when the word goes round like wildfire and we all hurry down to the bus station to buy as many as we can afford. Friends have taught us to cut them into thin slices to dry in the sun, to preserve them. When bread is on sale people queue for as long as four hours and many things are only obtainable with a ration card. But we find it is no struggle to live simply. All the worry is taken out of hospitality

– we all eat the same. Our little flat is warm and accessible and we are happy for it to serve as a place for the friends to come at any time.

In our first week one of our students invited us to join her Tai Chi and meditation class. A fortnight later, at the celebration of the Birthday of the Báb, both the Tai Chi teacher and our student declared their belief in Bahá'u'lláh. Mongolians are very eager to talk about spiritual matters and have no problem accepting the teachings and are eager to share them with others. Most of the declarations in Ulaanbaatar are the result of Mongolian friends teaching their colleagues, families and friends. Reverence is also natural to Mongolians. One friend, in describing his daily meditation, told us that after scrupulous ablutions he faces the Greatest Name and the picture of 'Abdu'l-Bahá and 'dances' with his arms raised in supplication, singing a Bahá'í song. Then he sits cross legged and reads from the writings and prays. Finally he meditates. 'And then,' he says, 'Bahá'u'lláh is as close to me as you are now. But if I don't meditate, I don't experience this.'

Now Local Spiritual Assemblies have been formed in Darkhan and Erdenet, the fruits of a teaching project set up by Semira Manaseki (Newcastle, UK), Jessica Shanks and Eric Dougherty (USA, from the Marion Jack project). Now we are just one soul away from forming the fourth Local Spiritual Assembly needed to elect a National Spiritual Assembly.

25
April 1993
Ann Dymond
Gibraltar

Ann pioneered to Gibraltar in December 1991 from Wallingford in Oxfordshire.

When I first heard Philip Hainsworth call for pioneers to go to Gibraltar for the Holy Year (1992) I thought 'this is somewhere I can go', there being no language barrier because most of the Gibraltarians speak English and there are a lot of British people living and working on the Rock. The currency is sterling so no problem with exchange rates. A big plus in favour of living in Gibraltar is the weather – mostly sunny and bright, with only a couple of months wet and windy. So I came over for a week and was bowled over by the friendliness of everybody I met. Perhaps they are really all Bahá'ís but don't know it!

On my second visit I was looking for somewhere to live and found the apartment I now have but before I returned home I discovered that Pari and

Mehraban Firoozmand from Watford were staying here too – a pure coincidence, as we did not know each other and this was our first meeting. We all went home, then after I had moved into this apartment they came and spent a week with me, and as we all enjoyed being together, we agreed to share, thus helping each other out in our pioneering goals. Before Pari and Mehraban moved in with me, two young pioneers, Rozita and Ramin Khalilian, with baby Carmel, arrived. Ramin had found employment and a home for his family during a week's stay in Gibraltar and had then gone ahead and let their home in England, giving up his very well-paid job to do what he and Rozita had promised themselves – to pioneer.

Together we all organized a public meeting for Philip Hainsworth to speak at, and while he was here visiting us from England books were presented to the Governor of Gibraltar. The local radio station gave him an interview and the daily paper, the *Gibraltar Chronicle*, published a large picture of him holding his book with a very good write-up on the Faith. Everything seemed a bit tame after Philip returned to the UK but we made contact with nearby Bahá'ís in La Linea, just across the border in Spain, and joined in their feasts. As well as making many friends here in Gibraltar, we have had visits from Bahá'ís from Scotland, Northumbria and from the Philippines. Since March 1992 we have placed a Bahá'í quotation in the *Gibraltar Chronicle* each week and we have hired a lecture studio in which to hold firesides. The National Spiritual Assembly of the United Kingdom kindly donated some books to the Gibraltar Public Library. We were all able to participate in the Centenary of Bahá'u'lláh's Ascension in the Holy Land and experienced the heavenly, unforgettable experience of it all.

What a year I have had! Living here as a complete Bahá'í for the first time, going to every feast, celebrating every festival, doing all we are asked to daily, and the best bonus of all, having such good loving friends to accompany me, would have made this year special even if it had not been the Holy Year!

26
April 1993
Lois and David Lambert
Mongolia

Pioneers in Ulaanbaatar since September 1992.

We feel very blessed to be able to be in the field of service in this country with its hearts, its mountains and its music so spacious and yet so much in need of the healing message of Bahá'u'lláh. At this time all thoughtful Mongolians are very concerned about the alarming increase in crime, alcoholism, begging, child abuse, vagrancy and moral laxity. They are eager for their children to learn moral and spiritual values.

Things have been moving really fast during the Holy Year in Mongolia. In January we accompanied 'The Amazing Travelling Roadshow' to Darkhan – organized on the initiative of Mongolian Bahá'ís who had been invited to perform professionally for a week in the Pioneer Palace, the largest theatre in Darkhan. Twenty of us set off late on the overnight train, and though only seven of us were Bahá'ís, there was very much of a Bahá'í spirit prevailing in the whole group. The musicians learned to sing Bahá'í songs and the director of the sponsoring company, a poet, promised to write a Mongolian Bahá'í song. In the meantime two of the group translated Joannie Lincoln's beautiful song 'Will You Give Your Heart to Bahá'u'lláh?' into Mongolian.

In Darkhan we were able to get in touch with six of the new local Bahá'ís, who were overjoyed to meet other Mongolian believers. The performance involved music, dance and a display of martial arts in a theatre that seats 800. At the end of the show, the organizer (our Tai Chi teacher who became a Bahá'í last year) came onto the stage, announced that we were Bahá'ís and told the audience something of Bahá'u'lláh's teachings. You can imagine our joy at seeing Bahá'u'lláh's message so publicly proclaimed and what an encouragement it was for the Darkhan friends to see the director's face so full of love for Bahá'u'lláh and so confident that His message is the healing message for the world.

Ulzeet is a small village in Bulgan Aimag where there are is now a Bahá'í community of 13. This community is very precious because it has grown entirely by the teaching efforts of one Mongolian couple who live there. They and their friends travel quite widely in their businesses to different parts of the country and also to China and Russia so there is great potential for travel teaching. Seven of the Ulzeet friends have been staying in Ulaanbaatar recently. Their excitement and enthusiasm are inspiring and infectious and provide an excellent opportunity for the Ulaanbaatar Bahá'ís to see that the Faith is spreading in Mongolia and that fellow Mongolians are actively teaching.

Ulaanbaatar continues to grow in size and maturity and it is unusual if a day passes when some of the friends are not meeting together to deepen, pray and meditate, sing songs and watch Bahá'í videos or just to be together. We are so grateful that we were able to find a home that is central and accessible for people to come to at any time. Not a week goes by without a new Bahá'í being introduced or, as in one case, discovered. One young university student, who is a Mongolian Buryat, met some of the Bahá'ís in Ulan-Ude (Siberia, Russia), where he has some family. On returning to Ulaanbaatar three months ago, he studied the Faith and accepted Bahá'u'lláh, unaware that there were Bahá'ís in Ulaanbaatar. This young man turns out to be our next door neighbour! He has already brought one of his childhood friends to the Faith. His father is the Deputy Secretary General of the Asian Buddhist Conference for Peace, which has in the past been in touch with Bahá'ís in Geneva. Our little courtyard now has eight Bahá'ís living here.

Mongolia has been given the goal of establishing its National Spiritual Assembly at Riḍván 1994, with the aim of opening every *aimag* (province) to the Faith. One of our new Bahá'ís is a part-time reporter on the same national newspaper which published an article on the Bahá'í Faith a few months ago, and he is planning to write a long article on the Faith, based on the World Congress in New York. We are also intending to translate the commentaries of the World Congress video and 'The Jewel in the Lotus' into Mongolian so that they can be available to be shown on Mongolian TV.

27
July 1993
Lois and David Lambert
Mongolia

Visit to Khovd Aimag and the Altai Mountains

In February Sean Hinton arrived in Mongolia, with his new wife Tebby, from Botswana. A couple of weeks after their arrival, the four of us took a plane to Khovd, a small town which is the provincial centre of Khovd Aimag in western Mongolia. When he left Mongolia last year Sean had promised the nomadic family with whom he had lived for several months during the summer that he would bring his new wife to visit them at Tsagaan Sar (Mongolian new year). Although the family lived in the Altai Mountains 400 km south of the airport, and it was the depths of winter and therefore a fairly crazy journey, we decided to do it. As a result we shared an amazing 10 days during which we experienced Mongolian customs and culture to an extent that is not possible in the cities.

Even the first leg of the journey (the easy bit) was pretty hairy. We were kept for half an hour on the tarmac before they let us on the plane, calling us in the order we had arrived at the check-in but very slowly, while everyone pushed and shoved as if their life depended on getting on that plane before their number was called. (As it was 30 degrees below zero this wasn't far from the truth!) But this was counterproductive because the air hostess would get very angry and go back into the plane and shut the door, so we all had to wait longer. When we finally got on the plane and our feet began to thaw we suffered 15 minutes of agonizing pain as frozen blood reacted with the warmth of the plane. Eventually the pain eased and Tebby (who is from Botswana) and I stopped groaning. Sean and David were more stoical but I suspect that was because they both were wearing fur-lined Mongolian boots!

The plane was a tiny, ancient machine that rattled as if it were about to fall apart. We flew for four hours over mountains and desert with only an occasional sighting of groups of two or three *gers* (the round Mongolian tents) nestling in the lee of the mountains. Once arrived in Khovd, we set about finding a driver to take us the 400 km through the Altai mountains the next day. This was more difficult than usual at Tsaagan Sar, when everyone prefers to be with their own family. We finally found someone who was not from Khovd who was willing to go and we planned to set off at 8 a.m. the next morning, hoping to stay overnight in a *ger* and arrive at our destination the following evening. Eight a.m. came and went and at noon there was still no driver! We were sorry to discover finally that the driver had been taken into hospital with acute stomachache. We had to find another driver pretty fast or we would have wasted a lot of money flying to Khovd at the wrong time of year. Eventually we found a driver willing to take us for rather large amounts of money and we set off in the afternoon, much later than intended.

Although it was the depths of winter and 30 to 40 degrees below zero, the sun shone most of the time. We were driving across the steppes, thickly covered in pure white snow so bright with diamonds and crystals that we had to shade our eyes. Sean had wisely brought sunglasses, but as the rest of us associated sunglasses with palm beaches rather than sub-zero temperatures, we had come unprepared. Soon we were in the mountains, edging along narrow snow-covered tracks hanging over gorges and rivers, crossing frozen rivers because the tracks on either side were impassable. Sometimes the rivers had begun to melt and the driver would get out and walk around on the ice – stamping up and down – and looking doubtful. Then we would all get out and watch him get into the jeep and drive across the river at high speed along his chosen route, while the ice bent and cracked behind him, and then the jeep would miraculously climb up the other bank!

All too soon it was dark. We were driving along rough tracks without any knowledge of whether we would find a *ger* in which we could stay the night. It is traditional in Mongolia for travellers to stop at any *ger* on the way, for refreshment or sleep, and when we finally found one, we discovered that the young family had only just moved in that day. They welcomed us warmly and gave us mattresses, but as there was no wooden floor to the *ger*, it was very cold indeed lying on the frozen ground. It was our first real experience of *ger* hospitality in the countryside and Sean guided us in the correct procedures: not to step on the threshold of the *ger* or to step over people's feet as they sit; to go around the *ger* in a clockwise direction and to sit in the appropriate places. The host sits directly opposite the door and as the oldest member of our group I would be seated on his right and would be the one to give out gifts – sweets, tea or sometimes a scarf.

The next day we set off early, travelling all day through spectacular mountain scenery, visiting several *gers* for rest and refreshment. Always we were given butz (meat-filled dumplings) which, politeness demands, you eat in as large numbers as possible, and Mongolian salted tea with milk. We were also always offered *arki* (Mongolian milk vodka) and fermented mare's milk. Guided by Sean, we would take the *arki*, put our ring finger in the liquid and flick drops to the sky and the earth, touch our forehead with the same finger and hand it back, without having drunk any but having satisfied the courtesies of Mongolian hospitality. Only one man, the head man of a village we visited, tried to make us drink but Erdene, our driver, who became a really good friend, explained in detail our Faith and gave a long tribute about how excellent Bahá'í principles were and what good people we were!

Because we were behind in our timing it was late at night when we arrived in the place Sean thought the family would be spending the winter. But they are nomads so it was not absolutely certain and we couldn't find them. The jeep was driving in what seemed to be circles across the empty steppe, sometimes finding animal tracks which we would follow, hoping they would lead to an encampment. Sometimes we would get out and stand under the huge bowl of the sky, studded with brilliant stars, and listen for a dog or any other sound, but there was nothing except the amazing sky. Eventually we found a *ger* by the roadside, the occupants of which knew the family we were looking for and so we finally found them. They were so happy to see Sean, whom they call their son, and we were all received with the usual very warm welcome, fed to bursting and given thick felt rugs to lie on. Sleeping in this *ger* was much warmer than the previous one because they had a wooden floor – also perhaps because of the rugs. You can imagine how very, very glad we were to have found the family at last.

The next day was Tsaagan Sar and there was a little ceremony some way from the *ger*, around a small tree which had been decorated with a few red and white rags blowing in the wind. They were burning dung and incense beside this tree, and food and drink was offered to the sky and the earth and shared between us. We walked three times around the tree in a clockwise direction and embraced each other in the customary way with a new year greeting. Later in the day most of their eleven children and their husbands and wives and children came to visit, dressed in their very best Dels, and greeting the elderly couple with a little customary ceremonial which was beautiful to watch. Only after this formal greeting did they greet Sean and the rest of us, even though Sean's reappearance after so long from the other side of the world was an amazing event for them.

Throughout this journey we had met and visited a number of families. With our still very limited Mongolian, we needed to find effective ways of communicating with our hosts. Mongolians are very generous and hospitable but do not initiate conversation readily and are happy to sit in companionable silence. I found a way of breaking the ice by making little origami flying birds out of waste paper and quietly giving them to the children, showing them how to make the wings flap. This would break the ice as both adults and children would gather round fascinated, wanting to learn how to do it. It was then natural to use the wings to mention the principle of the equality of men and women or the harmony of science and religion. We would also show photos of Conrad (our son) performing with the Bahá'í group 'El Viento Canta' – explaining that he visited Mongolia two years before we arrived, as part of their six month tour of former Soviet countries and China. Photos of our family at the Bahá'í World Centre also gave us a chance to tell people about the Faith.

Less than 24 hours after finding the family we had to begin our homeward journey. The jeep got stuck in snowdrifts many times but each time we managed somehow to dig it out and push it into movement. Often we had to leave the track because it was impassable but our driver instinctively seemed to know how to get through the dangerous mountain passes. Twice we ran out of petrol but obtained some from other drivers and we were on our way again.

Eventually we drove into Khovd at 2 a.m., very dirty and eight hours late for a dinner engagement with the Director of the Foreign Language Institute. Our plane was not until 12 noon the next day so we washed clothes, showered and collapsed into bed in the welcome (comparative) luxury of a tatty hotel!

28
July 1993
Margaret and Bob Watkins
Yugoslavia

Margaret and Bob pioneered to Belgrade from Totnes, Devon, in 1990, having previously served at the Bahá'í World Centre for three years.

Receiving *Pioneer Post* and the *Bahá'í Journal* for the last three years has made us feel that we were not forgotten by the British community. Originally we had planned to pioneer to Taiwan but before our departure, and having been inspired by a talk from a Counsellor about the eastern bloc, we decided to go on a two weeks' travel teaching trip to Yugoslavia.

When in Ljubljana we met an American Bahá'í, aged 75, who had sold her home and was heading for Belgrade with her heavy suitcase. Belgrade was the last place that we wanted to go to but we could not resist her enthusiasm and we changed our destination to drive her to Belgrade. While helping her to find a flat, I dialled a wrong number and found myself applying for a job as housekeeper to an Ambassador. I went for the interview and started work two weeks later! (Most of my life it has been my ambition to employ a housekeeper, not to finish up as one!) This enabled me to obtain a work permit and find a flat, which in those days was almost impossible.

Bob returned to the UK, closed down his small business and returned to Belgrade three months later. Within three weeks my job had collapsed because the Ambassador's country had a financial crisis. (The last member to join the Embassy was the first to be made redundant – me!) I was relieved because it turned out to be more of a cleaning job than that of the well-heeled housekeeper dressed in black standing at the door waiting to usher guests to the dining table (like you see in American films). However, the terminated job had served its purpose for now I had a year's work/resident's permit, banking account and a flat!

About this time an English-language weekly newspaper was launched in Belgrade and I finished up as a journalist with my own weekly column headed 'A Foreigner in Belgrade'. I changed my name in order not to disgrace the family! Bob became a member of the Regional Teaching Committee, organized the publishing of many books, travelled extensively throughout Yugoslavia and taught English. Our son, Paul, joined us later and became a photographic journalist and TV announcer. We were joined by Semira Manaseki and Meyher Badii from the UK plus two youth from Australia. Now we were seven pioneers and were able to contact all strata of society. Six out of the seven of us became teachers of English, which was a new adventure for us all.

The Faith really took off after the first book fair. We made many contacts and many good friends. Two new pioneers from the UK moved into Ljubljana and Meyher went to Zagreb. Unfortunately Semira had to return to the UK and was sorely missed by all her young friends.

The country then divided and chaos reigned. However, we were able to continue with our book fairs, concerts, firesides and public meetings in the southern part of Yugoslavia.

Bahá'u'lláh gave us plenty of opportunity to learn about detachment with our Serbian friends: 200 per cent inflation a month, queuing for petrol, some food shortages, strikes and no spare parts for repairs. Three months before we left we opened a Bahá'í Centre in Novi Sad, a town one and a half hours from Belgrade. We spent four days a week in Novi Sad and the rest in Belgrade. We seemed to be forever on the move.

We shall never forget Yugoslavia. We made many wonderful friends and we now have a Yugoslav daughter-in-law (Jelena, an electronics engineer) and about 150 distant relations. (What an experience it was when we attended a family wedding and met them en mass, especially as we never mastered the language!) The land is being tilled deep and seeds have been sown. The harvest is yet to be gathered.

29
October 1993
Janet and Ned Cundall
Tanzania

Janet and Ned pioneered to Tanzania in July 1990. From 1984 to 1986 they were pioneers in Papua New Guinea.

We are in Mtwara, Tanzania. Our young children, Alan and Alicia, are now able to travel with me and they speak Kiswahili like natives. They translate for us, correct our pronunciation and try to teach us new words every day.

In July the three of us left Ned to his cashew statistics and travelled most of one day to reach Mwitika village, near the Mozambique border. The local Bahá'ís there have been running a nursery school for 18 months. It was wonderful to hear the children sing prayers and songs and crowd round to look at pictures. They looked surprised about a picture showing that we should not bathe, wash clothes or fetch buckets from the same place that animals and people bathe. After an hour's class, they asked, 'Is that all?', obviously wanting more.

Several Bahá'ís from other villages came by foot and bicycle to help run a deepening conference. Alan and Alicia and I were given a house with a tin roof to stay in (most houses have grass roofs) and the children were very popular with the village people. During a discussion on 'Why do we pray?', Alan (aged 5) piped up, 'Because God loves us', so I was then sure I wasn't crazy exposing my children to malaria and filthy water (they did not get sick).

We stayed two nights in the village, glorious starry nights amidst melodious African Bahá'í music and laughter. The elderly chairman of the Local Spiritual Assembly, a key believer, was very sick and we were able to drive him (half a day's drive) on our way home to the nearest mission hospital where he was admitted. The hospital had no beds left for him so the mattress the children and I had brought to sleep on came in handy (we would not have needed it in the village as the home owners gave up their woven grass and post beds for us). Fortunately he recovered well.

The weekend before Mwitika, Ned had looked after the children and I had gone by bus and foot (our old Land Rover is usually broken down) to Mpindimbi village where there have been Bahá'ís since 1975, although they have been left to their distant selves for a long time. It was great to see how much they knew about the Faith, as usually we are with new Bahá'ís. At least ten women, carrying pots, food, tools on their heads and babies on their backs, came. All the Bahá'ís were keen to make cashew tree nurseries with the pots and seeds Ned gave me for them. A few days later, a colleague of Ned was working in Mpindimbi and was impressed to be asked for several hundred more pots and seeds. Now we are busy practising songs for our second Bahá'í wedding in this part of the world, held in Tulieni village. The people here are so musical and the songs they make up teach Bahá'í principles, history, laws and marriage counselling!

30
October 1993
Peter McAlpine
Thailand

Peter pioneered to Thailand in 1984, having become a Bahá'í a short time before whilst travelling through the Caribbean. He grew up in Epsom, Surrey.

In a copy of a *Bahá'í Journal*, someone suggested creating a garden to celebrate the Holy Year. So that is what we did. To give it maximum visibility, we placed it in the middle of the biggest roundabout in Phuket with a sign saying in Thai 'Peace Garden – Sponsored by the Bahá'í community'. All right, so a roundabout is not the most peaceful of places but we know its purpose. Also, as this roundabout is at an important junction to some of the main beaches in Phuket, it has meant that tens of thousands of people have seen the name Bahá'í many times. Furthermore, it has meant that most of the 300 staff at the Phuket Yacht Club Hotel where I work have now heard the name Bahá'í, and some have shown interest. Of course, most people don't know what Bahá'í means but at least it's a big step in the right direction.

As I live the nearest to the garden, I have become the gardener. At first people would hurl verbal abuse at me because they thought I was stealing flowers. Some would come over and look in my bag to see whether I was filling it with flowers or weeds. Some people even went to see my wife at her shop to tell her that they'd seen me stealing flowers. At 6 foot 9 inches, that made me the tallest flower thief in Thailand for sure! Then people got used to seeing me there and some would stop and give me drinks to keep me cool. Now I have made many new friends, namely the hundreds of people who call out to me or wave and say 'hello' as they go round the roundabout. Some stop their car or motorbike on the roundabout and have a chat with me. (Never mind the traffic flow!) Once a Jehovah's Witness stopped his car to throw out one of their peace pamphlets in the form of a paper dart. Twice the public relations clerk at the hotel has published a humorous article about the purpose of the garden and about me causing traffic jams, so the weed-pulling sessions are worth it!

Our next project is to start teaching schoolchildren about our views on the environment. It's a hot topic now in Phuket. We're going to create a giant 'Snakes and Ladders' board using sticks and, as snakes are common here, perhaps we'll use real snakes too. Then each pair of children will have to draw a number and answer questions about the environment, which will be on a hand-out, in order to progress. The game is almost ready in English but it has yet to be translated into Thai. We've also made a Peace Maze based on the Peace Statement but it needs simplifying.

31
October 1993
Mahin Humphrey
Travel Teaching in Albania

You are called upon to spread this life-giving message among your fellow countryman, to the prominent and the lowly alike, thereby imparting to them hope and enlightenment, and enlisting them under the banner of Bahá'u'lláh. It is only through the implementation of His teachings that mankind can hope to emerge from the perils of disintegration and chaos, and establish God's long-promised Kingdom on earth.

The Universal House of Justice[21]

Ever since I heard about the receptivity of the people in Albania, I wanted to visit. Travelling with Jan Mughrabi and Irandokt Talbot, we discovered the cheapest way to Tirana was to fly to Athens and then take the bus to Tirana. On the way we were very lucky to meet up in Athens with six members of the National Spiritual Assembly of Albania who were on their way back from the 1993 International Convention in Haifa. They were all on cloud nine! It was such a pleasure to get to know them and travel with them on the night bus (for 22 hours) to Albania.

On our arrival we were taken to a very lovely Bahá'í family (three generations) for refreshments and then we met with the Auxiliary Board member for two hours of orientation. The next day we were sent to a small town called Fier where we were met by Bahá'ís. We hired an apartment for the duration of our stay, which became the centre for all the friends we met and also the youth. We were very fortunate to meet the young lady who was secretary of the local assembly and also the town librarian. She knew everyone in the town and her library served as a meeting place and for firesides.

Many of the youth invited us to their homes to meet their parents. This was excellent for us, being older Bahá'ís, and a great advantage, for they respected us. We discovered many parents had been studying the Faith through their sons and daughters. They had only a few questions to ask us and then they would embrace the Faith as a family. In one home the mother was wearing a gold cross around her neck. As soon as she said, 'I love Bahá'u'lláh', she took the cross off her neck and put it on the table, saying, 'I don't need this now, I am a Bahá'í' with such sincerity that we just looked at each other and wept. Here was the power of Bahá'u'lláh which transformed this wonderful lady. She is a teacher and she told us that she would now tell all the teachers at her school about the Faith.

We met many VIPs in the town through our dear librarian friend. Her library was full of Bahá'í books and many Bahá'í pictures and posters were hanging on the walls. We had six to eight appointments almost every day but many days we had to see several more people. One thing would lead to another and sometimes we had to turn people away because we had no time to go through our book with them and we had to direct them to the LSA secretary. We were treated like royalty. One day we were visiting the maternity hospital and had to shake hands with many, many staff who were lined up to welcome us and show us around. I turned to Jan and said that I now knew how the Queen felt! We met many friends from the medical profession and also with teachers.

The last day of our stay we had an interview with the editor of the local newspaper. After half an hour of him asking us many questions, he said, 'I think the message of Bahá'u'lláh is the only remedy for the sickness of our time in Albania.' I asked him whether he considered himself a Bahá'í. He said, 'What else?' We discovered, when he put down his date of birth on the register, that it was 21st April, so we named him Riḍván!

The Albanian people are very receptive and sensitive to spiritual themes, such as Bahá'u'lláh and His station as the Manifestation of God, His sufferings and the spiritual nature of man. A direct invitation to become a Bahá'í seems very natural. It seemed to us that everyone we met were Bahá'ís at heart. They call themselves Muslims or Christians but in fact they know nothing about either. Life in Albania is very simple. The people have very little in the way of material possessions but they have a mine of spiritual qualities. I wish we could have stayed longer.

32
October 1993
Richard and Corinne Hainsworth
Moscow

Notes taken from a talk given at the UK summer school at Warminster, August 1993.

We arrived in Moscow in June 1982. When we first arrived we could only take a prayer book and we couldn't mention the Faith in any way or talk about it in our house because everyone was afraid of microphones that might have existed in the walls of the house. We did, of course, make friends with people and when we felt that some would be interested in hearing about the Faith we had to teach them outside in the street because we could not teach the Faith in our home.

In general people were afraid of us because we were foreign and people would avoid us. Richard was, and still is, working for a publishing house. The only foreigners allowed to work in Russia are those in Embassies or publishing houses using their native language. Richard got a job as editor in English for one of these publishing houses and we were in a unique position in that we lived in a Russian apartment block. Most of the foreigners live in special blocks with a policeman outside and they never meet an ordinary Russian but we were put in a flat and lived with Russians.

A Bahá'í came from Finland on business and he was responsible for the first Bahá'í to declare in Moscow in 1985. I started to give her English lessons as an excuse for her to visit us so that we could be together as Bahá'ís. In November 1988 two Irish pioneers came to Moscow but they were not allowed to visit us. In January 1989 the Universal House of Justice said that the time was now right for the Bahá'ís to start meeting at Feasts. However, communication was difficult and we were not informed of this. In February we had a phone call from the Irish friends and we invited them to dinner. They came with their two children. Having done this, we independently decided that we would start meeting with the other Bahá'í who was living in Moscow. By April 1989 we were seven Bahá'ís in the city. Also in 1989 the first Local Spiritual Assembly was elected in Siberia as a result of the visit of El Viento Canta to Ulan-Ude.

A month or two earlier two people from Moscow had 'declared' in Germany and they returned at Riḍván 1989 to find a Bahá'í community in the city. The Local Spiritual Assembly of Ishqabad was reelected and we actually sent one of our new Bahá'ís from Moscow to represent our community at that election. In 1990 our community had grown and we were more out in the open. One of our old Bahá'ís (he was from Azerbaijan) died that year and we were asked by his son to organize the ceremony. We had to bury him in a Muslim cemetery and it was the custom to have a big feast after the funeral. There were 19 of us present at the funeral and we were asked quite a lot of questions by his friends.

By 1990 there were 30 Bahá'ís in Moscow and the Local Spiritual Assembly was reformed in the presence of Hand of the Cause Mr Furútan, who had been a member of the Local Spiritual Assembly of Moscow that had been dissolved 60 years before! The Local Spiritual Assemblies of Tallin (Estonia), Ishqabad and Dushanbe were also elected that year. During the summer months of 1990 there were so many teaching activities that Local Spiritual Assemblies were being elected all over the place!

In 1990 a Two Year Plan was given to us by the National Spiritual Assembly of Germany and our goal was to form 19 Local Spiritual Assemblies – at that time there were only four. We thought it an impossible goal but in fact more than 19 Local Spiritual Assemblies were formed.

As there was so much activity in Moscow – all routes led to Moscow – we asked the National Spiritual Assembly of Germany if we could organize a conference for all the Bahá'ís in USSR. The letter never reached Germany! Eventually the Universal House of Justice heard of our suggestion and it asked the German National Assembly what could be done about it. In December 1990 this conference took place and Bahá'ís came to it from all parts of the USSR – from as far east as Sakhalin to Estonia in the west, to Ishqabad in the south and beyond the arctic circle in Murmansk. Thus the whole of the USSR was represented at the conference, the first time that Bahá'ís in the USSR had met each other. There were seven counsellors present and 17 nationalities were represented. Philip Hainsworth came from the UK and there were representatives from many other countries.

The outcome of this conference was the plan to elect a National Spiritual Assembly the following Riḍván. Thus the second gathering of the Bahá'ís of the USSR at Riḍván 1991 elected the first National Spiritual Assembly of the Bahá'ís of the USSR, only one year after the start of the Two Year Plan. The members who were elected came from cities covering eight time zones: Murmansk, Moscow, Kiev, Sakhalin, Baku, Azerjbaijan, Ulan-Ude. It is a nine hour flight to Sakhalin from Moscow!

Everything continues to go well. Each week someone in Moscow becomes a Bahá'í. We think that now there are about three thousand Bahá'ís in Russia, Georgia and Armenia (which is our NSA area). People are thirsty to hear about religion and are looking carefully at every religion. We have been asked by the Universal House of Justice to have two intensive teaching campaigns and we expect to enrol between ten and twenty thousand new Bahá'ís during the Three Year Plan. One of our plans is to teach children spiritual values in every school in Russia.

It took us seven days to travel to the National Convention this year. There were about 16 Bahá'ís travelling together on the train. When the restaurant car was free, we would go with pamphlets and invite people to listen to information about the Faith, holding firesides on the train! We even sold two thousand roubles worth of Bahá'í books on the train. Russians are great readers. If people feel the spirit of the Faith, they become Bahá'ís. An interesting point is that some communities have been formed for as long as two years but they have not enough adult believers to form a Local Spiritual Assembly. They have to wait for a youth to become 21 and then they elect their Assembly the next day!

33
January 1994
Susan and Shidan Kouchek-zadeh
Guinea-Conakry, West Africa

Pioneer Post gets more and more precious! It's a wonderful link with the rest of the Bahá'í world for we get very few Bahá'í visitors to Guinea – in 18 years we've had less than ten. Talking of 18, this is possibly Vadiay's last year here as she takes her baccalaureate in June 1994 and will go on to university in the UK, we hope.

This past year, for the first time, our National Convention (Guinea's sixth) was not held in the capital but in the Forest Region where most of Guinea's Bahá'ís actually live. It took those of us who were coming from Conakry two days to get there and when we arrived at the small house in Lola, the temporary home of a young pioneer from Burkina Faso, we were very impressed by a shelter of palm leaves that had been erected in front of the house. Alas, within 20 minutes of our arrival there was a downpour so heavy that the shelter collapsed. Nevertheless, it was up again the following morning and Convention was held under it. The exciting development at Convention was that for the first time a native Guinean woman was elected to the National Assembly. It makes for an interesting situation as she has no language in common with any other member of the Assembly! We have seven mother tongues amongst the nine members of the Assembly; perhaps it's not very unusual for Africa.

Our village schools project in this Forest area is a big item on the agenda of the National Spiritual Assembly. We have a French pioneer couple here who are teachers; although they work in Conakry they have established an Education Centre halfway between here and the Forest Region where they train young Bahá'ís from the villages, chosen by their Local Assembly, to teach primary school. The Local Spiritual Assembly is responsible for providing a building (sometimes just a bamboo and palm leaf structure) and benches; for collecting the fees (about 70p a month per child) and paying the teacher with the fees. Our French friends provide the programme and visit the classes as often as they can to support the young teachers. The National Assembly helps to finance the teachers' training and provides the pencils, paper, crayons, etc. for the classes. (Last year's educational materials for five classes were provided by a British Local Assembly).

There have been setbacks: one chosen teacher received his first month of training and then, just when the class should start, disappeared into the bush for an initiation programme; another village chose their man and then, on the eve of the training programme, he was given a scholarship to the capital and they didn't have time to chose another, and so on. But in the first village to start its school the young teachers are doing so well that teachers from the public schools (including their own teachers!) come to watch them at work and their students are way ahead of those in the public schools. Since the classes are strictly limited to 20 students the teachers only receive 70p x 20 a month – but that's another problem!

34
January 1994
Jo Harding
Greece

I have been in Greece two and a half years now. Time flies and there is so much to do! It was hot in Greece this summer – a sizzling 42 degrees C – and a busy one too. Our small Greek community has been out and about and has already fulfilled its goals for the Three Year Plan for travel teaching in the Balkans. Many helped with the famous 'open letter' project in Albania, which visited every village and resulted in some three thousand new Bahá'ís.

I went to Albania in July with a short-term pioneer to Greece, Californian Patti Berger. We were directed to visit a remote mountain village in the north, Puka, and stayed with the Islami family, who all became Bahá'ís. My first time in Albania, I was overwhelmed by the love and warmth of the people we met, and with their purity of heart, which enables them to recognize and love Bahá'u'lláh 'at first sight'.

Back in Greece I joined the third teaching project in Volos, where an international group and the local friends were together for street teaching and some clean-up jobs for the environment. While the latter were well received, the former roused some vigorous opposition from Orthodox Church folk who accused us of proselytising. We continued as before but there were no further attacks. Then the local Bahá'ís put a wonderful series of quotations in the paper, daily for 42 days, so that the wisdom and name of Bahá'u'lláh was read throughout the town. Here in Athens our numbers have increased as we keep coming across Albanians who want to be Bahá'ís! Our home is often a stopping off point for travel teachers coming through, especially for Albania and the Balkans; Haifa, too, with pilgrims coming and going.

We are to celebrate the arrival, 40 years ago, of Rolf Haug, Knight of Bahá'u'lláh to Crete, and the beginning of the Bahá'í Faith in Greece. This will be a festive gathering in true Greek style and we hope that many non-Bahá'í friends will come and learn more about us.

Another new experience this year was to find myself in the role of summer school coordinator and being responsible for the children's programme too. So it was an exciting week! The school was much enjoyed and we made an innovation in Greece by having daily workshops in small groups. It had been predicted that the Greek friends would not be comfortable with this style but it turned out very well with a much deeper level of contribution and learning than had been anticipated. Counsellor Patrick O'Mara spent a few days with us and we enjoyed the bliss of one of the best beaches in Greece. In the hottest of weather, the bluest of seas was full of happy Bahá'ís.

On the last evening a splendid festivity took place on the village *platia* under the huge plane trees. The next day as we gathered to say goodbye in a temperature of over 100 degrees F, the *platia* became the scene of a great water game, and most of us were delightedly wet to the skin as our youth (and some much older) scattered the cool water from the fountain in all directions. Some of the friends visited the village mayor and talked about the Faith in the tavernas and cafes; the response was good, warm and friendly.

We find that the Greek people are very pleased to listen to and acknowledge our explanations of the Faith but very rarely feel the need to go further and in the end remain steadfastly Orthodox. So we need pioneers with a lot of patience who do not mind waiting a long time for results. Perhaps this is one reason why we all like to go off to Albania or Bulgaria from time to time. It's enormously encouraging to find people who actually ask to become Bahá'ís!

The Greeks have recently elected a new government, so we are hoping that they will grant us the status of a recognized independent religion. Stephanie and Wesley Clash have decided to make their permanent home on Corfu and this has reopened this important island. Wesley intends to build his own house there when he is off duty from his unusual job of deep-sea 'saturation' – diving to construct oil rigs.

35
April 1994
Fiona Beint and Vicky Howarth
Swaziland

Fiona and Vicky (from Brixworth, Northamptonshire) are youth year of service volunteers at the Bahá'í Primary School in Mbabane, where they have been since September.

Our year of service is rushing by and the Bahá'í Primary School keeps us incredibly busy. We've been teaching art, music, reading, English and anything else that comes along! For the best part of our six week summer vacation we were involved in a very successful teaching project dedicated to the memory of Bahá'í pioneers Brian and Jennifer Bayliss killed in a light aircraft accident in October 1992.

We have been helping to reactivate the Bahá'í community of Gege. We held children's classes every afternoon at the homestead where we were staying. Each day more children would come from the village to sing songs and to hear stories about the Faith. On our last evening in Gege we walked with all the children into the village, singing all the way. The children would call out 'Alláh-u-Abhá' to everyone we met and then, when we got to the market place, we all stood (about 20 of us) singing every Bahá'í song we knew. Soon the market place was filled with people who joined in with the songs and eagerly took leaflets from the radiant children!

Of course the trip wasn't all heavenly experiences; we had no electricity, hardly any water (washing our hair was a problem and those of you who know us will know that this was a big problem!) and we had to share a room with tap-dancing, sweet-eating, toilet-roll devouring RATS! However, we are strong believers in the fact that without suffering you can't have blessings! We would definitely risk the horrors of pit toilets again if it meant we would be able to see 20 beautiful children standing in the market place of Gege, at sunset, proclaiming that 'Bahá'u'lláh has come!'

36
April 1994
Bill Brown
Ghana

Bill, a longtime pioneer (from Liverpool) in Ghana with his Ghanaian wife Paulina and three sons, wrote this harrowing letter on 5 February. Bill is in charge of the building unit for the Catholic Diocese of Tamale in the north of Ghana.

Since last Tuesday we have been in a war. 'Inter-ethnic' conflict is the label given to it. We hear of wars almost every day in the newspapers, on the radio, TV, then one explodes around you. People you know are manning road barriers, searching for weapons, searching for people to kill. Houses you pass every day are destroyed by mobs with sticks and fire. Bodies lie in the streets, stoned to death, outside the local supermarket. Areas of your town are 'no-go' and you are being shot at. Desperately you try to contact friends and those you know to see if they are OK. Lives are destroyed, communities irreparably damaged. Maybe our conflict is too small to capture the headlines, and I know that many are experiencing these things and worse on a daily basis, but it is simply in a newspaper, you read it and turn the page . . .

Then it is your neighbourhood.

In an area about 100 miles by 100 many of the villages and towns I know and have worked in have been destroyed and with them much of my hope for a better future for this people. My dreams are receding into a further distance, their suffering more immediate. Were those hopes never really shared between us? When their huts are burnt their seed for the next planting is burnt with it and those still alive will starve this coming year. The few possessions that you have (and mean so much when you have so little) are gone in a few screaming, terrifying minutes when the children have to be quickly swept up and you run desperately into the bush. The causes are not important in many ways and few would agree on them anyway. The future is gone or is at least a lot further off. I know those communities. I pass through them when I go to the sites where we are building schools, clinics, places to worship. Some of the people I employ are now trying to kill and burn.

I saw many trucks today burdened with people, young people, with guns, going off to kill. My car is searched by youth, children. Those eternally happy smiling faces in school are now etched with an eager hatred, a lust for destruction, which I am tempted to think will never be fully erased. A 14 year old boy is dragged from a priest's car and is beaten to death, a man returning to his office after lunch is attacked by a mob and his head crushed with a stone, another pulled off his bicycle and shot, a baby thrown against a wall. I saw this afternoon on TV (how it still works in this chaos I do not know) the carnage at Sarajevo market. I know of so many other massacres, so much hatred and destruction. It would be easy to despair and yet so wrong. There is a refugee camp about two miles from my house for members of one of the tribes. I have just heard it is about to be attacked. May God forgive us all, except I don't know why He should.

Yes, I know, 'the old world order will be rolled up' and I also know that the building of the new is largely in our hands. My brothers and sisters, I know now how urgent that need is and how much suffering can be avoided by speeding up that process by just one day. I have seen years of work of many good people go, years of hoping and dreaming shattered in the last few days. Every single day of suffering avoided can mean so much. Let us not 'put off till tomorrow' – let us do everything we can today.

37
April 1994
Na'im Cortazzi
Belarus
Youth Service

Na'im (from Leicester) is spending the best part of a year in service to the Faith in Belarus.

A year ago, of all the places in the world I never imagined I would come to was White Russia yet here I am in the last official communist outpost left from the USSR's collapse three years ago. Contrary to the official label of atheist, virtually everyone I've met, young and old, have some kind of faith in a Most Great Spirit.

For the first three months I was invited to speak at all kinds of schools, colleges and specialist language schools, so people could see, hear and talk to a 'real Englishman' (I am an English-born Iranian)! The first thing I did was to be a friend to the students. I wasn't supposed to talk about religion or the Faith but I did and I wish you could have seen how the students' eyes came alive and lit up with hope and vision after deprivation. I felt like Robin Williams in *Dead Poets Society* as they started to confidently express their beliefs and dreams.

Peristroka has brought a lot of hardship and confusion on top of suspicion and fear from the near 70 years of totalitarianism. Cut off throughout their history from the outside world, people are intensely curious about life beyond their national horizons. I have found that people are searching for hope, well-founded optimism, answers and, perhaps above all, a smile . . .

My stay in Belarus has been full of ups and downs and sometimes I feel so lonely but it really warmed my heart to know that I'm not alone when I read your letters in *Pioneer Post*. Although our teaching work via the masses is limited, I managed to get on TV here singing Eric Clapton's 'Tears in Heaven'! The Belarussian Bahá'ís are deepened and strong and united, and when more barriers come down, I hope we will have as much numerical success as in Albania and Romania.

The first signs of spring are finally here and the snow has stopped falling. Yes, the Russian winter that decimated Napoleon's army and froze Hitler's has not defeated this spiritual army! Yá Bahá'u'l-Abhá!

38
July 1994
Bill Brown
Ghana

Bill's second letter continues the harrowing account of present-day life in the northern region of Ghana.

We are safe now back in Tamale. We needed an airlift to escape at the height of the trouble; there was just too much lawlessness, looting and killing here. Dead bodies were lying at the barriers on the roads. As I am the deputy representative of the British High Commission here, it fell to me to organize the airlift. It was all done in a mad panic, suddenly having to pack, decide what to leave behind, never knowing if you would come back. My wife Paulina did very well as our family burden fell to her. I had two embassies, the US Peace Corps director, VSO field officers and who knows how many others on my phone (which by a miracle we had installed only four weeks before) all wanting to get their people on board. In all there were seven nationalities on that plane; you can imagine the sort of chaos inside our house with so many people coming in, the phone ringing endlessly and all the time we were trying to keep track of the fighting; who had escaped by road, who was where. So Paulina had a terrible job, packing, keeping coffee constantly on the boil and the children not too worried. We were in Accra (the capital) for a week, then we left for Kumasi where I left my family and I came back to Tamale. By then the worst had passed. On the day I drove in a man was stoned to death. There was only one illegal barrier left but manned by people who have killed at least 200.

Figures: 5,000 buried (and heaven only knows how many are left in the bush dead, how many buried in shallow graves); 260 villages burnt; 150,000 homeless; development projects cancelled; dreams shattered.

Although the bush east of here is still very dangerous, the road south is OK and I went to Kumasi to collect my family. We are all shattered by what has happened. Tales are coming out of unspeakable horrors. Most wrenching is the torture and slaughter of babies . . . Such hatred is beyond the understanding of all of us.

There is worse to come. In this entire agricultural region there will be no farming this year. Food prices have already doubled. Hunger will follow. Next year the tribes will take revenge for the babies and the old folks. More blood will flow and the cycle will deepen. How to talk to someone who left his friends and home only to learn the next day that it was all burnt, his friends from childhood dead?

As Bahá'ís we can only pray but we are too small a voice to matter politically. We all have some friends of some influence. We talk to them about reconciliation, the futility of revenge. They understand but their voices are drowned out by the tears, the anguish of a father who has lost his family, a mother her babies, the madness of a young man who has done and seen too much. We try to find out, one by one, if the Bahá'ís in the affected areas are safe.

The only solution is a spiritual one and even then do not expect such feelings of hatred and revenge to be swept away with a few pamphlets. More and more as a community we are going to face these immense human problems. Are we ready? Are we supposed to just sit back quietly and pray? As our community gets larger, the world more violent and the collapse of the old more total, we will need to find the answers. I cannot understand why so much suffering goes on, especially the innocent. God must have a good reason and maybe we do not have to know it. But I do feel that we do have to know how to be a part of the healing. Right now, after the prayers, I do not know where to begin. Please pray that we find a voice and the words to say.

39
July 1994
Helen Smith
Lithuania

*Helen writes about the contrast between two ways of life in eastern Europe.
She has been a pioneer in Lithuania since 1989 and is presently serving on
the Regional Assembly of the Bahá'ís of the Baltic States.*

A short time ago I visited the coastal town of Klaipeda (one-time German city of Memel), which I do every three weeks. I stay overnight in a hotel and try to hold a fireside with the few contacts I have made over the last few years, mostly university students and teachers.

The bus journey was not good. It was still winter and there was little or no heating in the hotel but I had taken my hot water bottle because I knew from past experience that the hotel would be cold. It was so cold I had to fill my bottle three times during the night. I carry with me a travelling immersion heater, fill a jug with water and pour the hot water into the hot water bottle. I was in Klaipeda for two days. Nobody came to the fireside so I went back to Kaunas on the midnight train. Not only was the train unheated, it was indescribably filthy and the guard was drunk, as were most of the other passengers.

It takes about seven hours by train and I had booked a sleeping berth. I was lucky there was only one man in the compartment and he was sober.

A few days later I had to go to Daugavpils, a town in Latvia. There was a new Bahá'í community there and I was going to help them organize their delegate elections. I took the bus to Vilnius and then the train to Daugavpils. I was so cold I thought I would die. When I arrived in the town there was no one to meet me. It was late in the evening and dark and I had no idea where to go. I went to the nearest post office to try to phone someone but the phones didn't work. I got directions to the central post office (my Russian improved that day) and after a very long time managed to find someone who knew someone who knew someone who knew they belonged to a new religion! By this time I was surrounded by people all talking at once and each one saying they knew where I had to go. Eventually I managed to get the phone number of one of the Bahá'ís, found a phone that worked and all was well. It appears there had been a mix-up in times. The joy of being with the friends in this new community more than compensated for the terrible journey. These lovely people were so warm and loving I was glad to be among them. I had to go back to Kaunas the following day on the 7 a.m. train. The train was unheated, the people already drinking their beer, and I sat and froze.

Two weeks later I was on my way back to Klaipeda. Determined not to be cold I wore five pairs of trousers (very thin), six sweaters (not so thin) and several pairs of socks. I also took with me a sleeping bag. The hotel was still as cold as before but I was quite warm, at least in bed. On the way back to Vilnius by train I bought the four bunks in the compartment and intended locking myself in. The train was still unheated, not surprising because some of the windows were broken, but the guard was sober and really a very sympathetic person. With all my clothes, sleeping bag, hat and gloves and the blanket that I got from the guard, I was quite warm. I didn't sleep because of the noise but the guard didn't try to sell the other three beds that I had already bought, so that was a blessing.

I arrived in Vilnius tired and hungry and went to the home of one of the Bahá'ís whom I had arranged to visit that morning. My problems disappeared in this family's home. They were so kind and caring, advising that I rest, filling me with coffee and food. What a treat. That day we had the delegate elections in Vilnius, and even though I was tired, it was a joy being with everyone and thinking to myself how far we have come in five years.

The next morning saw me back on the train to Daugavpils. I had on all my layers of clothing so was not cold. At the stop before the Latvian border the train filled with very busy people. Everyone had heavy bags and was rushing up and down the train. I was rather bemused by all of this activity. I didn't know what was going on. Suddenly a young man from the group of busy people took a screwdriver out of his pocket and started to take the cover off the heating panel that runs down the side of the carriage. I was stupid enough to think he was trying to turn on the heat! No way! He then unscrewed the panels on the side of the seats. Curiouser and curiouser! The people were putting their goods – butter, cheese, sausage, etc. – into these places. It seemed that many kilos of food products were being hidden away. I sat there with my mouth open then suddenly realized what was happening so got my head stuck way down into my coat collar and a book in front of my face. I was asked if I would take some bread over the border and I was most certainly not popular when I refused. One elderly lady had a bag full of litre packs of milk that she was stuffing down the front of her dress. She had so many packs of milk down her front that her dress rose well above her knees!

Shortly before arriving at the Lithuanian-Latvian border the people simply disappeared from the carriage. I was alone in this very long carriage. It seems that when you have hidden away your contraband you move to another part of the train in case the contraband is found, for if it is found you cannot be charged. At the border the customs people came on and asked everyone to declare what products they were carrying. The customs men knew where to look but they missed the heating and seat panels where the goodies were hidden. After they had gone and the train moved off the scurry started, the carriage filled up with people and out came all the contraband. Small bottles of cream were appearing from the hoods of coats, the sleeves of thick jackets, the inside linings of coats and so on. Along came the young man with his screw driver and off came the heating and seat panels and out came the goodies. I couldn't believe my eyes! It was obvious I had never seen this pantomime before because these folks kept whispering and nodding to one another and looking over at me but in no way did they try to hide what they were doing. The reason this smuggling goes on is because food is a little more expensive in Latvia than in Lithuania, so folks empty the shops on a Saturday and take everything to Latvia on the Sunday and sell it by the railway station or in the street. The profit cannot be very much. Even if the goods are sold at double the price they still have to buy train tickets and use up a whole day of their time because there are very few trains from Lithuania to Daugavpils.

I attended the Daugavpils Bahá'í delegate election and the love and joy that came from this lovely community took me to why I was where I was. Amidst all this cheating there is this lovely community where there are so many problems because of inflation and unemployment but at that time they were only concerned with electing their delegates. I didn't say anything to the friends about the scenario on the train because to them it is just part of living.

Next morning, back on the early morning train to Vilnius. It was still perishing cold but I managed to get back to Vilnius before my fingers fell off and was lucky to catch a waiting bus to Kaunas so didn't have to hang around the bus station for long.

40

July 1994
David and Manijeh Smith
Zambia

David and Manijeh set off on their pioneering adventure, starting in Leatherhead, Surrey, with their two very young children, Bayan (2½) and Holly (six months). The following is an extract from an account of their journey.

Arriving in Johannesburg, we looked for and found a Land Rover. This was our Africa machine and known as 'Joe'. God must have had some earth left over when He created the world and so spread it out between Jo'burg and Lusaka because it was a long way, a very long way! We arrived the first evening at a hostel near the Zimbabwe border. There was no security so we had to unload everything (including the potty). The scenery from the hostel to the border was stunning, almost alpine.

We were up and loaded early and reached the border at 8 a.m. We then had a nightmare of a day trying to get the correct paperwork to take the Land Rover out of the country. It was blazing hot, absolutely no shade, and the whole border complex was being rebuilt so there were no waiting rooms or refreshments. Poor Holly and Bayan really felt the cruel side of the African heat, in these circumstances relentless and unforgiving. Luckily we were able to drive back to a town half an hour away to stock up on cold water.

Finally, we crossed over the bridge at around 5:30 p.m. Another 90 minutes of Zimbabwean form-filling and we were on our way, the border gates literally closing behind us. There was no hope of reaching Harare before dark (too dangerous to drive in the dark because of large animals on the roads) and we were advised to stop at an old colonial-style motel, the only place of accommodation for 500 km. We arrived exhausted, hungry and desperate to get the children to bed. At the reception of the motel, we were told that they had no place for us and were in fact fully booked. Manijeh tried to reason with the owner, initially to no avail, but eventually the sight of her standing there with a baby in her arms, a toddler holding onto her skirt and some of our bags around her legs made him feel some concern, and he finally relented. 'There is one place but it is not in the motel!' We got in the car and followed him for a five-minute drive. When we got there the motel owner told us that he was letting us use his mother's room attached to his house!

When we woke up in the morning David opened the curtains to be faced with an ostrich the other side of the window looking straight back at him! From this window we could look directly into the African bush. Before breakfast David took Bayan to see some more ostriches. Soon after we left, the largest insect either of us had ever seen crawled up Manijeh's leg. She screamed! After a 30 second eternity we managed to kick it out of the moving vehicle. We don't know what it was but it was a taste of things to come!

It took us all day to get to Harare, where we stayed with dear Shidan and Florence Fat'he-Aazam. The next day we left at 7:30 a.m., arrived at the border in an absolute mayhem of trucks, buses and cars, and no order of where to stand or which office to go to. David, of course, being English, decided to stand in front of a door labelled 'Immigration Office'. After half an hour, an officer opened the door and started a queue behind him! While David was sorting out paperwork, Manijeh was trying to be clever and changed some South African rand into Zambian kwacha. She was so excited as she had managed to get 20,000 Kwacha. Two hours down the road we needed petrol which cost 18,000 Kwacha, leaving only 2,000 for two bottles of coke and a couple of bread buns, which left us the princely sum of 500 Kwacha as change. This was our first lesson in Zambian finances. It was another three hours before we arrived in Lusaka.

'Head straight through Lusaka and it's 80 km from the post office along the Great North Road.' These were our instructions to find the Banani School. 'And don't under any circumstances drive to the school in the dark as the road is a deathtrap of potholes.'

We set off thinking we had 45 minutes of light, which should get us most of the way there. Never can a strip of land have been so ill-labelled as 'The Great North Road'. We hit huge craters and after about six km we feared for the Land Rover's life. We realized that we could not endure 80 km of nerve-racking driving, so we embraced defeat and gingerly picked our way back into Lusaka with the sun setting in our rearview mirror. We went to the police station to use the phone to contact friends in Lusaka who might put us up.

The police station was a huge mausoleum with failing lights and incredulous staff who led us through dim passageways and over planks that covered holes which opened to lower floors. Manijeh had to sit and wait with the children in total darkness whilst David had to explain to anyone who demanded to know who we were, why we were in Lusaka, where we were going and how could we possibly know so many people in Lusaka if we had never been there before! The police were shocked that David couldn't understand Manijeh speaking in Farsi on the phone! We were met by one of the dear pioneers, Jamshid Yazahmeidi, who came to the police station and escorted us to his house for the evening.

Monday morning, around 9:00, on our fifth day of travelling, we set off for the Banani School. In the cool, fresh morning, whilst things were chaotic in Lusaka, our spirits were high. Bayan and Holly had accepted everything without a murmur of discontent and it seemed that they knew that this was going to be the last spell of driving. Around 10:30 a.m. we passed through a final police check and soon after saw the sign 'Banani International Secondary School'.

The school site is not large (90 students attend the school) but all around it is farmland and there is an abundance of fresh fruit, vegetables and meat. It is very peaceful, even idyllic. We know we will love it here.

41
October 1994
Bill Brown
Ghana

Bill has been writing about the effects of 'ethnic cleansing' and the consequent suffering in Ghana. Now, after 17 years, Bill and his family are about to leave Ghana to return to England.

There is still tension around but, oddly, it has drifted into a kind of unspoken background – like living next to a volcano or in an earthquake zone. Still people from the High Commission and aid agencies come asking for analyses. We hope it will all do something. An official cease-fire has been signed but the parties refused to sign it together in the same room so naturally people are sceptical. In Ghana, especially in the north, it is not so important what is said but rather what isn't!

As Bahá'ís we are holding the Feasts again as normal. We are planning a Unity Feast to which we will invite the religious leaders in Tamale. We not only have many Christian and Muslim sects but also Hindu and Buddhist. We will try to get all together for some prayers and readings. Maybe we can make it a regular thing, rotating around so that each will act as host.

The refugees are slowly going back to their farms and villages. They don't wander far; they go in groups and are very careful. The rains have been late.

People say there is too much blood on the ground and that it doesn't want to come down. Against all this there are broader problems in the country with the educational system. Reforms were instituted a few years ago and now the first batch of school leavers from the new system have finished. There was a 97 per cent failure rate in the exams. Obviously there is a huge scandal about it! This is why we have decided to come home, as our children's education has to be our priority. We hate to leave when there are so many problems but we do not see any options. It is very sad for us but we hope to return.

42
Bill Brown
Postscript

My two previous contributions written about the time we spent in Ghana only give one side of the conflict and the other side needs telling. The main purpose in writing about the tribal war and inter-ethnic conflict was that the government had a news blackout and was not telling the world the true extent of the fighting. I could not let those deaths go unrecognized. Their lives meant little to the world at large – to let them die without even an acknowledgment was one crime simply laid on top of too many others.

There is an extraordinary contrast between the conflict and normal life in Africa, where the daily struggle for food and health is undertaken with hope, dignity and optimism by the vast majority of people.

I saw, in those days, many extraordinary acts of bravery. One day an elder of one of the tribes came to my house and explained that they, the elders, had lost control of a section of the youth. He himself was hiding children in his house, an act of almost reckless courage, sustained, not in the heat of a battle but over days and sleepless nights, true courage indeed. He wept, a senior elder of a proud tribe – I never imagined that I would see such a thing.

I knew others that were hiding people in their homes and at times I was told I needed to get a message to someone as their house was to be searched that day. People were quietly moved to another location and at great personal risk those messengers did what they knew was right.

There were what I can only describe as miracles. A man showed up at my house. He was from Burkina Faso, the country to the north of Ghana. He was a driver for Oxfam and was delivering a Land Rover to their Ghana office. The road took him through the town that we were living in. He spoke little English and none of the local languages. How he ever found our house we'll never know. He had had a harrowing drive and was very scared. We gave him a meal and explained in our poor French that it was too dangerous to go on. We offered a place for him but he left, saying he was heading back north again.

Two young English teachers who had been teaching in a school in the bush were brought to us by the army. Again, how did they know? These teachers had been evacuated from their school with many others and had been living in a camp, scared and with little food, for a few days. The army had organized a convoy to rescue them and others and delivered the teachers to us.

Two English backpackers showed up. They had been on a bus and had wandered into the situation because of the news blackout. They had seen fellow passengers murdered and were in a state of shock. Again they just appeared on our doorstep.

A baby had been abandoned a few months before on the doorstep of the nun's house opposite ours. The traditional marks on the baby indicated that now he was of the 'wrong' tribe. He came out with us and the nuns got him to their Mother House in France. He was adopted in France and now lives there.

The real Africa has a culture that has been stable and functional for millennia, a culture that has developed a wisdom and understanding that is simple and profound and is now under great stress. I have spent many evenings with people, sitting under a baobab tree, listening to traditional stories that remarkably echo Bahá'í beliefs. I was welcomed and unfailingly treated as an honoured guest. This is the real Africa, away from the wildlife photographers and news reporters, but these are the stories that every pioneer is familiar with. The other story behind the violence I described is the courage of many people in those times and the years of friendship that a stranger was shown.

43
October 1994
Wesley and Stephanie Clash
Corfu, Greece

The Clash family from Shepway, Kent pioneered to the Greek island of Corfu one year ago.

After reading about the exploits of fellow pioneers and knowing the joy and strength of heart that these accounts bring, I decided to write about our own pioneering experiences.

My husband, Wesley, daughter Giselle, the cat and I came to Corfu a year ago in August. Shortly after arriving we received letters of loving welcome from the Greek friends; during the year we had the pleasure of meeting some of the Greek Bahá'ís and putting faces to names. We are a small community but enthusiastic, dedicated and very loving. We had come to our pioneer post as relatively new Bahá'ís, having been lovingly nurtured by the Shepway community in Kent. When we decided to pioneer to Corfu we had no idea of the Bahá'í situation on the island and wrote to the National Spiritual Assembly of Greece asking if they could supply us with the names and contact addresses of all the Bahá'ís living there. They wrote back to say we WERE the Bahá'ís of Corfu!

We are not the first pioneers to Corfu. Some years ago Ingeborg Weigelt, a German Bahá'í, was here and did valuable work 'preparing the ground'. The love and respect she left behind has made our work so much easier. Inge left Corfu for health reasons but has recovered greatly since we made contact and told her of our exploits here.

Our first year had its 'ups and downs'. Being fluent in Spanish I often wondered why Bahá'u'lláh should have made my husband fall in love with Corfu and not a Spanish-speaking country. However, having to learn the language has given us a sense of determination and achievement. At times I feel very frustrated and tongue-tied but then I remember Inge's advice: 'Just try to live the life and teach the Faith that way.' However, we feel Bahá'u'lláh has helped us with the language problem and opened so many other doors. I remember the first visit of our Auxiliary Board member and that we decided to hold a fireside in our apartment and put up posters in a few places I had discovered. The night of the fireside was one of torrential rain and thunderstorms but there were two knocks on the door and two soggy strangers appeared; they knew Inge from the past and had been delighted to see that there were Bahá'ís on the island again.

We have since got to know these two wonderful women very well. One of them, Britta, was a German Lutheran priest who was collared by Wesley one day and forthrightly asked when she was going to become a Bahá'í! Britta replied that she was seriously considering it but wanted to revise her Christian beliefs one more time before declaring. Sadly, Britta died of a brain tumour before she could do that but we truly feel her blessings and strength from the Abhá Kingdom. The other lady who arrived at our door has since declared her faith in Bahá'u'lláh and is a staunch and valuable member of our small group.

So what did I learn in my first year as a pioneer? Mostly the freedom to talk about the Faith in an uninhibited way; not knowing the exact social boundaries of the Greek people tends to open me up – unlike the UK, where 'religious talk' was often taboo. I respond to the natural curiosity of the Greeks about the Faith and the fact that religion is very much a part of their lives. Mostly, though, I have learned the importance of the writings and of being steadfast. I realize the reason why I'm here and my utter reliance on God.

44
October 1994
Lois and David Lambert
Mongolia

Lois and David (originally from Kirklees in Yorkshire) have been pioneers in Mongolia for two years.

During July we had a number of travel teachers in Mongolia, in particular Bijan and Sheedvash Farid and their family, all of whom had such a desire to serve Bahá'u'lláh and such a love for everyone they met that they really inspired those of us who were privileged enough to spend time with them. Every day we went out to teach and every day many people heard of Bahá'u'lláh's teachings and many became Bahá'ís.

Unknown to our visitors when they decided to come, it was the time of Naadam, the famous Mongolian festival of the 'Three Manly Sports' – wrestling, archery and horse racing. It was a wonderful time for visitors to come but presented challenges for a teaching team. Hotels were full, hotel restaurants were only serving meals to official residents and Zuulchin tourists, shops were closed and police offices closed for registration (for permission to go to the countryside, etc.). However, our visitors coped wonderfully well with the challenges and we attended all the Naadam events and met people to whom we could teach the Faith. The youth of Ulaanbaatar, whose lives have been transformed by their love and service, were wonderful teachers and translators. One whole family whom we met at the horse racing became Bahá'ís. They were all at the 19 Day Feast on 14 July, including their teenage daughter, who is a professional contortionist with the Mongolian State Circus.

One day we simply went to the children's park and while the children rode horses, Shiva, Sheedvash's sister, cut people's hair. While she did this, we sat and talked to people, sang Bahá'í songs and told them about the Faith. Another day we hired a bus and with two of our Mongolian Bahá'í friends went into the countryside around Ulaanbaatar to visit nomadic families, where again Shiva delighted everyone by cutting their hair. Another couple of days we travelled by train overnight to the city of Erdenet and visited a village where all the families came out to meet us and proceeded to offer us the most incredible hospitality all day.

One beautiful couple, who were our chief hosts for that day, were both completely blind and totally self-sufficient. They killed, skinned and prepared a goat for us to eat, milked the goats and the sheep, built the fire and even put up a tent for us to sleep in during the afternoon (but none of us was tired!). To watch them living so joyously and striding confidently across the fields, doing all these things as if they could see, was a humbling experience and it confirmed for us how important it is that these wonderful people who have retained their independence and purity of heart know of the message of Bahá'u'lláh. While we were singing a Mongolian Bahá'í song, we saw that Peljit (the blind lady) had tears running down her cheeks. She said that this was the happiest day of her life. Several of the Erdenet youth were weeping too. After we – and half a dozen families – had eaten the goat, we had a fireside and inevitably missed the bus back, so we were led by two young herdsmen on horse and bicycle through the Erdenet copper mine to catch a night bus for the workers – a bizarre industrial landscape after the paradise we had been enjoying all day!

45

October 1994

Payam and Shirin Foroudi

Guyana

Payam and Shirin (from N. Wiltshire) and their two small children, Layli (3) and baby Naysan, pioneered to Guyana in February of this year.

We are settling in very well and getting used to the Guyanese way of life. We are comfortable in our new home and have learned how to deal with the lack of things we take for granted in the UK, e.g. clean water from the tap, regular electricity supply and luxuries such as household goods of good quality and affordable price.

I was lucky to get a job with a British company and enjoy the usual privileges as an expatriate. When we compare our situation with the stories of other pioneers and their sacrifices, particularly the early British pioneers to Guyana, we feel we are cheating!

Guyana is an interesting place. The people are friendly and are mainly East Indians or black Afro-Caribbean. There are also other races such as Chinese and mixed Europeans. They all seem to get on well although in the past there was some racial unrest in the country. The climate is very warm and humid but there is often a cool breeze. The rainfall can be very heavy and quick and when the sky opens it can flood a whole residential area in a very short period of time. The land is very green and fertile. People say you can sit in your veranda swinging in your hammock, eating watermelons and spitting the seeds on the ground and they will grow. I haven't tried this yet, mainly because we haven't got a hammock!

The country is poor, the average income very low but with an incredibly high cost of living. The infrastructure, such as roads, water and sewage and electricity are in a total mess. Road pot holes are everywhere so cars are not likely to last long. Tap water is so bad that nobody drinks it. We boil and filter water ourselves mainly for washing food and cooking and also buy filtered water in five gallon containers for drinking. The crime rate in the city is high, mainly because of the poor state of the economy and social deprivation.

I am working as a coastal engineer involved in rehabilitation of the coastal defences (sea walls, dikes, etc.) for the entire length of the Guyana coast. As a result, for the short period that I have been here I have already travelled along the whole coast and walked several miles on its muddy shores. I have had to travel in single engine light aircraft in which I get airsick and in speedboats crossing vast rivers and choppy seas which make me seasick! The rough roads with pot holes also have a similar effect on me!

Bahá'í life here is pretty active. The officially registered number of Bahá'ís is very high but there is a great need for continuing education, nurturing and deepening. We are part of the Georgetown Bahá'í community and regularly go to 19 Day Feasts, holy days and other activities. We have also been travel teaching to some of the villages outside the capital.

Before leaving the UK a Bahá'í friend told us that we should act dumb for a while so that nobody would give us any Bahá'í work and we could have a good rest! Two weeks after we arrived the National Assembly met us in person and welcomed us, which was very nice, but also asked us to consult about ways we could be involved in the community. At local level, I was put on the Literature Committee and Shirin was put on the Child Education Committee, and at national level I was put on the National Teaching Committee and Shirin was put on the National Youth Committee.

We have started international evening gatherings at our house where we cook a particular type of food and invite various people. Our first one was Persian, the next Guyanese and after that Russian. We find that we already need a bigger house! The Bahá'í community is very active in social and economic development and there are several projects in health, literacy, training, etc. Shirin is planning to do some voluntary work at rural clinics as part of these projects. Layli goes to a nursery school and Naysan is growing rapidly. Wherever we go they both attract a lot of attention, which opens opportunities for us to meet more people.

46
April 1995
The Adventures of Stephanie, Gohar and Amelia
India

Stephanie Christopherson (Hertfordshire), Gohar Khosravi and Amelia Lake (Northern Ireland) all offered a period of youth service at the Bahá'í Vocational Institute for Rural Women in Indore, India. Stephanie writes:

In my first few days in India, nervous and excited, and before the girls arrived for the new term, the Institute was a solemn and strange place full of faces I didn't know and voices I couldn't recognize. Often in those early days tears would well up in my eyes and a burning desire to be somewhere else would flood over me. But slowly the Institute became a familiar place and as the days fell into a routine the tears dried up and I began to look forward to each new day and the adventures it would bring.

We spent a lot of our time in the office where we learned office skills and spent tedious hours making billions of paper corners for the photographs we were documenting. At these times we would have some of our best discussions, as the office with its still atmosphere would inspire us to sing – anything and everything!

As everyone knows, a year of service is meant to be a time of spiritual growth. One of the most personal experiences I had was in a village where we had gone to celebrate the Birthday of the Báb. There is a strange feeling, a mixture of excitement and exhilaration that comes over you when you find yourself sitting outside a mud hut in a sari, surrounded by the smiling faces of a hundred people. The warm glow that starts to grow in the pit of your stomach never leaves you.

At home in England when people organize holy day celebrations there may be a pot luck dinner or a quiz but never a procession down narrow village streets, through cow pats and led by flaming torches, with Bahá'í songs ringing in your ears.

This report of my time in India would not be complete unless I mentioned the people. Jimmy McGilligan has made the Institute a beautiful place with its low hedgerows, sweetly scented flowers, neatly ordered veggy patch and exotic trees. What really makes it a colourful and diverse place are the people – everyone from messenger to manager, garden hand to tribal girl. The friendship, unconditional love and pure hearts that these tribal girls possess are a welcome change from the cynical atmosphere of the West. Many a happy evening would be spent dancing in the dormitory, banging sticks.

Shortly after we arrived in India we attended a 19 Day Feast. At that time we thought it rather a strange occasion, far removed from what we were used to. It was then we decided we wanted to host one. As the time drew near we organized the music and English readings but of course none of us spoke Hindi nor knew what food to provide so we had to seek the advice of our neighbours. The next day our friend Vinal went back and forth ordering and buying many marvellous things. Our part of the Feast, the devotional, was a disaster (through no fault of our own) but the food was a success!

Things I have learned! Bananas are God's best invention! Always keep a secret stash of chocolate! Remember to tell your friends you love them!

A separate letter was received from Amelia and Gohar concerning the 54th training programme at the Rural Institute:

In September, 31 shy tribal women, girls and children from different castes and various surrounding areas began their transformation: from being illiterate, undernourished and lacking in confidence and skills, to becoming confident young women with a taste for learning.

We, also, had to learn new skills, such as coping with life in India – the heat, learning Hindi, cooking for ourselves, bargaining and dodging cows. One time we spent a three day field trip visiting the villages where the trainees came from. Our first night we slept in a traditional tribal home – very clean and plastered with mud and whitewash – with goats, cows and water buffalo for company. The life of these tribal people is so far removed from our lives. They are friendly, warm, hospitable and very welcoming. The field trip gave us a chance to see the life the trainees had come from and how the Institute's training is helping them. The highlight of the trip for us was late one night under the stars. From the light of a candle held by a boy standing on a stool, we danced tribal dances with the youth of the village. The girls were singing to music from three long wooden wind instruments, played by the boys amidst an amazing atmosphere. Then off to bed, to be woken a short time later by a rather loud and persistent rooster!

47
April 1995
Neda Azemian
Poland
Year of Service

Neda (from the Vale of Glamorgan) has been living in Olsztyn, Poland, where she has been doing a year of service since last August.

For as long as I can remember I longed to offer Bahá'u'lláh a year of service in Russia so I studied Russian in school but I ended up in Poland! Language-wise I was confused for a little while, forgot the Russian and fell madly and badly in love with Poland and most things Polish. This is really only a taster of pioneering but it's made me contemplate and appreciate the sweat and toil pioneers all over the world have put into building the Bahá'í international community. Of course, without divine assistance we'd be nowhere – it's the sweetness of those special miracles that is addictive.

When I arrived in Poland I had absolutely no idea what I'd be doing. For a few weeks I joined the Nowy Sacz project but I planned to live in another town where I left half my luggage. Then the National Teaching Committee asked me to stay in Nowy Sacz to help consolidate post-project contacts. Though Nowy Sacz is very pretty, with lovely Bahá'ís, I wanted to be in the other town, which was close to the Russian border. I soon realized that this was not *my* year of service but Bahá'u'lláh's. I left Nowy Sacz mid-December after four months of a kind of life I never thought possible. I taught English privately, did a lot of socializing, travelled many weekends to national teaching projects and seminars and was extremely busy. I lived with a unique American pioneer, Jane Czerniejewski, whose flat is an open house. I also taught English at the gypsy school. The gypsies became good friends of Jane and myself and we were often in their homes. There are many gypsies in Poland and some of them are very poor. Jane is trying to set up some sort of culture centre where the gypsy children can learn more and take pride in their heritage. We tried teaching them the Faith through songs and prayers.

The National Assembly asked me to move next to Olsztyn, in the north-east, nearer to the Russian border. The Olsztyn project was much smaller but six months wiser I now have a better idea of how to follow up contacts, etc. The language is no longer such a huge problem and I live with a retired Polish couple so my Polish is improving. The other pioneer here is Ester Bayaton, a young Filipina. Friends joke that the people in Olsztyn will think that 'Bahá'í' is a club for short, dark-haired, oriental girls, as Ester and I both fit that description! I haven't laughed so much since I arrived here. The more serious the problem concerning organizing activities, the more Ester and I giggle! And things always turn out fine. Olsztyn does not yet have a local Spiritual Assembly and that is our Riḍván goal. Sometimes the year has been rough. Everywhere one goes there are tests it seems, so beautifully prepared by Providence! I've learnt that there is no escape – if one has a weakness it's better dealt with sooner rather than later as otherwise it just shows itself in different ways in different situations. A year of service is a very good opportunity to reflect upon the future and to learn to trust in God.

Postscript: Neda has remained in touch with her friends in Poland. An exciting spin-off of her year of service was that a young Polish girl, Kasia, became a Bahá'í as a result of Neda teaching the Faith to Kasia's father on a bus trip from Nowy Sacz to Olsztyn. In 2008 an important article about the Faith was published in the Polish magazine *Cosmo* relating the story of how a young Polish Catholic girl (Kasia) became a Bahá'í as a result of Neda's youth service.

48
April 1995
Thelma and Ron Batchelor
Kathmandu Revisited

Kathmandu – land of temples – in the Himalayan Kingdom of Nepal.

Eighteen years ago, excited at the prospect of being pioneers in Nepal and with the blessing of the Universal House of Justice, we arrived in Kathmandu with our two young children, Simon (4½) and Suzanne (18 months). Had we known then the slings and arrows of outrageous fortune we were to suffer in those early years, I don't think we would ever have left for Nepal! In retrospect it was good we didn't know because in no way would we wish to have forfeited the priceless privilege we were given of being pioneers for nine years in one of the most beautiful countries in the world.

Teaching was restricted and those nine years (1976–85) were hard going. The best we could do was to try to 'live the life' and to share our Bahá'í lives with those Nepalese who had accepted Bahá'u'lláh. There weren't many and there was a handful of pioneers – one Persian, five Americans, one Malaysian and ourselves. We were a united community and we were happy to observe that the Faith was being built on very solid foundations. The Faith grew slowly and the Bahá'ís were firm, faithful and godfearing.

Ron's two-year contract with the British government, working as a structural engineer responsible for the building of 12 go-downs (grain stores) was extended to nine years – nothing was ever achieved quickly in Nepal! We had wonderfully happy and spiritually fulfilling years being Bahá'í pioneers in Nepal. When the time came for us to leave in June 1985 and return to the UK we were all very sad for we didn't know if we would ever come back.

Almost 10 years later, we did go back. It was our 25th wedding anniversary in February and it seemed right that we should celebrate it where, as pioneers, our spiritual bonds were strongest. We have just spent five wonderful weeks in Kathmandu and we were not disappointed. Kathmandu itself has changed – it is more dusty, dirty and crowded with people and cars than previously and the pollution is bad – but the joy in seeing our Nepalese Bahá'í friends again can't be imagined! It was as though 10 years had melted away – all that was different was that our children had grown up in the meantime! Instead of there being a few Bahá'ís, now there were many. At each Feast we went to, there were 50 Bahá'ís present and new believers welcomed each time. It warmed the cockles of an Englishman's heart to encounter such spiritual receptivity in a land far away from home. We stayed with our pioneer friends, were shared around with our Nepalese friends and were showered with love by our Bahá'í family everywhere.

When we heard in 1990 that the Hand of the Cause Collis Featherstone had passed away in Nepal we felt that this was fortunate – Nepal deserved to have a Hand of the Cause permanently in her midst. The Bahá'í cemetery has been made beautiful and it was good to be there. The Bahá'ís of Nepal are building a new Bahá'í Centre, which is nearing completion. It is a very large octagonal building, built with a vision of far greater growth in the Bahá'í community. The first Bahá'í youth has been accepted to work in the gardens at the Bahá'í World Centre. Much has changed in this Himalayan Kingdom – the Faith is growing and once again we have left our hearts in Nepal.

49

April 1995

Valerie Rhind

A Year of Service in Zimbabwe

Valerie has been a pioneer in Africa for nearly 30 years – in Zambia, Botswana, Zimbabwe, Tanzania – and is not quite sure where next! Gazing out through the palm trees at an azure blue sea (most people's idea of paradise!) she writes:

After 18 years working for one company in Botswana, my husband, Islay, decided it was time for a career move and joined Coca-Cola. We were immediately transferred to Harare in Zimbabwe and expected to stay for from two to five years. I quickly became involved in the local Bahá'í community life and was asked to work on a few national projects. But within a few months Islay was moved to Dar es Salaam in Tanzania and I remained behind to join him at the end of the year.

The Harare community organized many activities. I particularly enjoyed early morning prayers each Sunday at 7:30 a.m. Friends recited, sang or chanted, one by one in a circle, until it felt that we were being bathed by the power of prayer. Afterwards a light breakfast was served by the hosts. Another inspiring event was the Thursday study class, also hosted by various friends. Last Ridván the Local Spiritual Assembly commenced a word by word study of the Kitab-i-Aqdas which was very popular. Feasts and holy days are usually observed at the Bahá'í Centre, at weekends if possible, but weekly meetings are held just after work in order to give everyone time to travel home early in the evening.

As for the service part, well, I was asked to serve on one local committee and two national ones and was given an area to visit about two hours' drive from Harare, where there were several assemblies requiring deepening. In Harare our committee's goal was to reach as many school children as possible with the message of Bahá'u'lláh. My specific job was to approach head teachers and seek permission to give talks or show films. Fortunately, early on I discovered that all sixth formers have to write a general paper that included subjects such as 'Is world peace attainable?', 'Is there a need for a universal language/currency?' or 'The role of women in society' so it was easy to offer relevant talks and the students were also keen to discuss. In some schools we were invited back several times!

Deepening in the rural areas of Africa is most rewarding. In Zimbabwe the hospitality of the rural Bahá'ís is exemplary and their appreciation of your time and effort to visit them makes you want to return again and again.

Finally, 1994 was the year the Zimbabwean NSA hosted an international summer school, which they decided to combine with a music and drama festival. This was such an exciting project to be involved in. The National Spiritual Assembly assigned various committees to work on different projects and then pulled us all together during the latter weeks so that we had a unity of vision. As a result, last December we were able to host a gathering for one week for over 600 participants that included daily talks and workshops, separate youth and child education programmes, individual music performances before each session to awaken souls, plus public meetings. Afternoons were devoted to the music and drama festival and this brought all races and ages together in a most unifying and enjoyable experience. Our summer school choir, under the inspired guidance of Clare Mortimore, could have competed with the one at the World Congress. Sponsorships and bursaries were available so that no one was deprived of attending or eating together, and this wonderful experience was an appropriate ending to a most happy year.

At present I am with my husband in Dar es Salaam but am more or less cut off from the friends. I have no transport and am far away at the tip of Msasani Peninsula with little to do each day but pray and read and gaze out through the palm trees at an azure blue sea. Those who know me will understand that it is not my idea of paradise! However, I think we shall be moving again in a few months, so 'this too will pass'!

50
July 1995
Wesley Clash
Corfu, Greece

Two years ago the Clash family pioneered to the island of Corfu from Shepway, Kent.

Let me introduce myself. My name is Wesley Clash and I live on the beautiful Greek island of Corfu with my wife Stephanie, our daughter Giselle and the family cat. We used to live in Folkestone, Kent, but the British weather beat us, so we now live in sublime happiness with the hot Greek sun.

Stephanie has sent me a copy of the January *Pioneer Post*. I must admit I had never read it before and I must further admit that I had never heard of it either – although Steph assures me that we have been receiving it for the past two years! The reason for me telling you all this is that Steph mentioned that I might like to write about my Bahá'í experiences in pioneering.

At the moment of writing this letter I am not on my beloved Corfu but on an oilfield construction barge 100 miles off the coast of India. I am inside a deep saturation diving unit where I've been for 28 days. My bell partner and I have now finished our SAT (saturation) and are decompressing. It takes three days to decompress from our working depth of 250 feet. We have spent the 28 days in SAT helping to put together pipelines that carry crude oil from the oil wells to the gathering stations and then onwards to shore-side, India.

I must say pioneering offshore is a little difficult. Divers are not well-known for leading a sober or virtuous life, nor for the deep contemplation of the after-life, the before-life or, for that matter, this life! They tend to gallivant through

82

it all with great gusto and abandon and as a result tend to regard me as a bit of an oddball. Not drinking is very suspect and believing in God is truly odd, if not outright batty, to their way of thinking. I'm on safe ground chatting over motorbikes, where to go on holiday next or whether I will upgrade my PC. My favourite topic, and a safe one, is my beloved Corfu and Greece. At least on that subject I can try to convince them that I'm sort of normal and with 25 years of diving behind me, I've a plethora of stories that I tell to be one of the boys. I've been a Bahá'í since 1992 so for many years previously I was a heavy drinker and general nitwit. Once this is known and made apparent I am accepted and as I become accepted so my 'Bahá'íness' becomes accepted and as this happens divers and co-workers will, and do, ask me of my Faith, as on a recent evening in the inky blackness of an Indian ocean night dangling in our diving bell in 250 feet of water.

All in all a 'softly, softly' approach is my path. My prayer book lives beside my bunk in full view. We normally live four men to a cabin and the sight of a prayer book will sometimes elicit a query. I remember one chap asked me if I was a Muslim and I had a long chat with him telling him of the Faith. He now knows I'm not a Muslim but is still somewhat bemused. I find that people generally accept me as long as I do not push the fact that I'm a Bahá'í.

I'd like to say a big 'Thank you' to the lovely Bahá'ís of Shepway, especially to Jagdish Saminaden to whom I gave such a hard time prior to becoming a Bahá'í – God bless his cotton-picking socks! Thank you all for giving me such a wonderful gift through your patience, love and kindness. I feel I ought to tell you that despite the fact that my family and I are pioneering on Corfu, my prime reason for living here is my deep love for the island and Greece. Unknowingly, at the time we left England for Corfu we were actually fulfilling one of the goals of the Greek National Spiritual Assembly – opening Corfu again to the Faith. I've had a 'bee in my bonnet' about the island since my first visit in 1981 and we live here because we love the warm, generous, smiling and friendly Corfiots. That we became Bahá'ís is a tremendous plus in our lives and that we can pass on in some small way the gift of the Faith to those willing to listen and receive Bahá'u'lláh's teachings gives us great joy.

Those who know Greece will tell you that the Greek Orthodox Church and Greek nationality are perceived by the Greeks as being one and the same. Throughout the time the Ottoman Empire ruled over Greece it was the Greek Orthodox Church that kept alight the flame of Greekness in those dark days; the church was the glue that bound the Greeks to their heritage and their awareness of their culture. This it did for over 400 years. The Greek Orthodox Church is still very much alive in Greece. While the Christian churches in northern Europe are experiencing falling attendance as more and more teenagers and young adults, and not so young adults, are saying more openly that they do not believe in God or organized religion, here in Greece church attendance is still high and a belief in God is considered normal, not abnormal as in many parts of the world.

It may be that it is difficult to convince people of the authenticity of Bahá'u'lláh as the Prophet of God for this age, it may be that it is difficult to get people to take seriously the message of the Bahá'í Faith, it may be difficult to convince people that we Bahá'ís are a religion in our own right and not a sect, and it may be said that to do this in Greece is doubly difficult because of the strength of the Greek Orthodox Church . . . but who said it would be easy? Our job as pioneers on Corfu and in Greece is not to filch people from the Greek Orthodox Church or any other church or to undermine their beliefs or traditions. Our job is to strengthen peoples' belief in God and to convince them of God's love for them. If people can grasp the concept of progressive revelation and come to believe in the Báb and Bahá'u'lláh, all to the good. But, if people cannot grasp this concept and need to stay within the Christian church to stay within the parameters of a known concept . . . as far as I'm concerned, so be it. It is a joy to see people loving God through the Christian church in this country when in other parts of the world people live in a vacuum of disbelief and loneliness, possible victims of some of the oddball sects and rip-off pseudo religions that have sprung up around the world. The joy of being part of this island and this country is the knowledge that we live in a place where God is alive in the hearts of the people on a day to day basis.

51
July 1995
Susan and Shidan Kouchek-zadeh
Guinea-Conakry, West Africa

Susan and Shidan pioneered to Guinea-Conakry from Sierra Leone in 1975. They have been pioneers in West Africa for nearly 30 years.

I have loved the accounts in *Pioneer Post* of some of the youth on their year of service. Stephanie Christopherson writing about how participating in a 19 Day Feast in a village affected her expressed something of the magic of being with Bahá'ís in the villages. Nothing but the Faith would have got you to that remote place and nothing but the Faith gives you the feeling of oneness with people whose lives are so very different from your own.

We are plodding on in our rather schizophrenic Bahá'í life, alternating between a small struggling big-city community and visiting the larger village communities in the Forest Region 800 km away as often as is possible (at present four or five times a year). Here in the capital, which is 99 per cent Muslim, teaching the Faith is so slow. Up in the Forest, village communities are begging the Bahá'ís to come and tell them about the Faith but there are so few literate Bahá'ís, they can't get round to them all.

Last month I spent a day at Kotozou, 800 km from Conakry, for a deepening institute – so far off the main road that only one vehicle other than our chartered taxi reached it the whole day (and that one broke down!). We broke out into circle dancing, not quite the same as the Warminster summer school variety, at least three times during the institute! The friends went to great expense and cooked a whole goat to feed all the visitors; many Bahá'ís had walked in from neighbouring communities.

Shidan was named 'Consultant of the Year' in Great Britain last November. This was for the work he has done over the last few years on a project to upgrade Conakry's water supply. I'm so pleased he received some sort of recognition for all the gruelling work he does.

Here is an extract from an article in *The Times* (of London) entitled 'Projects that test the best':

> Shidan Kouchek-zadeh, who went to school in Bournemouth, and then qualified as a civil engineer at UMIST, was appointed chief resident engineer largely because of his experience on similar projects in Sierra Leone, Ghana, and Nigeria. He coordinated the work of the funding agencies, the client and the contractors. All communications were in French and all the contracts carried out under the French legal system. The contract was completed ahead of schedule, $10 million below budget, with no claims being made by the contractors and with the completed water treatment plant operating at 25 per cent above its design loading.

52
October 1995
Sylvia Girling
Poland

Sylvia pioneered to Poland two and a half years ago from Telford, Shropshire. Here Sylvia recounts her most recent adventure when she was visited by Bahá'í friends from the UK.

I'm buying a house in Poland but things aren't going too well. On my last visit to my lawyer, accompanied by my friend and her husband to translate for me, we talked over our latest disaster. She then says something and he translates:

'Would you like to buy the palace opposite your house, as my wife is selling it and would like to give you the opportunity of buying?'

'The palace opposite?' I say, a little stunned and unable to believe my ears.

'Yes,' he says. 'Would you like it?'

I laugh. I've always wanted to be Princess Sylvia, like my namesake (Princess Sylvia is a character on Polish TV).

'Well, now you can,' he replies.

'But isn't it too expensive?' I ask.

'No, it's not that expensive and even after the renovation it would be less than the house you wanted to buy,' he replies. 'A lot of renovation has already taken place,' he added reassuringly.

I thought for a moment. I had worked there. A small part had been turned over to house a business school and they had done a lot of renovating.

'It's far too big,' I say.

'Oh, there are many bigger palaces in Poland and you only need to use part of it until you require more,' he says.

I begin to dream. What a wonderful Bahá'í Centre . . . I know it has a grand ballroom, perfect for conferences. The beautiful grounds it is set in are just right for summer schools. It is perfect. Poland is in the heart of Europe and this is just what the Bahá'ís need. It's amazing what a few Fire Tablets can do.

He reads my mind. 'It would be just the place for your Bahá'í meetings.'

'It would cost too much to heat,' I say.

'Not much more than the other house you wanted, because the walls are so thick,' he replies.

It's true the walls are very thick and I have never been cold working there. But I think of the hundred or more rooms and wonder . . . 'But all that ground,' I say. 'Wouldn't the rates be too high?'

'No,' he assures me. He quotes a figure I don't understand. The Poles work in milliards (hundreds of millions).

Now I'm getting really excited as I can see the place filled with Bahá'ís . . . 'When can I have the keys?' I ask.

'A man will show you over the palace tomorrow.'

'OK,' I say.

We have a wonderful evening planning our new Centre. We would need a professional businessman to oversee it. Part of it could be a restaurant and we know someone looking for such a place. Part could be a hotel. It's so big and it's hard to plan that big.

As promised, the man comes in the morning to be our guide. The palace is over the road so we head on. He calls us back and points to the broken down old house in my garden – no windows, grass growing where there isn't any roof left. We look puzzled but think he wants to start by showing us that part of the estate and we follow obediently. No need for keys – no door – and we go in.

'That will do for the servants' quarters,' we say, and we're soon out.

Now we make our way across the road to what we are really interested in – our new Bahá'í Centre. We don't notice we're on our own until we're half way up the many steps. We stop. Where is our guide? We had better wait for him. But he doesn't come and, as we wait, the penny begins to drop. Oh no, it can't be true. We go over our conversation again and again. But already in our hearts we know the truth. All our dreams crumble. Not that old house, that can't be the place! We gallantly forge forward, laughing at our many plans. We make a tour of the palace and grounds but it is hard to believe that only minutes before we had truly believed it to be ours!

The next time I see my friend he asks me if I want to buy the palace. I show him a postcard with a picture of the palace.

'Is this the place?' I ask.

'Oh no, that's the business school.'

I ask whether it is the house in my garden, trying not to sound too foolish.

'Yes, that's right,' he says.

'But that's not a palace,' I say.

'Everybody calls it the palace,' he confirms.

I give up. This is just one of the hundreds of misunderstandings I have had since I came to Poland. But we had a wonderful evening planning the new Bahá'í Centre for the Bahá'ís of Europe!!

53
January 1996
Mojgan Agahi
Macedonia

Mojgan (from Northern Ireland) has been a pioneer in Macedonia since July 1995.

Two months after my arrival here I got to know a couple from Bosnia. Fatima and Stoyan had been living in Skopje for five months after having been expelled from their home town because they had the 'wrong' religion and nationality. (Here religion and nationality are counted as one). After having had to live under severe conditions for three years, without enough food, running water or electricity, they were forced to leave both their town and home either together or separately since each belonged to different religions. Through this couple I got to know other people from Bosnia living in Macedonia as refugees.

Being a Bahá'í gives us a vision totally different from what other people seem to have, or better not to have for that matter. The question for me was – how could I share with, or offer the healing message of Bahá'u'lláh to these people who have been suffering from injustice and are the victims of religious animosity? How could I talk about the establishment of the Lesser Peace to a group of people who for the last four years haven't seen much but killing and expulsion from their homes? How could I help them to restore their trust in God and in humanity where children had to choose between their mothers and their fathers because they belong to two different religions? The hardest of all for me was to see children wandering around in the limited space of the camp and who had not seen or heard much except the news of the war in their homeland.

After my second visit to the camp I came back home feeling disillusioned and helpless. I sat down and prayed and asked Bahá'u'lláh to show me a way at least to spend some time with them and get to know these children. I decided I could teach them English. For the first time I began to appreciate the popularity of the English language around the globe. Perhaps this way I could also learn their language.

I now have been teaching English classes to the children for the last few months and this way I have not only been able to get to know the children but also their parents. Progress is steady and the children's enthusiasm for attending the classes, their good manners, their respect for their 'Irish' teacher has all been very encouraging. It has made it worthwhile for me to walk up the mountain in order to reach the camp on Saturday mornings. Most of all, my effort was rewarded by just one comment made by one of the parents to my friend Mima, who said, 'The Bahá'í religion is the best religion in the world.'

54
January 1996
Tish Oakwood
British Virgin Islands

Tish has been a pioneer in the British Virgin Islands for the past two years with her 13 year old son Andrew.

Some people who receive *Pioneer Post* will know that I enjoy singing and since living here I have been singing a lot. I teach 'unity songs' in school to four to seven year olds. It always gives me a thrill to hear these non-Bahá'í children singing words from Bahá'í scripture. We have our class outside under a group of tamarind trees which have grown up around a cluster of boulders, so there is plenty of opportunity to speak about God's creation in between songs. To the older children in school I teach 'Earth-keeping', a class adapted from Wellspring educational materials, and we always round off the session with songs.

In the children's class that operates from my home we do a lot of the performing arts and the children are really very enthusiastic and quite talented. They have performed song, drama, puppetry and dance on several occasions. Most recently, for Bahá'u'lláh's birthday, their star performance was a dance to the words of the Guardian on the tape 'If you only knew' ('The world is, in truth, moving on towards its destiny . . . Adversity, prolonged . . .'[22]) to an audience of non-Bahá'í friends.

I must say, every time I work out a new song for the children containing words like 'black, brown or white from each and every land, like a beautiful garden, we're the family of man', it brings tears to my eyes and a lump to my throat as I look at this beautiful garden of children of all colours that I am honoured to work with . . . black, brown, white and every shade in between; children from Virgin Gorda, St Kitts, Barbuda, Venezuela, Guyana, Jamaica, Trinidad, America, Mexico, Canada, Italy, UK . . . truly a beautiful garden.

A precious friend of mine, a 90 year old local woman by the name of Viva (Life), was found stumbling over the dusty boulders between the church and my house in the midday sun on the holy day (the Birthday of Bahá'u'lláh). A younger member of her congregation observed her and went to her assistance. Viva told the younger woman that she had to go and see her friend Tish to tell her she couldn't come to the party because she was tired and needed to rest. The lady drove her to my house. I went out to the car when the lady told me what it was all about.

'Oh Miss Viva,' I said, 'you shouldn't be trying to walk over here. I really appreciate you telling me, but you didn't need to do that.'

Miss Viva looks me in the eye and says, 'Tish my chile. How can I tell you dat I love you an' den not show up to you' party? An' you be lookin' out fo' me? No chile, I can' do dat.'

Miss Viva is a singing companion too. I sit next to her every week at Community Chorus and I sort out her pages for her. For her 90th birthday I gave her the Hidden Words.

'You want me to change my religion, at my age?'

'No, Miss Viva, I want you to enjoy some beautiful words of God.'

'Well, tank you my chile. Dem is beautiful words fo' sure.'

55
April 1996
Lois and David Lambert
Mongolia

Lois and David have been pioneers in Mongolia (Ulaanbaatar) since September 1992.

Ulzi and I have just returned from a 4,000 km teaching trip to the far western provinces of Khovd, Bayan-Ölgii, Uvs, Zavkhan and Khövsgöl. Our trip had a number of objectives: to teach and to assist in the election of delegates in the electoral units where there were already Bahá'í communities, to contact local government and non-governmental organizations about the Convention on the Rights of the Child, and to teach the Faith in the Province of Zavkhan, where there were, as yet, no Bahá'ís. The five week journey was wonderful and very rewarding, although physically as punishing as anything I have ever experienced. In Uvs – the most northerly province – the temperature was minus 45 degrees Celsius. Everyone outside in these temperatures is white because breath immediately freezes on hats, eyebrows, noses, facial hair and scarves and as soon as the horses come to a stop, their hair freezes and they become snow horses. While we were visiting one *ger* (yurt, traditional Mongolian tented home) we heard a terrible yelping outside. A small puppy had licked an iron rod and his tongue had immediately frozen onto the iron. Our host was going out with a knife but kind and clever Ulzi thought of pouring water on his tongue and thankfully it worked.

We were travelling by petrol truck from one province (*aimag*) to another, through mountains where there were wolves, eagles and vultures. By the roadside we passed the body of a yak that had been attacked and eaten by wolves or vultures – not a pretty sight. On the way from Khovd to Bayan-Ölgii, which is on the borders of Kazakhstan, we stopped to visit a Kazak home in Bayan-Ölgii. The Kazak winter homes are little rectangular mud huts and very dark. The Kazak people are very hospitable and we were immediately invited to eat with them. Inside the home, one of the sons was kneading some rather unpleasant looking innards of some once-living creature in a bowl, his hands covered in blood. I'm pretty open minded about food in these situations but I did hope that this was not going to be our dinner. Of course, it wasn't! We had delicious cream, soup and meat off the bone – or to be more accurate, the sheep's head. Even Ulzi was rather reluctant to cut meat directly off the sheep's head so we were both rather relieved to have the men do it for us. Anyway, a few minutes after we had begun the meal the son put on a huge protective gauntlet and went outside. He came back with an enormous eagle with a black bag over its head sitting on his arm. He took off the bag and the bird gulped down the aforementioned innards in its huge beak, flexing its four inch long deadly claws. The eagle was magnificent and awesome, with a wingspan of between four and five feet. These birds are the pride of Bayan-Ölgii horsemen and they hunt foxes. The bird swoops down onto the running fox and grabs its back, and when the animal inevitably turns around, the eagle grabs its head and kills it. Then it waits for its master to come galloping up and a good time is had by all except the fox. I had heard of these amazing birds but never expected to meet one over dinner.

In the last week of January after leaving Uvs we made for Zavkhan, which we were hoping to open to the Faith. The petrol truck we were travelling in developed a leak in the radiator and every few miles we had to get out and melt ice to fill the radiator again. Our hands, feet and clothes were wet and frozen and we did not arrive in Uliastai, the provincial centre of Zavkhan, until after 11:00 p.m. at night. We went to both hotels and found that they were full because of a big political conference. The truck driver kindly took us to several families, hoping to find us a bed for the night, but each family was hosting politicians and had no room. Finally he took us to a house which had two *gers* built on the roof. This was Galtsentserren's home and the family received us with warmth, dried us out and gave us bedding.

During the next few days the house was always full of family and friends who had been invited to come and hear about Bahá'u'lláh and His teachings. The house seemed to attract people like a magnet. After three days we went to the top of a little mountain to say the Tablet of Aḥmad, praying that someone would accept the message of Bahá'u'lláh. When we returned, one of the teenage daughters told us she was a Bahá'í. When we told Galtsentserren that his daughter had just become the first Bahá'í in Zavkhan, he said, 'But I have been a Bahá'í since you first told me about Bahá'u'lláh!' It turned out that all the family considered they were Bahá'ís. It was simply that we had not asked them before. Thirteen people became Bahá'ís in the five days we were there and we arranged to hold the first Feast in Zavkhan on our last night.

56
July 1996
Colette and Vessal Ma'ani
Rhodes, Greece

Colette and Vessal with their family of three boys pioneered to Rhodes a year and a half ago from Northern Ireland.

We came to Greece in November 1994 and for all of us, Vessal and myself, Nason (11), Lewis (10) and Daniel (6) it has been a real 'learning experience'. When we decided to pioneer some years ago from Northern Ireland I naively thought the doors would fly open and the way made clear. Looking back, I can see an 'act of faith' was required. It was only when Vessal resigned from his job, we put the house up for sale and got our injections (for Africa?) that somehow all the obstacles began to disappear. I cannot begin to list them all. We wrote to Haifa for guidance and the day the faxed reply came from the International Teaching Centre giving us direction was the same day a couple arrived and bought the house.

So we arrived in Greece with no jobs, no home, three kids and six suitcases. The first night our eldest boy wept as though his heart would break. It has not been easy, and watching the kids cope with school in a completely foreign language has exercised our heart muscles somewhat! The first days leaving them in school where they could not communicate passed in a blur of tears and endless Tablets of Aḥmad (can one overdose on these Tablets?). However, the boys have emerged much stronger, much more loving and tender than I could ever have imagined. They have suffered a great deal but learned so much. Nason, our eldest, was in a state of revolt initially and as the months passed I used to wonder if he was a boy in a state of revolt or had adolescence transformed him into a revolting boy? However, he has emerged such a sweet soul and, ironically, of all of us, is speaking Greek like a Greek.

I'm ashamed to say I use the children for translation purposes, as my Greek is much, much worse than awful. One day at school the boys were led off to a Greek communion service at a nearby church. Unaware of what was going on Nason and Lewis filed in with all the other children. It was only when Lewis spotted the wine cup that he realized they could not participate in whatever was going on. He grabbed his brother from the queue and they refused to participate. It amused me later to realize that it was not the religious ceremony he objected to but the alcohol!

Our community on Rhodes has grown with the recent declaration of over half a dozen Russians, one Turk and one Greek. It has all happened very suddenly and community dynamics are in a constant state of flux (maybe that's the way they are meant to be?). We have been blessed with lots of love from fellow Bahá'ís and friends and relations. I could fill a suitcase with the letters and faxes we have received. So much love and support. Visitors have come and given us so much. I can honesty say I've learned so much about myself this year (not all of it good!). Pioneering is a very real experience. No boring routines, no complacency, no safety margins and very intense. Joy comes from very small things that surprise and delight, and every day is infinitely precious. It is a weird business this pioneering!

57
July 1996
Payam and Shirin Foroudi
Guyana

Payam and Shirin with their two very young children Layli and Naysan pioneered to Guyana from Swindon, Wiltshire, early in 1994.

A lot has happened over the past two years since we moved to Guyana. After a few months of uncertainty about our future here, we recently received confirmation that my contract has been extended for a further year.

The biggest event of recent months has been the new addition to our family. Shirin gave birth to a lovely baby girl on 19 January 1996 and we have named her Lian Sarah. Layli is five now and almost a lady. She is very vocal and talks nonstop. She loves saying prayers loudly at Bahá'í gatherings and is very confident. She is a great teacher of the Faith and always asks if so and so is a Bahá'í. When we say 'No', she says, 'Why not? We should tell him/her about the Faith!' Naysan is two years old and knows a lot of words but he is only understood by us!

The Bahá'í activities keep us busy as usual with various committee meetings and other activities filling up our busy calendar. In recent months our everyday life has become a bit more eventful, in that we get almost daily power cuts which last eight to ten hours, and although the Electricity Corporation gives their 'load shedding' schedule, they never stick to it and we often have fun trying to guess when the next power cut is going to be! Also, we don't have much running water (we are connected to the city's main supply but it is often dry!) and have to rely on water trucks delivering water to the house, which is not very healthy, but so far we haven't had any problems. We have been very lucky with the telephone services here and can phone anywhere in the world, quite easily and cheaply. I will go crazy if we lose this as well!

Locally, I am on the Georgetown Social and Economic Development Committee, which is responsible for undertaking some development projects in the capital. Amongst our activities are raising awareness of the Bahá'ís on environmental issues, literacy work and, more recently, on health. The Bahá'ís in Guyana are actively involved in some very successful health education projects in remote parts of the country and as a result the Bahá'í community is well known and well respected by everyone, particularly at high official levels.

Although the name of the Faith is well known, the current rate of growth of the community is slow. Guyana has a large Bahá'í population (on paper almost 50,000), and this was the result of a long teaching campaign some four to five years ago. A lot of people, particularly in rural areas, enrolled in the Faith but little attention was paid to sustaining the growth and deepening the new believers. There are now long lists of names in every village that need to be updated and followed up. I am sure this problem is not unique to Guyana and a lot of countries, including the developed ones, are experiencing this in one way or another. So we have a lot of work to do in the rural areas but our resources are limited. We can't really say we miss the UK but we certainly miss our friends and the Bahá'í community there.

58
July 1996
Fleur Mazloom
Thailand

Fleur (from York) spent part of the year as a youth volunteer at the Bahá'í School in Thailand.

I arrived in Thailand seven months ago, alone and extremely nervous. I didn't know anything about Thailand, I didn't know anyone, I didn't know what I'd be doing, I didn't know even how long I'd be staying. All I knew was that I'd left the people I love most in the world, and a place that was familiar and safe, for my love of Bahá'u'lláh and the hope of being able to serve His Cause in some small way.

I was only in Thailand two days when I was told that I had been invited to a Bahá'í institute. I didn't think too much of it until I got there and realized that it was for the National Spiritual Assembly and Auxiliary Board members. I couldn't believe it – within a week of arriving in Thailand I had met the most influential Bahá'ís in the country.

Through my time here I have been in contact with the majority of those people, who have given me much encouragement, love, friendship and anything I've needed. After a week and a half of orientation in Bangkok I was sent up to Yasothon, which was to be my permanent place of residence for my time here. I was extremely lucky that my move to Yasothon coincided with a major teaching project in the area. For that week I was able to go to the surrounding villages and see the beauty of mass declaration. However, for the rest of my time I got to see and know the problems that go along with this kind of declaration. It's been a good experience to see the pros and cons of such teaching, as I've always wanted to see mass declaration in my own community and now I've realized that the community as a whole is not truly ready and so it's a blessing that God has given us a little more time to prepare ourselves.

My service in Santitham School started slowly, as when I got there they had just started their three week holiday. However when the classes began things started to go very quickly. I was joined by three other youth volunteers, and even though the work was shared out amongst us, at the start I found it very hard going. I had never taught before and was very sceptical of how I was going to do. When I was looking for a place to do my year of service I had just one intention: I was not going to teach English! But yet I found myself doing exactly that and at first I really wished I'd stuck to my intention. However, after the first month I started to relax and the teaching became easier.

We just finished a ten day English summer camp and I found it to be so much fun. I love the interaction with the children and when it's obvious that they've learned something it's a very pleasant feeling. That's not to say that I've now found my chosen career in teaching, far from it! It's just reconfirmed my previous conceptions – it's not for me, unless it's only for a short period. Apart from the teaching, there have been a lot of other things that at the beginning I had not been too keen on and, now, feel very sad at the thought of leaving. One example is my place of residence. During the first two weeks I was in Yasothon I was moved twice and ended up staying at the school in some old class rooms. The place was . . . let's say, not in the best state, with spiders, ants, mosquitoes, lizards and flying bugs everywhere, with faulty electricity that kept cutting off, with a shower and toilets outside, with the toilet doors not shutting and only a curtain cutting off the shower, and sharing both with a few families of toads. The list goes on. Now the place is in exactly the same state, though there's now a door on the shower, and although the bugs can sometimes become a little overwhelming for my liking, I consider this place home. I'm going to miss waking up to the most glorious sunrises across the most beautiful scenery and the most spectacular sunsets I've ever seen and, most of all, the 'family' of volunteers who live here, the children at the school, the teachers, the Bahá'í community of Yasothon, the women in the market, the guy that I always get my iced tea from, the postman who finds so much pleasure in seeing the volunteers' smiles when the post arrives, the Thailand youth, the Thailand adults, the Laos friends, the Malaysian friends and many more. Even the thought of leaving any of them makes me sad but I know I'll always have them in my heart as I have so many wonderful memories of them all.

My period of service in Thailand has been the most wonderful experience I could have ever asked for. It's given me so much both mentally and spiritually. I only hope that my work here has given Thailand just a fraction of what it's given me. Lots of people have commented on the sacrifices that all us volunteers have made in our service here but all of us agree that it's no sacrifice being here, rather a blessing for us. That's not to say there haven't been tests as, believe me, there have been far too many to count, but as I've already said, I'll always be grateful for my time in Thailand.

59
October 1996
Arthur Kendall
Portugal

Over a period of two weeks in August, 22 all-singing, all-dancing Bahá'í youth and four adults travelled by minibus and ferry to attend and perform at a Bahá'í summer school at Monchique in the (Portuguese) Algarve. This account comprises the personal recollections of one of the drivers, Arthur Kendall.

Youth Travel Teaching Adventure

The first whimsical memory I have of events preceding last summer's youth travel teaching trip to Portugal was when Nottingham teenager Veronica Beales sidled up to me in the restaurant at the Whitby 1996 National Convention and announced, 'You're driving us.' In fact, there were three more adult drivers, namely Maureen Kerr (Oakham), Rita Green (Melton Mowbray) and the indefatigable Aberdeenshire-based Nick Sier, whose organizing thrust and tireless musical output proved to be the true 'driving force' behind the entire project.

And it thus came to pass that during the evening of Tuesday, 6 August, my little house in Solihull, West Midlands, became blessed to bursting point with sleep-bagging Bahá'í youngsters. At 4:30 a.m. the Solihull contingent departed in inky darkness in convoy with 'bus 2' down the M5 for the ferry from Plymouth to Santander, Spain.

Most of the 210 mile first leg passed without incident. Memories of last year's hot drive to the Czech Republic stirred uneasily in the back of my head. The outside temperature today was barely 20 degrees Celsius, so what could we look forward to in 32-degree Spain? I asked myself extremely quietly. We ended up in the queue for the Santander ferry with an hour to spare. Out of the hundreds of cars, lorries and caravans we were the very last on board despite being well up the queue. However, the last shall be first, and at the other end we were pleased to be about sixth to disembark.

Before that, though, 24 hours at sea resulted in some marvellous proclamation by our wonderful young singers. Led and encouraged by the guitar playing, singing and dulcet (his word!) Dewsbury tones of Nick Sier, the boys and girls sat in a semi-circle on the carpeted landing area of Deck 7 of the *Val de Loire* and infused the ship with several hours of musical entertainment to the surprise and delight of mums and dads and children who, like me, may have assumed 24 hours at sea to be largely boredom. Nick introduced a new song to the group – 'Thief in the Night' – which has a terrific rhythm and melody line and which the youngsters had a firm grip of within 15 minutes. That song in particular was to ring out joyfully many times across southern Portugal in the coming days.

A few dozen high-temperature red lights and an overnight camping stop somewhere later, we reached Monchique at about 7 p.m. on Friday, August 9th. We were not quite there however. Only the Bahá'ís, I mused, could have the confidence to travel a thousand miles without knowing their final address! We paused in the forecourt of a filling station and performed one of Nick's spiritual skyrockets. Piling out of the buses and linking arms in a big circle, we sang a few 'Remover of Difficulties' and set off in no particular direction, ending up at the local fire station. The only fireman to speak English went off with Nick and Maureen in number 2 minibus to help us find our destination! Twenty minutes sauntered by, during which I noticed, just as last year when we were lost in heavy rain 20 miles from Prague at 9:30 p.m. on a black night, with nowhere to stay, the young people, far from being concerned, chatted away happily, supremely confident of a sudden solution to the prevailing problem. Number 2 minibus duly reappeared with its occupants smiling broadly and Nick waving a clenched fist in triumph. They had found the location of the summer school and had announced our imminent arrival to the dozens in residence. Ah, the power of prayer!

We arrived at the venue, a villa on a mountainside, to resounding cheers and applause by the large crowd that had assembled to meet us. There was much singing and dancing and laughter that night – apparently into the early hours – though being well past 42, I had slunk away to our tented area at about 11 p.m. Shame I hadn't told the mosquitoes about the dangers of British beef though. I awoke the next day with a relief model of the Pyrenees down the right side of my face!

During the following four days we enjoyed the devotionals and talks at the school, and by about the Tuesday, when the school ended and the participants left, we were able to move up from our camp into the villa. Ooo – real beds!

We had an excellent interpreter, Tina Sanai, with a fine microphone technique, and wonderful support from the Portuguese Bahá'ís in general, who had planned and thought out a varied itinerary for us, even if a couple of times things came slightly unstuck. One example was when we were due to 'go on' in an illuminated square at 11:15 at night in the town of Chinicato but the preceding performers – a group of stick dancers – over-sticked by about 25 minutes. Our group, although tired by then, went on and were doing splendidly when the power to the locally-provided amplification was cut off. Apparently the electricity had been supplied from a shop and the occupant had decided to pull the plug, shut up shop and go home, right in the middle of our performance – and it was only 15 minutes past midnight! However, resourceful Nick Sier, aware that we still had lights, simply moved the whole singing dancing ensemble forward and close to the big crowd and carried on the show to the delighted applause of everyone. A few days ago Tina told me by email that a young man from that town has now declared his belief in Bahá'u'lláh.

I can't recall every incident in detail but in the tourist town of Lagos we attracted very big crowds of holidaymakers, many of whom were from the UK. There were also a couple of friendly locally-based Geordie street-performers who seemed to be able to juggle clubs, smoke, play the guitar and tell jokes all at the same time.

During the long haul back we sorely missed one of our drivers, Maureen, who had had to fly home to England a week early owing to job commitments, so for much of the return trip two out of three drivers were a bit tired – well, I was. Later we were to experience magnificent mountain views in the Sierra Ávila. Approaching Santander, I recognized feelings of attachment for Brittany Ferry dinners and reliable hot water but such delights would not be before a long night of driving in rain, with Rita doing a splendid job of negotiating the snaking mountain roads on dim headlights, following me as I pretended to know where I was going.

We trundled into Santander in torrential rain at 6:30 a.m. and parked by the gates of the still-closed ferry terminal. Within my bus descended a silence that passeth no understanding as 12 contentedly tired adventurers snoozed a couple of clammy hours away, oblivious of the rain spiking out of a leaden sky and rattling on the steel roof. The other bus remained in a state of similarly blissful repose. Ahead, the return 24 hour sea journey, a repeat of the 'on board' proclamation to even bigger crowds, and somewhere in the distance, warm showers, home cooking, fresh clothes, a stroll around the garden, and sleep.

60
April 1997
Heather Lansing
Venezuela

Heather pioneered to Venezuela from Peterborough in August 1995 to work at Escuela Campo Alegre, an American International School in Caracas.

My life has been a whirlwind since leaving England's shores last year. I am now settled in Venezuela. Culture shock has been and gone and now I just accept that each day is an adventure and appreciate that it takes time to get anything done. My Spanish is at the point where I feel confident in my daily life and can understand most of what is being said to me. Speaking the language is, of course, another matter but somehow I am able to make myself understood.

The city of Caracas is chaotic. I had vowed that I would never live in a big city but here I am! I can now decipher the difference between a gun shot and a firecracker. No longer do I hear the constant noise of traffic running through the city. And considering I have been here over a year now with nothing having happened to me, I do believe a 'band of His angels' came with me, especially after having a sawn-off shotgun aimed at me and some friends!

The Bahá'í community is small but truly wonderful. I live just a ten minute walk from the Bahá'í Centre. Last year the inauguration of the National Bahá'í Institute took place at our National Convention in a place called Barquiesimeto, between the two cities of Caracas and Maracaibo. It was built in just six months of the first meeting to raise money for it and has been built with simplicity, yet contains a beautiful tranquillity – it's so wonderful to pick a mango off a tree during break time!

99

My lack of Spanish has hindered me from getting out and teaching the local Venezuelans but the school in which I work has been getting a 'real education' on what this life is about! I remember Adib Taherzadeh saying that the word 'Bahá'í' should come up every day and it is indeed refreshing to mention the Faith each day. Last year our school hosted a conference on 'Global Citizenship'. A Bahá'í friend and I conducted a workshop on how to achieve this. The answers are so simple if people could just hold a vision and make a start.

This year sees me going off to the islands for which Venezuela is responsible – Curaçao, Bonaire and Aruba – with other Bahá'í girls. Everything has been incredibly good. Events leading to my getting from England to Venezuela were so easy and I do believe that I am meant to be here. However, my two year contract is due to end soon and I have to decide whether or not to stay. Pioneers are needed here but Africa is calling me still . . . I guess I'll do what I did last time and leave it in the hands of God and see which doors open.

61

January 1997
Karen and Tim Shrimpton
Philippines

Karen and Tim, with children Esme and Robert, left Norfolk in July to pioneer to the Philippines.

Living in a huge, noisy, polluted city wasn't exactly what we had in mind when thinking of pioneering but the teaching opportunities here in Manila are incredible. Tim and I are both teaching at the International School and are the first Bahá'ís ever to be employed there. The majority of expatriate teachers have already taught in many countries of the world. A lot of them have come across the Faith before and are interested to find out more. Others who haven't heard of it are very open-minded and world-conscious thinkers.

On a wider scale, I had the privilege to be invited as a Bahá'í representative to a Women's Forum where Hillary Clinton was the main speaker. She was here with her husband for the APEC (Asia-Pacific Economic Cooperation) Conference. There were many very influential women there including the First Ladies of New Zealand, Chile and Papua New Guinea, as well as many wives of mayors, ambassadors and diplomats. There were plenty of opportunities to mention the Faith and I made some very interesting contacts as well as met other Bahá'í women who had come from different parts of the country.

The National Spiritual Assembly also organized a dignitaries' dinner to celebrate United Nations Day. I was asked to emcee the event and it was lovely to meet lots of other Bahá'ís from Asia, as it coincided with a Bahá'í Institute being held in Los Baños (south of Manila).

In November a two day workshop on 'assessment' was organized at school in which 50 teachers participated. The workshop was led by Bambi Betts, a well-respected international educator and fellow Bahá'í, and between the two of us many teaching opportunities arose during the weekend. It was very exciting taking part in a professional development activity run by a Bahá'í.

Our local community consists of 11 adults and a few children but there are great difficulties in getting together for meetings. The major problem is the traffic! It can take over an hour to travel a very short distance, so meetings generally start very late. Communication (or lack of it) is also a big problem here. There is a wonderful Bahá'í Centre in Old Manila (our neighbouring community) and we are planning to hold an event there for World Religion Day.

62

January 1997
Michele Wilburn
Island of Skiathos, Greece

Michele lives in Hampstead, London, but is eager to explore the Greek islands with a view to pioneering.

It was my 10 year old daughter Romani who was determined to revisit and introduce me to this island where she had holidayed a year earlier with a friend. The warmth of the sun and the loving nature of the islanders had won her heart.

From the outset I had resisted purchasing air tickets. My initial reaction had been that 'such a holiday', as she painted it, seemed too luxurious a way to pass the time, let alone money set aside for travel teaching!

By the time I finally took the decision to go, there were no plane seats available. I was resigned to the fact – obviously this was the will of God! As days went by I was having trouble talking a disappointed Romani into other possible destinations. Imagine her delight when events suddenly turned! We received an unexpected phone call from a long-lost travel agent announcing he had found the perfect seats to Skiathos, at an unbelievable price. The choice was out of my hands!

With no time to book accommodation in advance, I decided to put the remainder of the trip into Romani's hands.

'You've got me into this,' I reminded her, as we headed for the airport. 'You'd better decide where we are staying tonight!' From that moment she and her company of angels led the way. Travelling with a child certainly opens many doors! And hearts!

As she would have it, two beds were waiting for us in the apartment of her choice. By the next morning I had sufficiently calmed down to count my blessings. We began every morning with prayers for guidance and teaching and set off to explore with open hearts, buckets and spades, and searching minds!

Day after day, from the moment we left the apartment, amazing doors opened – all in miraculous ways and with divine timing. Every conversation led to Bahá'u'lláh. Blessings and joy filled our souls as we shared His message.

We met people holidaying on the island of Skiathos from so many European countries. In such a naturally beautiful atmosphere people were relaxed and open to spiritual contemplation. I became convinced that much of the success of our teaching was due to the fact that away from the race and pace of hectic lifestyles, people are open to questioning the meaning of their existence – coupled with the fact that the heart is spiritually uplifted when living close to nature.

We were especially blessed in establishing friendships with the native islanders. In particular, through a fishing family – resident on the island of Evia – who invited us to spend time with them on their fishing boats.

Early one evening, several days into the trip, we were sitting in a fish restaurant by the sea, discussing the concept of pioneering when suddenly the sky began to flash above us. While we debated the cause of the flashing lights, lightning began streaking through the sky. A huge flash darted off the water only yards from where we sat. Suddenly the skies opened and rain poured down in torrents. We were forced into the local fish market behind us, where we shared a table with a couple from Norway and the Faroe Islands. Yet again, the timing was perfect! With all this happening in the middle of a conversation about pioneering, I was beginning to wonder if God was signalling a message!

On another occasion our plans were rearranged at the last minute. Because of high winds, we were transferred onto another boat, literally forced to take a trip we had definitely decided against. Sitting at the bow, within minutes we were in conversation with a woman from Germany who had also been transferred.

'God had other plans,' I joked with her, as she expressed her disappointment. 'Do you believe in God?' she asked intently!

To her amazement I mentioned I was a Bahá'í. As the story unfolded, it became apparent she had been investigating the Faith for years in Cologne. After a day at sea, tossed about by mighty waves, at the whim of nature, she was ready to declare. I was further reassured when she phoned us in London a week later, the hour she arrived home, to thank us. She was preparing to contact the Bahá'ís.

Where, but for Bahá'u'lláh, go we? About to embark on a study programme of the Greek language, I pray, if it be the will of God, that the doors will open for us to pioneer. Whatever way things go, I have committed to support the development of the Faith by focusing my attention on these wonderful islands throughout the Four Year Plan. I thank almighty God for having enabled us to become the recipients of such illuminating outpourings of divine grace and heavenly bestowals. And in so doing, I thank all those wonderful souls we met, with whom we were able to share the message of Bahá'u'lláh, for however brief a moment in time, to whom we were attracted by the spiritual magnet of the Holy Spirit.

63
April 1997
Guita and Shahob Youssefian
Japan

Guita and Shahob have been pioneers in Japan since 1988. They have two children, Shafa and Adora. They don't often get the time to write so I'm grateful to Guita's parents for forwarding me their latest news.

You might wonder why we live such busy lives! It is basically because we have all the occupations (and preoccupations) of any normal family, plus the fact that because we live in a very young community we are still the main catalyst for Bahá'í activities to take place. Thank God, a flow of travelling teachers in the past two years (including some of Japan's NSA members, Mrs Mehrangiz Munsiff twice in two years and my parents, Dariush and Mihan Ram (Gabriel) from Uruguay) has sustained us, each of whom prodded us along in their own wonderful and unique ways. Also thanks to the grace of God that has made our young Local Spiritual Assembly active and functioning, we have been able to keep up a string of events sponsored by our community, thereby familiarizing the good people of Akita with the lofty name of Bahá'í.

To the more seasoned pioneers among us there is no need to mention that in the course of all this we have witnessed a few minor and major miracles. Also in line with the recent call of the beloved Universal House of Justice to concentrate on a few key issues facing the world, our Bahá'í community has found it easy to approach the people through the subjects of the environment, education and women. Attending the Fourth UN Conference on Women in Beijing in September 1995 with my parents greatly boosted our activities in that direction.

The name of the Faith was clearly and frequently mentioned at a big public meeting to celebrate the fiftieth anniversary of the UN. This was considered a great victory for the Faith since the Japanese people and media are extremely cynical and suspicious about religion, especially new religions.

The fiftieth anniversary of Japanese women gaining suffrage was on 10 April 1996. This is one of the miracles, that out of all the women's groups and individuals and foreigners in Akita, the organizers, who had separately attended Bahá'í firesides at our house when we had our travelling teachers, asked me to write a report on my trip to the UN Conference on Women and not to forget to mention through which organization I took part! They knew fully well that it was Bahá'í. After double checking with another organizer who spoke English, I wrote two pages (they had only asked for one!) on Bahá'í viewpoints on the equality of men and women and included passages from 'Abdu'l-Bahá's writings. The article, translated into Japanese, with the word Bahá'í all over it, was included in a handbook printed for the celebration of women gaining voting rights and was given to all the 80 participants, many of whom were local government officials, including the mayor of our city.

In the course of the nine years we have been here there have been many occasions when the city has arranged events along the same lines as Bahá'í ideas and at which the Faith was not represented. It has been very painful to stand by and watch them celebrate something that Bahá'u'lláh first proclaimed without the views of the Faith being voiced. I thanked the grace of God that this one was not one of those occasions!

64
April 1997
Mihan and Dariush Ram (Gabriel)
Uruguay

In 1996, the International Year of Peace, the Bahá'ís in Montevideo decided to erect a monument in front of a tree planted for peace. On that monument was mounted a bronze plaque with words of Bahá'u'lláh about peace. Underneath it was buried a time capsule to be opened 50 years from

*then. The Plaza Fabina is located in the very centre of Montevideo. The
burial of the time capsule was the initiative of Mihan but could not have
been achieved without the help of the Bahá'í community.*

The Tenth Anniversary of the 'Time Capsule', 22 October 1996, and the Fiftieth Anniversary of the formation of the United Nations, 23 October 1996.

Bahá'í friends started to arrive at the Plaza Fabina at 10 a.m. The sound equipment was ready. There was someone to clean the bronze plaque of the 'Time
Capsule', someone else to inflate the balloons with Bahá'í words on them,
others to arrange the flowers and yet others to talk to non-Bahá'ís who were
gathering to see what was going on. At 10.30 a.m. the basket of doves arrived
and by 11 a.m. the balloons were suspended in groups, music was playing and
everything was ready. One thousand invitations had been sent out – for both
ceremonies in the morning and the next night – to ambassadors, consuls, pro-
fessionals, NGOs, members of the Town Hall and deputies and, in addition,
to those who had sent a message of peace for the 'Time Capsule' ten years
before, plus personal friends and Bahá'ís from Montevideo and other cities in
Uruguay.

There were almost 40 people present, of whom about 25 were non-Bahá'ís.
The history of the 'Time Capsule' was explained to those present, followed
by the laying of the first bouquet of flowers at its foot. The basket of 50
white doves was opened and they gracefully and beautifully circled above and
around the plaza before disappearing into the sky. Some Bahá'í materials were
distributed and then everybody was invited for refreshments in a restaurant in
the plaza where groups were sitting and chatting about the Faith.

The next evening, 23 October, a conference of Peace and Unity in Diversity
was held in the beautiful hall of the Parque Hotel in Montevideo. It was a very
important event, as it marked both the tenth anniversary of the 'Time Capsule'
and the fiftieth anniversary of the formation of the United Nations. Among
the audience of 200 guests was the Ambassador of Israel, a representative of
the United Nations, a member of parliament and various other high-ranking
officials. The most wonderful and unique feature of the ceremony, before the
programme of dances from different countries, was that of a group of youth
wearing their national costumes. They went onto the platform and each in turn
lit one of the 50 candles on a gigantic (one metre in diameter) three-layered
cake decorated with flowers and with a golden world symbolizing the planet
placed on top. It was a very dignified, beautiful and emotional ceremony. The
ceremony started with the UN representative who spoke very positively about
the Bahá'ís working for peace, and he read from *Gleanings from the Writings*

of Bahá'u'lláh about the formation of an 'all-embracing assemblage of men'. Then the key speaker for the evening spoke about 'World Peace and Social Economic Problems from a Bahá'í Point of View'.

65
April 1997
Charles and Sholeh Boyle
Queensland, Australia

Charles and Sholeh (recent long-term pioneers from the UK to the Solomon Islands in the southwest Pacific) relate their experiences of teaching Aboriginal people in north Queensland.

Following the highly successful 'global village' held north of Townsville last year, after which there were several declarations on the former aboriginal forced resettlement camp on Palm Island (which boasts amongst Australia's highest violent crime, youth suicide and alcohol abuse rates), there have been eight more declarations amongst Aboriginal people living in Townsville.

We had a group of visiting Maoris travel teaching on Palm Island. Of the six who declared their belief in Bahá'u'lláh, one – Philip – taught his mother. She likewise declared her faith just a week or so before she passed away. The weekend of her funeral we had visiting Bahá'í travel teachers from the Solomon Islands. Immediately after her funeral eight of her nieces and others in her family declared their faith. The Catholic sisters were quite concerned about this and pressed them to recant. Two of them returned to the Catholic Church but the remaining six responded with admirable courage that they had made their declarations of faith of their own free will and that if their aunt thought it was good, then they thought so too.

The following 19 Day Feast we were awash with new believers. What is amazing is that ever since the global village there have been strange stirrings in the land (as they would say). Because of aboriginal extended family connections, there is some expectation described by the aboriginal friends that more will join. Subtle threads link the various aboriginal communities, sometimes referred to as the footsteps of the rainbow serpent dreaming, so the phenomenon may be likened to nerves which, when excited in one location, trigger a response in another.

Our Assembly is trying to learn at 500 mph how to handle a completely new dimension to the community and is aware that for many indigenous people, their culture, their story and their knowledge are the only things that they 'possess'. Thus it has been at great pains to ensure that when the news of these declarations was more widely known, it was the declarations of faith, not their aboriginality, which was celebrated. We are aware that many of the assumptions we might make about our social customs, behaviour and the like may simply not mesh and, in extreme cases, may offend others, so we are taking things very slowly. We are also teaching ourselves aspects of Murri (the proper way to describe the Aboriginal peoples of Queensland) culture and society, and a history of Palm Island – surely one of the saddest places in the world.

Our new believers have been immediately reading all sorts of things – Philip is reading the Kitáb-i-Aqdas, describing how similar it is both in intent and detail to traditional Murri law. The others have been reading *The Seven and Four Valleys*, prayer books and so on. We have got to start running children's classes for 25 children now . . . and adult/new believers' classes.

We are also having to get pro-active about visitors as you can't just stump up to Palm Island for a visit (out of courtesy to the Palm Island Council, and by invitation from the Bahá'í friends there). We are soon expecting a visit from Kevin Locke (native American hoop dancer).

Our new believers are causing us to grow in more ways than we could ever have expected and at a speed far greater than we could have imagined – surely a part of the process of entry by troops.

Anyway, for what they are worth, the above are some comments on recent developments. I am sure you will read about them from a better pen than mine or hear the news from a sweeter voice but quite possibly not from one more enthused and excited by these events . . .

The global village was conceived as a part of the regional 'Ocean of Light' campaign whereby the Faith of Bahá'u'lláh was carried by traditional chiefs and representatives from island to island and tribe to tribe within the Pacific basin. It was an idea born of consultation between the islanders themselves and the Continental Board of Counsellors.

My own sense is that it is reawakening the spirituality within the people themselves. I look back at the anthropological evidence of continuous settlement within the islands and can sense that lost links of common cultural and spiritual heritage and ancestry are being polished up and rebuilt. Thus at the New Zealand conference last January, Kevin Locke could both figuratively and literally speak of a great 'hoop of unity' being made when his Lakota people, the Maoris and the Aboriginal peoples of Australia came together. It was awesome.

Anyway, this concept inspired the creation of the global village. We took over a bush camping site north of Townsville and invited representatives from the Pacific island communities, Aboriginal tribes and the Maoris to come and build their own 'settlement' within the campsite, and round the great fire and under the moon and stars or the trees in the hot sun, share their experiences of their past, present conditions and future expectations, and inspire each other by example.

The Bahá'ís deliberately took a completely understated position, not pushing the ideas of the Faith but simply facilitating the event. Nevertheless the Maori friends, outspoken as ever, shared their experience of the way their lives had been affected by the Faith and this ultimately led to two people declaring their faith in Bahá'u'lláh – one Maori lady married to someone from Tokelau (which presents interesting challenges in itself as Tokelau elected that each of their villages should choose one church only and all stick to it to avoid religious arguments); the other a man from the Torres Strait Islands north of Australia.

Also the Jalbu Jalbu local theatre group gave the inaugural performance of *Rainbow Serpent Dreaming*, which tells in dance and music the cultural history of the Murri people in this region. Afterwards the Bahá'ís were asked to be their managers, as they felt we were the only people they could trust.

It was after this event that the Maori group went to Palm Island and six people declared their faith in Bahá'u'lláh. Next year the Maoris will be holding their own global village which the Murri people on Palm Island will attend. The Torres Strait Island friends have asked to hold a global village in their islands and plans are afoot to make it a regular occurrence.

Some of the Murri people have spoken openly about their feelings that the rainbow serpent (which might be analogous to the Holy Spirit) has been awakened and is now stirring into life, according to aboriginal prophecy.

66
April 1997
Janet Rowlands
Republic of Ireland

Janet (from Tynedale) is an isolated pioneer in Co. Clare, Ireland.

My son and I have been in Ireland for seven and a half years. We bought a one storey house with two acres of land which is situated on the side of a mountain. The mountains around the lake are more like large hills. Their tops are tree-lined and covered in patchwork fields and topped with pine forests. When we first arrived with the removal van it was to a house shell without any of the facilities of modern-day living. For the first year we used paraffin lanterns for our source of light and a car battery operated a strip light which illumined the kitchen. I carried water for washing from the river a field away when the rain barrels were empty and drinking water I collected from a neighbour's well. I used to drive the one-third of a mile to the neighbours and went over what might be described as an assault course to get to and from the well. Since then I have installed electricity at great cost and a shallow well, and hot water and have converted a small passageway into a shower room. Our bathing facilities previously had consisted of a blue plastic barrel cut in half with a cork sealing an outlet. You can imagine the panic if the cork was accidentally knocked out but at least we were able to keep clean.

I'm sitting at the moment outside the house with my Jacob and Welsh Black sheep grazing around me and the donkey occasionally trying to shout for its feed. In front of me are the sloping green fields on the tops of part of the Slieve Bernagh range. It is very still and quiet in the sunshine, apart from the sound of the sheep pulling grass, the cat cleaning itself as it sits on the windowsill and the birds singing. Oh what bliss! A few weeks ago the rain lashed down so hard that many of the towns and villages were flooded. Streets in Ennis town were nearly three inches under water and the river was contained within its walls, which are higher than the car park alongside the river. A very rare occurrence.

When I first arrived in the area I made a point of mentioning the Bahá'í Faith in conversation with anyone I met. Most people had never heard of Bahá'ís. There were a few emigrant and Irish people who had met a Bahá'í, John O'Mahoney, received acupuncture from him and been introduced to the Faith. A few years on I was told one day, 'I had never heard of Bahá'ís before but now there are Bahá'ís everywhere.' This isn't quite true but since they have been made aware of the Faith they have become more aware of the name Bahá'í.

I invited the Bahá'í Limerick Roadshow to sing in the nearest small town a few years ago. They sang to an audience to help to raise money for the Steiner school which my son attended and they were well received.

Although it has been a great struggle both physically, mentally and financially living in Ireland, we have survived and I eventually managed to get a place on a Clare Employment Scheme, thus making us financially more stable. At present I am having a deep well and septic tank installed to make life more comfortable. Our shallow well which was installed two years after we arrived is full of manganese and iron and unfit for drinking. It is almost like having Quatermass in the attic when the water tank is cleaned out!

When we attend Bahá'í Feasts, holy days or Local Spiritual Assembly meetings, on average we have a 50 mile round trip to drive each time, unless they are held at my home or very occasionally at the homes of the two Bahá'í families who live about eight miles away.

Over the past seven years I have been involved with the setting up and teaching in both the Clare and Limerick Bahá'í children's classes. At first the Clare Bahá'í children met in a draughty caravan in John O'Mahoney's garden and then we moved to Villiers School in Limerick and joined the Limerick Bahá'ís to begin the Limerick school, where morning classes were held on a Saturday. Our next venue was the Unemployment Centre in Limerick city where I taught and also became a member of the board for a term. I am no longer involved with the school but often help out at summer and winter schools with teaching and entertainment.

A whole family of five, English friends of mine, became Bahá'ís and I still continue to tell everyone about the Faith whenever the opportunity arises. We have had stalls in my nearest tiny town and a display in the local library as well as in other libraries around Clare. I am now working on 'Thought for the Day' slots with a local radio station, Clare F.M. To the present date we have had three separate week slots reading Bahá'í writings for one minute, heard twice a day. Our fourth slot will be for a week in April. The first time that we recorded 'Thought for the Day', the priest who organizes the religious programmes was so overcome with the way in which the youth read their pieces that after a moment of complete silence he said, 'I wish everyone would record as well as all you young people did.' Everyone, including a monk who also is involved with the religious programmes, stood and listened intently to Bahá'u'lláh's words.

Later I discovered that on St Patrick's Day, a big celebration in Ireland with parades everywhere, Clare F.M. was in Shannon and was broadcasting live from the street. A huge crowd was waiting for the parade to begin and all the dignitaries were sitting in the large open container wagon waiting to judge the entrants when 'Thought for the Day' with our readings was broadcast over the radio for everyone to hear! What a captive audience! Hundreds of people heard Bahá'u'lláh's writings read by Amy Costelloe, a 12 year old Bahá'í. We were all so thrilled when we heard this news.

67
April 1997
Shirin Youssefian Maanian
Greece

Shirin was a pioneer in Romania from 1992 to 1994 until she met and married Socrates, currently secretary of the National Spiritual Assembly of Greece.

When I received *Pioneer Post* in the mail and was moved to tears as usual, I decided I must at long last write . . .

It is two years since I moved here to Greece – which is difficult to believe . . . I travel all over Europe so often for the Youth Council that it feels like I'm hardly here at all! (That's my excuse for being unable to speak Greek very well, anyway!)

It has taken me a long time to get over leaving Romania but as little miracles occur here more and more often, I'm feeling more at home! One of the biggest miracles is my work situation. Almost as soon as I arrived in Greece I found work, all in my own field. I set up an English theatre company with a lot of success (we just did a production in cooperation with the South African Embassy) and seem to find work all over the place selling my voice(!): audio novels, radio, even cartoon voice-overs! All of this has also led to wonderful contacts for the Faith in the theatre and diplomatic fields.

One of the biggest adjustments to make in moving from Romania to Greece was the number of Bahá'ís – Romania has over 7,000 and Greece has about 200 (including children). The steadfast, long-serving pioneers here are truly to be admired and need encouragement, as many of them feel that they never see 'results'. However no one can deny that even in Greece there is a 'new receptivity'. In Athens (the most noisy, polluted and hectic place I have ever lived!) we have a wonderful fireside every Monday where quite a few of our friends (Greeks and others) come regularly. We are very open about the Faith with them and a few seem quite ready to enrol.

A Counsellor member of the International Teaching Centre was just here and after spending some time with him I feel completely transformed (again!). He gave so many inspiring examples of reliance on Bahá'u'lláh in our personal teaching work and how we should be systematic and invite seekers to become Bahá'ís, that Socrates and I have already made plans for each of our contacts!!

I thank Bahá'u'lláh every day for being a pioneer – of course on some days when I can't understand a word that's going on around me, no one seems interested in the Faith, I miss my friends and family terribly and everything else is going wrong too, I really wonder . . . but then the next day I'll receive such a clear confirmation that I know that this is where I should be!

68
July 1997
Phillip and Ann Hinton
Australia

Phillip and Ann pioneered to Australia in December 1974 from Epsom with their two young sons Sean and Simon.

It is always a joy to read *Pioneer Post* – touching personal stories of brave souls in faraway places – some of them dear friends for many years. It reminds us of the sixties and seventies when we Bahá'ís inhabited a 'teaching culture' – we lived for teaching and winning the goals of the plans and not much else – alas, not so easy to revive that spirit these days, though the approach of entry by troops is perhaps stimulating the desire in more of us to teach.

The story of the dear Bahá'í friend in Limerick touched my heart. I went through there as a travel teacher in 1968 and cut my thumb quite badly trying to change a light bulb for Lesley Gibson (later Taherzadeh), who was a pioneer in Limerick. I was whisked off to the surgery of a young doctor who stitched me up – without a local anaesthetic – talking all the while about rugby, obviously his great passion! I remember almost passing out with the pain, so the joke was that I 'shed my blood for the Cause in Limerick'! It was not long afterwards that Stan Wrout came there and laid down his life as a pioneer. Stan's story is one that I often tell to inspire young Bahá'ís. Ann and I had known him quite well in London. You know how some people are easily forgotten – they pass briefly through your life and you forget their names and faces. Yet Stan is someone who is still clear in my memory and I think it was quite simply his sweetness, his gentle, modest personality and the depth of his devotion that imprints him in my mind so vividly. Such individuals are examples of what it means to be a Bahá'í.

It occurred to me that Ann and I must qualify as British pioneers though by now we have become 'dinky-di', as they say, Australian citizens and very much part of this place. Though Australia was not a pioneer goal for Britain, we wanted to assist British goals in the Pacific. When we were on pilgrimage in March 1974 with our two young boys and told House of Justice member Mr Hofman we were planning a move, he was quite emphatic we should come to Australia. We also mentioned to the Hand of the Cause Paul Haney we were considering moving to either New Zealand or Australia and he said very firmly, 'No, not New Zealand, go to Australia.' So we left London in late 1974 to head for Australia and after requesting permission of the House of Justice, stopped at the World Centre en route. Their letter had granted us a three day visit 'on the way to your pioneer post in Australia'. So, there it is, it was really dear David Hofman who gave us the final shove that sent us on our way here. We had some pretty solid backing, you might say, for the move. We arrived via Perth, Western Australia, on Boxing Day 1974 after a hellish 23 hour journey in a jam-packed 747. From a freezing English winter we stepped into the blazing hot Australian sun with two small children, Sean and Simon, two large suitcases, a bag of golf clubs, no work and just enough cash to get ourselves to Sydney. A new life beckoned.

We have wonderful memories of our time in England but no regrets at leaving. It has been a full life here. I guess we were never the heroic 'desert island' or 'derelict house in Limerick' pioneers – we have lived comfortably in the Greater Sydney area all this time, but we have been and still are in the thick of some exciting developments in the growth of the Cause and have been able to do our bit. Ann is an Auxiliary Board member, with 25 Local Assemblies to take care of in an area around the size of Britain, all the while holding down a full-time job as a teacher of children with intellectual disabilities! I get to travel around Australia quite extensively talking on the Faith and emceeing Bahá'í events, etc.

Also there have been many wonderful opportunities to present the Faith through the media, especially radio. Life is never dull. And most exciting nowadays is a growing awareness of the arts as a medium for spreading the message of Bahá'u'lláh. Inspired by the World Congress in '92, my one-man performance of *Portals to Freedom*, Howard Colby Ives's personal account of his meetings with the Master, has opened up countless opportunities to travel all over Australia and tell these lovely stories to the friends, as well as tours to the US, Canada, New Zealand and one performance in South Africa. Anywhere we travel, Howard comes with us, packed in a suitcase! In October '95 when Ann and I were in Haifa to visit our youngest son, Ben, who was at the World Centre for a year of service, I did two performances in the Seat of the House of Justice. Does an actor experience nerves after a lifetime in the acting profession? With two Hands of the Cause and half the members of the House of Justice sitting in the front row, you sure do! It has been a precious privilege to be able to use one's professional skills in a small way to serve the Cause. Sometimes when I am on stage in a small intimate theatre looking into the eyes of the people in the audience, telling them stories about the beloved Master, I think I'm about as close to heaven as I am likely to get in this world!

The Internet really is one of God's latest miracles, isn't it? We could not have organized our recent US tour without it and now we are working on plans to bring out performing artists to Australia to tour here and perform in all our major cities. We were inspired by Omid Djalili's recent visit. He was in Adelaide performing at a comedy festival and we got him to come up to Sydney for one night. He played *A Strange Bit of History* and his comedy routine to a sold-out house of mainly Bahá'ís and, needless to say, stunned everyone with his daring talent. We want to see Bahá'í artists cooperating with each other in their efforts to serve the Cause.

Perhaps the most satisfying thing at this stage of our lives though is to see our three boys, all so different in their ways, grown up and serving the Cause with such care and devotion. What more could one ask out of life? Sean is quite well known to the Bahá'ís in Britain – in fact they claim him, as do Australians, as 'their' Knight of Bahá'u'lláh for Mongolia. His connections with Mongolia continue. During the recent state visit of the Mongolian president to Australia, Sean was appointed as Honorary Consul General for Mongolia. We went to the little ceremony to mark the event and were all very proud of him. It is extraordinary to think it is only around six years since Sean confirmed the first Mongolian believer and now there are over one thousand Bahá'ís with a strong National Spiritual Assembly and 15 local assemblies!

Sean is married to Tebby from Botswana and Simon to Shabnam who grew up in the Solomon Islands. Simon did some marvellous work on tours to Asia and to eastern Europe with his Wildfire World Theatre group. Our youngest, Ben, who was born in Sydney and thus is the only genuine Aussie among us, is also a source of pride to his parents. He recently spent his university holidays walking the jungles of the island of Malaita in the Solomon Islands.

Ann and I are sometimes asked the question by young Bahá'í parents, 'How can I be sure that my children will grow up to be active and devoted Bahá'ís?' We usually tell them, 'You can never be sure, everyone has to eventually fight their own spiritual battles. But if you actively teach the Faith and take your children with you, they will be fired with a love for the Cause that will sustain them through tests and they will find their own way.' The balance is to mix Bahá'í community life with the other social and cultural activities children need and allow them to grow as individuals. Nowadays our boys all plan their lives around goals of service to the Cause and we thank God for that blessing.

69
July 1997
Tahereh Nadarajah
Mongolia

Tahereh and Silan arrived in Mongolia in February 1996, having been pioneers in Papua New Guinea since 1978. Here Tahereh writes about a recent travel teaching trip in Mongolia.

I went for four days to Sainshand province (10 hours by train) with Auxiliary Board member Narantsatsral (Tsatcha). On the train a wonderful tall and Genghis Khan-looking middle-aged man opened our coupé and asked if he could come in and talk to us. We said 'yes!' and that was the beginning of a five-hour fireside. He was a staunch Buddhist and he left our coupé absolutely floating in the Valley of Wonderment of Bahá'u'lláh!

Then he returned and brought two Mongolians, a musician and a singer, and we had two hours of blissful joy of Mongolian songs. They then asked me to sing and I told them I'd chant a Persian prayer instead. Our coupé had its sitting capacity filled with other people who wanted to know what was happening, including the two train inspectors who joined in the singing! This was a great prelude to the King of Festivals and the Riḍván election to which we were travelling.

The man then invited us to his *ger* (house) in Sainshand. Auxiliary Board member Narantsatsral accepted immediately and said, 'Tahereh, he is an important person there and if he becomes a Bahá'í he'll help the community tremendously.'

He did become a Bahá'í and we had a glorious two-hour fireside with his entire family. The same day he came and visited the Bahá'í community in a preparatory meeting for the Riḍván election. The Bahá'ís there are professional people, such as hotel owners and teachers.

Next day we went to visit a Bahá'í kindergarten teacher in her class of three to four year old absolutely gorgeous, adorable young Mongols! I held five on my lap constantly. They melted our hearts with their song and dance. The young Bahá'í teacher was a beautiful, calm young lady very keen to improve her class.

While we were there, Tsatsral's sister came and brought a beautiful-looking lady who was Tsatsral's teacher many years ago. She was apparently dying to see a Bahá'í and took us to her school. She is the course coordinator for grades seven to nine. She then called her 15 year old daughter. The daughter was searching for information about the Faith and wanted to come to Ulaanbaatar just to find it! It is absolutely impossible for me to describe the joy of the three-hour fireside we had in that office at her school (with 1,300 students!). The daughter was overjoyed and accepted Bahá'u'lláh after 20 minutes. When I asked what the mother thought, she said, 'How can I not accept if my daughter accepts it so regally!' That lady is live wire! and is such a great human resource for the Bahá'í community in Sainshand – she became a member of the Local Spiritual Assembly two days later!

I asked about her husband who is working at a TV station in Ulaanbaatar. She said, 'There are three Bahá'ís in our family now but I will tell my husband as soon as I see him.'

I asked, 'But you and your daughter are only two?'

'But my five year old son is also a Bahá'í,' she said.

You should see her face shining with such a joy. Truly, Bahá'u'lláh has come for people of Mongolia who are so noble to realize the realities of His message. Unfortunately our trip back to Ulaanbaatar was a midnight train and everyone slept, so no further chance of teaching!

70
July 1997
Anisa Turner
Tonga

A flavour of Anisa's experiences whilst a youth volunteer at the Ocean of Light Bahá'í Primary School in Tonga, as written home to her mother, Zoe, in Shrewsbury, Shropshire.

Naw-Rúz was so nice last night. After breaking the Fast we went to the Feast of Bahá at a little Tongan house where we sat on the floor on mats in an empty room before going to the Bahá'í Centre to join their Naw-Rúz celebration. Today the school is closed.

It was a lovely day at Utukelie beach. Bahá'ís in little groups under the trees sitting on mats sharing food. The beach was indescribably beautiful. I swam in the sea and sat in rock pools with the children. I had a little troop of kids following me down the beach as I collected shells, so we jumped over the waves together, which they found very amusing to see me, a 'grown up', doing!

The same week I set out on a teaching trip to three villages with some other Bahá'ís. We bought food from one of the local hut shops for the trip and I felt very excited walking to the shop in the dark, looking up at the expansive night sky, strewn with billions of bright stars.

We set off into the hot sun each with our own bags of bare essentials. We got to the first village early and waited under a tree while the lady got the house ready. The purpose of the trip was to find out if there were nine active Bahá'ís in each village so that a Local Spiritual Assembly could be formed at Riḍván. The little house or *fale* where we stayed consisted of just one room with a mat on the floor, so all seven of us slept on the floor. We drank coconuts and I watched several cute little black and white spotted piglets running about. Apparently the family was really pleased that *palangis* (foreigners) had come to stay with them and live in their Tongan way – sleeping on the floor, sitting on the floor outside and eating with our fingers.

After eating we went swimming in the sea in front of the house. Tongans swim in their clothes. I had a bucket bath afterwards in a three-sided lean-to type cubical. I walked with my friend Tesiola to the shop to buy bread for supper afterwards. It's very hard walking in the dark trying to avoid potholes and pigs with only the moon and starlight to guide you! Tesiola played the guitar and we all sang Bahá'í songs. There was a very nice atmosphere and I was so happy.

71
July 1997
Carol Spencer
Philippines

Carol (from Stanmore, Middlesex) pioneered to Palawan, an island province of the Philippines.

As a new pioneer it was lovely to receive my first issue of *Pioneer Post*, which really emphasized the Bahá'í Faith as one big family – something I had already been very grateful for on my arrival and receiving a warm (hot might be more appropriate!) welcome from the Bahá'ís in Palawan and also in Manila. Just before Naw-Rúz we were nine adults and now (owing to one 'coming of age', two declarations and two families moving into the area) we are 17 adults, plus 11 youth and children. Being the capital of the province, Puerto has quite a fluid population and I find it hard to keep track of everyone – a necessary task as I've been elected secretary – a real challenge to my Tagalog language skills, especially over the noise of motor tricycles, neighbours' radios, electric fans, etc., but one that I'm enjoying.

As well as establishing a regular programme of events in the community we hope eventually to raise enough money to build a Bahá'í Centre on the land here that the Bahá'ís own. In the meantime we squeeze ourselves into whoever's house, office or garden is available! Lots of the Bahá'ís enjoy singing and there seems to be popular support for a Bahá'í choir. My next challenge will be trying to set some Tagalog *Hidden Words* to music!

My work as a VSO occupational therapist is equally challenging but I'm surviving the stress and, despite the muggy weather, mosquitoes and mud (which is why my house is on stilts!), I'm having an exciting and wonderful time.

P.S. It was wonderful to hear Hugh Adamson speaking on the BBC World Service (May 29th). If it hadn't been a holy day I'd have been at work and missed it!

72
October 1997
David and Manijeh Smith
Zambia

David and Manijeh (Mole Valley) with their young children, Bayan (6) and Holly (4), have been serving at the Banani International School since March 1994. Here is David's account of a recent teaching trip to Northern Zambia.

I had packed the car the night before and made up beds on the seats for the children so they could sleep while on the journey. We were heading up to the far north of Zambia for a week of teaching. Needless to say Bayan was up at 3:30 with me, clutching his new Swiss army knife and wondering if his friend Sameen would have one with as many attachments! We kissed Mummy goodbye, Holly still more asleep than awake. The road was exceptionally straight and very quiet – we did not see a car for most of the 915 km from our door to the mission guest house in Mbereshi, Luapula Province.

A teaching project, named in honour of the late Isobel Sabri and funded by the International Teaching Centre, had been initiated four years previously in the neighbouring province. Much had been achieved and even more had been learned. This time round, and four months earlier, an orientation programme had been conducted for assistants by the two Board members living close to the project area – one had cycled approximately 350 km along dirt roads to the orientation. These Bahá'ís mean business! The assistants had undergone a spiritualization programme and then formulated the next phase of the plan. They had four months to go back to the area, deepen the local communities and get them to plan a teaching campaign – they had to devise it and execute it. We were going along as background participants – drivers, pamphlet deliverers, encouragers – not as principal organizers. At this orientation the assistants discussed the type of teaching materials they would need and one of the Board members and his wife agreed to make and print these materials. When we met in Mbereshi, they were reviewing the literature and discussing which villages to target, when it should be done and by whom. To my cluttered mind it didn't seem likely that anything would happen but the Board members skilfully picked through the dialogue and produced a recognizable 'plan' on a sheet of paper. It seemed there would be public meetings 'under the mango trees' in several villages. The Bahá'ís would use the teaching materials and invite the villagers to public meetings, where the Board members and three other 'visitors' would give talks about the Faith. We had also brought hundreds of copies of a thorough 'correspondence course' on the Faith. So that we could proclaim, teach, enrol and deepen, it was suggested that one person from each of the strategic villages be trained as a course facilitator. Things began to look feasible – we took our cues from one of the Board members who would fluctuate between depressed and euphoric!

The first meeting was with the big Headman – Headman Mano – who invited us back for two more long audiences. He gave us a cordial welcome and listened carefully to what we had to say. He did not embrace the Faith but many of his people did. Several days later he informed us that the bishop had expressed concern at our activities but that he had told the bishop to leave us alone. National radio announcements for the campaign had been arranged. We heard that the Bahá'ís would invite large crowds to come and listen to the 'communal' radio and when the announcements were made they would then begin spontaneous firesides. The Board members had also hired a mobile public address system and we would drive through the bush and along the main road from village to village and teach the faith. This was not proclamation but simple, concise, audacious teaching – the local Bahá'ís were so dynamic. Empowered by spiritualization, equipped with teaching materials, supported by radio and public addresses, encouraged by having visitors from other areas and consolidated by deepening course facilitators, they taught and taught and taught. In one village about 150 adults came to the meeting. A lot of souls responded to the call of the Faith and we quickly ran out of declaration cards – lists prevailed! We will now wait to see if the correspondence course will deepen the new Bahá'ís and lead to exponential growth.

We had to shower under waterfalls, catch fish in the rivers, drink very suspect water and burn coils to deter mosquitoes. We used Bayan's knife a lot – for fishing, cutting bread, spreading jams and opening cokes! Holly, Bayan and I saw the Faith in action and were greatly privileged.

73
October 1997
Farid and Mercedes Afnan
Summary Visit to Spain

*Farid and Mercedes live in the London Borough of Brent. For six months
in 1994 they were pioneers in the Solomon Islands.*

In August, Mercedes and I returned from holiday in Spain following the visit
of Rúḥíyyih Khánum there. While Rúḥíyyih Khánum was addressing the conference in Madrid for the fiftieth anniversary of the Faith in Spain, I was stuck
in the departure lounge at Luton Airport while spare parts were being brought
in for my flight. (If there is ever a time to repeat 'Is there any Remover of difficulties . . .' 95 times, it is when one is waiting at Luton Airport, sitting in the
cafe where the food looks like it is about to make an appearance on *The X-Files*,
looking out of the window while mechanics spend ten hours repairing one of
the engines of the plane you are about to board . . . and it only has two engines!)

Opportunities to see and hear Rúḥíyyih Khánum are few and far between,
so imagine my bitter disappointment. However, my disappointment turned to
joy when we heard that she would be attending the Basque Baháʼí Conference
in Vitoria, northern Spain, where many of Mercedes's relatives live. So we left
the children in her home province of Burgos with their grandmother and set
off on the two-hour drive north. There was a wonderful atmosphere at the
Basque conference. French and Spanish Baháʼís gave Rúḥíyyih Khánum and
Violette Nakhjavani a very warm welcome with traditional music and dance
outside the main conference centre in Vitoria.

Rúḥíyyih Khánum, in her address to the conference, said that one of the
main shortcomings of the Baháʼís is that we don't do enough to share the
Faith with the rest of the world. She used the analogy of inviting people to
a banquet where we prepare all the dishes and lay them out for our guests
to take as much or as little of whatever they want. She also said there are
great possibilities open to us to share the Faith through the media – radio,
newspapers, television, the Internet – and we must seize these opportunities.
She encouraged the friends at the conference to go to their local media when
they returned home, especially as this is the fiftieth anniversary of the Faith
in Spain. We left feeling spiritually invigorated by her words, her spirit and
her energy. The next day an article appeared in the Vitoria daily paper about
Rúḥíyyih Khánum's visit to Spain.

A few days after the conference we went to the city of Burgos to visit two
of the Baháʼís there, Marta and Manuel. The province of Burgos is one of the

largest provinces in Spain. The capital city (also called Burgos - so good they named it twice), was the medieval capital of Spain and is one of the most Catholic parts of the country. There are currently only five Spanish Bahá'ís and a newly declared gypsy family in the whole province.

Seated around a table drinking coffee and tea, we decided on the spur of the moment to go to the offices of the Diario de Burgos, the local daily newspaper, and see if they would print an article on the Faith. They were very interested in the fact that Mercedes was the first Bahá'í to declare in the province and that she had come from London to attend the conference in Madrid. Without us doing anything (except getting off our backsides to go to the paper) they printed a three-quarter page article on the Faith, its teachings and the activities of the Bahá'ís in Burgos and London (well, Brent actually), together with a photo of Mercedes in the centre of the page. This appeared in the paper the day before we returned to London. Since then the ripples have been spreading through Burgos. Manuel has been contacted by the newspaper asking him for another interview on the Faith and Marta has been asked to go on local television for 30 minutes to talk about the Faith. Last year Marta and Manuel appeared on local television on two occasions for nearly an hour in total, talking about the Faith! And all of this is happening in one of the most conservative, Catholic cities in Spain!

74
January 1998
Gillian Phillips
Republic of Ireland

Gillian (from Narberth in South Wales) has been a pioneer in Ireland (with brief interludes back in Wales) for the last 30 years. Here she goes down Memory Lane recalling very special memories of the early days in Limerick.

While attending the Intercontinental Conference in Frankfurt in 1967, I sat next to the chairman of the Pioneer Committee of the United Kingdom, Patrick Green. At that conference I made a commitment to pioneer to the south of Ireland. Pat said, 'It is a bonus being Welsh – Celts get on well together.' Being young and single I decided to throw in my lot with the Irish people. Crossing by boat, I made it safely over to Ireland in January 1968, feeling a little sick owing to an abscess in my front tooth. At that time no dentist resided in the Welsh market town of Narberth but I did not wish to delay my move to Ireland (as cold feet may have crept in).

I was met at Dublin railway station by Val and John Morley, pioneers to Dublin from the UK. I was greeted with so much love and taken directly to a dentist. The relief from the drained abscess made me very light headed, 'drunk' almost, as we drove to the Bahá'í Centre. As I looked out of the car window, the streets of Dublin seemed to swing like a pendulum.

After an unexpected week of hospitality and partying, I felt honoured and was determined to do my very best. At the end of that week I had a consultation with the then chairman of the Teaching Committee (Adib Taherzadeh, later a member of the Universal House of Justice). Limerick City was to be my pioneer post, where I was to join Lesley Gibson (later Taherzadeh), who had pioneered to Limerick from Northern Ireland in August 1967. The advice given to us by the Teaching Committee was to be patient, pray and live a Bahá'í life.

I found work as a nursery nurse with children with special needs in the same clinic where Lesley worked as a speech therapist. The atmosphere in Limerick City was grey and oppressive. Dublin was the only Local Spiritual Assembly and three more Assemblies had to be raised by 1971 to enable the National Assembly to be established by Riḍván 1972. The third pioneer arrived on his Honda motorbike in the winter of 1969. Stan Wrout, a distinguished man of 40 years old, was so cold that he needed help to get off his bike.

We formed our Bahá'í group. Sadly, on 9 August 1970 while taking his holiday driving around the Ring of Kerry, Stan found a beach, went for a swim and got into difficulties in the water . . . after nine days his body rose to the surface and was washed up onto a small cove called Kilbaha, where his remains are laid to rest at a special spot looking out onto the Atlantic Sea.

Other pioneers arrived from the UK – Ann and Fred Haliday, Jim Bradley, Roberta Strain and Jim Elliot; from the USA – Miss Hordy Bradehorst and Mrs Mary Lou Martin; and from Switzerland, Mrs Doris Holley (wife of the Hand of the Cause Horace Holley), who replaced Jim Elliot who returned to the UK after a few months. The Limerick Assembly prayed and prayed for inspiration for teaching, reciting together five hundred 'Removers of Difficulties' on several occasions.

In the winter of 1971 the ice broke. Youth in large groups began attending the fireside at Lesley's flat and the atmosphere was as if Bahá'u'lláh had walked into the meeting touching the heart of each person. Many embraced the Faith with firm resolve and went off pioneering to other towns in Ireland, forming the Local Assemblies. In 1972 the National Spiritual Assembly of the Republic of Ireland was established, having a large, youthful, active community to guide.

Last August (1997) Lesley and Adib returned to Limerick to commemorate the 30th anniversary of Lesley's pioneering and arrival in the city. A party was organized by the Local Assembly. Many of the youth who attended those early firesides at Lesley's flat were there with their children and youth. Stories of the early firesides were recalled and much laughter permeated the air. In those early years the newly-enrolled youth were taught to become lovers of Bahá'u'lláh. They were showered with love and guidance and were given a thirst for the revealed words of Bahá'u'lláh, myself included in this process.

75
April 1998
Sandra and Philip Cooles
Dominica

Sandra and Philip pioneered from Aberdeenshire, Scotland, to Roseau, Dominica, in 1982.

We have been pioneers in Dominica for the past 16 years but in a couple of months we will be the only pioneers left, so as you can gather there is never a dull moment! As I write, I have on my desk the minutes from the last National Spiritual Assembly meeting and all the accompanying letters, the newsletter to be finished, another Feast package to get out to the villages, the money to be sorted out from the last Feast and then, of course, there is always the village teaching, children's classes and Institutes to support!

Just now we are trying to get a new fire of activity going by visiting all the different communities. We are using the Ruhi Institute material, which can be very challenging indeed for poor readers, but it is having great results. A guy in one village thought it was the 'ointment' of honesty. I felt almost sorry to tell him it was 'ornament'! But as we gird our 'lions' and drink a deep 'drought', one can only wonder at the power of the revealed word which overcomes all these difficulties and many, many more.

For a couple of years now we have been sending out Feast packages to the different villages. They say exactly what to do and include a selection of short readings with all the 'hard words' explained. It is having great results. Last Riḍván six Local Spiritual Assemblies elected themselves because of the constant contact with the Feast letters and now we have nine 19 Day Feasts organized by the friends themselves, a tremendous result when you think that a year ago we only had one. One of the Feasts is even being held by the side of the road. It is the only time when all of the friends in that area can get together, as most of them are street merchants and have to sell food, etc. in the evening. Alice, the organizer, explained that people who come to buy always stop to listen! Last Feast, she said, there were eight adults and seven children, all organized by her. Tremendous!

Last summer we went to the Shetland summer school. It was the first summer school we had ever been to and it was just fantastic. It showed our girls who, as far as the Faith is concerned, live a very isolated life, what being part of the Bahá'í family is all about. I cannot thank the friends in the Shetlands enough for all their love and care.

76
April 1998
Peter Smith
Thailand

Peter has been a pioneer in Bangkok, Thailand, since 1985.

Work at Mahidol continues as ever. I now teach introductory psychology, sociology, anthropology and world history there. This keeps me busy. We have recently acquired a new boss who wants us to go out more often, which is fun. The campus – at Salaya – about 40 km from where we live, has been undergoing a building spree, with masses of new buildings to dispel the former rural quiet. The road out there has also become part of Bangkok's urban sprawl and the traffic has correspondingly increased. Add to this two major transport projects being constructed along the way and my journeys to and from work have become even more time-consuming. My record for a journey home is from six to seven hours! That was exceptional but three to four hours is quite normal. To avoid a similar nightmare in the morning, I get up at 4:30 a.m. and set off at 5:30, thus narrowly missing the beginning of the morning rush hour. Thus I am often at work by 7:15 or so. I leave work at 3:30–4:00 p.m. but if the traffic is too bad, I now frequently abandon the journey half way and watch a movie or go to a tea shop and do some work. I then resume my journey after the traffic in that area has lessened (7:00 p.m.) and get home at 8:00 or 9:00 p.m. All of this is quite normal by Bangkok standards: one really has to be crazy to live here!

When we first came here, Bangkok buses had much lower roofs than they do now so that when I stood up – which I invariably did because there is no theoretical or practical limit on the number of people that can be crammed on to a Bangkok bus – I often had to stand with my head tucked to one side like an owl, or alternatively with the crown of my head sticking up into the ventilation hole. Or I could hang on the outside and feel the refreshing awakening breeze as the street furniture rushed towards me. Bangkok buses also have the interesting habit of not fully stopping when people are trying to get on or off. This leads to many interesting situations, including in my case once being dragged along by the bus for 200 yards at increasing speed until we got to a stop light. Only one of my big toes was broken! Apart from that, I had a suspected broken kneecap, a severe gash to my shin and numerous minor abrasions all courtesy of Bangkok buses. Perhaps I should get a job with their PR department!

77
April 1998
Tanya Jones
Youth Service in Poland

Tanya grew up in a small village in North Wales.

I spent my first eight months in Cieszyn, a border town in the south of Poland, or the north of the Czech Republic (depends which way you look at it) and the last four months in Olsztyn, in the north. In Cieszyn there is a community of seven, two of whom are long-term pioneers. Both of them work as English teachers and during my time there I would often go into the schools with them. At the beginning I would go into the schools as a 'guest from Wales' and would be asked questions and, usually, be asked to play my guitar and sing them a song. Later in the year I would go in as an assistant teacher. Performing songs in the schools gave me a good reputation and I was asked to play in two concerts. The first one was in the student bar at the university and the second was at a local club. Both were very successful, especially the second one where there were a hundred people or more. All this happened within the first two months and it was therefore a great opportunity to make friends and to meet some of the local youth.

Soon after I arrived in Poland I was asked to be an assistant to the Auxiliary Board in order to encourage the youth and the arts. I didn't know what this involved but I accepted gratefully. I was asked to go on a two-week teaching trip to Bialystok, where I would go and hold firesides, give public and private concerts and be of assistance to Siona Neale who came from Canada to give concerts and tour Poland, visiting Bahá'í communities on her way. In Bialystok both Siona and I had some very successful concerts with great media coverage. To join in our teaching efforts another Bahá'í youth came down from Olsztyn and we went out on the street with our guitars and sang some Bahá'í songs.

In May I was invited by one of the schools in Cieszyn to go on their school trip to Budapest, which was a great time to talk to the students and to visit some of the places 'Abdu'l-Bahá had visited.

In July there began the ongoing project of teaching in Bielsko-Biala (twinned with 'Akká in the Holy Land). During this project we did some cross-border teaching and were invited by the Slovakian community to participate in their fireside as they were working towards getting their own National Spiritual Assembly. This involved taking part in another concert.

During the past year the Bahá'í community in Olsztyn doubled in numbers, many of them youth. I was asked to help by being an active member of the workshop institute, to train the youth to become strong teachers of the Faith through the performing arts. These workshop meetings would always start with prayers, then we would either sing or consult on where the workshop was going, then on to warming up, learning dances, rehearsing, etc. Mei-Ling Leong, a youth volunteer from Australia who had recently been serving at the Bahá'í World Centre, was the facilitator and driving force behind the workshop. Her workload was massive so as part of my duty I would assist her in any way I could. As all the youth were still very young Bahá'ís some consolidation was needed. My part in this would often be on a one-to-one basis and my friends and I would talk about the laws of Bahá'u'lláh and the reasons behind them. We would study the writings together but usually on a really informal basis. From this a weekly youth deepening came about on a slightly more formal level. The text would be in English and Polish and these weekly meetings were very nice. We would all squeeze into my box of a room, and it was all nice and cosy. We would often deepen for at least three hours until my landlady kindly asked everyone to leave!

Other activities I have been involved in here in Olsztyn have been working with a music group. This was a wonderful experience for me. In November the workshop felt ready for its first teaching trip. We went to Gdansk and it turned out to be a very successful weekend. We gathered together for prayers and consultation and then went onto the streets. We did three street performances in the freezing cold and invited people to our evening performance. Around 15 non-Bahá'ís came to it (two from the street!) and it was such a good night, the sense of success really uniting the group – all the hard work, effort and sacrifice paying off. The following week we held another performance, this time in our own town of Olsztyn. This was a big test for the members, performing in front of their friends and families. However, again it was very successful and over 40 non-Bahá'ís came this time! It was an excellent way to end our 'winter season' and now we are praying that the youth will keep the workshop going, ready for a big summer project.

I thoroughly enjoyed my year of service in Poland and I honestly feel that I have gained a thousand times more than I have given.

78
July 1998
Jimmy and Janak McGilligan
Bahá'í Vocational Institute for Rural Women, Indore, India

Jimmy (from Northern Ireland) and Janak have been working at the Bahá'í Vocational Institute since 1986. This is Jimmy's report of their participation in World Environment Day.

The ex-trainees of BVIRW in Gangpur, a remote village in Dhar district of Madhya Pradesh, in consultation with the Institute, decided to host a conference on World Environment Day, so they invited us to be the guest speakers.

When the Institute started in 1985 a project sponsored by a funding organization of the government of India had been implemented for three years, so recently this organization decided to evaluate this project. They wanted to go to the villages to see how many of the trainees from that time were still using the skills they had learned. We decided to take their evaluator, Dr A Tiwari, Professor of Botany, University of Gwalior, with us on this trip to the villages. As most of the trainees at that time had come from the neighbouring district of Jhabua, it meant that we would have to make a long circular trip to visit some of these trainees and get to Gangpur on the fourth evening.

This being a very hot summer, with the average temperature in the mid-40s, we knew it would be very hot in the villages so we planned to leave Indore at 4:00 a.m. on the fourth morning. We had two volunteers from Canada and the US, one Bahá'í youth from another district and Dr Tiwari in our jeep, a 10 year old Susuki 410, along with enough water for at least one day. Like all good plans that are made, we finally left Indore at 5:30 a.m., heading west to Jhabua. The 180 km drive was quite pleasant, though the road was quite rough, and those in the back of the jeep had a hard time. We visited some ex-trainees in the villages in and around Jhabua town. As Dr Tiwari had his own list of names of the trainees that he wanted to meet, it became a little difficult as some of them were now married and gone to another village. We compromised and took him to some villages that were near the main road. By now we were already behind schedule as we had planned to do most of the driving up to 11:00 a.m. and then try to find somewhere to hide for a few hours from the midday and afternoon sun. However, it was not to be. About 11:30 we left Jhabua to drive 95 km south to another area where some trainee had come from. By now we had left the main road and to make it a bit more comfortable for those in the back had to reduce the speed on the barely surfaced road. By now the temperature in the jeep according to my Casio watch was as high as 48 degrees C, so everywhere we found water those of us who had hats would soak them in water to stop our brains from being cooked.

We reached a town where there was a government rest house – a system set up during British rule and still existing today. There they have rooms with beds and fans. Janak and I got our guests settled in and we went to the market to organize some late lunch and get some fruit, etc. We all had lunch and then got a couple of hours' rest – even though there was a power cut for some time, we still could get some rest. Still heading south, we reached the large village of Umrali where some of the trainees lived. This episode is a story in itself so I will be brief . . .

While Janak and the doctor went to visit the trainees' houses, our foreign volunteers and I went to the market area to try to find some cold drinks. Though the cola wars have hotted up in India, Pepsi and Coke have not reached the interior areas. We found a small hut with a fridge and there we asked for cold drinks. We got bottles of Thumbs Up, an Indian cola, that went down in seconds. When we asked for more, we were told, sorry, it was finished!

After Umrali we left the road for a few kilometres to visit the family of one of our trainers, then we headed southwest towards the district of Dhar. As the sun had now gone down it was becoming less hot. Near the district border the road gave way to a dirt track with lots of dust. Passing through a small village where a bus was unloading goods from its roof, one of our volunteers sitting in the back said that someone was running after the jeep. It was a youth from Indore who had gone travel teaching about a week earlier and was sitting in the bus when he saw the jeep pass by! He was very happy to see us as he had picked up a bug and said he not eaten any good food in three days. We eventually stopped in a village, and at the house of our ex-trainees we cooked dinner. Our Bahá'í youth was happy to get something good to eat, though he still had diarrhoea.

About 10:00 p.m. we reached Gangpur and met some of our staff who had spent the last three weeks in the villages meeting the trainees and doing other follow-up work. We spent the night there and that was a lot of fun, as we slept under the stars with no interference from the lights of nearby towns, which is an experience in itself. The starlit nights are truly heavenly. As the cattle shed was near by, our volunteers kept us laughing most of the night by talking to the cows and goats or mimicking the sounds they were making. Next morning almost everyone had a bath beside the well, whose water was just visible about 80 feet below.

Dr Tiwari, Keykhroso (from Canada) and I went for a tour of the village fields to see the improvements that had taken place over the last few years. Though a lot of work has to be done in this highly eroded area, the improvements are impressive.

The conference was scheduled to take place at 4:00 p.m. so we had to spend the day hiding from the sun in a place where there is no electricity, no fans, etc. We found a place where there was a natural air flow and the villagers cooked us lunch – a type of bread cooked over burning cow dung, and dal (lentils), some specially prepared non-spicy food for us foreigners. Later, helping the girls set up the conference site in the grounds of a school, one problem was trying to decide where the sun would be at 4:00 p.m. so that all could sit in as much shade as possible.

The conference was very successful, with more than 150 villagers and ex-trainees attending. The jeep, which was used to power the P.A. system, was strategically parked to provide the participants with the most shade from the setting sun. Also, some saris, etc., were hung from trees and buildings to provide shade. The programme was well-organized, starting with prayers and songs on the environment and health. Then Janak introduced the concept of World Environment Day. Christina from the US and Keykhroso from Canada spoke about the Bahá'í Faith. Dr Tiwari and I congratulated the villagers for the improvements in the area and spoke about the environmental issues affecting the area and how we have to pass it on in better condition to our children and grandchildren. Then there was an open forum where our trainees spoke about what they have achieved and what they are planning to do for the environment of their villages.

At about 7:00 in the evening Janak, Dr Tiwari, Keykhroso, Christina and myself drove to the nearest small town about 25 km away to return the P.A. system and give press releases to the local representatives of newspapers. About two km from the village, while changing from four wheel drive to two wheel drive, the jeep rolled to a halt! The nearest town where we could get to a workshop was 50 km ahead and the nearest spare parts were in Indore, more than 200 km away. First we panicked a little, then had to do something! Dr Tiwari and Christina walked back to the village to get a torch. Keykhroso and I started taking things apart but without light we couldn't do much. Luckily, I had replaced all the bearings in the transfer box about three years before, so I knew what was in there and what had possibly gone wrong. After about an hour Christina and Dr Tiwari returned with my glasses and a torch. Then a bus came along the road and loaned us a lamp to attach to the battery. I eventually got the top off the transfer box and found that a pin had come out of a selector. We were soon back on the road and back to Gangpur.

Janak and I drove into the town, arriving after midnight, and gave the light back to the bus wallah with many thanks. We then woke up the newspaper wallahs and the P.A. shop. This work is done with no hassle as all these people know us and are very helpful. Then we found a shop selling cold drinks and we got Pepsi at 1:00 a.m., with the temperature still around 40 degrees C. It tasted like nothing on earth.

By the time we arrived back in the village most everyone was sleeping. Two mattresses had been put out on a stone platform for Janak and me, so we slept soundly until 5:00 a.m.

The drive back to Indore was relatively uneventful compared with the previous day!

79
July 1998
Nina Harvey
Panama

Nina (from Norfolk) pioneered to Panama in 1995 to serve as caretaker for the House of Worship.

On Easter Sunday (yes, I know this sounds quite off the wall but Bahá'u'lláh is full of delightful surprises that are both awesome and fun at times!) I was asked to help a crew of armed guards that suddenly rode up and wanted to camp in our cabin (but thankfully found alternative rooms, as I explained to them our feelings as Bahá'ís about guns in our home). I was about to learn that they were signalling the arrival of the president of the Republic of Panama. Anyway . . . there I was with our kids and neighbours, standing about in shorts and T-shirts in a very non-glamorous atmosphere, when 'himself' and his entourage arrived. The helicopter, which had not heeded the rather erratic chalk powder circle drawn with an arrow to define where the helicopter should land (and in which direction so that the skids would not sink in the mud and cow muck), began to sink and so had to elevate and land according to the arrow previously missed! A path of sand that had very quickly and roughly been created from the pasture to the beach, to avoid any muddy feet, was lined with the guards and all of us. We were in the province of Bocas del Toro on the Island in an area called Boca de Drago, which was named after Sir Francis Drake.

As they swept through to visit a house on our 'point', 'El Torro' (the Bull) as he is affectionately known, wrapped his arm about my son Aaron's shoulders and addressed him in Spanish saying, 'And how are you my son?' to which Aaron proceeded to chat back in perfect Spanish (amazing to me as when he left the UK in '95 he knew not a word). The first lady, the 'Primera Dama' of the country, who had sent a very nice substitute to represent her at the 25th anniversary at the Temple, slowed her step and pointed straight at me. She asked who I was and was quickly told that I had been at the Bahá'í Temple for a while. I thus had the privilege of hearing the word Bahá'í on other tongues before I even got my mouth open. I then spoke up and found myself in a very short but powerful conversation with the first lady. I thanked her for her support at our event and she wanted to know if her substitute had been satisfactory to us. She had had a report back that our event had been quite breathtaking and wonderfully spiritual, and she was glad to have been in some way a part of it. I thanked her again, admitting that as administrators we had been too busy to hear the talks but that we also had felt the power of the moment and hoped to see some video tape of it. I then backed in fade mode into the crowd as she continued on to their destination.

I just find it so awesome that after two years of service and efforts to teach, and feeling many times quite inept and unworthy and unable to reach the levels that one sets oneself, there I am in shorts, in flip-flop sandals, on a windswept paradise of beach land, in the middle of a small oasis in a jungle area, and in a moment the most powerful human being in this country and his wife suddenly drop out of the sky, hug my son and ask me if their efforts for the Temple were satisfactory. Need I say more?

80
October 1998
Audrie Reynolds
Petropavlovsk-Kamchatsky, Russian Federation

Audrie (originally from Chester) has served as a pioneer with her husband Johnathan on Indian Reservations in the USA, including Alaska, and since 1991 has been living in Kamchatsky.

At the World Congress in 1963 I met Johnathan Reynolds, a Bahá'í from Massachusetts, USA, and we were married in Chester. We intended to pioneer to Africa but didn't have the money for the trip, so decided to go to the States and save up. Well, it didn't work out that way. The Bureau of Indian Affairs offered Johnathan a teaching position as music director on the Standing Rock Sioux Reservation in North Dakota and we found ourselves already in a pioneering post.

It was quite a change for both of us, far out in the prairie on the Missouri River, with only Indians and a few white ranchers. Johnathan, used to singing opera and playing the organ, found no organ existed within hundreds of miles. We acquired a raccoon that was a good public relations figure and attracted many people to our firesides. We learned Indian dancing and some of the language that had almost died out. They were interested in what we believed and then asked if this new religion would divide them as other groups had done and if it would forbid them to practise their culture. After hearing favourable answers they decided this was like what their grandfathers had always believed. We stayed there for seven years and an Assembly was formed at Fort Yates Indian Agency.

This was a time of great learning for us as neither of us had encountered native people before. We tried to be as natural as possible, knowing that we were being closely observed. One Indian said, 'We can tell what you think of us by the way you sit down in our homes.' We were greatly enriched by learning their culture and value system that is said to be the same across North and South America. We also learned how to listen. Finally we realized that we couldn't both continue school teaching. I gave it up and with Indian friends and a visiting black Bahá'í, travelled as an interracial team to all the Dakota reservations and issued a newsletter to those we visited. The Indians were to write it themselves but they were usually too shy and so we interviewed them on different topics and wrote exactly what they said. The newsletter was distributed to Indian areas in the lower states, Alaska and Canada.

In 1970 we were asked to carry out mass teaching and wondered how the reserved Indians would accept it. But we followed directions and it worked wonderfully. Several new Indian Assemblies were formed, one in the Cheyenne area where six months later the tribe refused to accept new 'white' religions – and found that all Bahá'ís on the Assembly were Cheyenne!

Then Johnathan was transferred to the Navajo Reservation in the Southwest, to a completely different tribe of sheepherders in the desert. Only 60 per cent spoke English, so an interpreter was essential, usually a schoolchild. It would take us all day to collect everyone from the mesas, hold the Feast and return them by van at midnight. At first we were part of an Assembly that stretched one hundred miles across the desert, then we moved to a school at Kaibito Trading Post near Flagstaff. The older Navajos still wore their costumes daily and I remember one impressive gathering in Phoenix when Hand of the Cause Mr Khadem addressed them and referred to 'Abdu'l-Bahá's promise that the Indians would enlighten the world. The translator hesitated, not knowing how to explain this and Mr Khadem said, 'Go ahead. Translate it. 'Abdu'l-Bahá didn't give this promise to the Persians or anyone else.' I was sitting at the back of the room and as Ben Kahn translated, it seemed as though everyone grew six inches higher in their seats.

The Navajo Assemblies included medicine men and hand tremblers, those whose hands shake over patients as they diagnose illnesses. Their old ways were very different from the Sioux. For example, they would destroy a home where someone had died and people were buried far out in the desert, whereas in Fort Yates they held all night wakes before a funeral and we were able to say Bahá'í prayers at all their services. Sometimes we travelled with native Bahá'ís to other reservations in the West and took part in mass teaching in California and the Pacific Northwest.

After seven years in the desert and having by chance acquired a sled dog and taught her to pull a sled, we moved to an Eskimo village in northern Alaska, still under the Bureau of Indian Affairs. Again, a big change. Our sled dog had lost her undercoat in Arizona and arrived in Unalakleet shivering in the cold of March 1978. The Eskimos couldn't understand a sled dog that shivered. By this time we also had a pet skunk which is not native to Alaska. They were afraid of her but referred to her 'good pelt'.

It was sad to find the Eskimos had completely lost their old ways and despised dancing and the old songs. Unalakleet, a village of 500 people, was the Alaskan centre for the Covenant Church. Several Bahá'í teams came in during the summer and we joined them, travelling north of the Arctic Circle, to Kotzebue, Kiana and Ambler.

Finally Johnny was transferred to Juneau, the capital, in southeast Alaska, and a time of continuous air travel came when, having ascertained that a Bahá'í pilot was available, a couple of families bought a small four-seater plane. Thus we followed the Yukon River each Riḍván from one Assembly to another. This was a time when Bahá'ís were allowed to take the whole 12 days of Riḍván to form Assemblies. Sometimes, in the air, the pilot turned to us and said, 'Pray now!' so we knew there was some danger ahead, either bad weather or no radio communication.

It was all a great change from England and the US east coast. Johnny said the only place we had ever lived in that had a bus was Juneau, as we were always far out in the bush somewhere.

Since Alaska is considered the backdoor to Russia, it seemed natural, having learned some Russian, to move there when the door opened in 1991. Actually it was forbidden by law to mention the Bahá'í Faith in Russia until the law was changed in 1988. Our move was supposed to be to Vladivostok but they didn't give foreigners a visa whereas Kamchatka did, so we now live among the many volcanoes and earthquakes of the Far East of the Pacific Rim. It was especially interesting to be here before the Soviet Union broke up. There were no Bahá'ís in Kamchatka at the time and people were very interested, so that now there is a community of 50 adults and 20 youth and children, only one Assembly as yet, in the main town of Petropavlovsk, also two Bahá'í Centres, one, hopefully looking ahead, as a centre of learning. Bahá'u'lláh planned the move to Kamchatka so well, for this area has native people while Vladivostok does not. There are Bahá'ís of the Even and Itelmen tribes now, very similar to the native tribes of Alaska.

Johnny has taught English at the regional library since 1991 and I taught at the Teachers' Improvement Institute. At first, life was hectic with food coupons, clothing rationing and empty shops but the people were very friendly and hospitable. Everyone brings food to the Feast. Many speak English and it helps to have the equivalent writings in Russian. I don't speak Russian well but can read and understand the National Spiritual Assembly letters.

I am not a US citizen so every year we return to Alaska as legally required for non-US citizens who have 'green cards.' We have permission to stay in Russia till 2003 and they say the permission can be renewed. Last year we flew to the Moscow Convention and to England where we met wonderful friends in England and Wales. England in spring was full of flowers and blossoms while in Kamchatka flowers appear only in June. Actually one Bahá'í said she had never seen a tree in blossom. But what can compare to bears and earthquakes? (Have just experienced a tremor while writing this letter.) Isn't life wonderful - thanks to Bahá'u'lláh!

81
October 1998
Irene Taafaki
Marshall Islands, North Pacific

Irene and her husband Falai-Riva from Tuvalu have been serving the Faith for a great many years in Kiribati, Panchgani (India) and now in Majuro, capital of the Marshall Islands in the Pacific.

It has taken a while to sit down and write – but l do want to keep my promise and share a little of what we have been doing here that might be of interest to the friends who read *Pioneer Post*. I actually began a letter three years ago! Somehow the experience here has been so intense it has been hard to encapsulate in a single letter, not fully understanding all the mysterious processes at work myself!

Falai-Riva, Justen (12) and I came to the Marshall Islands almost four years ago, after spending 11 years in the United States and, before that, ten years at the New Era School in India. Our purpose in coming to the Marshall Islands has been to serve as project managers for the Majuro Public Schools Project. Falai-Riva had been visiting the Marshalls on and off since 1992, working on the negotiations and arrangements for the Memorandum of Understanding between the Majuro local government and the National Spiritual Assembly. Justen and I visited with him shortly after the World Congress and assisted with the development of the first School Improvement Plan.

So, in November 1994 we left our grown daughters Muni and Jane in their respective universities in Massachusetts and DC and moved permanently to Majuro.

I spent the first year working for the Asian Development Bank as a teacher training consultant. After about nine months Falai-Riva was asked by the late President Amata Kabua to be a full-time member of his staff. Much of his work has to do with analysing issues and preparing statements on international affairs and education.

That first year was quite heady – all the usual settling into a new home and readjusting back to Pacific Island life (after being away for almost 25 years). The Schools Project is a major undertaking. We have three wonderful professional staff implementing the Improvement Plan but there was enough to keep us busy most nights and weekends on top of our own professional work! Being so far away from our family was the usual test. Muni married in Amherst, MA, and we couldn't share her wedding day. My mother (Rose Jones) in Devon had a horrid fall – lots of separation pain! However the rewards have been indescribable. To see the Project win the hearts and support of so many, despite all the obstacles placed in its path, has been wonderful.

When my contract with the ADB finished I spent three months back in Massachusetts enjoying the first months of life of my sweet granddaughter, Naima. Whilst there I was appointed by the President to the position of Secretary of Education and I returned to take up the challenge. The President and Paramount Chief Amata Kabua, inspired by the 1985 'Promise of World Peace' and by his visit to the Seat of the Universal House of Justice in June 1990, had great confidence in the Bahá'ís to take his newly independent country forward. Particularly, Amata Kabua wished the Bahá'í principles to permeate and uplift the national education system. Together with his daughter Amatlain, the Mayor of Majuro, he was a prime mover behind the Memorandum of Understanding between the local government and the National Spiritual

Assembly. He especially desired a Bahá'í-inspired moral education curriculum to be taught in the schools.

We were moving along quite nicely with a range of improvements, including the Ministry of Education's approval of the Framework for the Moral Education Curriculum (itself an important and integral part of the Memorandum of Understanding) when, unexpectedly, the President passed away in December 1996. It was a terribly sad event, from which the country has yet to recover. However, the Project is secure and that is most important. We are responsible for the seven public elementary schools on Majuro, which has one third of the country's children and a third of its teachers.

Falai-Riva continues to serve the new President. As for myself, this year has been, on reflection, a great bounty. For the first time in many years I have been able to work at home – being of greater service to the Project developing the second School Improvement Plan and beginning the texts for the Moral Education Curriculum. I have continued to do some work for the National Education Task Force in the US, revising some of the Core Curriculum materials, helped with the establishment of the Training Institute here, worked with Falai-Riva in teaching Youth Institutes and, overall, had a useful time. It has been helpful to Justen to have his mother at home – his GPA (grade point average) went up to the top – and I was able to have the luxury of spending five months with Muni and her family in Los Angeles, helping when their second child, Taafaki, was born almost a year ago. Jane graduated from George Washington last year and decided she also preferred the Pacific, so has been with us here.

I was invited to apply for a couple of positions but for months heard little after the first invitations. Just when we were thinking that we might have to move (Falai-Riva earns a local salary so I do still need to make a living!), I was elected onto, and then made secretary of, the National Spiritual Assembly – perhaps a sign that we should stay? I came home, overwhelmed by the spirit of the National Convention, the Riḍván message and my new responsibility, and found an email from UNESCO firming up my work for at least the next year. What more can I say? We have no plan except the Four Year one – and pray that Bahá'u'lláh will assist and guide us to use our time wisely for His purpose.

We love the Marshallese people. As India was for Muni and Jane, this is a wonderful place to raise Justen. After a couple of years' initial difficult cultural adjustment to school after being in Connecticut, Justen understands his friends and is understood. The Bahá'ís here are strong in the face of great opposition, and outstanding in their fields. We have seen ever-increasing maturity and the power of the Training Institute to strengthen the friends and carry the teaching work forward. The members of the National Assembly who attended the International Convention returned transformed. They were so happy to be able to visit Shoghi Effendi's resting place in London and meet some of my British friends en route.

Two weeks ago we went across to a neighbouring atoll called Arno. The Bahá'ís there have built their own Centre themselves and the whole Local Assembly was there, singing their own song about the Centre's significance to the spiritual and material progress of their island. It was a very beautiful dedication and, hopefully, the first of many similar evidences of progress.

We worry about my mother living alone in England. Just when she finally decided she would like to live with us here in our little house on the beach of the bluest of blue lagoons, she says she feels unable to undertake the long journey. We hope to persuade her yet.

Life in the Pacific now is so different from the early seventies when we were in the Gilbert and Ellice Islands (now Kiribati and Tuvalu). We have the BBC, email and reverse osmosis machines to help overcome the el Nino drought. But the work is as, if not more, challenging – the opposition and opportunities greater as we see before our eyes the intersection of the Major and Minor Plans of God.

82
January 1999
Karen and Tim Shrimpton
Uganda

Karen and Tim moved to Kampala, Uganda, in August, after having spent two years as teachers at the American School in the Philippines.

We just have to tell you some incredibly exciting news!!! We have been looking into adoption for several years now and had no luck at all in the Philippines, where there is very strict legislation against foreign nationals living in the Philippines adopting children there. We started making enquiries about the process in Uganda as soon as we knew we were coming here and things seemed much more hopeful. We made contact with two orphanages when we got here but little did we know how quickly things could happen.

Yesterday, as well as being the Birthday of the Báb, Tim and I attended court in the morning and received a care order for two gorgeous Ugandan babies, a boy called Kenneth and a girl called Jasmine. They are about two years old and were both abandoned in different parts of the city within three months of each other. They were estimated to be around the age of three to six months (nobody knows for sure) and were both in pretty bad shape. They are not blood siblings and we are now trying to make up birth dates for them. We will probably wait a month or so until we have a better idea of their actual ages.

Both these children were on a list to be taken away from the orphanage last week to make room for more tiny babies. Once they are taken to the villages, they grow up in a sort of community home as orphans and there is virtually no chance of adoption. Because we were willing to take older ones, the process was speeded up so fast that our heads are still spinning! The entire process from the first day we went to visit the orphanage to the granting of the court order was a mere 16 days! The court hearing was very quick and we proceeded directly to the House of Worship to take part in the Holy Day celebrations. This was a Birthday of the Báb that we will never forget! As you can tell, we have really got stuck into Ugandan life and it's wonderful!

83
April 1999
Sammi Anwar Nagaratnam
Thailand

UK pioneer in Bangkok, Thailand, since 1985.

Towards the end of September 1998 the Spiritual Assembly of Thailand made the bold decision to invite a member of the Royal Family to the opening ceremony of the new National Centre in Bangkok. The decision was to invite Her Royal Highness Princess Soamsawali. When this invitation was accepted, the feeling of success, rejoicing and delight among the Bahá'ís was tremendous. There was a great sense of confirmation. This would be the first time that a member of the Royal Family would be coming to the Bahá'ís of Thailand.

The External Affairs Office set out the working groups needed for the opening of the Centre. Each coordinator in turn could select a team to work with Bahá'ís from all over Thailand. In this way the concept of using the talents and services of believers from all around the country was put into operation. The working groups were: children's programme, catering outside, catering inside the building, flower arrangements and corsages, cleaning and beautifying, exhibition and book displays, welcoming, ushering, accommodation, photography and videoing, sound system, media, and parking.

Work went into full swing. Members of the Royal Protocol Department came to visit our Centre and met with the Bahá'ís to discuss the programme and every step of the event. They arranged for tents for the Princess and our guests, flags and decorations for the Centre, chairs and refreshments for the Princess, gold-coloured curtains for wherever the Princess was to sit. At some points work was a true frenzy, with office staff staying at the Centre until midnight.

Letters of invitation were written to all Local Assemblies, some communities and some isolated individuals. Five hundred invitations were printed, about two hundred were sent to prominent guests, including the Prime Minister, members of the Cabinet, governors, heads of organizations, women's organizations, police chiefs, educators and so on. Ten Bahá'ís were invited to represent the Bahá'í Community of Thailand and be presented to the Princess – old, young, year of service volunteer, an educator, Bahá'ís running projects, the head of a Bahá'í school and a representative of the Bahá'í International Community. Counsellor Zena Sorabjee was invited as a guest of honour by the National Assembly and graciously accepted the invitation.

The National Office sent a notice and invitation to all National Assemblies. The National Assemblies of Japan, Malaysia and Singapore, and a Vietnamese Bahá'í, accepted to be present. Other international guests from Laos and Malaysia also responded. Accommodation had to be arranged for about 70 Bahá'ís in Bahá'í homes around Bangkok. Friends offered space for anything from two to 15 people. Everyone was allocated a place and a few asked for hotel accommodation. Two weekends were taken up with detailed cleaning, so that the Centre really began to sparkle!

As a two day Institute conference was to be held following the opening, as well as a meeting for the Day of the Covenant and the Ascension of 'Abdu'l-Bahá, there had to be consideration of those as well. The prayer room in the Bahá'í Centre was furnished and decorated and looked beautiful, and areas were set up for the friends to sit and rest and eat.

The National Office contacted the municipal offices and told them of the visit of the Princess. In no time they came and cleaned up some wasteland across from the Centre, which had become a garbage dump, and permanent signs were ordered for major street corners showing the direction to the Bahá'í Centre.

Packages of three books were prepared for guests, to be given as gifts. They all received a deluxe edition of *The Hidden Words*, the compilation on Education and a book on the teachings of the Faith. A label was printed to commemorate the occasion and had to be stuck into 200 books. Friends from all over the country started arriving and helped tie each package with gold ribbon.

The Reading Room was cleaned, every book was dusted and a display set up. Two hundred chairs were borrowed from a school and many tables from a temple. At the last minute it was realized that we didn't have enough tents so one more was rented. One of the tents was set up as a media centre, ready for a press conference. Press kits and a book display were prepared for the press.

The flower arranging team worked two nights non-stop. The Centre was like a garden of orchids. Flowers had to be bought at the midnight market so that they would be very fresh. A plaque commemorating the event and dated the Day of the Covenant was placed on the Centre wall.

Finally the great day arrived. This was the day of rehearsing all roles – how the Spiritual Assembly members and then the performing children should sit with Her Highness for the two permitted photographs. The readers of the holy writings had to practise their reading. Final seating arrangements were made.

Friends started arriving from all over the country. Bahá'í friends from the Karen tribe were the icing on the cake. They brought gifts of woven cloth to present to Her Highness. Other friends brought flowers to be presented to her. One friend was to present a cheque for the Royal Charities.

Everyone was ready and dressed. Everything was ready and in order. The Royal car arrived as the Royal anthem played. Her Highness was welcomed by members of the Spiritual Assembly and she was presented with flowers. She listened to readings from the writings of Bahá'u'lláh and to the report presented by the Spiritual Assembly. A gift of books was presented to her, including the Kitáb-i-Aqdas, 'The Promise of World Peace', a statement from 'Abdu'l-Bahá's *Secret of Divine Civilization* and *The Hidden Words*. Her Highness then pressed the button that officially opened the Bahá'í Centre sign. She then entered the Centre, signed her name in a guest book, looked at the exhibition on the Faith and asked some questions. Next she met the ten friends to be presented to her. Her Highness went up to the meeting room and watched the children's performances. Then two photos were taken with her and she left, thanking everyone at the car before she sat down. The Royal anthem played and the official ceremony was over.

Perhaps this whole process can be said to have been a great community-building exercise for the Bahá'ís. Many believers worked together as they had never done before and saw each others' strengths and weaknesses but everyone was forgiving and understood the stresses involved. It was also the greatest proclamation event in the 50 year history of the Faith in Thailand, as six TV channels carried news of the opening and some of the teachings of the Faith in the evening news programmes.

On the same day as the opening ceremony a wonderful, confirming, ennobling message was received from the Universal House of Justice.

Dear Bahá'í Friends,

On the joyous occasion of the formal opening of your new National Bahá'í Centre, the Universal House of Justice wishes us to extend to the Bahá'ís of Thailand its warmest greetings. It gives the House of Justice immense pleasure to witness the efforts of your community to diffuse the divine fragrances among the spiritually minded people of Thailand. It hopes that, as the institutions of the Faith are further consolidated and the range of the community's activities expanded, the Bahá'ís will come increasingly to be known throughout the country as the promoters of the highest ideals and the upholders of human dignity. The people of Thailand possess great capacities that must be realized so that they may rise among nations and make a distinctive contribution to the advancement of spiritual and material civilization.

84
July 1999
Nasrin Boroumand
Azerbaijan

Nasrin left the UK (Ealing) in September 1997 to visit her sisters in Uruguay. She was invited by the Counsellors to visit Azerbaijan for three months and attend the National Convention in May 1998. She went to visit her son, Lee Fawbush, a pioneer for the past three years, in Tbilisi, Georgia, a neighbouring country to Azerbaijan. Since then she has been teaching English at Baku's prestigious Western University and at the Bahá'í Centre. Now, having spent more than a year in this Muslim country, Nasrin writes of her global family (recently printed in an English newspaper in Azerbaijan).

It is quite rewarding to work here at the Western University, where students are learning many different languages. People who ask me where I am from are often amazed by my reply. I usually draw a circle symbolizing my country, the globe! As a child I memorized the following quotation from the writings of Bahá'u'lláh: 'The earth is but one country, and mankind its citizens.' This belief in the oneness of mankind and the essential unity of all religions has made my family global.

It all started with my grandfather. When he learned about the Bahá'í Faith and its universal principles, trying to put them into practice he consented to the marriage of one of his daughters to a Muslim, even though he himself came from a Jewish family. That first interreligious and interracial marriage, about 70 years ago, and others that followed later on, have resulted in his having great-grandchildren of numerous nationalities and racial backgrounds who speak in over 20 different languages!

What has happened to my own immediate family is truly amazing too. Though British by nationality, I was born in Tehran into a large family of eight sisters and one brother. I left Iran about 30 years ago to study in India. At that time one of my sisters was working in England and eventually married an Englishman. I married an American in India and have a son who has both Indian and American nationality. He is at the moment studying in Tbilisi, Georgia, speaks Russian fluently and understands Georgian too. My brother is married to a Chinese girl and lives in Hong Kong. My parents settled in Panama a long time ago. My mother, however, is buried in Jamaica, where one of my sisters lived, but my father is buried in Uruguay, where my other sisters live! My youngest sister, who married an American, lived in Colombia and speaks Spanish fluently, taught in the School of Nations in Macau for many years but now is living in the heart of China learning Chinese! My eldest sister lives in Iran, and besides having many beautiful Iranian grandchildren, has a Panamanian daughter-in-law. One of my nephews married a Norwegian and his children have lovely golden hair. His sister has lived in Japan for over 15 years and her children speak Japanese like their mother tongue! My other sister's daughter is married to a radiant black man from Benin. Her other daughter lives in Australia and her children have sweet Australian accents! Her son has married a tall American girl. Another sister of mine, married to an American too, lived in Bolivia for many years, speaks Spanish fluently and at the moment is in the United States conducting workshops on racial harmony. One of my sisters who lives in Uruguay has a Bolivian grandchild by one of her daughters and a Uruguayan by another daughter. There are people from New Zealand, Germany, Switzerland and many other countries in our family, living in as diverse places as South Africa, Samoa, Italy and France!

Our family includes Muslims, Jews, Zoroastrians and Christians. Our children are world citizens and from childhood learn to respect all religions, understand the idea of progressive revelation and the fundamental oneness of God and all His messengers.

Communication is not a big problem as every one of us speaks Farsi and English fluently. But there are problems when it comes to real communication among the grandchildren. Here one truly appreciates the need for an international, auxiliary language. Travelling in over 30 countries of the world, during and after the International Year of Peace, has reaffirmed my belief in the need for a universal language. Our family meets every now and then and keeps in touch through the Internet that has made the world a global village, a small blue planet among many other planets.

85

July 1999

Stephanie and Wesley Clash

Corfu, Greece

Stephanie and Wesley, and their daughter Giselle, formerly from Shepway community in Kent, have been pioneers on the island of Corfu for six years.

Spring is well and truly here, with fields and fields of gorgeous pink, purple, yellow and white wild flowers! It is also Greek Orthodox Easter time and, to Greeks, Easter has more significance than Christmas. On the Friday before Easter the mournful processions carrying the garlanded coffin of Christ wend their way through the villages, towns and cities of Greece to the accompaniment of sad and dirge-like music. (The light of Christ has left the earth.) Late on Saturday night everyone goes to church and towards the end of the service the priest lights his candle. The congregation then light their candles from his and there is a procession of lighted candles and singing to the village square. At 12 midnight the priest declares, '*Christós anésti*' (Christ is risen) and the cry goes up, '*Alithós anésti*' (He is truly risen). For us, as Bahá'ís, it is a poignant moment as we believe the spirit of Christ has risen for this time in the person of our beloved Bahá'u'lláh. After this, the dimmed lights are switched up. Fireworks are let off and men on the edge of the crowd let off shotguns. There can even be dynamite further off! The bigger the bangs, the bigger the smiles! The reason for this delight is the fact that the Greeks believe that the light of Christ has returned to earth.

When we first came to the island almost six years ago, our main money came from Wesley's deep-sea diving. However, that has dried up somewhat and we have been doing antique restoration, interior design and painted effects on floors, walls and furniture, etc. We have also begun to design and make furniture and are very proud to have had a commission from our new Bahá'í Centre in Athens; we produced a sofa, coffee table, side tables and a buffet table for the main reception rooms.

Do you ever find that, as Bahá'ís, you are constantly thinking up new ways to interest people in the Faith and almost cajoling them into attending firesides? This has sometimes been the case here on Corfu and so you can imagine

143

our great joy when we met like-minded, spiritually aware and questioning people at an Alpha course run by the local Anglican church. The new vicar, Stuart Broughton, who was very impressed and positive, having met Bahá'ís in the Falkland Islands, invited us to attend an Alpha course on Christianity. At these meetings we made good friends and had deep and meaningful discussions on the individual's need for communion with God. At the end of the course there was a dinner at which we two Bahá'ís were commended as being the most faithful participants of all the Alpha groups. Also for us, as Bahá'ís, it was wonderful to hear people who had attended our course stating that the most interesting part of the course for them were the questions asked by us and the discussions that ensued! Our group have now become such close friends that we meet every week for a fireside.

86
October 1999
Jo Harding
Greece

Jo has been a pioneer in Athens, Greece, for eight years.

It's been a hot summer in Athens, sometimes around 45 degrees. The Greek summer school on a hillside site overlooking a cerulean sea gave us all something else to think about. Some 140 folks, Bahá'ís and friends, created together a very special atmosphere of connecting love, and this proved to be the catalyst for four wonderful declarations. We do not have many of these in Greece, so four all in one day was an occasion of great joy, which spread like fire around the campus.

In Athens we have been having a systematic fireside programme for over four years, working on specific themes with a printed card with all the subjects for discussion and reflection – about ten weeks on each theme. Gradually these have attracted a circle of friends, between 12 and 19 people come each time, often more than half of these are non-Bahá'ís, who love to explore these Bahá'í concepts together and to be exposed to the spiritual atmosphere which is generated around the word of God.

The months and years rolled by and we wondered if anyone would ever feel moved to declare themselves as Bahá'ís! Now, in this last year of the century, we have had four new believers from this group – one for each year of the programme! We just needed a bit of patience. This community has the enormous bounty of some inspiring visits from travel teachers coming through at fairly frequent intervals, which encourages us and enlivens our faith and trust in the outcome for our efforts here. This year also saw the opening of the National Bahá'í Centre in Athens, which is a huge asset.

Now, this week came the earthquake. All the Athens Bahá'ís are safe, though, alas, some of our contacts have had their homes condemned as unsafe. I was in a trolleybus at the time and some sturdy pneumatic tyres cushioned the shock. The passengers were packed in tight, standing and hanging on anyway so no one fell over. Also we did not hear the horrendous noise, which adds to the terror of those inside buildings. My own home in central Athens is built on solid rock and has already survived two major quakes.

We are all deeply touched by the evident signs of a blossoming Greek-Turkish friendship, as both countries have greatly helped each other and acknowledge their common fragility as humankind in the face of such suffering. Its a very special providence out of this solemn calamity, for two countries locked in conflict for over four hundred years.

87
October 1999
Greg Akehurst-Moore
Czech Republic

Greg, from Dumfries and previously a volunteer for some years at the Bahá'í World Centre, has been teaching at the Townshend Bahá'í School in Hluboka for a little over a year.

Pioneering in the Czech Republic is not apparently as difficult, materially, as in other parts of the former communist world. Here there is no shortage of food or most consumer items. The countryside in southern Bohemia is stunningly beautiful, with plenty of lakes and the very attractive Bohemian Forest nearby. People are friendly and kind and there seems to be little crime.

Like most pioneers in this area, I work at the Bahá'í-inspired Townshend International School. The school takes up a lot of time and energy. But it also means that the local Bahá'í community is probably one of the most diverse in Europe. Currently there are members from Czech Republic, Slovakia, Germany, Austria, Italy, Albania, Ireland, Britain, Iceland, Greece, Russia, United States, Canada, Australia and the Philippines.

Much of the Bahá'í work at the local level is taken up with managing the quite large Bahá'í community, the majority of which consists of youth. The youth are full of energy and enthusiasm and crave novel and interesting activities, which can be quite a challenge! It also means the community does not easily become stale or boring! Most successful has been the local Bahá'í youth dance workshop, which tours giving performances to all kinds of audiences. It has been extremely popular with both the youth themselves and the Czech people.

In general, Czechs are curious about new ideas and beliefs, while slow to change their own. There is a predictable caution stemming from the old communist days. Unfortunately, one legacy of the old political regime which does not change so easily is atheism. Many people here admit to this belief. They are also looking to the West and its capitalist ideologies for inspiration. The Czech nation is trying to strengthen its economy with eventual membership in the European Union as a main goal. Consequently, a great many people here are interested in accumulating wealth and increasing their standard of living, and admit that religion and spirituality are not a priority in their lives. On the other hand, at most local firesides there are anywhere from six to 16 seekers. There is a strong curiosity, and spirituality, among the people. Quite a few want to join the Faith but don't take the final step. We have had some declarations, the latest being our Australian primary teacher at the school.

It takes patience and sincere kindness to make headway in teaching. People here are thinkers, generally highly educated and not easily fooled! Next time you open your prayer books, spare a thought and a prayer for those who work at the Townshend School. The workload is great and the workers too few! The challenges and tests can be hard but the fruits are very sweet!

88
October 1999
Maureen and Nick Sier
Samoa

Maureen and Nick and their family pioneered to Samoa from Banff, Scotland, in August 1997.

The last two years in Samoa have just flown by. Life is pretty busy most of the time. It is hard to pinpoint the highlights of our stay so far. Of course, we are lucky that we have the bounty of praying at the beautiful Bahá'í Temple whenever we want. We live in a village called Pui Paa and it is part of a wider village area called Toamua. This Riḍván the first ever Local Spiritual Assembly of Toamua was formed and Nick and I are privileged to serve on it. Assembly meetings are held about one and a half miles down a beaten track and into the forest.

The family where most of our Spiritual Assembly meetings, Feasts and firesides are held live in a simple Samoan home, known as a *fale*, with no doors or windows, yet the family and the rest of the community are wonderfully hospitable despite their obvious lack of material wealth. Our Feasts often consist of freshly-killed chicken, taro (a sort of potato) and coconut cream, followed by a drink of strong Samoan cocoa. This week two new Bahá'ís joined our small community. They declared after three firesides and their background, like that of most people here, is Christian.

On Sunday afternoons we pick up some of the Bahá'ís from this community and drive to another village called Faleula where we hold children's classes – they are great fun. I am on the National Child Education Committee now and help organize material for children's classes on the Islands of Upolu and Savaii.

Once a month there is a children's activity day at the Bahá'í Centre in town and children come along from villages all around. It's a pretty full day, with the children doing performances, art, games, study, etc. Nick helps the youth in a dance workshop programme. Nick doesn't do the dancing but assists in other musical aspects of their performances. These youth have performed to schools, universities, the general public and in villages, taking the spirit of the Faith to hundreds of people. Sometimes they are joined by other dance groups. In fact, quite recently an amazing group of youth from Hawaii joined our Samoan youth and performed literally to thousands of people. There is a steady stream of youth year of service volunteers – four here at present – two from Australia, one from the Solomon Islands and one from Ponopei.

Nick is working for the Australian High Commission and I'm working on my PhD and also, on occasion, for a secondary school and recently at the National University here too. Our children Zoe and Tom are doing fine. Tom loves to surf and Zoe loves to dance and luckily they can do both here! Zoe has been asked to choreograph an evening of dance, music and song with a Scottish theme for her school. She attends a Samoan school called The Robert Louis Stevenson School and in celebration of Stevenson, and thereby the school's Scottish connection, they are holding a concert – so Zoe will be teaching the Highland Fling and Scottish songs to her Samoan classmates!

Occasionally we climb a hill called Mount Vai and visit Robert Louis Stevenson's grave – mostly because the view from there is spectacular.

In Samoa there are 42 Local Spiritual Assemblies, which is not bad for a population of only 160,000. Nearly everyone here has heard of the Bahá'í Faith and, generally, when they know what the teachings of Bahá'u'lláh are, feel warm towards the Faith.

It's been an incredible two years here in Samoa. To give you an idea of what sort of things can happen, at 5:00 p.m last night eight 50-seat canoes began a race from our village to Apia (the main town). The Fautasi Outrigger Canoe race is held each June. The canoeists race along the north coast of Upolu, finishing in Apia harbour. The day coincides with Samoan Independence Day, with dancing and festivities held outside the Samoan Parliament. Not only did the race start from our village but it was from our back garden (which is the ocean). It looked so spectacular and the shouting and drumming only added to the sense of occasion. Then in the evening Ben (our oldest lad, who is visiting at present), Zoe and Tom headed into town to watch some fire-dancing and further festivities. Today they went surfing and Latin American dancing and listened to Nick playing with four very talented local musicians.

We feel that we are more like visitors here than pioneers. The true pioneers are the wonderful people who came here 30 years ago and made Samoa their home. What exists here now in Samoa is the legacy of the long-term pioneers in this country.

89
January 2000
John Lester and Barbara Stanley-Hunt
Travel Teaching in the Faroe Islands

There is rock and there is grass and there is water. There is rock and there is grass and there is water. There is . . .

The ferry methodically transports the airport bus from Vager to Torshavn, the capital, wending between lofty crags, half-cloaked with stubborn green. At frequent intervals streams tumble down in a headlong plunge so that it seems that the land has just been heaved out of the ocean and the waters are still running off. Higher hills are sprinkled with snow as if prematurely aged. Occasionally a house, settled determinedly at the foot of a cliff, stands lonely and forlorn with the air of being the first to arrive, thinking others would join it. It is rugged, gaunt and magnificent.

Torshavn buildings cluster about the harbour as if afraid it will escape. More trusting houses head away into the hill. This is Europe's smallest capital, with 16,000 people. No other settlement reaches five thousand and most are less than a thousand.

Blue sky proclaims, 'No rain today – trust me!' We venture out and the ambush is sprung. From over the hills, where it seems to have been lying in wait, leaps a huge dark cloud that empties itself over the city. Half an hour later the blue sky is back. 'No rain today – trust me!'

The grave of Eskil Ljungberg, Knight of Bahá'u'lláh, is prominent in the cemetery, a miniature of the resting place of his beloved Guardian. He was here for over 30 years, half of them as the only Bahá'í, and was nearly 99 when he died at his post. When he arrived he was regarded with suspicion. Some people thought he was a spy or an agent of the devil and would cross the road when he approached. He began this greatest phase of his life at the age of 67 and gradually wore down the suspicion with his steadfastness and love. Now the older Faroese refer to him as 'Eskie' with affectionate memory. There is now an attractive Bahá'í Centre, royal blue, where all visitors are welcome on Friday nights.

The Faroe Islands have only 45,000 people but still hold three Local Spiritual Assemblies, all of which need to be stronger before giving thought to National Assembly formation. Torshavn is one and the others are close neighbours (Runavik and Toftir, the latter with only a thousand people). Both nestle one side of a fjord with a settlement just across the water (but 20 miles by road) gazing wistfully across. Sometimes the mist prevents it. In the evening both sides of the fjord twinkle with a multitude of lights that merge at the bend so that it is hard to tell where the water runs. It gives the illusion of a huge bay of speckled light, its lands united in darkness where they were separated by day.

The Faith progresses slowly here but dedicated pioneers, hailing from all parts of Europe (Norway, Iceland, Denmark, Sweden, Germany, Spain, Bulgaria, United Kingdom), America and Iran are daily and gently easing away opposition and moving more and more people towards respect for the Cause and acceptance of it. 'I have nothing against the Bahá'í Faith,' one lady tells us. She knows Sue and Roy Philbrow, who have been here since 1972.

Long-standing patience and steadfastness are watchwords here and every action is noted so that to mirror forth the attributes of a true Bahá'í becomes even more paramount a duty than it is already. As travel teachers we try to make friends wherever we can to aid this process. We walk about the villages whenever the weather permits and say prayers in appropriate places when there are no people to meet.

Suduroy is the southernmost island, which depends on a ferry battling its way across a frequently heaving ocean. The lone Bahá'í here comes from Sweden and all the island seems to know her, thanks, in part, to the international language of music. In many ways these are innocent islands. Houses are often left unlocked during the day. The postman opens each door and drops the mail inside. Small girls wheel their baby siblings about the streets with no cause for fear. At a mothers' meeting prams are parked outside in an orderly line, their occupants well protected against the elements but needing protection against nothing else. A visit here is memorable, the warmth of the people more than outweighing any thoughts of the northerliness of the location. 'Come again,' they say.

90
January 2000
Corinna Mills
Papua New Guinea

Corinna (née Twiname), originally from Northern Ireland, and her husband, Jalal, are both dentists in Papua New Guinea.

I have been in Papua New Guinea for three and a half years, moving here straight after I got married. It is a Commonwealth country, the official language is English, we drive on the same side of the road and our government system is the same but that's where the similarities end – it could not be more different from the UK! It's a tropical island – palms, sandy beaches, high mountains. The weather is hot and humid in the coastal areas and Mediterranean-style in the mountain regions. The people are from seven hundred different groups or tribes, each with their own language, customs and beliefs. They are innately religious and all believe in God and accepted Christianity readily. There are over 60,000 Bahá'ís here also. Ninety per cent of the population (of four million) live in the villages and survive by subsistence farming. The ground is mostly very fertile, rain is plentiful and there are four crops per year.

We live in the capital city with half a dozen other pioneer families and about four hundred Bahá'ís in total. Our community has the most wonderful community life. We have weekly meetings on a Sunday and Feasts are also held on the Sunday (because of security issues). There is a culture of singing and the songs are melodious and uplifting. If you go feeling down in the dumps (spiritually) you always leave with your spirits soaring! The people are quietly spoken and gentle but life here is far from boring. PNG is called the land of the unexpected and I never can say, 'I've seen it all' or 'Nothing can surprise me'. People often ask me when I go back to the UK if I like it there. I suppose it is hard to live here in some ways but I can say that I have never been so happy as I have been since living in PNG. The Faith is part of our daily life and the Bahá'ís are our closest friends here. I have a little baby boy who is a year old now and he is a constant source of joy to us both.

Well, what do I do day to day? We live in a pleasant area, a compound where it is safe to walk about and it's been easy to get to know our neighbours. I stay home, most of the time, with my son Thornton, and try to get out to play-groups, swimming and even a quilting class! We are very lucky to have home help, which makes a big difference to our quality of life. Despite this, I always have more to do than I have time to do it! Another Bahá'í lady and myself are writing the children's classes (ages three to 12) for the National Assembly to send out – a mammoth task which we are struggling with as neither of us is a trained teacher, but it has to be done and we'll do our very best. Also, I have been allocated the national archives to collect and organize, and more. But aside from that it's easy to make friends and you can talk about religion quite easily. The people know about the Faith here and most people know we are Bahá'ís, even most of our patients. People like the Faith, like the Bahá'ís and watch us closely.

We have a dental practice and are soon to be opening another branch in a new, more prestigious location. Both my husband Jalal and I are dentists. I only work one afternoon a week and we see the full variety of people residing throughout the country. We also have a clinic in the Highlands (Hagan) where my husband has his responsibility as Auxiliary Board member. It has been amazing to see how this community, which not so long ago was unable to get a quorum for Local Spiritual Assembly meetings, overnight kicked into action, as if a certain critical mass had been reached and an irreversible process established, as it ripened and arose to action. They have now started their own part-time permanent Institute of their own accord and run it almost all on their own. Before we got married Jalal took me there to show me to them. When we got married they held a traditional ceremony where they killed and cooked a whole pig in what is called a *moo-moo*, and told my husband that his legs were, from then on, broken!! (they have always been my good allies!) – that means that he has his duty at home and cannot leave and go 'nabout, nabout', as they say in Pidgin. Then, when we had our son Thornton we went up, again for another celebration, so they could meet him, and again we had another pig. Thornton loved it, as we celebrated his arrival together with the other five babies who had all made their debut in and around this last year into the small community there.

91
January 2000
Philip and Lois Hainsworth
Travel Teaching in Uganda: A Country Re-born

Philip writes:

After an absence of 33 years, Lois and I flew to Entebbe, Uganda, on 29 July 1999, just two days after my 80th birthday. We arrived on the morning of the 30th to be met by Bill Ogeuna, Chairman of the National Spiritual Assembly of Uganda, who escorted us quickly through Immigration, Baggage Reclaim and Customs with me in a wheelchair. We entered the Arrivals Hall to be greeted by a wonderful reception party carrying a large banner which displayed a large picture of the Kampala Bahá'í Temple and the words 'Lois and Philip. Welcome to the Heart of Africa', along with many local designs.

Among those who greeted us were George Olinga, son of the late Hand of the Cause and Secretary of the Uganda National Spiritual Assembly, and Mrs Dawn Belcher, who was to drive us to our accommodation in Kampala. It was explained that there would have been a much larger party at the airport but many friends were away in Rwanda at a Bahá'í Youth Conference!

We immediately had a meeting in Kampala with members of the National Spiritual Assembly and the Local Spiritual Assembly of Kampala to review the detailed schedule planned for us – some activity for every day of our three-week stay – it was fantastic. Actually, as it worked out we had some free time and the arrangements were superb. After this briefing we had the afternoon and evening free to catch up with the sleep we missed during the crowded and not very comfortable flight from London Gatwick.

The following day we had our first visit to the Temple, the Bahá'í Centre and cemetery and then back to Kampala to have lunch with Iranian pioneers Mr and Mrs Ebrahimi at the first Uganda Bahá'í home – 3 Kitante Road, the home of the Bananis and Nakhjavanis from 1951. This home was the one in which Enoch Olinga and many others accepted the Faith; from which Hand of the Cause Musa Banani was buried; in which Enoch, his wife Elizabeth and three children were murdered; which was passed to the National Spiritual Assembly of Uganda and which is now the home of the Ebrahimis and the place where the Kampala Feasts are often held.

The next day, being Sunday, found us at the Temple service, which was followed by a 19 Day Feast but in which we were unable to participate fully as a press conference and TV interview had been arranged in the Temple grounds. It was a moving occasion once again to sit in the Temple facing the Qiblih, participate in the readings, listen to Lois sing a prayer and the choir sing in English and vernacular languages and to greet Crispin Kajubi, the first Muganda to accept the Faith in 1951 (whose son was in the TV team). On being questioned as to our first impressions on our arrival, we spoke of the vast changes to Entebbe and Kampala we had already seen, the great increase in population and African housing, the bad condition of the roads and the crazy driving in the heavy traffic all around Kampala. Should we have had these interviews later in our visit we would have given much more emphasis to the wonderful advances made in the educational system, the role played by the women of Uganda, the enlightened system of government and the freedom of the press – all of which became clear to us as time went by. One of the significant changes in Kampala, which made it impossible for us to recognize our way around, was the way in which high security walls, hedges and fences surround every property compared with the open gardens of the days when we lived there.

Monday morning was dedicated to a visit to Auntie Claire's Kindergarten where, under the direction of Janet Lever, the school continues to flourish. On the next day we visited a school in Buganda developed and run entirely by a Local Assembly. We were taken by Dawn in her four wheel drive vehicle and accompanied by Mary, a Muganda Auxiliary Board member. In the evening we attended a 'deepening', where we had a fine presentation of the work on Mount Carmel by an engineer recently arrived from there.

For the following six days we were taken by George in his car visiting Jinja; Mbale; Pallisa; a Bugisu Local Spiritual Assembly; Tilling, Teso and the scene of the first village teaching in 1952; and Kalapata (Teso). During this time we met about a dozen of the early Bahá'ís, including Kolonerio Oule and Oloro Epyeru (retired Counsellors); Mrs Olinga (George's mother and pioneer to Cameroon, now living in Tilling); Mrs Isimai, wife of the late Sosipoteri Isimai, long-time Secretary of the Uganda National Spiritual Assembly, also living in Tilling; Mrs Oloro and Mr Mutambo, one of the early Bugisu Bahá'ís. What was a cause of real happiness was to meet with many of the children and even grandchildren of those early believers and find them active in the Faith – some Auxiliary Board members and members of the National Spiritual Assembly. In Dussai (Pallisa) and Tilling we were royally entertained in the Louis Gregory Memorial Bahá'í Schools and in Tilling we had a press interview with a Bahá'í journalist from Soroti.

During the four days following our return to Kampala Lois spent a most exciting day with women's organizations which had resulted from contacts she had made at the United Nations Commission on the Status of Women earlier in the year in New York and who were delighted to meet her again. We also had visits arranged by George with government officials and met some most impressive people. All knew of the Faith and thought highly of it, indicating that good public relations had been carried out by the Ugandan Bahá'ís. By now, from these interviews and a study of the local press, we were beginning to realize just how big the problems were which are facing the Ugandan government and how high were the ideals which they were attempting to achieve. We purchased a copy of the new Constitution (1995) and realized that the potential exists to make Uganda a leading country of the world. It is unfortunate that publicity in the West is centred on disasters, coups, scandals and corruption and that really good developments pass unremarked.

On the third Saturday after our arrival we were privileged to meet with the National Spiritual Assembly and to attend some of the sessions when the National Spiritual Assembly and Counsellors Edith Senega and Garth Pollock and several Auxiliary Board members participated in launching four new Regional Bahá'í Councils. On the following day there was a full choir at the Temple service and almost all the seats were occupied. When Lois and I were Secretary and Chairman respectively of the committee responsible for seeing to the construction of the Temple between 1957 and 1961 and were responsible for the organization of the choir which sang at the opening public service, we never believed that we would be able to experience such a moving service some 38 years later. For me it was perhaps the highlight of our visit.

On the Monday and Tuesday we were taken on visits to Besiege communities with Mr H. Sabet accompanied by the son of Egos Epyeru and were joined on the second day by Mrs Sabet. (The Sabets lived in England, pioneered in the Middle East for many years and travel taught in a part of the USSR and are now caretakers of the Kampala Temple.) The township of Jinja where I had lived from 1951 to 1956 was as unrecognizable to me as Kampala, with its large expansion in housing, shops and population. The large hydro-electric installation which dammed the River Nile at its source, shortened the river by about half a mile, extended Lake Victoria by the same amount and obliterated Owen Falls, produces electricity for some parts of Uganda and Kenya but is far from adequate and large dam extensions are being built and new ones proposed at other falls along the course of the Nile, particularly at Bujagali.

On Wednesday we had a memorable lunch with the Senogas, one of the many fine meals we had with individual families – the Olingas in Mbale and Tilling; at the Chinese restaurant in Kampala as guests of Fataneh; the Ebrahimis; the Burristons; the Assembly of Kalapata, Teso; the Ekoots; the Shrimptons and the Sabets.

During the last few days we also had some time for rest. Lois met with more women's organizations, while I went to meet with the Minister of Health for Primary Health Care (a lady veterinary doctor) and with a retired judge from Kenya who had been called in by the government to prepare legislation on matters of personal status – marriage, divorce, etc. – which he assured me was presently before government and would allow Bahá'í law to be observed.

On the final day we had a last visit to the Temple, where the local press took some pictures for a feature article, and had lunch with the Sabets. Lois consulted with the Bahá'í Women's Committee and we attended a memorable 19 Day Feast before leaving for Entebbe to fly home.

Our overall impression was that Uganda is a country with a recent history of bloodshed and disruption which has left it struggling with an ailing economy and much work to be done but that it was making great progress, has an enlightened leadership and is ambitiously tackling its many problems in education, health, environment, communications, transport and public morality. In all this progress the women are making an outstanding contribution both in public life and within the Bahá'í community and we are following the news from this 'Pearl of Africa' with eager anticipation. It was for us a most wonderful experience and we are deeply grateful for all the help and encouragement we were given to make it a reality.

92
January 2000
Valerie Rhind
Angola

Valerie has recently arrived in Angola, after serving as a pioneer in several countries in Africa – Zambia, Botswana, Zimbabwe, South Africa and Nigeria. This is Val's first letter from Angola.

I'm cooped up in our apartment for most of the day and we seem to have builders hammering above and to one side of us, which doesn't help. My one consolation are the dear Bahá'ís who do so well under the most trying of circumstances. The Holy Day celebration (12 November) was a real treat for me and the way the friends organized a potluck – with just one candle amongst us all – would give the western Bahá'ís wonderful inspiration. The National Centre has no running water, no windows and at present no electricity. However the Birthday of Bahá'u'lláh was honoured with a lively programme of prayers, readings, talks, performances by the children and youth, music, games and a big feast. There was a kind of game where each person chose a paper and, according to the number read out, he would be given the task of presenting a short talk on such subjects as the meaning of certain Arabic words or heroes such as Quddús and Vaḥíd. I was so impressed by the knowledge revealed. I couldn't understand that much as it was all in Portuguese but could follow the gist of the talks. I wouldn't even have been able to read my number in that light, let alone give a talk! The music was inspired and the programme lasted over four hours. The way that the offerings of food were displayed in such simple surroundings was attractive and all the children were served first.

Every Sunday there are prayers and deepening at the National Centre. At present the friends are studying the Hidden Words using the participatory word-by-word method. Studies are always interspersed with a few hearty songs. I've noticed one couple who always attend and discovered that they are a brother and sister who have been Bahá'ís since 1959. What steadfastness, even though they have suffered persecution for the Faith in earlier days.

A very happy footnote to our holy day celebrations: Our driver helped me to bring in some food and books and so he saw our Centre in the gloom but he must have liked the atmosphere. A few days later he asked me in Portuguese in which language the meetings are conducted. I replied Portuguese, the language of the country. He has been reading a Bahá'í pamphlet which he said he loves and then he said, 'The Bahá'í Faith is my religion!' So he has become a Bahá'í! What a blessing that I've been enabled to teach the Faith to one soul.

93
April 2000
Richard Hainsworth
Moscow

Long-time pioneer in Moscow with his wife Corinne and three children, Richard had the privilege of representing Russia at the funeral of Amatu'l-Bahá Rúḥíyyih Khánum in Haifa. He wrote this at the request of the Russian National Spiritual Assembly for the 'Russian Bahá'í Express'.

And the Heavens Wept

The rain poured down as great gusts of tears, black shards of gauzy fabric ripped from the substance of the clouds, the heavens crying as memories of the last of the Holy Family passed through the hearts of those gathered near the Shrine. Yet between the clouds, the sun shone brightly. And for us, those who met below, our profound sadness at the occasion was pierced by the joy of seeing well-remembered friendly faces from distant lands.

Without the rain and the clouds, the holiness of the Báb's mausoleum and the beauty of the gardens would have removed all cause for sadness, and but for the spiritual power of the surroundings, the downpour would have been unbearable.

The round white stones of Galilee crunched beneath my feet as I stepped upon the path towards the House of the Master just after one o'clock. I glanced up to direct my steps and saw on my left the faces of the pilgrims and World Centre staff. For a moment I hesitated, only members of the National Spiritual Assemblies and Counsellors were to enter the building, whilst the majority of the mourners would have to stand in the rain. Yet here was I, at that moment serving on an administrative institution, acutely uncomfortable to be elevated to some form of elite. An inner voice reminded me, I was but a representative, a symbol of an entire community of believers; it was not me the individual being honoured but all those who could not be physically present at this final parting. And in that instant came an image of the very person we had come to honour.

Rúḥíyyih Khánum was, according to the emphatic words of her husband

Shoghi Effendi, a high representative of the Bahá'í religion. She held the highest rank bestowed upon a believer, she was the last remaining link with the family of 'Abdu'l-Bahá and yet at the same time she was a lady who disdained fawning reverence.

High rank, and the need to be polite to vain and power-wielding individuals, is a burden to a soul who longs for truth and the beauty of nature. No wonder she preferred the Amazon rainforest or African plains, the peoples of the mountain village or the remote hamlets, to the sophisticated denizens of concrete conurbations.

Atop the three or four marble steps the doors to the Master's house were wide open. Within, rank upon rank of chairs were tightly ranged facing to the right and beyond the polished wooden coffin to 'Akká. Before the coffin, sitting silently and alone when I entered, was Violette – Amatu'l-Bahá's constant companion. The ushers – Rúhíyyih Khánum's devoted staff – beckoned and the steady stream of mourners were guided to their places. Every single seat was filled, late arrivals (like the Counsellor and National Spiritual Assembly members from Uganda, who had been travelling for most of two days to reach Haifa 15 minutes before the service started), pushing their way gently through the tight mass to the remaining empty places. Not a person spoke, not a single whispered conversation could be heard, during the entire 40 minutes it took to fill the hall and the adjoining rooms. My place was on the 'mandar', a bench running along the side of the three solid walls of the tea room.

The last time my family and I had been there, it was to have tea with Rúhíyyih Khánum. She had aged considerably since the time we last met, when she had visited Russia. She talked about her recent book, *The Ministry of the Custodians*, and other projects she was undertaking. On the next day of pilgrimage she noticed some of the children had only managed to get seats on the second and third rows, so she scolded the adults sitting in the front and insisted on a rearrangement to allow the children to sit where they could see her and talk to her. On the wall opposite was a wooden frieze of village women, redolent of the African country where it was carved, and to the left a portrait of Bahíyyih Khánum, Bahá'u'lláh's daughter and 'Abdu'l-Bahá's sister. This had been her house too.

Above my head, two plates had been suspended; handmade, decorated and individually fired, I have not seen such fabulous pieces of ceramic art in a private collection. Each permanent item in the room, from the mandar, which she described how to make in *A Manual for Pioneers*, the wooden frieze, the portrait and the plates, each reflected an aspect of the personality now departed from the mortal plane.

The clock arm clicked on two o'clock and the service began. Unable to see the readers, the voices came out over the loudspeakers and somehow the disembodied spirits had a more profound effect than had I seen their lips move. Members of the Universal House of Justice, the International Teaching Centre and Rúḥíyyih Khánum's staff and companion each read one of the pieces that had been chosen for the programme. The obligatory prayer for the departed was chanted by Mr Ali Nakhjavani. His voice strengthened as the ending verses were each chanted 19 times. As I listened and counted the repetitions, it seemed to me that each redounding verse reflected the passing of time. Our memories change as life moves on, the grief of parting is assuaged and we recognize that sadness is for those who stay and not those who pass beyond.

A silence of a few moments passed into the movement of feet, as the coffin was taken to its final resting place in the gardens on the other side of Haparsim Street. We fell into line behind the coffin and walked the short distance from the House to the graveside. By chance, I ended up in the front row before the coffin. As witness for the Russian-speaking community, it seemed right to be in such an honoured position. And yet our religion is so egalitarian. For while our National Spiritual Assembly represents an area spanning nearly half the radius of the earth, it has no greater privilege over the National Spiritual Assembly of a small island people, fewer in population than one of our medium cities.

Thunderstorms had blasted the eastern Mediterranean since the day Amatu'l-Bahá passed away, making work on digging a grave tiring and dirty. None of the suffering of the labourers could be seen, except the calm dignified result of their efforts. A path of red stones led to the grave site, which was surrounded by flowers and rose petals scattered on green matting. Even the cavity prepared to receive the mortal remains was walled with flowers. On the outside, we too only saw a scented bloom. Yet how much suffering was hidden from view! Between the lines of her books, and in the broken places between her words, we would often perceive the love Rúḥíyyih Khánum had for Shoghi Effendi, and her desperate loss when he passed on and she was forced to continue living. How could we be sad to know she was reunited?

The first prayer – 'From the sweet-scented streams' – is one my mother always sang to a setting by Charles Wolcott. I could hear her voice, as she must have sung it at the dedication of the Temple in Uganda. Tears could not be restrained. Who would open Temples in the future?

The last link to the Holy Family had broken. Humanity is now bereft, on its own, without a living symbol of the closest family of the Greatest Name of God. The remaining prayers seemed to have finished before my heart started beating again.

Mourners could now pay their last respects. Returning to reality, I realized that next to me the lady from Korea, dressed in exquisite national costume, had just raised her umbrella. The rain, which had held back until the end of the ceremony, could no longer restrain itself and flowed like waves against the shore. Together, we found our way to the grave side, picked up roses and cast them onto the coffin. My rose was sent in the name of all Russian-speaking peoples. The funeral was over, Amatu'l-Bahá was now gone, life will not be the same without her.

94
July 2000
Eric and Margaret Hellicar
Cyprus

Eric and Margaret pioneered to Cyprus 30 years ago from the north of England. In Cyprus they brought up their six children. Here are Eric's reminiscences.

This suddenly seems a time for reappraisal, with new life around, a new millennium beckoning and a feeling of imminent change in our Bahá'í community, our island and our small planet.

First, within our family, there's the brilliant new life that grandchildren bring. Then there is the strangely beautiful sadness that comes from the loneliness now that our Rúḥíyyih <u>Kh</u>ánum has gone. At her funeral there were so many pioneers gathered round the flowers in the rain, each of us with hearts she had touched but feeling it in ways blessed by the new lands we love. Each of us felt it in different ways but for me it was the mad wheeling of jackdaws in a midnight valley of wild wind that gave me the courage to live on, lonely but not sad. And then Adib Taherzadeh went to complete the hiccup in our history. Adib, with whom I'd learned the fierce power of pioneer dedication to the Faith on that National Spiritual Assembly of the British Isles back in 1967 – how often I remember him and others – Joe, Betty, Adib, Owen, the Johns (Long and Wade), Abbas and Philip – now that I seek new patterns of unity among the Greeks and Turks (and pioneers from US and UK) in Cyprus. How often as I wonder how to chair an NSA meeting so that simple faith can overcome blind eagerness, do I think of Joe Jameson in tears as chairman of the UK NSA, bless him. (Is the Cyprus National Assembly the only one that meets in a UN hotel in the buffer zone between armies?) Our National Assembly at last has a secretary who is Cypriot, which also means new days ahead – with a local language. So I'm in the valley of bewilderment, with the children grown up and new freedom ahead in retirement next year. How to serve family, country, Faith as a once British (still red-faced) activist almost transformed into a Cypriot who accepts their peculiarities more readily than English ones?

Pioneering is a privilege – how else would my children walk the world with such openness? – but it also can so easily evaporate into the local air. We have watched so many magnificent Bahá'ís overcome so many troubles and weep for them but then remember our own settling years with such warmth! But we are blessed, for in a land where so few have so far accepted the Faith, those few are such shining friends.

Can I thank you pioneers for nearly always writing so truly (for I shun the occasional exaggerated peon of praise that describes a pretty good Convention as heavenly choir of consultation!) and make a plea for such refreshing honesty as we face our bewilderment. The Bahá'í world is without doubt about to welcome (and be panicked by!) the troops that will finally muster and then attack on the creeping arrogant materialism that is suffocating true joy of life – Great! – but as we pause before that amazing multi-cultured mass of angry, desperate people, we seem to talk of them as if they will be a few extra at our mild monthly firesides or hilarious picnics in the rain. Our inspiring K͟hánum, our history-inspired Adib, and even many of our over 40 ex-pioneers from Cyprus, who are writing books or making films with great vision, these give me hints of how to be ready, but in the gentle suburbs of our pioneer posts, at least in places like here where we only have four armies, our prejudices are quite modern and there's lots of money around (no one starves here, so hatred seems tamed), it is not easy to live at the ready. So many Cypriots struggle with divorce, disunity or doubts yet can often seem so much better than we are.

Our adult children are all vibrant and delightfully independent-spirited and pride in them is such a satisfying vanity. Margaret is the mistress of our wonderful old mud-brick and stone complex of buildings in the quiet village of Pera at the foot of the mountains – though the local priest's chanting (broadcast for the whole village but we are right beside his church!) rouses us at 5:30, along with our cockerel and our granddaughter Katia.

95
July 2000
Rita Green
Solomon Islands

After 10 months' service with VSO in the Solomon Islands, Rita's time came to an abrupt end when a military coup in the islands meant that she was evacuated back to the UK in June.

I drove for six hours through mud swamps, torrential rain, floods and heat to reach my first National Convention here in the Solomon Islands. It was a journey never to be forgotten as I set out in my one ton, four wheel drive truck plus various delegates, not realizing just what the journey would hold. I have travelled widely in Europe and Africa but never on such bush paths and through such wild terrain as I encountered on the journey to the north Malaitan village of New Kwaiola situated at the furthermost tip of this island.

The route into the village was the most treacherous as torrential rain had wiped out the path and left mud and swamp and we still had a very steep hill to negotiate. Luckily the Solomon Islanders are very strong and determined and were able to push, pull and lift the truck when we were repeatedly stuck. Once at the village, which is 90 per cent Bahá'í, the spirit of the occasion soon took over. We were warmly welcomed and I soon had the feeling of coming home and being a part of the worldwide Bahá'í family. Delegates had gathered from all nine provinces to elect the National Spiritual Assembly and the spirit in which the election took place was truly magical. Out of 38 delegates, 31 attended and the others had not been able to attend because the boats had not been running to schedule over Easter. This attendance and participation was the largest ever recorded. It was a privilege to be a part of this event and to see the administration working at the real grass roots level. No one was excluded. Delegates who could not read or write were assisted by the Auxiliary Board members and Counsellor who were in attendance. Everything ran on time and in perfect order and the new National Spiritual Assembly voted in was, I think, wholly composed of native believers.

Another moving occasion was the reading of the Riḍván message which had been discussed in four language groupings prior to the reading so that the message was clear. The silence and concentration throughout was wonderful to experience. To round off a wonderful day, the Bahá'í youth group 'Nightingale' sang and danced for the conference and each area represented performed a musical piece. It then only remained to sleep in a hut with 20 others and start to worry about the return journey home. Needless to say, we made it – Yá Bahá'u'l-Abhá!

96
October 2000
Melissa Parsons
Youth Service in Costa Rica

*Melissa embarked on this particular Bahá'í social and economic develop-
ment project so that she could use the experience as fieldwork for her degree,
and also to serve the Faith wherever possible.*

During my time here I've had the chance to study Spanish for a month (and
then use it), visit the Bahá'í Temple in Panama, get some fieldwork done in
the indigenous reserve of Talamanca and learn about Bahá'í concepts of social
and economic development.

When I arrived in Costa Rica I had only a vague idea of the nature of an
'indigenous reserve', one that I had gleaned from spending time in northern
Canada. There the people have western-style housing, electricity and many
modern conveniences. I thought I might be going somewhere like that because
I had been informed that the Bribri people were 'acculturated' and integrated in
several ways into national society. However, I found that the reserve itself is like
another world. I was joking with some of the other people who work there that
we should make a *Lonely Planet Guide to Talamanca* because it almost constitutes
a country in itself. The edge of the Talamanca universe begins at Suretka, a small
sleepy town which forms the last outpost of mains electricity and bus transport.
Here you find a mixture of races: Bribri indigenous people, Nicaraguans, Ticos
(Costa Ricans), and black people who originated from Jamaica, although you
can't tell them apart anymore. Once you cross the mighty Telire/Coen river,
however, you are clearly in Bribri territory, a valley that extends west and north
into the mountainous wilderness. Go 12 hours further into the mountains
by foot and you may encounter the Cabecare indigenous people, said by the
Bribris to be more private and perhaps more 'traditional'.

Both the Bribri and Cabecare peoples speak their own languages and deal
with life very much on their own terms. I have been living with an indigenous
family who also are Bahá'ís. The father's name is Elias and he is an Auxiliary
Board member who has had many opportunities to travel for the Faith – to
the rest of Central America and to the Holy Land. He is a great source of
information about Bribri culture. Through living with a family I have come to
see how the two sexes balance their activities to have productive and healthy
lifestyles. Most women have their own *'finca'* or farm which provides a lot
of the family staples and they share childcare responsibilities with their own
parents (who rarely live very far away).

As well as still practising subsistence agriculture, hunting, fishing and gathering are still means of ensuring the survival of themselves and their culture. However, they also rely to a fair extent on the '*pulparillas*' or local stores for some products like rice, salt, sugar, batteries, soap and other luxuries. Of course, in order to be able to afford to 'buy' things, they need money, which many get from selling bananas to national and multinational companies.

Being here primarily as an anthropology student, I am studying the effects of these incursions of money, products and ethics from national society and beyond on the traditional forms of social organization of the Bribri people. This has meant getting to grips with the 'traditional' society, which is not an easy thing to do. It's not like there's a written code of laws or a records system that I could use to glean something about their values and collective aspirations. Rather, there's the work of other anthropologists (which may be crucially flawed owing to the fact that anthropologists used to try to fit American indigenous cultures into African 'tribal' kinship patterns), or my own research and observations. And that's what it's really all about – using my own eyes and ears to come to some understanding of what is going on in the minds of these people, how 'culture' manifests itself and whether there is some pattern running through it all – the traditional anthropological experience.

Another goal I had was to learn about Bahá'í concepts of social and economic development. I have been lucky to be closely integrated into the life of the development project here through regular visits to the office in San Jose and consultations with the project's director, and through its regional educational centre in Talamanca. I have come to understand that the concept is multi-faceted and draws on the distinction Shoghi Effendi made between Bahá'í-inspired development activities and teaching the Bahá'í Faith. The latter may only draw on Bahá'í funds whereas the former may use non-Bahá'í funds to achieve its economic and social objectives associated with the humanitarian institutions of the Ma_sh_riqu'l-A_dh_kár. This reflects the principle that Bahá'í development is for all people, regardless of background or religion.

Despite this, Bahá'í social and economic development is predicated on the awareness generated by the Bahá'í writings that humans are essentially spiritual beings created to 'carry forward an ever-advancing civilization'. This is the essential difference between Bahá'í-inspired development and some of the other development projects around the world. One of the most interesting aspects of this Bahá'í-inspired development is the principle that each 'people' or community must walk their own path to development, which reflects the principle of 'unity in diversity'. This can be achieved principally through the use of consultation to make decisions about a community's aims and objectives. Asociacion NUR uses a 'rural university' methodology which advocates all of the above but specifically contains a deep respect for traditional knowledge and culture. For example, in Talamanca the project employs indigenous people who read up on modern farming methods and consult with the community about the best way to proceed. Then they put their findings into action. One current project is the '*huerta indigena*' or the indigenous garden. This seeks to provide a sustainable way to grow subsistence plants, medicinal plants and bananas for sale. Another is the control of pigs. This uses pigpens to keep the swine from eating all the crops (sounds simple but it is actually difficult to get the people to comply because when pigs are in pens they must be fed, which requires growing a special amount of crops to take to the pigs). These kinds of everyday problems can have far-reaching solutions when the community decides to think and act together, for example, to control to what extent they comply with the multinational banana companies or allow state educational authorities to decide their children's curriculum.

I am really enjoying my experience with the Bribris, who have such a unique and clear perspective about what life on earth really means. It is comforting to just lie in a hammock when the sun is beginning to set at 6:00 p.m. and hear the squeaks and cries of the children at play, the grunts of the pigs coming from under the house (which is made of trees and bark, and on stilts), and then listen to stories about their culture. It is also a memorable experience, if somewhat unreal, when I consider that at 2:00 a.m. on 29th May I was walking ankle deep in mud through the rainforest to reach the Bahá'í Centre in time for the commemoration of the Ascension of Bahá'u'lláh. I remember Elias proudly but humbly telling everybody that exactly eight years ago he'd been at the Shrine of Bahá'u'lláh for the same occasion. Needless to say, every time I am there I learn new things, not just about their culture, but about their spirits too and about how to live closer to nature (for me, this means to suffer more!). Obviously they have their problems too, and they shouldn't be romanticized, in fact can't be . . . but the time I spent with the Bribris over the summer of 2000 is certainly an experience that I will never forget.

97

January 2001

Greg Akehurst-Moore

Czech Republic

Greg, previously from Dumfries in Scotland, is in his third year teaching at the Townshend International School in Hluboka.

Life seems to fly by and this is never more clear than when you read *Pioneer Post* and see the names of youth on a year of service whom you remember as small children, or hear of friends who have moved on to distant lands and whose lives have changed so much. One is also very conscious of the march of time as a teacher in a school, where each year the faces behind the desks get a little older and new young faces appear to replace the older ones who move on. The start of this academic year at Townshend School seems to have produced a good crop of new students. There is a real positive buzz, and most of the students appear to want to be here, which must say something for a school! This is in spite of the fact that a major disappointment has been that the hoped-for move into new and impressive purpose-built premises, scheduled for September, did not happen owing to the financial situation.

The Bahá'í community in the Czech Republic reminds me of the stories heard from older members of the UK community about the time when the number of British believers was a lot smaller and everyone in the whole country knew each other. Here there are about 300 to 350 believers. If you attend events, it is easy to meet everyone and get to know the members of the National Assembly, the Board members and so on. And like in Slovakia, where it seems that most community members are below the age of 30, the majority of this community is young. There are some older pioneers and a few believers from pre-communist days who kept their faith throughout the 40 years of the communist regime with only a few prayers to live by!! Attend the summer school here and you will find a vibrant and close-knit band of intrepid souls who seem to gain much strength and pleasure from one another, although knowing that they are still such a small minority amongst their countrymen.

This summer was a special one here. The National Assembly arranged a series of teaching projects in the east of the country (Moravia). A major focus of events was the singing group 'Patchwork', based in Belgium but gathering singers from the Netherlands, Luxembourg, Germany, England, Belarus, USA and the Czech Republic. The effect of the choir on the local population was electric! Audiences at performances often gathered in as many as 60 non-Bahá'ís. Many were so enthusiastic, they appeared at more than one performance. A fireside held at the choir's hotel in Prostejov drew quite a few interested people. As well as discussions and questions, there was also singing, and seekers said such things as 'The spirit here is much greater than I find in my church' and 'Even your silence speaks – it caresses the heart!' The fireside itself was amusing, as at first the doorman would not let us use the dining room as had been promised and the event started (with permission, of course) in the corridor on the second floor where all the choir, travel teachers and members of the European Bahá'í Youth Council were staying. Improvisation was the watchword as chairs, crockery and refreshments were hauled from individual rooms into the passageway! Not content with this, a couple of Bahá'í women silently descended to a room on the ground floor where they started praying. Within minutes the phone in the reception rang and the manageress spoke to the doorman, assuring him that we had her blessings to use the dining room after all!

The spirit was really high during the choir's tour, which also took them to the Polish summer school, literally just across the border in the Polish goal town of Cieszyn. At the last performance, there were many red, tear-stained eyes, and no one wanted to part. Afterwards, at a Bahá'í's squash club, everyone stayed together until about 1:00 a.m. that night! Some National Assembly members felt that the public's response to these projects was the best since the days just after the iron curtain fell. It does seem that music is the key to hearts here. Surely it is the same where you live too!

An ironic footnote: We heard after the tour that some of the enthusiastic local believers who had been busy the week before sticking up the 'Patchwork' posters all over the place had been caught on police video cameras unwittingly sticking them up in a place where that was not permitted! They were fined. The sacrifices of the friends!

98
January 2001
Jeremy Fox
Pays Basque

Jeremy's 20 years as a pioneer in the Pays Basque, southwest France, has drawn to a close and he has returned to live in Scotland.

Reflections on 20 years' pioneering in the Basque Country

In October 1980 my late wife Denise and I, with our two daughters, left the Isle of Mull after 12 years, having opened the Inner Hebrides in 1968 and left behind what we imagined to be a firmly-established Assembly. We had decided to open the French Basque region where there were at that time no Bahá'ís (in fact we later discovered a Bahá'í who had been out of circulation and who became very active again until his passing). There were, however, Bahá'ís on the Spanish side. It was in many ways our greatest time of tests – financially, health-wise and at times community-wise, so I cannot join those who entrance you with miraculous stories of great breakthroughs, even though we had our exciting moments. We had a few declarations, regular

Feasts, deepenings, firesides, picnics and public meetings, with regular reports in the papers. Some of those who declared fell by the wayside but a few grew to be pillars of the community, particularly one Basque family – husband and wife with their two sons and the husband's brother.*

For many years we concentrated our efforts on the goal town of Saint Jean de Luz, which for a while made progress but then largely dispersed. It remained a goal town for the coming Five Year Plan. Cambo-les-Bains was also a goal town for a while but nothing much came of it, although one friend died and was buried there, providing the first Bahá'í funeral in the French Pays Basque. He had also, shortly before, had the first Bahá'í wedding, held in Saint Jean de Luz. Saint Jean de Luz is a delightful but small town and the formation of Assemblies outside the big cities is particularly difficult in France owing to the smallness of the administrative areas, the 'communes'.

With time, despite becoming a community of about 25 friends who met regularly, we were scattered over eight administrative areas. More recently various friends moved into the main town, Bayonne, and the first Assembly was formed there at Riḍván 2000, almost 20 years after our arrival. This made me feel a little better about leaving my post to return to Scotland! So, though declarations of indigenous believers may seem thin on the ground, the Bahá'í presence had, by that time, moved from zero to about 30, including children. There was by then a Basque Bahá'í Council, unique in that it ignored politi-cal frontiers and governed the whole of the Basque region under the aegis of both Spanish and French National Spiritual Assemblies. In order to work together the Council used French and Spanish with some English and Basque, so Council meetings were sometimes quite complicated, especially for the recording secretary! By the time I left there was a promising Bahá'í Sunday school in Bayonne serving a wide area.

I have many thoughts, reflections and feelings as I look back over these 20 years and am reminded of a visit I made in 1969 to the first pioneers in Niger. At the end of my stay, just before my departure, one of them said, 'Before you go I'll take you to visit a Bahá'í that, if one day the government expels all the pioneers, will remain faithful at his post.' He then took me to the grave of his young son. I feel the same about Denise's grave (she died of cancer in 1996) situated in the beautiful cemetery in Sare, the village we lived in during the last few years of our time there, for surely she fulfilled the Guardian's appeal to certain pioneers to leave their bones in their pioneering post.

Even if two-thirds of the present Bahá'í population consists of incomers from other regions, it seems to me to illustrate the fact that once friends move to an area for the sake of the Faith and persevere, it sets in motion certain spir-itual forces which, sooner or later, attract people, both Bahá'í and non-Bahá'í.

This sets in motion a dynamic spiritual process. God's time is not ours and it is impossible to know now what will grow from all the seeds sown or indeed when they will grow. I remember the words of the Hand of the Cause Mr Faizi in 1963 at the World Congress at the Royal Albert Hall in London, speaking of the mass declarations in India and reminding the assembled friends that such developments did not sprout from nothing. Before things took off there, pioneers since the time of Bahá'u'lláh had laboured for over a period of 60 years, many dying without seeing any visible fruits from their labours. As the Hand of the Cause Dr Mühlschlegel so often repeated, 'Ve must keep ze vision of the Faith', and as the Little Prince said, 'L'essentiel est invisible.'

* Now, in 2010, they are still the only indigenous French Basque believers. Parents and both sons remain devoted and active believers.

99
January 2001
Marion and Alan Pollitt
The Gambia

From Burnley in Lancashire, Marion and Alan pioneered in October 1977 to The Gambia, where they lived in the village of Kerr Serign.

Loving greetings from The Gambia, where at present we are experiencing the dry season when the days are hot and sunny and the evenings and early mornings cool – wonderful!

Over the past two years we have seen many developments. In April an 'all Gambian' National Spiritual Assembly was elected for the first time. Perhaps our most joyful news on a personal basis is the success we have met with in a nearby fishing village, Ghana Town. As the name suggests, 90 per cent of the residents are from Ghana. The fishermen go far out to sea in small canoes for days at a time; they bring back stingray, hammerhead sharks and other big fish which are salted and dried for export to Ghana, Mali, Benin and the Ivory Coast. The majority of the villagers are Christian and in this small village there are ten churches (from Roman Catholic to Pentecostal). There's also a mosque – mainly attended by the resident Gambians. The reception to our small Bahá'í teaching team has been warm and friendly and we are put through our paces on biblical references. And when Muslims attend we are put through our paces on the Qur'án!

Our first declarant was a young man, Godsway (what a name)! He is quite remarkable and very enthusiastic. Now we have ten Bahá'ís (all male) though a few women do attend our firesides.

Another 'coincidence' is that the Bahá'í Temple land is in Ghana Town, though no one knew this when we first decided to visit the village 'spokesman' and ask permission to share God's word with the villagers. Every Sunday we sit under a huge shady mango tree on the Temple land and hold firesides and deepenings, in the form of a study circle. Even the government has helped our efforts by constructing a new coastal road through to Ghana Town, which means it takes us only ten minutes by car rather than one hour through the 'bush'!

Another development here is a Bahá'í socio-economic project initiated by the Bahá'ís in the area of Bakau. At the local Bahá'í Information Office free computer classes are held, run from Monday to Friday. To qualify for the course, students have to have reached Grade 10 level of ability. Already over one hundred students have 'graduated' at level 1 and perhaps 25 at level 2. Both ceremonies were televised.

The second project has been to offer lessons in English and Maths at Grade 7 level of ability to the television company and a literacy course for adults. Shortly computer courses will be televised too. In this way we hope to be accepted as part of the Gambian community life.

Our celebrations of World Religion Day and International Women's Day organized by our National Teaching Committee were also televised and very well attended. Together with our regular firesides and teaching projects we are making the Faith known in this coastal district – but there is still a lot to be done, especially in the rural areas.

The majority of declarations still come from other West Africans living here in The Gambia who, away from their families and restrictions, are free to follow their own conscience. At any one gathering there may be 11 or 12 nationalities represented, truly the epitome of the Bahá'í Faith – unity in diversity.

100
January 2001
Robin Bell
Marshall Islands

Robin left Manchester in October 1999 to give a year of his time to the National Spiritual Assembly of the Marshall Islands. October just past he weathered the rain and storms of England briefly before returning to serve a further two years in this Pacific outpost.

On a hot and sunny afternoon in July I was lying on the floor of a large wooden porch overlooking the vast Pacific Ocean. The gentle noise of the waves lapping against the shoreline was accompanied by the sounds of both traditional and Bahá'í songs from the Kiribati friends who had come to the Ocean of Light conference.

The conference, which had finished a few hours earlier, was the largest international Bahá'í event ever held in the Marshall Islands – and to help with its organization was one of the primary reasons for my being over 11,000 miles away from the UK.

The conference, which ran for five days, consisted of drama, dance, song and deepening and was preceded by a three-day youth conference with the same theme: In Marshallese this was '*Jake Enra Eo Elutoklok Kin Naan Eo An A Bahá'u'lláh*' or 'Share the Basket overflowing with the words of Bahá'u'lláh'. In addition to the Marshallese friends, Bahá'ís came to Majuro, the nation's capital atoll, from all parts of the Pacific including Hawaii, Guam, Tuvalu, Kiribati, Fiji, Chuuk, Phonpei, Australia, Saipan, New Zealand and mainland USA. In total, over 250 friends attended. Their motive: to share their cultural presentations of Bahá'u'lláh's teachings.

It was a wonderful and spiritually uplifting event and to many was a great celebration of 'being a Bahá'í'. It also received presidential blessings as the country's leader, Kessai Note, was present and spoke at the opening ceremony. Our wonderful Counsellor, Betra Majmeto, the first indigenous Marshallese Bahá'í, was also there to offer her spiritual insights and words of wisdom. The days were full of energy, love and complex catering requirements! There was an incredible diversity of cultures and a wonderful spirit of unity, which only seemed to grow through the course of the proceedings.

For me, there were several outstanding elements. The friends from Hawaii provided the musical 'glue' with a plentiful supply of gentle island songs. In some contrast, the dancers and singers from Kiribati were exuberance personi-fied and the Marshallese Bahá'í youth group from the island of Ebeye danced and sang their hearts out. Around the conference hall, tears were prominent as the National Spiritual Assembly presented Counsellor Majmeto with a gift to honour her years of selfless service.

We had wonderful speakers too, each presenting the teachings of Bahá'u'lláh on specific virtues synonymous with the Pacific peoples (e.g. hospitality, gen-erosity, uprightness, etc.). Such speakers included Marsha Gilpatrick from the USA, Margot Macphail from New Zealand, and more familiar to *Pioneer Post* readers may be Irene Taafaki and her husband Falai-Riva, who have pioneered in the Marshall Islands for several years and who also shared their knowledge with the conference participants.

However, as I believe Shoghi Effendi said, the success of any such conference should be based on its results. Well, motivation was renewed and a
number of the participants stayed in the country after the conference to help
with teaching activities, which resulted in new declarants to the Faith. Some
friends sailed or flew to neighbouring atolls to spread the word, taking their
energy, ukuleles and grass skirts with them! One trip on which I accompanied
the Hawaiian Bahá'ís (across a very rough Pacific!) was to an atoll called Arno.
Coconut palms, sunshine and access to a beautiful lagoon – pioneering can be
tough! All the atoll's inhabitants seemed to be present at the evening's musical
fireside. Not quite inside – but faces pushed against where windows should
have been.

So, back to that wooden porch immediately after the conference and, for
one lasting moment, the delights of my earthly senses transformed into such
a greater sense of spiritual calmness. It was almost four years since I had consciously heard of the Faith and here I was quietly marvelling in the effect such
a discovery had made. It was perhaps appropriate at that moment that the
Kiribati friends dragged me off the floor to dance . . .

101

January 2001

Joe Donnelly

Bulgaria

*Joe and his wife Atieh and their two children, Neysan and Melody, are
pioneers from the Republic of Ireland to Plovdiv, Bulgaria.*

We first thought of pioneering overseas when we were on pilgrimage in the
Holy Land in January 1992. It was as if being in proximity to the holy shrines
reminded us of the great privilege of pioneering. Meeting pioneers at the
World Centre and learning of their experiences was really thrilling and somehow on a different level than anything else. Coming from a community like
Ireland, where practically everyone has at some stage in their life pioneered on
the home front, we often wondered what it would be like to leave everything
and pioneer overseas. My wife's parents were veteran pioneers, having moved
several times to goal towns in Iran.

When we came across the booklet *Quickeners of Mankind* and read the
words from Bahá'u'lláh's immortal Tablet, 'They that have forsaken their
country for the purpose of teaching Our Cause . . .'[23] we began to realize the
great station that He conferred on overseas pioneers. We were further inspired

to focus on serving the Faith in this way. We also learned that many of the Hands of the Cause of God were themselves pioneers and we wanted to emulate them in our own small way.

After attending teaching conference in Ireland in the autumn of 1994, we decided to send our CV to the European Pioneer Committee in Germany, and they sent a copy of our letter to a number of countries which included Albania, Bulgaria, Greece, Hungary and Romania. We definitely had a country with a warmer climate than Ireland in mind! Of course, the children were a major factor in coming to a decision about wanting to pioneer. We thought that if we didn't go then, while they were still young (Neysan was 11 and Melody 9) it might be more difficult later on. We waited for a few weeks to receive replies. By far the warmest and most welcoming replies came from Bulgaria, suggesting that we consider coming for a visit to get the 'feel' of the place and, hopefully, that would make it easier for us to decide.

So we took up the offer and travelled to Sofia in March 1995. Before the week was over we had decided to move there. What made our minds up? Well, I guess it was a combination of things. Firstly, I think it was the friendliness and genuine love of the Bahá'ís, and secondly, the great need for pioneers in Bulgaria. (At that time there were only about nine pioneers in the whole country – pop. nine million). Thirdly, it was the genuine receptivity to the message of Bahá'u'lláh by the Bulgarian people. Also, and on a more practical level, the cost of living was much lower than in western Europe.

When we got back to our community in Ireland there was a mixture of joy and sadness at our decision to leave. Joy that we were serving the Faith on a new level and sadness that we would no longer be a part of Co. Cavan (a border county) community where we had spent the past nine years and where our children had grown up and developed their Bahá'í identity. We put the house up for sale (we still had a mortgage), got the rest of our affairs in order – tax, debts, etc. – and left for Bulgaria on 14 August 1995, stopping off in London for one night before arriving in Sofia on the following day. If I remember correctly we carried *16* pieces of luggage with us!

They say first impressions are the most lasting. Well, the first thing I noticed was how incredibly old the cars and taxis were. The next thing was the amount of litter in the streets. And the third was the way people stared at us everywhere we went! It could have been something to do with the way we dressed, looked and spoke. I suppose, on reflection, it wasn't that surprising, considering the country had more or less been 'locked up' for 50 years. Almost straight away we went to our first Bulgarian summer school in the north of the country, very close to the River Danube (involving a train journey of about eight hours, overnight – that was an experience in itself). By the way, the Danube is not blue, at least not anymore. The summer school was quite lively with youth from many western European countries, all fired up after a teaching project. As a family, it was our first encounter with the Bulgarian mosquito, a small, hardy and persistent little creature.

Another strange feature of Bulgarian life is that when Bulgarians say 'yes', they will move their heads from side to side as if saying no! It took us quite a while to get used to that one. Well, pretty soon we had to think about getting jobs (we had completed a TEFL course in Ireland just before we left). In late September I went to the local university to find a job teaching English, not knowing a word of Bulgarian and trusting in Bahá'u'lláh. I met a Bulgarian teacher who spoke perfect English. She introduced me to the Head of the English Faculty a few days later and I began working the first week in October (still hanging in there after five years).

We placed our children in a Bulgarian school so they could integrate quickly into the school system and we began taking private Bulgarian lessons ourselves. We would like to mention something here about parents' worries over the quality of education when you pioneer overseas. The school system in Bulgaria and in the rest of eastern Europe is quite good, in some ways better than the West. Discipline in the classroom, drugs and teenage pregnancies are not the huge problems here that they are in western Europe and the States.

It wasn't long before we had our first Bahá'í visitor early that October – Foad Kazemzadeh, our Counsellor at the time. This remains a feature of every pioneer's life – the visit of friends and travel teachers who make such an important contribution to supporting the task of pioneers. The Irish NSA, of course, was, and still is, wonderful. It continues to encourage us all the time.

The Bahá'í Faith is one of the officially recognized religions in Bulgaria, along with Judaism and Islam, and is gradually developing a relationship with leaders and prominent people. The name of the Faith, this year alone, has been proclaimed on television and radio and to hundreds attending open-air concerts. So the future looks promising for the progress of the Faith here. Bulgaria is largely unspoiled by materialism and the teachings of the Faith have a more profound effect on the hearts of the people.

As a pioneer family during the years we have been here, we have always felt that Bahá'u'lláh was protecting us and that whatever happened was all for the best. Atieh and I really feel that Bulgaria is our home and we intend to stay, God willing, for quite a good many years. Another bounty I forgot to mention up to now is the close proximity (three hours by car) of the Roman city of Plovdiv, where we live, to the house of Bahá'u'lláh in Edirne (or Adrianople, if you prefer the old name).

102

April 2001
David Renwick Grant
'Bahá'í Viking'

From May to September 2000 David (from Scotland) kayaked from Sweden to the Black Sea, following a Viking route through northern Europe, and visited Bahá'í communities.

I was ten days into my journey, sitting in my Klepper folding kayak, Bahá'í Viking, in a fresh breeze and moderate sea, sailing across the Baltic from mainland Sweden to Gotland. Getting this far had entailed carting a mound of equipment by train and ferry from Scotland via Bergen (and the Feast of Jamál), Oslo (and the Viking Ship Museum) to Stockholm, where I had stayed with friends, making final preparations. Departure had been from the small fishing village of Arkösund on 20th May last. I had paddled through the Swedish Archipelago, then across to the island of Öland, from where I had set off for Gotland. My idea of kayaking the old Viking trade route from Sweden to Istanbul had been conceived during our family's seven-year expedition around the world by horse-drawn caravan.* It had only become reality on leaving Arkösund.

During the horse-drawn caravan expedition we had spent a winter in Ulaanbaatar, capital of Mongolia, and there I had become a Bahá'í. My present journey had the twin aims of following the Vikings and visiting Bahá'í communities en route. Initial contact was made, via our own National Spiritual Assembly, with the National Spiritual Assemblies of the countries I expected to visit: Norway, Sweden, Latvia, Belarus, Ukraine, Romania, Bulgaria and Turkey. My mode of transport made fixing dates difficult but everybody knew roughly when I should arrive.

Circumstances curtailed my visit with the friends in Bergen to a couple of hours. In the flurry of pre-departure work I had not been able to seek out anyone in Stockholm. I had arrived exhausted in the harbour of Visby, Gotland's capital, at 1:00 a.m. and slept on the pier, so was greatly relieved when I telephoned next morning to find my contact there, Ola Okfors, at home.

Ola, Swedish-Finnish, was married to Katinka, an east Greenland Inuit. They had five boys, ranging from 12 to early 20s, and lived in a modest house in Bokbindergatan amid a tangible atmosphere of warmth. Somehow they found room for me as well. Ola took me sightseeing and we discussed the Faith while examining prehistoric ship-burials and Viking picture-stones. On

5 June I had the opportunity of meeting many of the rest of the community at the Feast of Núr, Light, as well as telling them about my journey and giving a tune on the shuttle-pipes.

The Okforses were about to move, to pioneer in Lapland. With bad weather delaying my progress and more storms forecast, I decided to take the passenger ferry to Pāvilosta in Latvia.

Two days later, paddling up the Latvian west coast, I nearly came to grief in Ventspils harbour. A rising wind reached gale force and I ran in for shelter – only to find that the wide harbour basin offered none. Ignominiously I had to be rescued by the harbour cutter. My life was not in danger but Bahá'í Viking had been at imminent risk of being pulped against the harbour wall. Storms remaining on the menu, I entrained for Riga in Latvia. At least from there onward I should be on rivers and no longer weather-dependent.

My stay at Riga Bahá'í Centre coincided with a series of meetings, giving me the chance to meet many more friends than might otherwise have been possible. I gave what was to become my standard talk, starting with the horse-drawn trip, how my conviction that we had been protected had led to my adopting the Faith, to the present excursion. I also spent a day with the Jelgava community, a hair-raising 40-kilometre bus ride out of town. Newspaper interviews had provided a good forum for public mention of the Faith. The last of these took place while I reassembled the kayak on the banks of the Daugava, just before setting off again.

Some hard paddling, portaging around hydro-dams and towing through shallows eventually brought me to Daugavpils. I was again accommodated in the Bahá'í Centre and again gave a talk, followed by discussion, while further media attention gave more opportunities to promote the Faith.

A week later I was in Belarus. The frontier crossing had gone smoothly, after several recitations of 'Is there any Remover of difficulties . . .' and I spent my first two nights at Vrhnedvinsk. The difficulties to be overcome, teaching the Faith in a country that is still almost Soviet, are huge. Nevertheless my welcome was especially warm and I reflected, not for the first time, that adversity often brings out the best in people.

I had an adverse time myself, paddling through the abandoned canal system that joins the river Ulla to the Berezina, before arriving at a wonderful reception from the Bahá'ís of Borisov. This was followed two weeks later by an equally great time spent with the friends in Bobruisk.

Berezina flowed into Dneiper. I crossed into Ukraine, passed close to the evacuated area around Chernobyl and eventually reached Kiev. There I stayed in a borrowed flat, sorted out the matter of getting my passport stamped (there had been no border post on the river), had a marvellous evening with the Bahá'ís at their new Centre, was interviewed by newspapers and TV. It was almost a relief to get back to paddling.

The Dneiper was polluted with algal bloom as thick as paint in places and had six hydro-dam locks to negotiate. I had passed one before Kiev but had to tackle three more before Dnepropetrovsk, my next Bahá'í port of call. I stayed five days, meeting Bahá'ís, making minor repairs, restocking provisions and visiting the Zaporozhye community by bus. Then it was off again on the last lap to the Black Sea.

The weather broke, becoming changeable with contrary winds. The open sea could be hazardous. One day, calm became storm in 30 minutes; I had struggled for hours to reach shelter. When I arrived at Odessa, I decided not to risk continuing to Istanbul. It was just too late in the year for safety. Disappointment was tempered by another delightful encounter with local Bahá'ís. As for Istanbul, there is always next year . . .

* Grant, David R. *The Seven Year Hitch: A Family Odyssey*. London: Simon & Schuster, 1999; Pocketbooks (pb), 2000.
The full story of the above trip is related in Grant, David R. *Spirit of the Vikings: A Journey in the Kayak Bahá'í Viking*. Long Riders Guild Press, 2008.

103
July 2001
Silan Nadarajah
Mongolia

Silan and Tahereh have been pioneers in Mongolia for nearly six years. For many years previously they were UK pioneers in Papua New Guinea. Here Silan describes a wonderful 19 Day Feast in the capital, Ulaanbaatar.

First 19 Day Feast in Ulaanbaatar in the Fifth Epoch at the Ulaanbaatar Bahá'í Centre

Temperatures at night are between minus 25 and minus 40. This year has been unusually cold. The Feast was scheduled to start around 6:30 and friends came in trickles, all wrapped up like a 'pillow' to protect themselves against the cold – children, mothers, fathers and youth. Chimgee, who just had a baby (born on new year's day), also turned up with her two sons and the newborn all wrapped up so tight like a 'cushion'. Around 65 people were there, sitting on chairs and on the floor, all huddled together. The hosts for this Feast were the Ulaanbaatar youth.

The Feast began with the Youth Committee chairman welcoming everyone and introducing a new declarant, a youth and a recent university graduate. A beautiful devotional programme began, with prayers and readings intermingled with the chanting and singing of prayers in unison and this went on for about 30 to 40 minutes. Though readers are prearranged for the devotions, in Ulaanbaatar (as in all Mongolia) the option is open for anyone to say a prayer and this happens in most Feasts. Why should we deprive a soul that wants to pray?

The administrative part began and Bolorchimeg, a member of the Local Spiritual Assembly, chaired the session. The Feast letter from the National Spiritual Assembly was read. Ulaanbaatar has an area growth programme and has been broken up into districts. The chairman announced (based on an Assembly decision to have group consultative meetings) that we need reports from each district and so the Feast gathering is broken up into groups (by districts) and the friends had to consult on the number of firesides and study circles we have had and our plans until the next Feast – we were allocated 10 to 15 minutes. There was a big shuffle of people in the room and in the meantime the newborn baby was being cuddled and everyone was 'kissing and welcoming' the newborn to the Feast. In our group (district) meeting, suddenly everyone clapped because one of the girls (another youth) decided to join the Faith. We consulted (all the talk was in Mongolian) and the translations were whispered into my ear. Then everyone came together again and each group gave a report. There were reports of firesides, study circles, dawn prayers, declarations, English classes, children's classes and goals. Then a Board member who had just returned from the historic meeting in Haifa gave her report. The Youth Committee gave a report and their plans for the next 19 days included a request that each youth develop a virtue.

A member of the Teaching Committee pointed to a wall chart showing the number of new Bahá'ís for this phase of the Twelve Month Plan, reminding everyone of the dedication of this plan to our beloved Amatu'l-Bahá Rúḥíyyih Khánum.

Since Riḍván we have had 43 declarations and our two new Bahá'ís were called upon to write their names on the chart. Our Local Assembly treasurer announced the fund and friends put their fund money in envelopes and gave it to the children to place in the fund box. The Local Spiritual Assembly always announces the number of friends who attend the Feast, the number of contributors and the amount collected. The goal is to get everyone at the Feast to contribute. There were suggestions and recommendations and the time was past 9:00 p.m. In the meantime the newborn baby was still being cuddled and greeted . . .

Closing prayers were said and devotional songs sung (this took another

20 minutes). Then the youth announced that they had prepared a skit, and as refreshments came, we saw their performance and we laughed and clapped them. People then stayed on talking and chatting. Two members of the Local Assembly were in a corner counting the fund money . . . and soon everyone started to leave to catch their late bus.

What a *Feast* . . . it was full of life, all had participated and taken ownership, had contributed to the discussions and all were in very high spirits.

104
July 2001
Jody Koomen
Swaziland

I recently arrived home from youth service in Swaziland. My sister, Jonneke, told me once that everybody wants to go home while they are doing a year of service, well at least at some point during their time away. I didn't realize how true this statement was until I'd spent six months working in a school in Swaziland. And the only reason I'm saying this is because I don't want it to appear like everything was good about Swaziland. When I look back – sorry, I'm gonna churn out a cliché – the last year has been the worst and the best year of my life.

One of the most beautiful experiences I've had in my life was a funeral. There are a lot of funerals in Swaziland due to the rise in the percentage of people with AIDS (the United Nations calculated that half of the people who are sexually active – between the ages of 15 and 55 – are infected with the HIV virus). In the last few months three people who worked at the school where I was have died.

In Swaziland funerals are conducted at dawn and the night before the funeral everybody stays up all night to sing, pray and talk about death and the person who died. It was really a joyous experience: people laughed, sang, danced and cried all night. Just before dawn everybody went into the room with the coffin, said prayers and sang beautiful, gentle songs. After this everybody stood outside the room with the coffin and waited for it to be carried out. First came the youngest daughter, a girl who was about 16 or 17 years old. On her head she carried a grass mat and a pillow; the coffin with her mother inside was carried behind her. After walking a few paces the coffin was put down, a young lady knelt on her knees and said a few prayers, and then we all sang a soft song. The song carried on as the coffin was picked up and the young girl led the way to the grave site. As we walked I realized how many people were present – the number was huge. When we reached the grave site, we continued to sing songs while the grass mat and the pillow were placed inside the grave and the coffin was carefully lowered into it. The songs continued while the grave was filled up again and rocks were placed on top. Then, when everybody sat down in a beautiful reverent manner, the father began to talk.

Of course I didn't understand a word during the entire funeral but I did have a beautiful experience. The first few funerals I attended, I just could not see any light in death and it never really inspired me to watch friends being buried, but that morning I looked at the amazing blue sky and felt something glorious. God, death is such an amazing thing. I realized my friend had just been released into glory, and I was happy for her.

105

October 2001

Shohreh Azarkadeh

Tanzania

Shohreh arrived at the Ruaha Secondary School in Iringa, Tanzania, in April where she plans to spend a year of service.

I feel very much settled and have fallen into a daily and weekly routine. There is little stress – there seems to be more time here and people take time for each other. People always shake hands with big smiles and take time to ask about every member of the family. As much as time is important in the West, here relationships are important. A couple of weeks ago I was waiting for the school's pick-up van that was supposed to pick me up from the market and I was getting rather impatient and looking at my watch. A passer by commented, 'In Africa you don't worry about time.' I realized I was in Africa and just relaxed.

It is wonderful to be here – I am so lucky to be living among so many amazing people, in particular the pioneers. I have my own privacy and when I want company there are always friends around, so I don't feel lonely or crowded – it's just nice. I don't have to drive two hours to get to work, only two minutes. My work is going well and I enjoy it.

Sunday mornings we have Ruhi study circles. It is organized so that everyone in the community is in a study circle. We meet at 9:30 for a devotional and then everyone goes to their own groups at the same time. We sit outside under the shade of a tree in the school yard in our own groups until almost lunchtime. On Sunday afternoons we usually go teaching in the villages and I love that. Most of the tutors are our Bahá'í youth from the school.

Every day is a sunny day here and it is beautiful. I have not yet seen a full cloudy day. It is now our winter (more like an English summer!) and days are pleasant, and sitting in the sun is so comfortable, although a little cool for my liking. As soon as the sun goes down it becomes cold and we don't have any heating – in fact, nobody has any heating. The sky is always clear at night, full of stars and the Milky Way is so clear. I am looking forward to the summer when I can sit comfortably outside and watch the sky.

Dressmakers sit outside the shops with their very old sewing machines – the old Singer machines operated by hand or foot – it is such a delightful sight to watch. I guess it reminds me of my childhood and my mum's sewing shop.

The battle of bugs goes on! There only needs to be one crumb, or a dead fly, for a whole army of ants to start marching in. Ants are the 'goodies' – the 'baddies' are the invisible ones! The good news is that the real 'baddies' are out of season for the time being so I have stopped my malaria drugs, which didn't suit me. There are also living bugs in most of the foodstuff that we buy, such as rice, grains and flour. We used to throw out the food but now we just look for them and debug the food – so cooking takes longer. I am eating things that I never even used to look at in England – chilling out with a bottle of Coke is one of my treats now. We just don't have many treats, so any treat, even if it never used to be a treat, becomes a treat. Local donuts and samosas are sometimes nice and we serve them as refreshments at our feasts. Then we either serve tea, which is so sweet, or we serve bottled juice made of sugar, colour and flavourings. It is very sad that there is so much fruit here but no industry to make fruit juice. Juices are imported from South Africa and they are more expensive than they are in England. Most restaurants make nice fresh juice at a reasonable price.

I am a member of our Programme Committee, which means we arrange programmes, venues, refreshments, etc., for all the Feasts and holy days and most other events. At least 80 people attend the Feasts and most of them are youth (40 Bahá'í students from our school) and at least 20 children. Arranging the programme is relatively easy – we just ask the choir to sing and the quartet to sing the Hidden Words and excerpts from the writings that they have beautifully put to their own music. And then there is the children's choir – they love to sing and say prayers. Africans love long devotionals. They feel cheated if they go a long way to a short meeting with a short devotional.

106
October 2001
Nichola Davis
Mongolia

Nichola (from the UK but presently a pioneer for Canada) is working for an international organization in Ulaanbaatar.

This is my first assignment working for an International NGO in the development field with children. In listening to my heart, it is daily becoming clearer to me that I need to change the environment in which I pursue my dream. In Mongolia I have been given an amazing opportunity to learn that without a spiritual vision and aspiration, it is very difficult for people to transform their lives and grow. So what I would like to do is to find a Bahá'í context in which to continue working with children and women in Asia after my contract expires in April 2002.

The weather has been magnificent and I am enjoying the warm sunny days with quite a few showers and some heavy rain that has made the surrounding hills beautifully green, unlike last year when they remained brown. Unfortunately, many parts of the country are not getting any rain and so the animals and herdsmen continue to suffer. The predictions are for an even worse winter, as the animals will not be able to find enough grazing during the summer. The weather patterns are not helping with this, the third bad summer following two very heavy winters. However, those in the know tell me that there are far too many animals for the land to sustain. There are over 30 million animals and 2.6 million people in Mongolia. The tragedy is that the herdsmen have large families and then divide their herds among the children. Fewer than 100 head does not provide enough of a living for one family and more than 100 head for each of several children results in over-grazing in the valleys. Although the herdsmen's life is very harsh, it is all they know and there does not appear to be an alternative way of generating income in the countryside. Nobody wants to acknowledge the problem and the situation gets worse.

On 4 July and with some friends I flew early in the morning from Ulaanbaatar to the east Gobi. Our four-day trip was magnificent, intensive and most enjoyable, despite the poor health (flu, headache and digestive problems) that afflicted some of us. We saw lots of wildlife while being bounced around the wide-open and sometimes rocky terrain in two jeeps. We experienced a magnificent sunset while sitting on the high sand dunes. Another highlight was hearing an excellent folk concert performed by some wonderfully talented musicians and dancers in the very intimate setting of the restaurant in the tourist *ger* resort, with only a small party of Japanese enjoying the concert with us.

On the first day of a three-day summer festival called Naadam many country folk and herders come to town to compete in three sports: horse racing, wrestling and archery. The horse racing takes place very near the airport. Again with friends, I stopped to watch a horse race, parked, with others, on the brow of a hill, as we did not have the correct pass to get nearer to a good viewing spot.

However, we decided to fetch some binoculars and return with a translator friend. This took just over an hour but there was nobody around when we got back to the area by the airport. So we checked with the few remaining police and army recruits to discover that the next race was not for another two plus hours. We were able to park in the reserved lot for those with passes and settled down to play cards while we waited. Unfortunately, the seven hundred horses took more than an additional two hours to get to the start area and I expect the race was further delayed until the President arrived at the same lookout spot where we and all the foreigners and important Mongolians (including famous wrestlers) had been brought by bus and car. The race was 30 km long and young boys rode the winning horses. Although it was a very long wait with the course in the distance and the horses hard to see in the dust they kicked up, it was exciting – so our patience paid off!

107
October 2001
Vafa Kouchek-zadeh and Andrew Wilson
Youth Summer Teaching Project in Russia

There were five of us youth from England, including ourselves, who left for Russia on 19 July to participate for five weeks in the Russian Youth Summer Teaching project. With all the Russian youth and two Canadians, we were about 30 youth altogether.

The project started in the Bahá'í 'dacha', the Bahá'í summer residence just outside Moscow, with a ten-day intense and well-organized training programme run by the National Youth Committee of Russia and the two members of the Canadian 'Generation of Hope' team. There were lectures on the running and coordination of a teaching project, junior youth study circles and plenty of dance training. Youth between the ages of 13 and 26 from every part of Russia took part. At the end of the training three groups left for Murmansk, Maykop, Ryazan and Penza.

We were lucky enough to join the Murmansk group, which involved a 36-hour train journey heading towards the north. We slept on benches and ate '*lapsha*' [Russian noodles] for breakfast, lunch and dinner. We passed woodland and plains and lakes and the train stopped for 20 minutes for us to get food if we needed it. It seemed that everyone lived in flats in tall tower blocks and there were a lot of cars in the cities. The toilets in the train were in a very 'interesting' state but the inadequacies were largely compensated for by the amazing scenery of rivers and forests. We found the Russian people very, very friendly.

After the first few difficulties of settling into a new town and learning to live with nine people in the small but cosy apartment that was the Bahá'í Centre of Murmansk, things started running smoothly. There was a good variety of food but we lived mainly on boiled potatoes with ketchup and salad, and sometimes pasta or soup, and for breakfast we had spaghetti in boiled milk.

Every day we performed on the streets and each evening we held firesides. As we progressed, we moved from the streets into schools where the teachers were very impressed by the messages we were getting across to the pupils. Our firesides turned into deepenings and eventually into a study circle. It was a beautiful experience, knowing that we were trying to serve Bahá'u'lláh every day, praying constantly for the success of the project and having the opportunity to share the teachings of the Bahá'í Faith with so many others.

The people of Murmansk were extremely talented and friendly. Quite a few were instantly attracted by the unity present amongst our diverse group. We had the privilege of catching a glimpse of an understanding of Bahá'u'lláh's words 'So powerful is the light of unity that it can illuminate the whole earth'.[24]

We always had a good turnout for the firesides. People were very receptive to the Faith, which was very interesting; you so rarely get that in the UK. It felt great because you knew they would ask questions back when you told them about it. It was the same for both youth and adults.

The experience we had was fantastic! It was hard work but worth it. We made good friends and the Russian participants were nice to work with. A lot of the Russian Bahá'í youth we met had found the Faith for themselves; they were extremely devoted Bahá'ís and a great inspiration to us. The best thing about the experience was going somewhere completely strange, not knowing what to expect and finding out that we loved Russia! The worst part was saying goodbye to everyone.

108
October 2001
Wesley Clash
Corfu, Greece

*Wesley (UK pioneer with his wife Stephi and daughter Giselle in Corfu)
has written this letter from offshore Qatar in the Arabian Gulf where he is
a professional diver.*

I am writing to you, not from my beloved Corfu, but from inside a deep
diving saturation complex, offshore Qatar, constructing oil fields once again.
After three years out of the diving game, I'm now back in it for three years.
Stephi, my wife, and I worked at helping our daughter through school and
we started an antique restoration and hand-painted furniture business, which
was hard work and financially very difficult – plus there were difficulties in
our marriage.

Behavioural problems and financial problems sometimes go hand in hand
throughout such difficult times – times of reappraisal, self analysis, long and
hard discussions, and a determination to overcome all obstacles.

As a pioneer there is, I feel, an obligation – to God and to Bahá'u'lláh.
Once you start on this most beautiful and glorious adventure of pioneering, you have, in my opinion, to do all in your power to keep the adventure
moving and alive from day to day and from year to year.

Ingeborg Weigelt first opened Corfu to the Faith and Stephi and I try our
best to follow in her footsteps. Our presence there is the physical foundation
of the Faith on Corfu and we intend to stay through thick and thin, offering the Faith to all who care to listen – the words and hope of Bahá'u'lláh,
organization of the venues where possible for dance groups, speakers, travel
teachers, etc. plus personal teaching when and where we can. To have had a
lovely person, Beverley Gongakis, declare was a great blessing.

Stephi and I are now closer together than ever before. This closeness, this
staying together, I attribute to the Faith more than to ourselves. We tried very
hard to see each other's point of view but sometimes we failed. I feel it was the
spirit of Bahá'u'lláh and the Báb ever present through the power of prayer that
allowed us in times of extreme stress and anxiety to keep on walking hand in
hand down the path of increasing maturity and spiritual awakening.

The reason for my telling you all this is to let other pioneers know if you
are facing difficulties, as we did – including the difficulty of educating our
daughter in a foreign language plus feeling guilty for taking her out of the
British system into one that may not have been as adequate.

Remember that when rising up to be a pioneer there are blessings given to you that do not become apparent until later on – financial hardships, problems, discord are no fun. But the people you meet along the way, the courage, humility and kindness in others are truly amazing and the love and hospitality shown to you is humbling. The intense satisfaction one gets from seeing the Faith progress and blossom eventually puts the problems to flight, and strengths you never realized you possessed come to the fore. The spirit of Bahá'u'lláh enhances your resolve. At least this is what Stephi and I have found.

109

October 2001

Danielle Pee

Albania

Danielle (19) from Surrey, spent the summer months travel teaching in Albania.

The Albanian Experience

The pilot announced we were about to land at Tirana airport, the only airport in Albania. I looked out of the window expecting to see something with some kind of resemblance to an airport but to my amazement I saw nothing. In fact, all I could see were fields of sheep, cows and other farm animals. As the plane started to descend I noticed a small road, which I soon found out was the runway! Well this was Albania! Home to me for the next three months.

I arrived on Tuesday, the day of firesides. It was also my nineteenth birthday, and so for me it was a great way to start my service! First I visited Tirana, the capital city, which was so interesting and different from the town centres one sees in Leatherhead or Camberley! I soon realized that this country, like many countries of the world, is one of extremes. One side of the street has grand fountains, a luxurious hotel and rich, plump people walking around, while directly opposite is what looks like a disaster bomb site with a dump yard and half torn down houses all around where the poor people live. It was here that I had my first meeting with poverty. It really shook me to see young children walking around without an arm or a leg, or who were so thin and malnourished that they couldn't walk properly. Amidst the extremes of poverty one could see a banner of hope, for in bright lights in the cultural centre of Tirana was a huge Bahá'í sign and at nightfall this sign was the main thing visible in the centre of town.

I soon found out that when visiting Albania for Bahá'í service you need to take your own initiative with you. You have to make your own service and push your activities forward. So I set up a dance workshop of which the attendants were non-Bahá'í pre-youth. I walked around some poorer areas of the city with a self-appointed translator and found some junior youth. We asked them to meet us on a particular date at the cultural centre. I was so worried that no one would come; in fact I waited at the centre for about 15 minutes, then I thought I had better ask for some divine assistance. Sure enough, after I had said a few prayers and closed the book, a crowd of pre-youth boys entered the culture centre. I talked about the Faith, briefly explaining the principles. When I saw a few of them getting a bit bored, I started the dancing and it became a hit!

We started every session with prayers and then would say 'Alláh-u-Abhá'! In the beginning during prayers the junior youth would giggle or behave inappropriately. But eventually, as they became more familiar with prayers and their importance, they changed. The children soon learned and became shining examples. In fact, when new recruits joined and would behave inappropriately during the prayers, it was the original attendees who would tell the newcomers off for acting wrongly!

Originally the dance workshop was for one hour, two days a week. Eventually it became every day for seven hours, with the numbers rapidly increasing and the youth's eagerness to know about the Faith intensifying. Every time I saw them in the streets they would say 'Alláh-u-Abhá'. Every time they saw anyone, in fact, they would say 'Alláh-u-Abhá'!

Later that summer the Youth Committee of Albania ran an arts seminar. Luckily I was asked to help out. It was such an amazing experience to serve with the Albanian youth – I learned so much from them. The arts seminar attracted an international audience. The Italian 'One Family' dance workshop arrived and there were Albanians, English, Czech, Swiss and many more different nationalities attending. For me this was the most exhausting week. I had to chair the seminar, patrol the corridors in the evening to ensure everyone went to bed and prepare for my own talk. This I did with three hours' sleep every night, as I managed to get to bed about 3:00 a.m., having then to wake up at 6:00 a.m. This was because there was no running water between 6:30 a.m. until 4:00 p.m. every day. The fact that there was no water, nor electricity, was a great motivator for the participants to get up in the morning to get ready and then attend dawn prayers!

After the arts seminar was a series of teaching projects in various villages throughout Albania. I was in the town of Fier for only one day but this one day was the most uplifting, inspiring and fulfilling day of the whole Albanian experience. The 'One Family' workshop had been asked to perform at a nearby small town. There were no Bahá'ís living there and I don't think anyone there had even heard of the Faith. I arrived with Bahá'ís from Tirana, one member of the National Spiritual Assembly, one member of the National Youth Committee, one member of the European Bahá'í Youth Council and one member of the Local Spiritual Assembly of Tirana. As we got out of the car, there was a very different feeling to this place – a feeling that the time was right to spread our beloved Cause.

The 'One Family' workshop attracted attention by starting to play music. All of a sudden hundreds of children came to investigate what was going on. As the workshop performed, during the magical hour that evening, it attracted many crowds of people to hear Bahá'u'lláh's message. I cannot put into words what I saw before my eyes. Bahá'ís who were not performing were networking during the performance, speaking to people in the audience to ultimately teach.

Directly after the 'One Family' performance a woman declared and we announced that a fireside would take place the following weekend. The next weekend was the start of the teaching and consolidation process. A town that had never been opened to the Faith now had three children's classes and two study circles!

In a place called Korca the junior youth dance group I had set up in Tirana went to perform at the local park. It was 7:00 p.m. and everything was going wrong. First of all we couldn't get any electricity to play the sound system as there was a power cut. Then when power resumed the wire was not long enough to extend to the nearby café. There was a beggar child who wouldn't leave us alone. In fact he managed to steal a few items of equipment. Then it started to rain . . . we all just got together and said a few prayers. About five minutes later someone lent us an extension cord that they just happened to have with them. It stopped raining and we managed to perform. It was a good performance with many people attending and afterwards we managed to speak to the members of the audience about the Faith. We then saw the same beggar child, who this time instead of asking for money, started dancing the steps he had learned in the poverty dance! We couldn't stop laughing and so we took him out with us for byrek, the traditional Albanian pie.

So . . . to sum up the 'Albanian experience': I learned so much, I got robbed twice, and I managed to get food poisoning . . . But Albania is like a private school: you pay to get education. In Albania you pay through your material possessions or the tests you receive from Bahá'u'lláh (trust me, Bahá'u'lláh provides loads of them out there!) and what you gain is, hopefully, spiritual growth, guidance and a deeper love for the Faith.

110
January 2002
Maureen Sier
Samoa

Maureen and Nick (from Scotland) pioneered with their family to Samoa in October 1997.

We have been living in the beautiful islands of Samoa for four years. It's hard to believe it, as time has flown by so quickly. Tom and Zoe have spent their secondary school years in a local Samoan school. Zoe has just finished her time there and is now working as a pre-school teacher at the Bahá'í Montessori school.

There are so many wonderful things that have happened to us since arriving in Samoa. We have had two audiences with the Head of State Malietoa Tanumafili II. One of those visits was to present a beautiful solid silver Scottish quaich (cup of friendship), hand carved with greetings from the Bahá'ís of Scotland; the other was to do with my research. His Highness, although getting old, is full of love and humour and it is always a pleasure to be with him.

We live only ten minutes' drive from the Temple where devotional services are held every Sunday and where many hours have been spent in quiet prayer and meditation. On 15 September a memorable service was held to pray for all the victims of aggression throughout the world. Of course the service was prompted by the acts of terrorism in America. Particularly moving moments during the service came when the American Peace Corps director read a beautiful Bahá'í prayer, followed by his Cuban wife, who read in Spanish with tears in her eyes, followed by a Pakistani Muslim reading from the Qur'án, asking for peace and justice. There were prayers from many world scriptures read in six different languages, interspersed with the beautiful singing of the Samoan choir. Members of government were present along with Bahá'ís and their friends. The following week a special service was held for the UN International Day of the Elderly. The Temple continues to be a very effective sacred tool for touching the hearts of all who enter with the spirit of the teachings of Bahá'u'lláh.

Throughout Samoa study circles, children's classes and devotional meetings are increasing. Along with the Feasts, Local Spiritual Assembly meetings and social and economic development projects (five pre-schools and a Bahá'í youth workshop), the basis of true community life is evolving. As an Auxiliary Board member I am often out in the villages where it is a joy to spend time in these Bahá'í communities. One week a women's conference is held at the

Bahá'í Centre, the next week is a training meeting for assistants and the following week there is a children's conference – life is very full.

During the year Samoa has been visited by some incredible souls. Wes Baker, a Bahá'í from Uganda, graced Samoa with his musical presence. Wes has the most amazing voice and sang his way into the hearts of hundreds. The first indigenous Australian to serve on the National Spiritual Assembly of Australia, Philip Obah, also came to Samoa to share his vision of indigenous spirituality. Many others have visited too but these two souls stick out in my mind.

My work at the National University continues to be challenging and interesting. Sometimes it amuses me to think that a Scot is teaching 'Pacific Island Society and Culture' to Pacific islanders – most of the time I feel that I am the one doing the learning. This year I was elected onto the executive committee of the Samoan Association of Women Graduates and I am delighted to work with these dedicated women in the educational field. Our family loves being here in Samoa and would encourage those who are able to visit this remarkable country.

III
January 2002
Joy Behi
Poland

Joy pioneered to Poland ten years ago and is currently serving on the National Spiritual Assembly of Poland.

Yesterday I was in Krakow. Next weekend the community is celebrating ten years of having a Local Spiritual Assembly. It was the first Local Assembly in Poland so it is the first of similar celebrations in Poland.

It set me to remembering what it was like touring this wonderful country in 1991 with the dance group 'Vision'. We were in Krakow over 19 August during the attempted coup in the Soviet Union and the incident with Gorbachev. The world was still pretty much in the Cold War and we were uncertain of the outcome of daily happenings beyond Poland's eastern borders.

Many of those youth who recognized Bahá'u'lláh during that trip and the visits of other groups just before and soon after are serving the Faith today in several ways. They are on Local Spiritual Assemblies in Krakow, Warsaw and places throughout the world or they are Auxiliary Board members for Counsellors on different continents or they function on Institute Boards and countless other services for our Faith.

At our National Spiritual Assembly's table last weekend, we reflected with our beloved Counsellor, Nicola Towfigh, how the Five Year Plan again puts emphasis on process rather than events.

This summer during our Ruhi training courses here in Cieszyn, we had friends who had been introduced to the Faith by pioneers from the United Kingdom, the United States, Iceland, Ireland, Canada, Germany and other countries. I thought this weekend, where would the Faith in Poland be without the sacrifice of those pioneers and travel teachers? Those wonderful souls, Jane Cierniewski, Sylvia Girling, Miguel Watlers, Patrick and Sara Crowley, Anis and Laleh Samandari, Jane Sadler, a whole gang from Ireland – and the list could go on and on – who came to share the message with their lives in Poland. It became obvious as the Ruhi courses were being held that everything is interconnected and we are very much a part of the process of the entry by troops.

Now as we witness the development of study circles, community devotional meetings, systematic children's classes, we recognize the impact of entering the fifth epoch and the need to align our plans with divine processes.

Yesterday as I sat in the spacious square of a sunny and warm Krakow with Polish and Czech friends, I remembered being there recently with my daughter Krista, and just before visiting this beautiful city with my eldest son Bud and his family. I thought of Wales and being with my family and Bahá'í family there in September this year.

Yes, so much has changed in the world since the 11th of September. It had a big impact on our lives and the reality of detachment and relying on God is more and more important. Psychologically I must be prepared for being cut off from my children, and yet somehow, sitting in Krakow and knowing that we are witnessing the development of God's plan, I don't feel alone at all but in awe of this mighty Cause.

112
January 2002
Thelma and Ron Batchelor
Thirty Years On . . . Solomon Islands

Ron and I were pioneers in the Solomon Islands, South Pacific, from 1970 to 1973. The other day, while searching through some boxes in the attic, I came across something I had written after a teaching trip to a remote island in December 1970. It brought back some incredible memories . . .

Teaching Trip to Sawa (island off the north tip of Malaita) Solomon Islands

It was Christmas Eve and we were on a flight from Honiara in Guadalcanal to Auki in Malaita in the Solomons. We flew in a brand new ten-seater plane which took 28 minutes to fly over the Coral Sea and was one of the most beautiful flights we have ever experienced – flying over the Florida group of islands from which it was easy to spot palm trees and gorgeous white sandy beaches, bush, strips of coral and turquoise water in lagoons glistening in the sunshine.

We landed in Auki on a grass landing strip with a hen and her chicks scratching about underneath the wings as the plane came to a halt. We were met by some of the Bahá'ís in Auki and then driven in the back of a truck through the bush until we reached the little town of Auki and Fassy's store and home. We had a wonderful evening with the Fassy family (with many intervals of the islanders singing Christmas carols at the door). The next morning 16 of us were ready to journey to the north of Malaita and so in the back of the truck we drove off to the north of the island where we were going to attend the first teaching conference in a new area opened up to the Faith.

We drove through the bush, passing a few scattered villages along the sides of the road, where the people came out of their leaf huts to see us go by – the women topless, chewing betel nut and smoking pipes. It took three very hot hours to reach the road end, about 70 miles further on, crossing rivers on rickety old bridges. When we got north it began to rain and when finally we could go no further by truck we climbed out and were ferried across a river by some Bahá'í girls from the island of Sawa who had come to meet us. We were greeted with a tremendous amount of love, which was overwhelming. After being paddled across the river, we walked along for another mile or so until we reached the lagoon at the northeast end of the Malaitan coast. Then for half an hour and in two leaky old canoes we were paddled across to the artificial island of Sawa where we were going to stay.

The canoes leaked so much that we had to put our fingers to the cracks in the wood to prevent too much water from pouring in, while one of the Solomon Islanders busily baled out with a saucepan lid. Piled into these two old tree-trunk-like canoes with us was our luggage, a generator that we were taking with us to show movie films, a ciné projector, tape recorders and much of our material wealth accumulated in the rich outside world – to take over to a people who had nothing (but spirit)! The canoes nearly sank with their loads but it was a bit like the Oxford and Cambridge Boat Race as ten of us in each canoe slid gracefully over the lagoon. Far out to sea we could glimpse the white Pacific rollers curling gracefully, forming white foam as they crashed onto the coral reef at the edge of the lagoon. Here there were many man-made islands where a hundred years ago, in order to escape the mosquitoes and sand flies on the mainland, the Malaitan people collected rocks and dumped them into the lagoon. On this foundation they built their leaf and bamboo huts on stilts. Surrounded by a few palm trees, these islands now stand rock-like in the peaceful waters of the lagoon.

Dusk approached as we were paddled into the slipway of Sawa. Carefully trying not to tread on sewage (we had arrived at the wrong end of the island) as we clambered out of the canoes, we were greeted like royalty with hundreds of loving people wanting to shake our hands as the two hundred or so islanders came to greet us – none of them wanted to be left out from welcoming their Bahá'í guests from the outside world. Everyone on this island was a Bahá'í and the love they showed us was tremendous – it had even overwhelmed the Hand of the Cause Enoch Olinga who had visited Sawa just a few weeks previously. A huge feast was laid out for us on our arrival. We ate from a tablecloth of banana leaves. We were amply fed with coconuts, sweet potatoes and taro pudding. Trying to avoid the cockroaches, we made an effort to eat a substantial amount of the feast provided. What was not eaten was recooked and eaten the next day and so on until it was all gone!

In between the leaf and bamboo houses narrow lanes led off in different directions (to one area taboo for men and another taboo for women), usually ending up at slipways where the canoes were housed. There was no such thing as electricity on the island nor sanitation but this didn't matter, as we had taken the generator with us so that we could show films to the islanders, many of whom had never seen ciné films before. We showed the old silent movies of Laurel and Hardy, and Charlie Chaplin. The Solomon Islanders thought they were hilarious and insisted on seeing them over and over again. It was late before they finally tired of watching films. Finally a small group of islanders began to sing some South Sea island songs, which became intermingled with Bahá'í songs.

A Bahá'í Centre had been recently erected on Sawa and in this large leaf and bamboo hut jutting out onto the lagoon about 20 of us bedded down for the night on the hard stone floor – surprisingly we slept well. All night long a relay of people would stand guard watching over us. At dawn we were woken by happy islanders who had come to see how we slept. They just couldn't give us enough attention!

Early in the morning large groups of us were ferried over to the nearest stretch of mainland in the bush where the teaching conference was to take place. First we washed in fresh water streams and then joined the two hundred people who were attending the first ever teaching conference to be held in this area. Ron spoke about the Faith in England and our journey out to the Solomons via Haifa.

The idea was to convey to the people living on these man-made islands the importance of they themselves taking the message of Bahá'u'lláh to others, and the effect was electrifying. It was like teaching conference at home. About 25 humble people offered to go teaching, offering two weeks out of every month. There were also 19 declarations, one from a man who had held out from declaring until he was sure that the Faith was right. Many people spoke of their fine impressions of what Bahá'í means, as they saw love and unity in action and how the Europeans were happy to be partaking of their food and visiting the local homes that weekend.

After each talk food was brought round until it seemed as though we must forever be eating! Meantime we were bitten unmercifully by mosquitoes and sand flies until we burned bits of wood, the smoke from which helped keep the insects away. By the end of the day, and when the conference was over, we were ready to paddle our canoes back to Sawa. By then it was dark and we had a five-minute canoe ride through channels of phosphorescent luminous fish and then we were back, clambering about in the sewage which was the slipway for our island home. The conference continued for a short time the following morning, and afterwards many of the islanders put on a show of custom (native) dancing for us just because they felt like dancing, and decorated themselves with palm fronds and other leaves which they cut from the bush.

When the time came to leave Sawa the rain was coming down hard and we got very wet in the old leaky canoes. We were drenched to the skin after half an hour of being rained upon in an ominously cloudy and drizzling rainy wet lagoon. When we reached the shore, we had to walk some way back to where the truck had been left, which had taken us to the road end. We piled back into the truck, dropped a few Bahá'ís off at their village called Potato and started for home. No easy matter. What we hadn't known was that back on the coast of Malaita the rain hadn't ceased for three days and, as a consequence, we discovered that the rivers were flooded and the bridges barely holding. After we had gone some way we came to a gap where a section of the road had been swept away. We all very ably jumped out and patched up the road enough to enable the truck to continue on its journey. That was all right until we came to a large ford when again we discovered that part of the road was missing and this time in too bad a way for it to be repaired. We also heard that bridges had been washed away farther along the road, so with this sad news we decided to turn back and return to Maluu, where there was a small store where we could have some food and shelter for the night.

As it was holiday time (it was Christmas) there was not much hope of any repairs being done to the bridges or washed away roads so we wondered what would happen as there was no other means of getting back to Auki. We decided to have a swim in the morning in a nearby river. It was a good excuse to shampoo our hair and wash off some of the dirt and grime of Sawa. Some of the Solomon Island lads found the kind of white rock that is the substance used, when wetted, for rubbing white marks on the skin to turn themselves into tribal warriors! A loud whoop of laughter was heard as our Solomon Island friends came charging along the river dressed up as savages! It was great to see them like this and so Ron, not to be outdone, was eager to have the same body markings made on him. White paint on semi-white skin doesn't show up too well but he was made up as well as he could be, with his shampooed hair stretched into a long point on top of his head. Looking for all he was worth like the return of Dracula, who should come along in his Land Rover but the local Catholic priest, who wanted to know who the person was who had wanted a message sent on his radio to Honiara in Guadalcanal to say he would be late back for work!

After this incident and we had returned to the store, some local boys came along to tell us that a boat had been sent from Auki to collect us at Maluu, which would take us back to Auki. By now the weather was getting worse and the boat, the *Krista*, couldn't come right in to collect us from the shore, so we had to go out to the boat in a canoe, leaping over high waves as we did so. It took four rough hours of being tossed about on rollicking waves before we got back to Auki and meanwhile most of us were seasick.

The next morning we were able to fly back to Honiara, only in fact one day late for work. The next day we were informed that the boat that we had been travelling on had struck a reef at Maluu, the point where we had embarked the day before, and had broken in half.

113
April 2002
Ann Dymond
St Helena, South Atlantic

Ann (from Oxfordshire, and a grandmother) was one of the first pioneers in Gibraltar during the Holy Year (1992). She stayed for some seven to eight years. Recently she was inspired to go short-term pioneering in St Helena for three months.

Physically getting to St Helena takes time and planning. It has no air link, no airport and only the Royal Mail ship *St Helena* sails there regularly. It is the last and only mail ship in service in the world. Connections have to be arranged between flights to, and sailings from, Cape Town or Ascension Island.

I opted to fly to Cape Town and had three days to wait before boarding the ship. After landing in Cape Town I was met and taken to the home of a Bahá'í family, Gregory and Tahirih Matthue. The whole family – grandparents, parents and children – were an example of true Bahá'í family life and I felt I was privileged to spend time with them.

Sailing time to St Helena is five days, so during the time on board I met lots of St Helenians (they call themselves 'Saints'). Most were returning home from working away or being on holiday. Some had also been to Cape Town for specialist medical treatment not available on the island.

Each time the R.M.S. arrives in St Helena is special to the 'Saints'. It's their connection with the outside world. It also carries loved ones, stores and mail. Everybody that can goes to the front to see who is arriving, even if they are not meeting anyone themselves.

Three of the six local Bahá'ís met me and took me to the apartment I had arranged with the help of Barbara George. Later that evening I was driven 'up country' to have supper with them and for us to get to know each other.

My first week there was easy because the friends I had made on the ship were spending a week in famous James Town near me and we kept each other company and explored together, but when at the end of the week they sailed away, I felt really lonely. Still, I got busy introducing myself to my near neighbours, and as everyone was friendly, it was easy to do. The Saints are very good natured and greet all the people they pass in the street with a 'Hello Mam' or a 'Good day Mam'. If I asked, 'How are you?' they would answer, 'Not so bad' with a lovely drawl.

St Helena has an excellent Bahá'í Centre which young Bahá'ís from New Zealand, Ireland and the UK helped to construct and landscape. The local Bahá'ís have a continual stream of visitors – which they need – as St Helena is the most remote place I have ever been to. Five days sailing away from the nearest land mass with no sight of another ship, and once on the island, all you see wherever you stand looking outward is sea and sky, both a most fantastic blue. But inwardly I felt isolated and as though I would never see home again. It was impossible to express this feeling because I did not want to hurt other peoples' feelings and I thought if I said it out loud it really would come about. However, since returning to the UK I have met and talked with others who have visited St Helena and they too had this weird feeling.

It was suggested that I might start up some Yoga classes as a way of getting to know people and to keep me occupied. With the help of Gay Denbow, a Bahá'í I had met ten years before in Haifa, we found a venue and advertised on the local radio station. The class turned out to be very popular and continued until the day before I sailed home.

There is only one radio station and they broadcast everything that goes on in the island. Each night just before the 10 o'clock news, they have a short Epilogue. This is written and read in turn, a week at a time, by each of the different church ministers. That is Protestant, Roman Catholic, Baptist, Methodist, Salvation Army, etc. Some years ago the then governor felt that the Bahá'ís should also be included in broadcasting an Epilogue.

It takes quite a time to plan seven readings, each lasting three to four minutes and each complete and giving a message. The seven had to be recorded at one sitting and left to be slotted into the evening broadcast when it was our week. I did one of these when I was there and one evening they made a mistake and introduced it as from the Baptist Church!

At the Bahá'í Centre each week a devotional meeting is held to which the public is welcome and once a month a public meeting is advertised and friends are invited. I was asked to give a talk on Gibraltar, as the Saints admire the Gibraltarians for their independent attitude to the British Foreign Office. I called the talk 'Multi-cultural Gibraltar' and drew on the oneness of the moral teachings of the different cultures.

The governor is the Queen's representative in the territory, and he and his wife are friendly with the Bahá'ís. Throughout the island the Bahá'ís are very respected and well thought of. This might have something to do with the fact that they have all been connected with the education system of St Helena and one Bahá'í, Jenny Corker, is a magistrate.

There is very little work on St Helena and what there is is poorly paid, so most of the young people leave to find work elsewhere. While I was there the last young Bahá'í left to take up work on Ascension Island, and that left just six adult Bahá'ís, all past retirement age. So it is very difficult to interest the young people in the Faith.

On 24 December the *Duyfken* sailed into St Helena with two Bahá'ís on board. She was two weeks earlier than we had expected, which was a great pity because the Heritage Society had planned a reception, but wind and sails wait for no man. Delia and Cliff Huxtable and I dashed down to meet them when they came ashore. We gathered them up and showed them the island. They only had a short time ashore but we gave them tea and heard about their adventures. That trip from Australia to the Netherlands was going to take one whole year – and that put my three months into a different perspective altogether.

The practicalities of living on St Helena are such that things we take for granted in the UK are not always available. Owing to infestations of a variety of bugs and animals, the local flora has been badly infected, little food is grown and not much of the land is suitable for agriculture. A great deal of basic foodstuffs has to be imported from the UK or Cape Town, all via the R.M.S. It really is the lifeline for St Helena, and when it breaks down, as it has on occasion, it causes hardship on many levels.

I particularly longed for green vegetables and fresh fruit. We could get those pale white cabbages but I needed green stuff. Funnily enough, the local bananas (if you could get them) were always green and had to be wrapped in brown paper and put into the dark to ripen for a week or two. Then they were very tasty, that is, if they had not gone rotten.

Christmas and New Year was a time of great revelry. A few days before Christmas a large number of people were invited to Plantation House, the governor's residence, for cocktails and carols (soft drinks were available). The singing was wonderful and Gay Denbow played for us. Usually if I was going up into the country away from James Town where I lived, the Bahá'ís would pick me up. This time, however, the governor's wife arranged for me to travel with two of the local priests who were also invited – Father Fred and Father Joe. I sat at the back of the car listening to these two old friends talking. One was Protestant and the other was Catholic. Presently I heard Father Joe, the Catholic, mention Kampala, so I asked him if he had seen the Bahá'í Temple there? What a surprise and thrill it was when he said, 'Oh yes, and I knew and was great friends with Enoch Olinga (the late Hand of the Cause) for over eight years.'

Although I was looking forward to coming home, everybody made parting quite sad. All through the morning people kept coming in with cards and farewell gifts. We all had lunch at the cafe on the front before our last goodbyes were said and big hugs all round. Then onto the ferry and last waves to St Helena and her 'Saints'.

114

April 2002
Peter McAlpine
Thailand
Opening a Hotel in the Seychelles

Peter has been a pioneer in Thailand since 1984.

I've been having my first 'sort of' holiday for many years – opening a hotel in the Seychelles! It's tough but someone has to do the dirty jobs! The villas at the Banyan Tree Seychelles are mere loose change at between US$750 to

US$1,200 a day plus ten per cent service charge. Lean closer and listen to what's going on at the hotel. Lean closer . . . that's it . . .

Dear Friends

We have a choice of 20 pillows. Which would you prefer? Would that be silk, satin or cotton sheets? May we tempt you with our Jacuzzi menu or bath menu? Shall we set up candles and fizz beside the Jacuzzi? Which CD of Banyan Tree music would you like me to turn on while you have dinner? Or if you'd prefer, we'll set up a table for you anywhere along the beach and prepare a barbecue for you. Ripe mangoes? I'm very sorry but they are out of season in the Seychelles at the moment. Would you like us to fly some in for you? You'd like to hire a plane? I know all the details. Where would you like to go? Please try our spa. We provide a wide array of treatments – several kinds of massage, aromatherapy. You have back pain? We can put that right. We can send a buggy to take you to the spa. If you'd prefer, I could arrange for a therapist to massage you beside the pool . . .

When you sit on the sun-bed beside the pool in your villa, watching flowers drift across in the warm breeze, and listen to the gentle Banyan Tree Spa music, with the sound of the waves breaking onto the white sand beach nearby, you will start to feel why the hotel is called a sanctuary for the senses. All this for mere loose change, dear friends!

In addition to living in conditions far beyond my means, I've been doing something useful for the Faith. Because the global level of customer service for the rich is becoming unreal, one is now touching on mind reading and spiritual values. Indeed, the level of customer service has moved deep into the realm of spiritual values, and to get the concepts over, I use stories that are very emotional and which basically move people to tears. (I have a terrible time telling the stories!) We talk about love, religion and read Bahá'í quotations. Every middle manager and new member of staff has to ponder the meaning of quotations by Bahá'u'lláh and 'Abdu'l-Bahá and practise them in his or her job. The training courses all have Bahá'í quotations built into them and the departmental orientation manual, which new staff have to be trained in for four months, is full of them. So although I'm not in the Seychelles, the managers are continuing the teaching work for me. (Very decent of them!)

I couldn't have done this five years ago. I'd have been locked up!

115
July 2002
Ramin and Rozita Khalilian
Gibraltar

Ramin and Rozita and their three children are UK pioneers in Gibraltar. They went there ten years ago in 1992.

Gibraltar's Memory of Philip Hainsworth

The passing of Philip Hainsworth was a great shock to our community in Gibraltar. He played a significant part in promoting Gibraltar at the time when no Bahá'ís were present here. It was through his many efforts that Gibraltar was finally opened. During the National Convention in 1991 it was announced, by Philip, that pioneers to Gibraltar were urgently needed and it was through his enthusiasm and encouragement that my wife, Rozita, and I finally decided to choose Gibraltar as our first pioneering post. Mrs Ann Dymond was also present at the Convention and was similarly inspired. I still remember Philip's excited voice when my wife Rozita and I rang him from Gibraltar saying that I had found a job and we were going to stay in Gibraltar as pioneers. The three of us had only been here a few weeks when Philip phoned us offering a whole week of his precious time and we jumped at the opportunity.

In no time at all we were scouring Gibraltar for a suitable venue to hold our very first public meeting. After Philip's arrival we were busy arranging a meeting with the Gibraltar *Chronicle* which resulted in a half page article about the Bahá'í worldwide community together with a large photograph showing Philip holding a copy of his own book. He was later interviewed by Christine Clifton of the Gibraltar Radio Station. There were two other items on his agenda, one to make a presentation to the Governor of Gibraltar, Sir Derek Reffell, and the other a public meeting. The public meeting was held at the John Mackintosh Hall and a surprisingly large number of people attended. His talk was interesting and inspiring and ended with many searching questions from the audience. His memory for facts and figures was prodigious; he could reel them off without reference to his notes. Philip's expertise and energy compensated for our inexperience and the public meeting was a success.

Philip has a special place in our hearts and we shall miss him very much. He gave of himself a hundred per cent; whether his audience was one or a hundred, you had a full shilling's worth: 'A true Yorkshire man'!

116
July 2002
Sandra Cooles
Dominica

Sandra and Philip are longtime pioneers in Dominica in the West Indies. No doubt these thoughts that Sandra is sharing here will assist others who may find themselves in a similar situation when faced with having to make important family decisions.

Perhaps the most difficult and worrying time for longtime pioneers is over for us, at least I hope so. Three years ago we sent our three daughters back to the United Kingdom to finish off their education at university and sixth form. At that time we were in a real dilemma. What were we to do? Follow them and leave our post? They really need us here – all other pioneers have had to leave and the doors have seemed to stay open only for us. But then the girls really needed us over there. Should we abandon them to a very corrupt society, certainly amongst the youth, praying that they would be protected by the Faith, or should we join them?

I should maybe fill you in a bit with their background. They had been educated totally at home, finally taking open exams in O and A levels. This way of education had proved necessary so we could stay at our post. I had seen too many foreign families driven from the island by the treatment meted out to their children in the schools to risk the same thing happening to us. Though they had lived in a sheltered environment, they had been surrounded by drink, drugs, child abuse, murders, AIDS, teenage pregnancies, etc. but they had to a great extent been protected from having to deal with the reality of it in their own lives. In our Bahá'í community they were active and dedicated, holding children's classes, youth groups, weekend Ruhi institutes (where I only did the cooking), attending Bahá'í conferences in the region and, above all, teaching.

So you will understand that it was with a lot of trepidation that we decided to send them back alone to what was a completely alien environment, for though they looked white they were in everything else black. We were unable to rely on relatives back in the UK for they were virtual strangers; a visit of two hours every two years was not enough to form any long-time bonding. The culture shock that they experienced was profound. They were horrified by the attitudes of the non-Bahá'í youth of their own ages and also by the morals of some of the Bahá'í youth who were also unable to include or accept an outsider. I felt we had made a big mistake and was thinking of returning to give moral support. Thankfully, with constant phone calls from home and visits, they have coped, stayed strong in the Faith and now are members of their respective communities.

Why I am saying all this is to, hopefully, help someone else learn from our mistakes. When your children are growing up, and if they will be returning to the UK for higher education or to live, try and take them to the summer schools there, so that they will make friends who can be kept from year to year. Never think that this transition from one country to another will take place easily – prepare them from the age of ten on. Even though your children will not leave home until they are 18, prepare. We have been very blessed, and only now do I see the pitfalls we have missed. My heart aches for all the pioneer children who have done such a wonderful job pioneering with their parents, who have cheerfully coped with, and become accustomed to, hardships, and then are suddenly asked to meet the reality of the world today. Prepare.

117
October 2002
Valerie Rhind
Zambia

Val has been a long-time pioneer in Africa. Her previous pioneering posts on the African continent have been in Zambia, Botswana, Zimbabwe, Tanzania, Nigeria and Angola. She is now living in South Africa.

Bahá'ís of Zambia celebrate their fiftieth anniversary at the William Masetlha Foundation

I was so pleased I went to the fiftieth anniversary celebrations in Zambia. For me it really was a trip down memory lane.

Celebrations to mark this happy event were held in various localities but the ones I attended were held on 29 and 30 June at the William Masetlha Foundation, about one hour's travel by car north of the capital, Lusaka. They were opened by the Honourable Minister for Home Affairs Mr Mapushi, who praised the Bahá'ís for the work being done at the William Masetlha Foundation because the wonderful institute programmes, such as rural health and trades for those who were not able to continue in the school system, have a wide appeal, both to Bahá'ís and others. The Minister also commended the Bahá'ís for establishing a high school of international standard for girls which promotes the Bahá'í goal to advance the status of women.

He told us that the area where the William Masetlha Foundation is situated was formerly called the meeting place of lions, as in the past it was a traditional spot for lions to encounter each other in battle as they moved over their territories, so it has always been a famous place! He asked the Bahá'ís to redouble their efforts to guide the community spiritually because society is in a state of crisis.

The celebrations continued with singing and dancing both from local Bahá'í groups and the National Dance Troupe, interspersed with presentations and reminiscences from Bahá'ís who taught during the 1950s and '60s. There were also talks by earlier pioneers and visitors, such as former Counsellors Shidan Fat'he-Aazam and Lally Warren and present Counsellors Firaydoun Javaheri (from the International Teaching Centre), Enos Makhele and Maina Mkandawire.

A highlight was a glimpse of photographs of the early believers which filled a whole room. In her closing remarks, wife of the first principal of the Banani School, Jane Richmond, took up the lion theme suggested by Minister Mapushi and encouraged the friends to become like those lions of the past and conquer the hearts of the rest of the people of Zambia.

The British Bahá'í community has significant tradition of assistance to Zambia over the past 50 years. It was an Englishman, Eric Manton, who first brought the Faith to Zambia when he moved there as a widower with his young son, Terry, back in 1953. Slowly other friends came to share in the teaching work and Eric met and married Jessie, also from England originally, in October 1956.

I had the privilege of pioneering to Zambia in the late 1960s and stayed for over six years. During that time I met and married my husband, Islay, and our first son, Matthew, was born in Kitwe in 1974.

118
October 2002
Lois Lambert
Mongolia

Lois and David have been pioneers in Mongolia for ten years. For many years Lois served as Auxiliary Board member but at the present time she is serving on the National Spiritual Assembly as treasurer.

Our community is growing steadily, doing its best to follow the guidance from the Universal House of Justice. Any growth that takes place is a result of following the institute process over the last few years. This summer we have been involved in intensive Ruhi 6 and 7 courses happening in each of the clusters, and Cluster Conferences are taking place to plan for the next phase of this year.

We have been away from the UK for 14 years, having moved to Mongolia from China in 1992. David is now the longest serving VSO in any one place in the world! During this year I have been travelling backwards and forwards to the Philippines, planning and facilitating a series of four radio drama training workshops for the first Bahá'í radio station in Asia, in a rural area of the Philippines. Radyo Bahá'í is funded by the Bahá'í Office of Social and Economic Development (as are the workshops) and the purpose of the radio station is to support the institute process and entry by troops. It has been a challenging but very stimulating assignment, involving the development of new materials and approaches. It has been a joy to work with a number of radiant and dedicated young Bahá'ís from the Philippines, many of whom are second and third generation Bahá'ís. I have learned a great deal in the process and am still learning. To travel to diverse communities around the world, such as the Philippines and Yakutia, and to share their vision and experience is a precious privilege.

Semira and Ian Manaseki Holland are now here from the UK with their two little boys, Rodan and Daryon. Semira's mother recently arrived from Iran for at least a couple of months' stay with them. Also living with them is Nika, the first official pioneer to leave Iran since the troubles. It is a delight to have them all here. In 1992 Semira came to Mongolia on a six month travel teaching trip and it was a team she assembled that opened Darkhan and Erdenet to the Faith and established Local Spiritual Assemblies there. So she is part of Mongolia's history and that she and her family should have returned here is great. Semira has set up a research project on the practice of swaddling and the way it affects respiratory health, while Ian is a VSO, like David, and is working on a capacity-building project with UNFPA.

David and I continue to balance a busy Bahá'í life with professional lives and we find the first gives us energy and commitment to the second. David is project director of a nationwide in-service teacher training project, and my current work with UNICEF is documenting the responses of Mongolian adolescents through film and written media to a global project to meet the participation and development rights of adolescents. It is inspiring because it involves meeting and talking to youth and junior youth throughout Mongolia about their visions and dreams, and links with the work of the Bahá'í community with junior youth. Some of the youth I meet in the rural areas are Bahá'ís, and of course, our perspective as Bahá'ís is always the key factor in helping us to focus on the important issues in our work, whatever it is. At the moment, several of us are enjoying studying the first unit of a specialization course on development called 'Constructing a Conceptual Framework for

Social Action', which has been developed by FUNDAEC in Colombia. This was introduced to us by Dr Farzam Arbab during a dynamic visit he made to Mongolia in September 2001, when he was the key speaker at a high profile seminar on the need to recognize the spiritual dimension in the development process.

One of my colleagues at UNICEF is Burrenbayer, who was the first person to translate the Hidden Words into Mongolian and who had the privilege of meeting Rúḥíyyih Khánum when she visited Mongolia both in 1990 and in 1994. He spent six months in the United Kingdom, where he met many Baháʼís, and knows Sean Hinton very well.

119
October 2002
Lois Lambert
Mongolia

Residential Intensive Institute in Ulaanbaatar

19th July was the closing ceremony of a two-week residential intensive institute course for Ulaanbaatar Baháʼís, studying Ruhi 4, Ruhi 6 and Ruhi 7. Our institute building is called the Wade Institute (named in memory of our dear John Wade), located in the hills on the very edge of the city. Most of the participants have become Baháʼís while studying Ruhi 1 in study circles. Now, just a few months later, they have become trained facilitators. Immediately following the course a two-week teaching campaign is taking place, for which they have all made personal plans to hold devotional gatherings, study circles and children's classes in many districts of Ulaanbaatar and daily at the local Baháʼí Centre. Their goal is to have 69 devotional gatherings, 21 children's classes, to have four new study circles established during these two weeks and to have at least 30 declarations during that time.

It was such an inspiration to see the radiance and dedication of this group of people of all ages, which included two 13 year olds, one 15 year old and one aged 16. During the ceremony it was announced that one of the participants had been elected to the Local Spiritual Assembly of Ulaanbaatar in a by-election to fill the place on the Local Assembly that was made vacant when someone was appointed Auxiliary Board member. I looked around that room in which there were Auxiliary Board members, National Spiritual Assembly members, the National Coordinator of the Day Star Centre of Learning, a Mongolian international pioneer on a visit home, members of the National Teaching Committee, the Local Spiritual Assembly of Ulaanbaatar, trained institute facilitators (and if she had not been travelling in Russia, there might also have been our own Counsellor, Uransaikhan), all of whose lives are dedicated to the systematic acceleration of the advancement in the process of entry by troops and the development of human resources. All of them had become Bahá'ís within the last ten years. It is impossible to describe adequately our gratitude that we have been given the opportunity to learn from and grow with such radiant servants of Bahá'u'lláh. Although I was born a Bahá'í and as a little girl had the opportunity to be a tiny part of the growth of the Faith in the British Isles (my lovely mother, Alma Gregory, pioneered repeatedly in the Six Year Plan and subsequent plans) and though I often heard stories from many of the heroes and heroines of that era of the Faith, I did not really begin to understand the reality of being a Bahá'í and the bounty of service until we came to live in Asia and ultimately Mongolia.

Recently Nichola Davis, another British pioneer, who worked for the Christina Noble Foundation, has left to take a post elsewhere. We miss her very much. While she was here she had regular firesides, devotional gatherings and study circles at her home, where many people declared. She also approached her professional work in the development field with a constant application of the principles of Bahá'u'lláh. One of her significant achievements was to bring the various development agencies that work with children together in a regular consultative meeting where they shared experiences and expertise. This had never happened before and one of the successes of uniting their efforts was that they were able to remove a number of orphan children who had for years been shut away in a mental institution, where they had absolutely no stimulation and were severely malnourished. These children were found places in various shelters and care centres and are now living normal lives and discovering the joys of being children in a caring environment. I am constantly meeting people, in both professional and social contexts, who say how much they miss Nichola.

120
October 2002
Brian O'Toole
Guyana

Brian and Pamela have been pioneers in Guyana for the past 24 years.

It's early morning here as I write this letter which provides an opportunity for reflection on our experiences. About six per cent of the population in Guyana have accepted the Faith. Everyone here knows about it. Many, many of the fifty thousand plus persons here who have become Bahá'ís now live in New York and Toronto. Many others knew little about the Faith when they 'signed their acceptance'. Many too have been 'inoculated' against the Faith. However there are many others who appreciate the Faith and undoubtedly have the capacity to become lovers of the Cause if given the necessary loving nurturing. Like many other countries, I am sure we struggled with how to translate that nurturing process into action. Now with the emergence of the institute process we are beginning to see a path to draw numbers of persons closer to an understanding of the Faith they have embraced.

Guyana has undergone a number of upheavals over the years. It is a country composed of two major ethnic groups – descendants from Africa and from India – this is a historical circumstance that has sometimes been used to divide people. Despite this it provides an opportunity that has the potential to reflect what unity in diversity can mean in practice – once we begin to celebrate our differences. The economy has been slow to develop and many people see their future in terms of other lands. Despite these factors, it is a land of tremendous opportunities. The Faith has established a firm foundation here – the administration is strong, there is a pool of dedicated youth, the people are educated and the recognition for the need for fundamental change is strong.

It is a land that presents many opportunities. Seven years ago we started School of the Nations here – the school now has 500 children, representing more than 30 nationalities and has been called by one parent 'an oasis of peace' within the city. The school offers pre-school to A level. At times the school has been exasperating and exhausting but now, as we enter our seventh year, the school has established a reputation as one of the best in the country and is proving a wonderful medium through which to try and paint a vision of what education means.

Pam and I are part of a Bahá'í-inspired NGO, the Varqa Foundation. In response to guidance from the World Centre, a literacy programme has been developed, 'On the Wings of Words', which has now trained over seven thousand facilitators. This looks at both the mechanics of reading and the spiritual process of establishing change. Three years ago a youth leadership programme was created called 'Youth Can Move the World', which looks at challenging social issues (alcohol, drugs, suicide, poverty, etc.) and tries to help youth draw on the inspiration of the holy writings from the major religions represented in Guyana – Islam, Christianity, Hinduism and the Bahá'í Faith – to see how to respond to those challenges. Youth from every region of the country have now been trained in the programme. UNICEF has now requested that we focus on the prevention of HIV/AIDS in the next phase of the programme. We are hoping to begin to develop a series of video programmes as one element of the intervention.

For six years Varqa worked deep in the interior of the country, on the border with Brazil, in developing an integrated development project with the native Amerindian people of the country. A remarkable surgeon from Canada settled in that region for many years and provided the most noble example of work as worship. The development initiatives are opening up the hearts of a number of people.

As in so many countries, one of the real challenges is the higher education of one's own children. We have one university here – I worked there for nine years. A number of youth, however, feel the need to attend university overseas with more facilities. As a result we 'lose' some of our most dynamic youth. For our own part we have two boys who were both born here and see this as their home. Presently they are both in Canada studying. Liam (20 years) did a year of service in New Caledonia in the Pacific and is now in the third year of engineering at McMaster University and Cairan (18) has just completed a memorable nine months in Ethiopia and is now pursuing water resources engineering in Guelph. A next challenge may be to try and develop some form of university here that may allow more of our youth to stay in Guyana.

I am not sure whether when we arrived here 23 years ago as newlyweds that we thought we would still be here in the next millennium but it has been a rich experience. For so many countries, that line from a recent Riḍván Message [1988] – 'to restore vision where hope is lost' – is such an eloquent presentation of the challenge for the Bahá'ís.

Every time we get a copy of *Pioneer Post* everything else is put aside for a few minutes as we read of what the pioneers are doing – often in very challenging environments – and it is truly inspiring and humbling.

121
October 2002
Helen Smith
Lithuania

Helen Smith pioneered to Lithuania in 1989 from Guernsey, Channel Islands.

During these last 13 years we have seen many changes in Lithuania. Leaving the Soviet bloc to become an independent republic, this small country of 3.4 million (it was 3.85 million before independence in 1991) has gone through many upheavals, social and economic being the greatest. It is true that a large minority of the population, mostly pensioners, is very disillusioned with its newfound freedom. In Soviet times the pension was sufficient for one's needs; now it is not. These elderly folks have spent the greater part of their lives praying that their country would one day be free of the Soviet yoke but at the same time knowing and expecting that at pension age, about 58 years, they would retire and have enough money to continue with their current lifestyle, however good, bad or indifferent. The young, too, feel they have been cheated. Why is their country not on a par with other western European countries, or better still, like the USA? Those in their middle age have a hard time coming to terms with this independent and free society. Where is the easy life and more money, better jobs and more free time, less corruption and more safety for ourselves and our children; surely this should have come with cessation from the Soviet Union? None of this came with independence, only smaller pensions and money to be stretched to enable us to buy all the glitzy goodies now flooding the shops and which we have been denied for so long. Corruption is at an all-time high, the streets are empty after dusk because it is not safe. This makes for a very confused and sad society.

A predominantly Roman Catholic country (98 per cent), the churches have seen a massive increase in Sunday attendance at Mass. Catholicism is taught in most schools, other religions are not – it is not allowed. While most people profess to being Roman Catholic, their knowledge of and love and obedience to the teachings border on the negligible. This would lead us to believe that we should have a ready market for the Cause of Bahá'u'lláh. Not so. Those who are interested in the teachings – and there are many who are genuinely interested and agree with the teachings – find it difficult to face change, to be different, to face the criticism and scorn of family and friends. Why do people need another religion? We are happy being Catholic. To be a true Lithuanian one must be Catholic. Lithuania converted to Christianity in 1368 – at the sword of the Knights Templar. Then there are those wonderful souls who throw caution to the wind and willingly and lovingly accept the Cause of God; who face up to the scorn and censure, finding their strength in the prayers and writings. We do not have many but who we have are strong and sure. This small band (of course, we have a great many registered Bahá'ís whom we rarely, if ever, see) is involved with the training institute, projects, firesides, constant advertising of Bahá'í activities and serving on the various committees.

Our most recent task was to deliver and distribute the message 'To the World's Religious Leaders'. In my community, Kaunas, we had the bounty of delivering the letter to the Hassid Rabbi of Lithuania and the Roman Catholic

Archbishop. It was impossible to meet with the Archbishop; he was either on holiday – more weeks than we could count – or some other reason. We mailed the message to him but received no acknowledgement. Rabbi Lopianskis was a different matter. We had studied the message ourselves ensuring that we were well-versed should he ask us any questions; studied the information from the Bahá'í World Centre and prepared ourselves by saying prayers before the visit. We met with the rabbi at his workplace. He welcomed us, graciously received the message, asked us to join him for coffee – which we did – and spent a pleasant hour chatting with him about his life and the history of the Hassids in Lithuania. It was difficult for us to talk about the Bahá'í Faith because this man had a captive audience to whom he could talk to his heart's content. We took our leave, agreeing to invite each other to special occasions and celebrations. Our feet were a few centimetres off the ground when we left.

122
January 2003
Helen Cameron Rutstein
Albania

Helen with her husband Dale and three children have been overseas pio-neers for over 20 years – from Papua New Guinea to Pakistan – to the Bahá'í World Centre – and more recently – Albania.

In January we move again! This time from Albania to Manila in the Philippines, still with UNICEF. It is always exciting, wondering where in the world we will go next. My eldest son a few months ago came to us and said he felt he had missed out on not growing up in an American suburban neighbourhood like some of his cousins. We didn't know how to make him realize all that he'd gained. Then one day I asked him to sort out all his photos from babyhood till now. After a couple of hours he came to me and thanked us as parents for, in his words, giving him a *National Geographic* childhood. He had pictures of himself taking his first steps in a remote highlands village in Papua New Guinea where he spent his first seven years and where we left part of our hearts. Pictures of himself surrounded by Afghan refugees in a camp where we had gone for teaching when we lived for two years in Pakistan. Pictures of himself in Haifa where we spent three wonderful years and where we all left yet another part of our hearts. And Albania, pictures of a European country in transition, deeply wounded and yet so receptive to the Faith.

Working in the UN system has not enabled us to be long-term pioneers in one country and establish the kind of roots that are so important in teaching work but it has given us a frame of reference that is useful and a flexibility that we try to keep when we move to a new community. And we have learned never to say, 'In our last post, we . . .'!!!

123
January 2003
Karen and Tim Shrimpton
Bangladesh

Karen and Tim are now new pioneers in Dhaka, having previously been pioneers for four years in Uganda and before that for two years in the Philippines.

After four years in Uganda our contracts came to an end and we now find ourselves in Dhaka, Bangladesh. Tim and I are both teachers and Tim is teaching science in a very exciting school, which is only in its third year. It is owned by four wealthy businessmen in Bangladesh and has been set up as an IBO (International Baccalaureate Organization) school in English medium, mainly for Bangladeshi students. The school is managed by ECIS (European Council for International Schools) and the majority of the teachers have been recruited overseas. Our two youngest children, Jasmine and Kenneth (both in first grade), attend the school and are learning to play tabla, sing songs in Bangla and play cricket, among other things.

We had not been able to contact the Bahá'ís before our arrival in August, but having arrived, we were able to attend the 19 Day Feast of Asmá just days after arriving in the country. The first things that hit you are the crowds of people, the heat and humidity and the colourful bicycle rickshaws (hundreds of them). The script is totally unrecognizable and relatively few people understand English. The people are lovely and smiley and the Bahá'ís made us feel completely welcome. The Feast was very interesting as it was conducted almost entirely in Bangla (with a few bits of translation especially for us). They are already a 'B' community and are aiming to have 'A' status by Riḍván. There are 18 study circles presently being conducted throughout the city and 28 people have pledged to host regular devotional meetings. One gentleman used the analogy of 'Blessed is the Spot'. He said that every spot where mention of God has been made is blessed, so let's create hundreds of these spots throughout Dhaka. It was a very simple but beautiful idea.

After just three weeks we got news that our dear friend Forough Olinga would be visiting for a few days. Luckily we had settled in enough to be able to take her around and visit some of the sights of Dhaka. The last night she was here was the 19 Day Feast of 'Izzat (Might) and she was very touched by the Bahá'í community here. She made lots of notes to take back to Kampala as suggestions for the Local Spiritual Assembly there. One of the ideas implemented here which I have never seen anywhere else is that a huge fund box (about the size of a pillar box) is wheeled out immediately after devotions and contributions are made then and there. It is beautifully made out of wood with beautiful lettering FUND BOX – LIFE BLOOD (in English, interestingly). By the end of the consultation the amount of contributions received is announced. In some ways, things are done very traditionally here, with everyone sitting in rows and the speaker at the front with a microphone and podium, but in other ways they are very advanced with the institute programme and all the committees in place. Unfortunately, the Bahá'í Centre is located near downtown and the volume of traffic can make it very difficult for us to get there. Also, owing to the troubled situation of the world, there have been almost weekly anti-American/Israeli demonstrations in the downtown area and we have been advised not to travel far from our homes on these days. Thankfully, we have discovered another Bahá'í family who lives not too far from us and we have taken it in turns to host the last couple of 19 Day Feasts in our homes. We are also holding children's classes in English. Although it means that we don't see so much of the greater Bangladeshi community, our children are gaining a stronger Bahá'í identity.

The food is exquisite here and for vegetarians the choices are plentiful. It is also very interesting for us as Bahá'ís because of the restrictions on alcohol. Alcohol can only be served in private homes or clubs and cannot be purchased easily. Therefore restaurants have huge selections of 'mocktails' (non-alcoholic cocktails) and we have been able to indulge in virgin pina coladas, banana daiquiris and hundreds of new names I can't remember. Although there are many challenges here, I think our time in Bangladesh will be very positive.

124
January 2003
Janet Fleming
Faroe Islands

Janet (from Surrey) spent a week travel teaching in the Faroe Islands in September.

Towering cliffs, vivid green hillsides and tumbling waterfalls, little black wooden houses with turf roofs, the evocative call of geese flying over the house and a school of dolphins swimming and leaping ahead of the ferry to Vagar Island – these are some of my memories of the Faroe Islands.

Having lived for several years in island communities in various parts of the world, I had felt drawn for some time towards travel teaching in the Faroes. So when the opportunity arose last September I was keen to travel there and share my experiences of island life with the pioneers while at the same time, I hoped, teaching the Faith to any waiting souls that I might meet.

I went to the Faroes for one week, flying there from Aberdeen, and spent the first five days in the capital, Torshavn, where I stayed in a comfortable and homey guesthouse. Many people speak English in the Faroes, especially young people, and Danish is also widely spoken. The proprietor of the guesthouse, however, hardly spoke any English at all, so we communicated in pidgin Danish. Most Faroese people are Lutherans and about 20 per cent of the rest belong to sects such as the Plymouth Brethren, Jehovah's Witnesses and Seventh Day Adventists. Torshavn has an abundance of churches, including several evangelical missions.

I had a warm welcome from the Bahá'ís in Torshavn, most of whom are pioneers, and spent my time exploring the picturesque narrow streets perched on the hillside overlooking the sea. There are two museums and several small but interesting art galleries, and I visited these in the hope of finding someone to chat to about the Faith. As I'm a librarian by profession I visited the public library and talked with one of the staff about the possibility of adding Bahá'í books to their stock. I also went to the National Library where I had a long and friendly talk with one of the librarians about libraries in various parts of the world and was able to present a copy of the book *Visions of a New World Order* to the National Library. This beautiful book has recent photos of the buildings on the Arc including the Seat of the Universal House of Justice and the Centre for the Study of the Texts which now houses the Bahá'í World Centre Library. My Faroese colleague was suitably impressed and full of admiration for the elegant classical style of the buildings.

One day I walked out to the cemetery on the outskirts of Torshavn and visited the grave of Eskil Ljungberg, Knight of Bahá'u'lláh for the Faroe Islands. Torshavn is small enough to make walking around it a comfortable option but there are frequent buses and also taxis. The weather in the Faroes changes constantly and you can start out on a walk in bright sunshine only to find that heavy rain has set in – in which case it's comforting to know that you're on a bus route.

Torshavn has a fine, modern Bahá'í Centre and I was invited to give a fireside there as part of the regular Tuesday evening open house programme. We started the evening with prayers and at eight o'clock, in answer to our prayers, one Faroese lady, one Dutchman and an Icelandic lady with her six year old daughter arrived for the fireside. Two young Bahá'ís came from Runavik (a journey of an hour and a half) to swell the numbers. As these young men were half Swedish, half Greenlandish they complemented my theme of unity in diversity very nicely.

My presentation lasted about an hour. I talked about how I had become a Bahá'í in Fiji, talked about the Fiji Islands and the unity of races and religions that I had experienced there and showed slides of Fiji to illustrate my theme. The talk was well received with lots of audience participation. After extensive refreshments I finished by showing some slides of the Bahá'í holy places in Haifa, Bahjí and 'Akká.

The next day I left Torshavn and travelled by bus to Toftir where Sue and Roy Philbrow, long-time pioneers in the Faroes, have made their home. Toftir is on the next island and I was able to enjoy the beautiful fjord scenery and many spectacular waterfalls as the bus followed the coast road, went through a long tunnel through the mountain and crossed to the island of Eysturoy via the 'Bridge over the Atlantic', which connects the two islands.

At Sue and Roy's home I met up again with their daughter Sóley and we were able to exchange memories of our service together at the Bahá'í World Centre. That evening there was a gathering of the Bahá'í pioneers and their friends at the Philbrows' home. I was invited to give a very informal talk and spoke for about an hour about my two years in the Maldive Islands. I felt this would be of some interest to the Faroes pioneers because the Bahá'í community in the Maldives is very isolated and cannot teach because it's a Muslim country. I also mentioned going to India from the Maldives for the dedication of the House of Worship in Delhi in 1986.

The following day I left Toftir for the airport on Vagar Island. The journey to the airport involved taking four buses and a ferry and I was most impressed by the efficiency of the transport system. Whenever I had to change buses, which seemed invariably to be in the middle of nowhere, the next bus that I needed would appear over the horizon just at the desired moment and we would rendezvous successfully in the midst of the moors.

I thoroughly enjoyed my trip to the Faroes and felt blessed with divine assistance throughout. It has its own unique culture and is not so very far away from the shores of the United Kingdom and therefore relatively easy to go and assist with the spread of the Faith of Bahá'u'lláh there.

125
January 2003
Michael and Mahin McCandless
French Guiana

Michael and Mahin pioneered to French Guiana one year ago from Hastings.

Our pioneering adventure started in the spring of 2001 when Mahin's brother-in-law in France called to say there was a notice in *Objective*, a French Bahá'í publication, that might be of interest to us. An American Bahá'í pioneer family in Kourou, French Guiana, needed to return to the US and was offering to turn over the family business, The English Institute, at no cost to a Bahá'í pioneer family that could replace them at their post. Mahin immediately felt it was the right move for us and called French Guiana for additional information. It took me a little longer to reach the same conclusion but the next morning I staggered sleepily into the lounge of our maisonette in Hastings and found myself looking at all the stuff there and asking myself, 'Do we ship it or sell it?' The die was cast.

Lots of emails later and six weeks after paying more than £8,000 for a knee replacement operation that I should have been able to get for free under the National Health Service, we made an exploratory visit in late October to Kourou, best known for its proximity to Devil's Island and as Europe's spaceport. The Institute checked out OK, we met a number of the Bahá'ís and we felt confirmed in our decision to pioneer to Kourou. It was rather sobering to realize that many small Bahá'í communities in the United Kingdom have as many people with some degree of administrative experience as exist in the entire Bahá'í community of French Guiana (about 15 Local Spiritual Assemblies at the time).

In late January 2002 we arrived in Kourou – just in time for the grand opening of the new McDonald's in Kourou (only the second in French Guiana). We expected to have a three month overlap to properly prepare ourselves for teaching the classes, handling all the administrative details, etc., but the family's 15 year old son was having health problems that defied all efforts of various specialists here to treat him. So in early March the whole family headed back to the United States. The next couple of weeks were, uh, memorable, but we survived and learned what we needed to know much more quickly than otherwise would have been the case. Such are the benefits of the 'sink or swim' approach to training.

We had hoped to gradually get involved in Bahá'í activities but then we made the 'mistake' of attending the National Convention and suddenly

Mahin found herself elected to the National Assembly. Shortly thereafter, the Assembly elected her as the new secretary. So much for settling in gradually.

In a rather bizarre turn of fate, I was elected president of our Local Assembly even though I don't understand any of the languages used during our consultations. I can express myself tolerably well in French, so I manage to introduce a topic and then the local friends talk it over in Taki Taki or Saramaca. (They're all from Surinam, where the Faith has spread much more quickly than in French Guiana, which has a much higher standard of living since it's a *department* of France, and many come, legally or otherwise, as economic migrants.) Then they tell Mahin and me in French what they've decided. It actually works pretty well that way but recently it's been difficult to get a quorum together for meetings. Mahin currently offers a French literacy class for several of the local friends, including two members of the National Assembly, but it's proving to be a considerable challenge to get a programme of children's classes, study circles, prayer meetings and teaching activities up and running. At least our personal efforts to make friendly contact with the Amerindian community are off to a good start and we have become friends with an elderly and apparently well-respected man here in Kourou.

A recent two-weekend study course for Ruhi book 2 was a big success, with more than 20 people taking part from all the main Bahá'í communities. There was a wonderful sense of friendship and unity, which bodes well for our future efforts to reach all strata of society here.

We've definitely had more than our share of blessings since coming here, many of which have been artfully disguised as 'opportunities for spiritual growth' and as lessons in coping with life during times of insecurity.

126
January 2003
Karen Jamshidi
Mariana Islands

A year ago Karen Jamshidi from Northern Ireland was occupied doing youth service in the Mariana Islands (North Pacific). With Karen's permission the following is something she wrote for Communiqué (the Northern Ireland Bahá'í newsletter).

Last year I went through the most amazing experience of my life. I went to assist in the Brilliant Star Montessori school on the island of Saipan, Marianna Islands, with Lucie Hanrahan from the south of Ireland. Little did we know that it would be such a nourishing and life-changing time. Before I went on my year of service I never really spent much time thinking about prayer or the power that it held. To be honest, I never really thought about anything more than my A levels or what I was doing at the weekends!

Don't get me wrong. I prayed, and did so with faith, but my journey to the other side of the planet really opened my eyes to the full potential of prayer and spirituality as a whole. At the moment I'm at university in Edinburgh at Queen Margaret University College and I am having the time of my life but the one thing I think of every morning when I get up is the life that I lived a year ago. People would say to me before I left, 'You will be sent so many tests when you are on your year away and you will receive so many blessings!' – so I shouldn't really have been surprised when I was confronted with what I thought were insurmountable tests and difficulties. At night I would sit in my room and nearly go mad over some of the things that I came up against and the only place I could turn to was my prayer book and Bahá'u'lláh. It's hard to explain and I really think you have to experience it to really appreciate the true power and wonder of it all. But, literally, the next day the problem would have in some way been eased or have simply disappeared. This automatically brought me closer to God and Bahá'u'lláh. Even if I had resisted I would have eventually realized that Bahá'u'lláh is looking out for me and when there is no one else, He is there. It's such a comforting thought and that thought stayed with me throughout my year of service and has now made me a stronger more independent individual.

127
April 2003
Robin Bell
Marshall Islands:
Neither here nor there

Robin spent three years as a pioneer in the Marshall Islands and has only recently returned to live in the UK. I asked him to share his feelings, having left his pioneer post – all I can say is that almost every returning pioneer will know what Robin is going through.

I felt a strong sense of anticipation as I left the chemists in Wetherby with my newly-developed photos encased in their colourful packets. The package contained the last two films that chronicled my three-year period of service in the Marshall Islands. Up to that point, my departure from the Pacific and my arrival back in England had been a relatively smooth and exciting process. Yes, I was sad to leave but I was cheered by the thought of seeing my parents, my friends in the Manchester communities and my growing nieces and nephew, who had existed only via digital photos on email. I knew that doctors and nurses would figure at some stage – because of a rather inconvenient, minor medical condition that had precipitated my return – but, largely, my feelings were positive. The Báb's advice contained in the *Dawn-Breakers* was also uppermost in my mind in that on departing we should merely 'shake the dust from off your feet'.[25]

So, I opened the packets of photos. Pictorially they began with the Fire in the Pacific conference held in Hawaii which celebrated one hundred years of the Faith in the Pacific region. The conference started with a march from the resting places of Hands of the Cause Martha Root and Agnes Alexander to the conference centre. Colourful photos followed including those showing the national costumes of Yap, the Solomon Islands and Tonga. I'm sure there were more. On stage the Marshallese dancers, in their ocean blue dresses, performed a traditional mat dance. The photos prompted other memories: the endearing liveliness of the French Polynesians, the dignity of the Solomon Islanders, quiet moments at the resting place of Martha Root, Falai-Riva Taafaki (pioneer in the Marshall Islands) addressing the conference, too many mosquito bites at the National Centre and the sheer number of friends gathered in this geographic paradise.

The conference was followed by the Ocean of Light teaching project. For me, this was such a joyous occasion and my first travel teaching experience! Gary Sterling's beaming face recalled his wonderful music and humour; the smile of Chris Cholas, surely disguising logistical complexities; pacing the streets of Honolulu with our invitations; the haunting sound of indigenous North Americans at one of the teaching events; the camaraderie of friends staying at the National Centre; a public picnic on Ala Moana beach.

Thousands of miles of air travel became contained in a turn of a photograph and I was back in the Marshall Islands. Familiar faces attending Ruhi training, youth gathering around Betra Majmeto – the first Marshallese Bahá'í – Karen Olin Parrish facilitating teacher training for children's classes, the children of Arno atoll, the Rairok youth group singing at the national youth conference. The colourful clothes, the perpetual sunshine, the coconut palms and deep blue Pacific conveyed the physical warmth. The smiling faces, the spiritual warmth.

The photographs hinted at other activities: the dissemination of the Message to the World's Religious Leaders, Local Assembly meetings, a busy National Convention, Sunday devotions, a little stream of declaration cards, cluster gatherings, training institute board meetings, my sense of tranquillity when the National Assembly was in session, the never-ending challenge to obtain adequate contributions to the national fund and the production of a weekly radio show which aired every Sunday on the national radio station.

The theme of the photographs soon changed and it was time for goodbyes: friends enjoying the pot-luck dinner at the Outrigger Hotel, me being decorated with leis (Polynesian garlands of flowers worn round the neck) and traditional handicrafts, a bowl full of dollars, Helly and Jabjen in mischievous mode – maximizing my embarrassment, so many hugs; and a final airport farewell.

The photos have since been viewed by my family and the friends attending the 19 Day Feasts in Manchester and Leeds. They are carefully contained in a sky-coloured album that would happily suit fellow Manchester City fans. From time to time, between the job hunting, the hospital appointments, the cold country walks and the coming to unfamiliar terms of being an isolated believer, I take a quick look.

There's one photo especially that I find myself gazing at. It's one of the goodbyes. I guess it epitomizes how I now feel after the excitement of seeing friends and loved ones in the United Kingdom has subsided. I'm embracing one of the Marshallese friends – a devoted and enthusiastic Bahá'í and one who has recently suffered many tests and challenges. The way Irene Taafaki (UK pioneer to the Marshall Islands) took the photograph suggests I'm holding on for dear life. It's as if this friend that I'm clinging to represents the whole Marshall Islands community. It's difficult to let go.

The photo seems to convey the deep love and affection I feel for the friends out there. My time in the islands, as I expected, was full of tests and challenges, but the biggest of all is the one I'm experiencing now. It creeps up on you. I miss the friends so much. I miss the closeness to the administrative order. I miss missing England.

I know that all these feelings are familiar for returning pioneers. The International Pioneering Committee's guidance on this subject is a great help. My friend Chris in Hawaii says that he used to dream of his pioneer post. Maybe I do too.

I return to the words of the Báb that used to hang on the wall of my Majuro apartment. I'm still shaking off the dust . . .

128
July 2003
Eric Hellicar
Cyprus

Eric and Margaret and their first three children arrived in Nicosia on 18 December 1969 (some 35½ years ago)! Eric wrote immediately after the exciting events which signalized the coming together of north and south Cyprus on 21 April.

You should have been in Cyprus at Riḍván! It was the best place to be as suddenly the rigid division that has hurt our island and made Baháʼí community life so difficult for the past 29 years began to crumble. To be here was one of the unexpected blessings of pioneering. How well I remember the misery when after five years of pioneering and somehow seeing the first Local Spiritual Assembly of Nicosia re-established, we were shattered by the division of the island and a number of pioneers having to leave. That was 1974. Then we learned to live with it and concentrate on 'spiritual unity'! The greatest moment was when I watched Greek and Turkish Cypriot Baháʼís praying together in the shrines but now another day rivals that, no, it completes that picture. Those four were in my house praying together in a Feast, something unbelievable just four days before! In July we celebrate 25 years of our National Spiritual Assembly (and independence from our mother National Spiritual Assembly of the United Kingdom) and 50 years since the arrival of the Knights of Baháʼuʼlláh in 1953. This is really a blessed year and as I write Greek Cypriots are visiting Turkish Cypriot Baháʼí homes for the first time ever! The celebrations have begun!

The Baháʼís of Cyprus were hoping for something special this year but we could not have dreamt of a more joyous gift! On Sunday 27 April, on the seventh day of Riḍván (and Easter Sunday for the Orthodox in Cyprus), a group of 41 Baháʼís and friends came from the north across the newly opened 'Green Line' and went to the Baháʼí Centre, where we had the most uplifting prayers and messages. Fourteen Baháʼís from the Nicosia area (and four visitors from France) greeted them and provided the first of the day's many refreshments. The Turkish Cypriot Baháʼís had never been to the Baháʼí Centre before, nor to the three homes they then visited during our bus trip. It was all the more delightful because the week before the Nicosia cluster meeting had met to celebrate the completion of the redecorating and renovating of the Centre. We climbed onto the roof and stared across the once impenetrable line. Later we heard that over thirty thousand Cypriots (twenty thousand Greek Cypriots and ten thousand Turkish Cypriots) had crossed over on that precious day (and seventy thousand expected to cross the next day)! And not one unpleasant incident was reported, while there were hundreds of stories of real joy and sincere hospitality. This was not a protest but one of those world-shaking peaceful expressions of 'people power' by ordinary people who crushed under their feet the walls of superstition and fear that have held them apart for 29 years or more. They are demonstrating, without banners or slogans, how powerful their longing to live together in peace is! More powerful than all the well-meaning but so far unsuccessful plans and negotiations of the United Nations and so many politicians and nations.

In our prayers we praised God in Greek, in Turkish and other languages. We celebrated this evidence of the power of God's Major Plan that will break down every barrier. We felt the momentum of the Lesser Peace. We just loved being together. Special gifts (framed photos of the four Knights of Bahá'u'lláh arriving 50 years before) were given to the Centre from the friends in the north. The Board member, Eren Orac, spoke of the significance of this historic day; Antonia Antoniou welcomed the Turkish Cypriots on behalf of all the Greek Cypriots; and messages were read from Counsellors and members of the Universal House of Justice and the International Teaching Centre. It was a truly spiritual gathering of love, unity and fellowship.

The hired bus then took the group, with some 'southern' friends squeezed in and others following in a car, to Limassol where we all had a marvellous lunch (for 56) at the home of Lesley and Ramin Habibi. Then, after more prayers and photos, we toured Limassol, invaded the first shop we found open on Easter Day and filled the garden of Marion and Takis Pnevmatikou with our excitement, more prayers and Turkish, Greek and Bahá'í songs. Marion had had 25 guests for lunch who had stayed on to serve us with more refreshments. Children shouted joyfully in Greek, Turkish, English and Dutch as they played football and everyone felt a winner that day. Then we drove on to the home of Margaret and Eric Hellicar in Pera Oreinis – though the bus proved it was just too big to get to the village centre – and after another meal we held the Feast of Jamál (Beauty), which many felt was just the right name for this day. One of the Turkish Cypriot families had come from the nearby village (Arediou) and Maria, a Greek Cypriot Bahá'í who had come after their family celebrations to join the friends, took them there. There they found the granddaughter of the woman who had been their loving neighbour over 40 years ago – who turned out to be a relative of Maria!

We ask Bahá'ís throughout the world to give prayers of thanks and to pray that we may be guided to use the wonderful opportunities now before us wisely and powerfully. At present we are too stunned to take it all in but the experience of the Bahá'ís finally meeting together physically to express the spiritual unity they have maintained through all these years of division is something we will savour forever.

Before, Greek Cypriot and Turkish Bahá'ís had only been able to meet together on a very few occasions at the Ledra Palace on the Green Line and in other countries. The members of the National Assembly had therefore been longing to go to the International Convention in Haifa so that Turkish Cypriot and Greek Cypriot members could meet together for the first time in many years. The cancellation of the Convention, which had at first brought disappointment, now meant that they were still here in Cyprus and able to meet each other and take part in this amazing day's events. Moreover all Bahá'ís in Cyprus should now be able to attend the National Convention for the first time ever after 25 years of the National Assembly. Twice the Convention was held in the Ledra Palace but even then some friends were not permitted to attend – now all can go to the Centre in the north and all but a few (the pioneers from Turkey) are able to come to the south. Now Turkish Cypriot Bahá'ís will be able to come to the summer school in Limassol. Many opportunities are now opened up for teaching and community development. It is truly a wonderful time to be a Bahá'í in Cyprus and we send our special love to those pioneers who were not able to be with us on this historic day.

129
July 2003
Lois Lambert
Mongolia

Lois wrote the following at the end of March before the Bahá'ís in Mongolia knew that International Convention was definitely cancelled.

We had a National Spiritual Assembly meeting at the weekend. It is always a pleasure attending National Assembly meetings but this one was really special. The International Convention had not, at the time, been cancelled, but the Universal House of Justice had asked all National Assembly members to vote and to send their votes no later than 18 April in case the world situation made it impossible to hold the International Convention. So we voted at this weekend's meeting. We wanted to mark it as a very precious occasion, so we set up a special table with flowers and arranged the seats in a half circle. All the National Spiritual Assembly members wore national costume and we sat in alphabetical order. The Counsellor and our four Auxiliary Board members, who were consulting with us that day, sat together to the left of the ballot box, and the young people who worked in the national office joined us. We began with prayers and the Counsellor spoke to us for a few minutes. Then the Board members read prayers and we voted, taking a long time over it. When everyone had finished, each member went up to the ballot box and touched the ballot to their forehead as a mark of respect and reverence before putting it in the box. Then we shared a happy feast of fruit and juice that the office staff had spontaneously arranged for us and ended by taking pictures. It was a really moving and beautiful occasion.

In the end we were unable to go to the International Convention but we felt that we had nevertheless experienced something of the profound spiritual significance of the election of the Universal House of Justice. Our consultations during the day were so inspiring, both before and after the voting. It really is a lovely National Spiritual Assembly. We are so fortunate to be given the privilege of serving on it.

130
July 2003
Mahin Humphrey
Fiji

Mahin is always on the move somewhere – to the benefit of isolated Bahá'ís scattered around the world. She visited Fiji with Sylvia Girling who, until a couple of years ago, was a UK pioneer in both Poland and Slovakia.

When I attended the Fire in the Pacific Conference in Hawaii in December 2001 there were many friends there from the Pacific. I was invited to visit their islands but I had no idea at the time that I would have the chance to visit Fiji a year or so later. The Australian National Travel Teaching Committee invited me to visit Fiji for a month or more, so with my friend Sylvia Girling – already in Australia – we flew from Sydney to Suva, the capital of Fiji (a five hour flight).

We were invited to stay with a pioneer family in Suva for two days and also to consult with the National Spiritual Assembly and National Teaching Committee. We were asked to visit Levuka on the island of Ovalau which was once the (British) capital of Fiji. It used to be a port with one street full of pubs! Now they have a fish canning factory where most of the local population work. We were asked to visit the Bahá'ís and schools and, if possible, to study Ruhi book 1.

We enjoyed our first two days in Suva with friends at the Ayyám-i-Há party where everyone danced and sang and where there were lots of children. We took a small plane to Levuka where we were met by three friends. We slept in dormitory accommodation of the only hotel (British-owned) there. We had the use of a kitchen and could cook for ourselves and boil our drinking water. The heat and humidity were intense so we bought two big umbrellas to protect ourselves from the sun and carried cool flannels to wipe away our perspiration.

The population were mostly Fijian and Indian. In general, Indians owned the shops and businesses and the Fijians were mostly small farmers and factory workers. We met a group of Bahá'í friends and asked them what they would like us to do in order to help with the teaching. One couple wanted to study the Ruhi book in one of the villages. Sylvia helped with that while I concentrated on meeting the Bahá'ís and their friends in different locations. We walked just about everywhere, only occasionally taking a taxi, though once we had a ride in a police van!

We visited schools, colleges and churches and made many friends. After a week almost everyone in Levuka knew us and called us by name. The advantage of having dormitory accommodation was that we were able to meet lots of travellers, mostly youth who were taking a year off from study and work to travel around the world. Levuka is not a holiday island; it has no beaches so people usually stay only a night or two in order to go diving. They were surprised when we said we were staying four weeks, so we had lots of opportunities to tell them why we were there on the island.

We met four ladies from the capital who were well up in the field of education and who were staying in the dormitories with us. They were there to run several courses for all the women from the villages around the island – teaching them flower arranging, child care, cookery, agriculture and other skills. They became our friends and we were invited to join them and get to know the village people, all of whom speak good English

One day when we were visiting a family in the distant village, Napoleon (that was his name) asked us to pay our respects to the chief of the village. The chief was an old man and was sitting on a throne like a king. It was an honour for us and we were served with delicious fresh coconut juice. Afterwards we had to walk all the way back in the heat but it was worth it. Our dorms had a surrounding garden in which were oranges, lemons and avocados (as big as melons) and there was also a swimming pool. Sylvia and I, both early risers, would be seated by the pool at 6:00 a.m. for prayers and meditation. It was the best time of the day as it was so hot. One day we took a dilapidated small boat to another island to swim in the sea and that was a real adventure for us. The only family living there provided us with a delicious lunch of fresh fish cooked in coconut milk with local vegetables.

When we left Fiji we felt sad to leave our beautiful friends who had all gathered to say goodbye. They pleaded with us to come back some time and to tell other Bahá'í friends to come and visit the islands.

131
July 2003
Simin and Bruce Liggitt
Zambia

Simin and Bruce pioneered to Zambia in 1996 with a year's leave back in the UK (2000–1). Once again they are leaving a country that they love and, with their young daughter Tajalli, are on their way back to England.

We left Zambia on 9th April after a stay of 19 months. This was our second turn of pioneering in Zambia. Already we miss the very special people we have left behind and feel very privileged to have been part of that special community once again. We miss the singing at the meetings and all the happy and joyful faces.

This time in Zambia we were based 400 km north of Banani International School. The first 15 months we lived in a lovely small town called Chililabombwe (the town of the croaking frogs!) which is close to the border with Congo. The Bahá'í community was made up of two jewels, two of the most devoted and deep Zambian Bahá'ís we had ever met and had the privilege of being with. We would meet three days a week and were most uplifted by these gatherings. Gradually, some of the inactive Bahá'ís came to meetings and we had two declarations and so our numbers grew. We then moved to a neighbouring town called Chingola where Bruce was transferred for his work. Here there was an excellent children's class. The teacher of the ten children was the mother of six of them and she was dedicated to bringing up her children as strong Bahá'ís.

We were fortunate to be in Zambia when Mr and Mrs Nakhjavani visited Banani International School on their African trip. The school was named after Mrs Nakhjavani's father, the Hand of the Cause Mr Musa Banani, so their visit was especially significant. We were also very lucky to be able to participate in the fiftieth anniversary celebrations of the coming of the Faith to Zambia. The conference was held at the Banani International School and many old-time pioneers had come to join the celebrations. Looking at the glorious history of the Zambian community we felt very honoured to have become a very small, tiny part of it.

When we were back in the United Kingdom in the year 2000 and had suddenly been given the opportunity to return to Zambia (out of the blue), we thought that it was all too good to be true and that we must be prepared to face many tests! It was not possible that it would be just SO easy!!! Well, we were right as we experienced some of the most trying times of our life but we learned a lot from these experiences. Bruce's job, though most interesting and enjoyable, became difficult and challenging. Also I had a security test and became a recluse for a while but eventually I managed to pull through.

Tajalli and I were able to spend a lot of time with the expatriate community. Tajalli had lots of company and enjoyed the warm climate again and became a very good swimmer during this period. I joined art classes and fitness groups, making friends with lots of the expatriate ladies. The very last week that we were in Zambia, at the ex-pat ladies' monthly meeting, I was asked to speak about the Faith. It was the best teaching experience of my life. There were about 20 ladies present and it was interesting to see that though I had got to know them quite well over the months, they had not shown much interest in the Faith until a formal talk was given! As I knew we were leaving I decided to just go full-force and tell them everything! We went through the principles, teachings, laws, personal development, progressive revelation, the writings and administration and ended with the life of Bahá'u'lláh and Edward G. Browne's account of his meeting with Bahá'u'lláh – all in one talk! There were endless questions and the literature I had with me was all taken or bought up and some orders taken for more. So we really ended our time on a high note and feel so lucky to have had the opportunity to teach in this way.

132
October 2003
Helen Smith
Lithuania

Helen left Guernsey in 1989 to pioneer in Lithuania.

The Training Institute Board in Lithuania organized a five-day youth summer camp for the middle of July – fairly sure of good weather. This was our first youth camp so we were not sure how it would work out. We need not have worried – it was a magic camp.

One of our main concerns was cost. It had to be cheap so the youngsters would be able to afford it. The Training Institute Board covered part of the expenses, so keeping down the cost to the youth to a price they could afford.

This meant that everything – food, travel, venue, even band-aids and insect repellent, etc. – had to be finely budgeted.

Our venue was a converted watermill – lovely grounds, basic kitchen, garden toilets and beds so close together it was not possible to put a penny piece between them. However, there was a lake close by and with temperatures in the high 90s this was just perfect for keeping everyone happy. Having the beds so close together wasn't really a problem because the heat and the incessant bombardment by armies of mosquitoes drove everyone outside to sleep in their sleeping bags in the garden. We bought hundreds of insecticide candles so everyone could surround themselves with lighted candles in an effort to ward off the mosquitoes. After dark, when everyone was in their sleeping bags surrounded by lighted candles and lying all over the garden, the place looked like a cemetery on November 1st. The food was simple but lots of it, and provided there was plenty of bread, jam, ketchup and mayonnaise to ward off midnight starvation, the youth were happy.

The ground rules were made by the youth themselves. Each morning there was consultation and the misdemeanours (some of them) of the previous day were discussed and dealt with. Sure, we had some problems but the youth consulted, decided and put right the wrongs. Work details were organized on a volunteer basis, each one signing up for a particular task each day. I might add that the kitchen was cleaner when we left than when we arrived.

The study programme was, I think, a bit too much. With hindsight we should have had less study and more swimming and dancing and games. But the youth didn't complain. They entered into the programme with topics such as 'Role of the Youth', 'Relationship with the Institutions', 'Modernity' (sounded less severe than 'A Chaste and Holy Life', and into this topic we could include relationship with parents), 'Systematic Planning', 'Prayer and Meditation', 'Vision' and 'Consultation'. The consultation programme was deliberately at the end of the camp so that by the time we came to study it we had some hands-on experience of the subject. The programme really was too intensive but it seemed the only people who were in any way worried about this were the two organizers. The youth took all of this in their stride and considering that 90 per cent of them were non-Bahá'ís, we were more than happy. On the last day, amidst the weeping and wailing of 'Why can't we stay for another two days', we decided that this had been a magic camp and we would need to keep it as a regular event – but not for ten days as the youth wanted.

No, we did not have youth wanting to register as Bahá'ís; this was not the purpose of the camp. But after the first couple of days they were looking for prayer books at morning devotionals and joined in with prayers. Later, some of them took part in a three-day teaching project and most of them have stayed firm friends with each other, Bahá'í and non-Bahá'í. They are already looking forward to next year's camp. I hope the organizers have recovered enough by then to organize it.

133

October 2003

Thelma Batchelor

Back to Kathmandu via the Delhi Temple

Nepal for my family is home. Despite the health hazards at the time when we were pioneering for eight and a half years from 1976 to 1985, they were wonderful years. Our children were young then. Such years don't come again. They were years full of privileges, being Bahá'ís in a beautiful country with happy, cheerful Nepalese people – surrounded by the Himalayas as a backdrop to the Kathmandu Valley.

Eight years ago Ron and I returned to our pioneering post for our twenty-fifth wedding anniversary. Not much had changed. Our Bahá'í friends were still there and we enjoyed five weeks in their company.

On 14 September 2003 I flew out to Kathmandu again but this time with my daughter Suzanne, about to embark on a year's travels around the world starting in Delhi on 1 October. She wanted very much to recapture her childhood memories of growing up in Nepal and suggested that we return together to Kathmandu. That suited me! My only anxiety was that my 92 year old mother was in very poor health.

However, we flew out via Delhi so that we could visit the beautiful Lotus Temple. Amidst the chaos and confusion of the traffic there, and amidst the dust of India, suddenly we saw it. The Temple looked small from the road but once we started walking along the path towards it, we realized how large it was and how magnificent. Outside the sky was overcast and the air sultry and humid. Inside we felt cool and refreshed and looked in amazement at the simplicity and beauty of the Mother Temple of the sub-continent. We sat and reflected and prayed. It was later I learned that it was at this very time that my mother passed away.

As we came out of the Temple and walked between the pools of water, coloured turquoise from the brightening reflection of the sky turned blue, we marvelled at the steady stream of people, almost all Indian, who thronged the path leading to and from the House of Worship. Ten thousand visitors each day and thirty thousand at weekends. We had seen the Temple during the early stages of its construction some 20 years earlier and were reminded of Charles Macdonald who used to oversee the building work at the time. It was very different then. Since its completion in 1986 it has become one of the most frequently visited sites in the world. The new Bahá'í Information Centre, opened six months ago, is amazing. Seldom have I seen information displayed so well and colourfully anywhere in the world.

We flew up to Kathmandu two days later. The Himalayas, home of the gods, lay beneath us as we flew over the highest mountains in the world. We were met by Bahá'í friends and over the next two weeks we were feted and hosted by Bahá'í families whom we knew 20 years ago and for whom we are forever part of their extended family. Like so many other countries in the world, Nepal is no longer so safe and terrorism is becoming part of the day. In June 2001 the Royal Family of Nepal were assassinated. When we used to live there it was very safe, though in some respects like living in medieval times. It was hard to purchase a telephone. Now our friends are connected to the Internet, correspond by email and speak to their kids who live overseas by means of the webcam!

Those of you who have seen the video 'Building Momentum' will remember that Nepal is the last of the seven countries featured. Bahá'í-wise there is lots happening there now. When we used to live in Kathmandu we were just a handful of believers meeting in a very small Bahá'í Centre. Now a new Bahá'í Centre has been built, is big enough to house several meetings at once and hums with activities every weekend. A reception for us was held soon after we arrived. We met with many old and new Bahá'í friends and also some Nepalese year of service volunteers who were preparing to go out to different areas of the country for teaching purposes. There's so much more happening now.

Our love for Nepal and our Bahá'í friends continues to grow and strengthen. Pioneering for us was a privilege and a very special time in our lives and we cherish the times now that we can return to our pioneering post and be blessed by the love of our worldwide Bahá'í family.

134
October 2003
Sylvia Schulman Benatar
South Africa

Sylvia and her husband 'Sue' became Bahá'ís in 1955 in Southern Rhodesia. They moved to Cambridge in 1963 with their family and returned as pioneers to South Africa in 1977. Sylvia lives and works in Johannesburg.

We have a new National Bahá'í Centre here in Johannesburg! The deed of sale was signed on 12 September. It cost a great deal of money (although in terms of American dollars or English pounds, it is a snip) and the friends are coming forward with sacrificial contributions and pledges. The sellers have bent over backwards to make it as easy as possible for the Bahá'ís to have the place and have given us nearly five years to complete the structured payments without interest! The property itself is 22 acres with an administration block of offices, a prestigious reception–conference facility with dining room and professional kitchen, a large warehouse with partitioned off rooms suitable for office and archives area and a mezzanine storage area, staff quarters, book sales and storage area, maintenance workshop, large garden shed with equipment, an accommodation block with ten double bedrooms and en-suite bathrooms, professional laundry room, linen room, an entertainment building, a rondavel that can sleep eight people, a five bed-roomed farmhouse and one bed-roomed cottage, swimming pool, and four other houses on the site. In addition there is masses of parking space, beautifully laid-out gardens and plenty of unused space, some of which is suitable for a future House of Worship. The Universal House of Justice is in agreement with this move, which is likely to be a permanent one. Of course, we will have to continue to make sacrifices to keep up the payments and to cover the upkeep but the South African community is very excited about it.

A little story about this property. Just over two years ago the friends were asked to look out for suitable property for a new Bahá'í Centre. I decided it would be very good if it could be closer to where I was living (!) so I hunted around in my spare time, of which I don't have a lot, and found various places, including some huge properties. One, in particular, was very beautiful but would have needed a lot of converting to be useful. Then I was shown the property we have now agreed to buy. I fell in love with it straight away and took several other friends to see it, who agreed it would be wonderful for us, but as the owner was running a training centre for literacy there at the time, he wanted to sell it as a going concern and the price was out of our reach. But this property continued to haunt me and after two years of the National Assembly trying unsuccessfully to purchase various other properties, some with buildings and some without, I suggested we go back and see how 'my' property stood now. This time the circumstances had changed considerably. The owners were reluctant to sell to developers as the property had many trees and so many buildings and they didn't want to see it all destroyed. The original owner had built the place himself over ten years and had met Bahá'ís in Hawaii some years back who had impressed him greatly. He had been to Haifa and had seen the World Centre. Being a spiritually inclined person, he was very keen for us to buy the property. So after much negotiation, the price landed at about half the original amount of two years previously! I forgot to mention that the owner has even built a lovely little non-denominational chapel with stained glass windows at each end! It all goes to show that when the time and circumstances are right, the doors open and everything works out. All praise to Bahá'u'lláh for this wonderful gift!

135
January 2004
Judy Finlay
Marshall Islands

Judy (from the Isle of Skye in the northwest of Scotland) spent six months pioneering in the Marshall Islands.

The transition from Scottish island life to Pacific island life was fairly smooth. Already used to island life, it wasn't hard to take on board the change from cold to hot. The loving welcome and support given by the Bahá'ís here has been incredible. They are generous with their spirit, their knowledge, their homes – and not just for a few days. It is sustained throughout. An experience in Bahá'í life, in reality, that I am privileged to have.

The Five Year Plan has increased the feeling of familiarity that is there when you travel as a Bahá'í. The rhythm of 19 Day Feasts and holy days is expanded to take in study circles, devotional meetings and children's classes. We all speak one language.

The Marshallese are holding study circles with enormous enthusiasm, racing through the process and producing devotional meetings and children's classes as a result. In a compact community like this, the influence and impact the Bahá'ís have is plain to see. They are highly respected and looked to for advice by a wide range of people from government ministers to students. Frustrations and lessons are inevitable when you move out of your 'comfort zone'. But prayer and a sense of humour are the best defence and these abound in the Marshall Islands.

Some of the lessons: cockroaches don't bite, even when they land unexpectedly on you from their seat on the ceiling; bananas that are fresh from the tree and haven't travelled around the world have retained all their nutrients with devastating results when eaten in profusion; fishing is a serious business here, do not shriek when a barracuda is on the end of your line, it disappears; don't overreact when your Auxiliary Board member disappears out to sea after a fish during a holy day celebration.

All in all, this is a fantastic experience where I feel I am receiving all the bounties from the Concourse on High as well as this earth.

136
January 2004
Susan Kouchek-zadeh
Guinea-Conakry, West Africa

Susan and Shidan have been pioneers in West Africa since 1966 and in Conakry since 1975.

Here in Conakry the community is struggling to come to grips with an ever-changing situation. When we first came to Conakry in 1975 it was minute for a capital city and was a ghost town – what had been shops were all shuttered and the centre of town closed down by about 3:00 p.m.

From about 1980 onwards it began to grow – entirely without the benefit of any town planning – and is now several times the size in area and population. The centre of town is on the tip of a long thin peninsula that gradually widens inland. Whereas built-up areas used to stretch about 14 km inland from the town centre, now they go for nearly 50 km. Roads meanwhile remain about the same size, so you can imagine the congestion. Only the principal ones are tarred so all the others are winding rock and puddle-strewn lanes. Most people have a walk or bone-shattering drive of about a kilometre or more before reaching a main road where they may have to wait hours to get transport.

All this means that journeys that used to take ten minutes can now take anything up to an hour or more because of traffic jams – and that's if you possess your own means of transport. Our Bahá'í community, which is very varied in its composition – in race, age, education, literacy, language, depth of knowledge of the Faith, etc. – is scattered over this now large area and getting together for a meeting of any sort poses new problems. We have all the problems of the large city with few if any of the advantages. Are there any? And like everyone else we are struggling to establish study circles and devotional meetings.

Being on the National Spiritual Assembly ensures that one gets to enjoy the countryside as well – as our secretary found out. She tried to go to the National Assembly meeting overland and spent the night in the car bogged down in mud. The next morning the vehicle was hauled out of the mud and STILL she tried to battle on but by midday, still 200 km from her destination, realized they were not going to make it so headed back to Conakry which she reached at midnight and found herself locked out of her apartment so spent a second night in the car – this time in the garage!

I had opted for the plane, which has its own pleasures and excitements – gold and black lace curtains are the most recent improvements but at least one of the tires still had a great bald patch. You get on the plane at midday, by which time the interior is just short of bread baking temperature and the ventilation system is such that shortly before arrival (one and three quarter hours later) it has just cooled down to a reasonable level. Another improvement was that on arrival at N'zérékoré one was no longer allowed to wait in the shade of the wing and leap forward to claim their bag as it was dragged out of the hold. You had to go direct to the airport building and wait till the baggage arrived jammed into the back of a small van. The porters opened the door of the van and called out the numbers of the pieces of baggage one by one. This meant that all 50 passengers crowded around the back of the van in an effort to be close enough to hear their numbers – under the broiling sun of course! Mine were among the last and I gleefully shouted bingo when I heard my number!

I always feel pretty gleeful to be alive when I arrive at N'zérékoré airport. And very grateful to those wonderful Russian pilots. They are so subtle! The plane went up so very gradually that for the first 15 minutes I expected us to be about to circle and land again in Conakry. And it never did start to come down. Ninety minutes into the flight when I KNEW it should have started its descent I decided that the pilot was lost (it's always difficult for me to believe someone can do something that I can't – so it was quite easy to believe he couldn't find his way to N'zérékoré) and was wondering where we would be by the time we ran out of gas. Then I managed to convince myself that the trees were fractionally larger than they had been a while ago - we WERE imperceptibly on our way down.

The disadvantage of the plane is that one arrives in N'zérékoré without means of transport, bags to carry, and in my case being the treasurer, much cash secreted about my person, and have to find somewhere to stay and a means of getting to the village where we have a permanent institute and hold our meetings when in that area. Better than sleeping in the mud I have since decided.

The difficulties and the apparent slowness of the spread of the Faith always loom large in one's mind. So it's good to be reminded that 50 years ago there were no Bahá'ís in all of French West Africa, which was an enormous area comprising what are now Senegal, Guinea, Mali, Burkina Faso, Benin, Togo, the Ivory Coast, Niger, Tchad and Mauritania. The fiftieth anniversary of the Faith's arrival in French West Africa is being celebrated by a conference in Dakar from 26 to 28 December. For 35 of those years we have been associated with French West Africa because although we pioneered initially to

Sierra Leone, it was then under the jurisdiction of the National Spiritual Assembly of West Africa, which included Guinea, Senegal, Ivory Coast, Mali and Burkina Faso.

137

January 2004

Nichola Davis

India

Nichola (born in Madras to English parents in January 1947) returned to her roots last November after an absence of almost 50 years. Not having enjoyed her childhood years in India, she now finds India most challenging and rewarding.

In October I returned from a wonderful four weeks visiting Bahá'í institutions and development projects where I was useful and able to contribute. It was delightful to have to address, consult, pray and handle challenging issues.

Departing Chennai by overnight train on 18 October my plan was to spend a week in three locations: Panchgani at the New Era Foundation; Pune, participating in a youth workshop; and Indore at Barli, a development institute for rural women. Arriving at midnight in Pune (four hours by train southeast of Mumbai), I spent the night in a hotel before catching the bus that takes three hours to Panchgani the next day at noon. This is a small village high in the hills renowned for the 20 or so private schools located in its vicinity. New Era High School (NEHS) is probably the oldest, having started with a handful of students in 1945 and now has eight hundred co-eds with seven hundred boarding. I arrived just in time for the celebration of the Birth of the Báb, which took place in the outdoor amphitheatre with a stunning view of the valley and lake below.

I had wanted to spend time at the New Era Development Institute (NEDI) that offers one- and two-year programmes to rural youth who have completed 10th standard. Although vocational skills are taught along with English, many graduate as teachers but with a very different set of skills from the government-run teacher training colleges. They are in great demand and easily get jobs in schools, some as the principal or head of department in smaller schools. Of those that return to their villages, many start rural schools. The future emphasis of NEDI will be teacher training and administration with ongoing support for starting rural schools. Only 50 per cent of children in India complete eight years of school and many never get to attend, especially in the rural areas.

It was wonderful being back in an environment where meetings start with a prayer and there was a separate prayer room open all day. Less than half the students and staff are Bahá'ís. Ramadan started while I was visiting and special arrangements were made for the Muslim students. There is a Muslim school in Panchgani, and we were invited to attend their English theatre performance, but regrettably we did not have the time. Although I was kept very busy with only one sightseeing excursion to a village consisting of less than ten huts, I had lots of fun.

I showed my Mongolia video to many students and teachers. About one hundred students in standard 10 and above were studying child rights, so I was asked to speak about child abuse for one hour. Quite a challenge and rather worrying, as you never know who in the audience has been a victim of abuse.

After promising to try and return as a volunteer early in 2004, I finally caught the overnight train to Indore (north east of Mumbai, in central India and south of Delhi) where Janak McGilligan met me. Janak is an amazing individual who in 1985 established and is Executive Director of Barli Development Institute for Rural Women. She has shared and pursued this dream with another amazing individual, Jimmy, an Irishman, who is her husband. They are a very special and talented couple who complement each other and have a great partnership. I am still in awe of what they have achieved, and continue to accomplish, as it is so varied: literacy, health practices, agriculture (vegetables, spices and lentils), composting, rain water harvesting, near zero waste, solar cooking and lighting, tailoring, computing, fabric design, weaving and tribal crafts.

Barli is a common name for tribal women in the area and is also the name given to the central pillar of the tribal hut. So Barli is a beautiful and powerful metaphor for women being the pillars of the family and community. Barli offers six and twelve month residential programmes to young, usually illiterate, women from the scheduled tribes and castes of the rural villages within a radius of 200 km of Indore, Madhya Pradesh. The major problems faced in the region by these marginalized women are illiteracy, lack of water, poor nutrition, lack of fuel (there are no more trees to chop down), few medical services, unhealthy traditional health practices, poor hygiene, family abuse, and low or no income.

The Institute uses parabolic and box solar cookers. The smaller parabolic cooker is good for a family and about 40 have been locally manufactured, subsidized and sold to graduates who return to their villages. They pay about ten per cent of the actual price and recover this in one year on fuel saved. The larger parabolic cooker is used to feed a hundred trainees and staff most days (average of three hundred sunny days in the year) for lunch and dinner. They are also testing a new solar storage cooker that is used to cook chapatis and breakfast for the trainees. Many educational and energy-conscious Indian organizations visit Barli to learn about the cookers. I was very impressed, especially since the electricity goes off for a scheduled hour each morning and evening, and for numerous other unscheduled periods in a day. If it is this bad in Indore, a large city, I cannot imagine what it is like in the villages!

A group of 60 to 75 trainees graduated while I was there, and although the chief of police was the local dignitary present, I was asked to be the guest of honour! There were at least 150 guests from the government, technical and nursing colleges, social workers and two professors of biotechnology with their postgraduate researchers. Janak and Jimmy have developed and enjoy great relations with city officials and a variety of academic, professional and business organizations and individuals. I was amazed to watch half a dozen trainees get up and address the audience in Hindi and others sing and read poems they had composed. Apparently they were explaining the different subjects that they had learned and what they planned to do on their return to their communities. I felt that I was witnessing a miracle. When it was my turn to speak I kept it short, as two hours had passed and we were all hungry. I congratulated them on the great courage they had displayed in being willing to leave home, become literate, learn new life skills, speak and perform in front of an audience and encouraged them to be even more courageous in sharing their new skills and knowledge with family and community. It was an inspiring experience, especially as the women had arrived six months earlier with no knowledge of their own worth and abilities.

Realizing how much more Spartan my life will be in Panchgani (no imported cheeses and dark chocolate, no variety of veggies, no club, pool and gym, and decent restaurants are a 30 minute bus ride away), I am relishing the luxury of my existence in Chennai and making the most of my remaining weeks here!

138
April 2004
Pippa Cookson
Macedonia

Pippa, from Northern Ireland, departed for Macedonia in November 2003.

I first visited Macedonia in 1960, when it was part of Yugoslavia. At that time I learned quite a bit about the whole country, and a little Serbo-Croat, which is quite similar to Russian, which I was then studying.

In 2003 I kept reading the International Pioneering Committee's appeals for pioneers and travel teachers to the Balkans, and I thought, 'There's not much doing in July and August – I'll go then.' I didn't fancy Serbia, Bosnia or Kosovo because of the war, so I picked Macedonia and went for five weeks as a travel teacher. Two days after I decided to go I received one of the promised confirmations: I went to a meeting at a venue close to my home in Belfast and there was another group in the building. I asked where they were from and was told 'Macedonia'! After my meeting I talked to some of them and made four contacts, three of whom I visited.

On my travel teaching trip I spent some of my time in Ohrid, which is an interesting city on a large and beautiful lake, and some in Bitola, near the Greek border. The Equal Wings course, which I put in my baggage as an afterthought, was a winner. I did a bit of it with a group in Ohrid and it went to two women's groups in Bitola, one in Struga, one in Tetovo, and an NGO support group in Kichevo.

I liked this little country and realized that pioneers are desperately needed because there are very few active Bahá'ís. So I decided to come back to live and help Deni in Bitola. There are probably less than ten active Bahá'ís in Macedonia. I arrived back at the end of October and shared the 'Bahá'í flat' with a German lady who was very good at languages and at making and recording new contacts, which was a great help. She was there for three months. In Ohrid there is a youth service volunteer, whose family were in Ireland until they pioneered to Bulgaria, so he speaks Bulgarian, which is close to Macedonian. I go over there for the first part of every week to help him.

In Bitola I have been 'finding my feet' as a permanent resident. Deni and I are trying to establish a weekly devotional and an international conversation evening every other Sunday. We have attractive little flyers, a place to meet, two Bahá'ís to host the events – all we need now is people to attend them!

Macedonia is slightly larger than Northern Ireland, where I was living before, and has a population of two and a quarter million - about 70 per cent Macedonians, 23 per cent Albanians, and one to two per cent Turks, Roma, Vlachs and Serbs. The Macedonians and Serbs are mostly Orthodox Christians, the other groups are Muslims. There are tensions between Albanians and Macedonians – the similarities between here and Northern Ireland are quite striking. (Oddly, it makes it feel more like home to me!)

It's an attractive little country, with lots of mountains of all shapes and sizes – the biggest one, Mount Pelister (2601 metres) is visible from my balcony. In winter, there is skiing. There are two big beautiful lakes, Ohrid and Prespa, with crystal, aquamarine water, in the southwest corner and smaller lakes elsewhere. Towns and cities all seem to have their own characteristics and are often an extraordinary mixture of new and old, all jumbled together in a way that would give a town planner the heebie-jeebies!

Roads are well designed – not too many hairpins in the mountains – but are often in need of repair. There's a good, cheap bus service (though the buses are often decrepit), and a limited rail network through Skopje, down the Vardar Valley to Thessaloniki (here called Solun) in Greece. Taxis are cheap (except in Skopje, the capital).

The cost of living, for most items, is pretty low and in summer there's a profusion of fresh vegetables and fruit, especially peppers. Most towns seem to have good, clean, drinkable water. Bitola (next to the power station) has a good power supply – other places, e.g. Tetovo, aren't so lucky!

The main language is Macedonian, which is a Slav language with a Cyrillic alphabet similar to Russian. However, people below the age of 24 have learned English at school, and many others know a bit, picked up from the films on TV, or in other ways. The National Spiritual Assembly of Germany is in charge here but it likes its pioneers and travel teachers to speak English. The local Bahá'ís are mostly very good at English, and a lot of events are conducted in it, but they mostly can't speak German. Albanian is a second language spoken down the northwest strip of the country. It's totally different from Macedonian, with a modified Latin alphabet and a softer sound. Many notices are written in English as well as Macedonian; road signs are often in Cyrillic and also in Latin characters, such as are used in Croatia.

139
April 2004
Sylvia Girling
Australia to Thailand to Malaysia

Sylvia now lives in Australia but she was a UK pioneer to both Poland and Slovakia.

I moved to Australia a year ago and found, like everywhere else, that there's plenty to do here Bahá'í-wise. I've joined a small, very nice, friendly and active community consisting mostly of families. We have children's classes and an ongoing project called 'Kidz 4 Peace', which is open to all children between the ages of five and 15. We cater for nearly 30 children and they learn through the arts, prayer and the holy writings about how to make this world of ours a better place. Many of them come through the religious education classes we give in local schools. In Australia parents can choose which, if any, religion their children are taught at school and the Bahá'í classes are proving very popular.

Not being a resident here, I have to come and go, so there's plenty of opportunity for travel teaching, which suits me as I love visiting my worldwide family. Mainly I help out at a Bahá'í social and economic project in the mountains of Thailand. It's a very remote area where the hill tribe children are given a home at the Bahá'í Centre, which enables them to go to the local high school. They are children who, along with their parents, want a better education than can be provided in their even more remote villages. Their parents provide them with rice, if possible, but all other expenses are met by the Bahá'ís. At the moment there are ten girls and seven boys between the ages of 13 and 18. The plan is to double the numbers this year and again next year.

Their day begins at 5:30 a.m. with prayers. It's still dark and quite cold, so some come huddled in their blankets and they sit on the cold tiled floor in a circle. One begins to sing and then they all join in and soon I'm transported to a higher realm as the holy writings and prayers flow from their pure souls. Some of the music they compose themselves and lasts for about half an hour. Next they split into groups to share the workload of cleaning, cooking and gardening. Then all gather outside around an open fire to eat their breakfast of vegetables, rice and lots of chilli. They also cook over an open fire. Then back to work as they wash the dishes and clean the kitchen, which is also in the open. Full of smiles, they wave their goodbyes or use their own greeting (*wai*) by putting their hands together in front of their face as they leave around 7:30 a.m. for school.

I also had the pleasure of teaching some of them at school, as during the day I taught English at two primary schools as well as at the high school. It was great fun for me and the kids, as they had never experienced my way of teaching before. The same as in the Faith, actions outdid our words. The children look for the fun in everything they do, so where they are you will always hear laughter. It could be from the bottom of a well they are cleaning out or washing their clothes down at the well and taking a shower at the same time. Or it could be chopping wood or a simple game of ball where they use their head or feet to pass the ball to each other over the gate. I just love to sit and watch them. If only the world at large could experience the joy they find in their work and play!

My trip was not without its adventures – one being taking the local bus to town four and a half hours ride away. The buses are very old and infrequent.

I was returning from Chiang Mai and the bus, as usual, was struggling up the hill when a smell of burning became pronounced. The driver got down and looked underneath the bus. This was repeated several times as we continued our uphill climb. Finally he gave up after a prolonged look and a bit of banging with his tools. We seemed to have come to a full stop. Out came the mobile phones and slowly the bus emptied as vans came to collect friends and family. Now there was only me, the driver and the lady conductor. It was dark and cold and my lack of Thai and their lack of English meant I had no idea what was to happen next, as there were no other buses along that road.

Eventually a man got on the bus who spoke a little English and asked me if I would go home with the lady conductor. So off we set back down into the valley to her home, which was very basic by all standards. I noticed they slept on straw mats on the floor. I could see I was in for a very long night. Out front was a bar, two tables and a few benches. I joined the jovial men who had lost their inhibitions and tried out their few words of English on me. I lifted my eyes heavenwards and asked why, being under Bahá'u'lláh's protection, this place had been chosen for me. Then suddenly I was asked to come to 'sister's house'. The other sister had fetched her English book in order to speak to me. They took me by motorbike to another village and, to my great surprise and delight, 'sister' had a house and could speak English. I was given a room of my own and had a good night's sleep. In the morning we spoke about the Faith and she seemed very interested, so you never know what is in store for you or others when you set out from your home trusting in God.

In Malaysia I was able to attend the fiftieth anniversary celebrations of the first enlightened believer there, Uncle Yan Kee Leong. It was another wonderful experience with over two thousand Bahá'ís present. Many pioneers came from all over the world to join in the celebrations and were honoured one evening by the youth, each youth taking the hand of a pioneer and in the other hand holding a candle. The room was darkened as the candlelight procession wound its way through the hall in song to the words of 'Abdu'l-Bahá 'Look at me, follow me, be as I am'. It was a very moving experience and I think we all had tears in our eyes.

I hadn't realized that Malaysia has such a diversity of cultures – all united under the banner of Bahá'u'lláh – celebrating in song and dance their diversity, not only culture but all ages – there were children who looked no older than four years right up to the not-so-young like me. The main focus was on the history of the faith in Malaysia, so there were lots of stories that made us want to laugh and cry at the same time. One of the great joys for me was meeting relatives of Pauline and Isaac de Cruz (from Liverpool) and hearing stories about them. Having the pleasure of knowing them for many years, it was very special to me to see their father on video and hear the many tributes to his generosity of spirit which has helped Malaysia to grow into such a vibrant community (now being one per cent of the population).

140

July 2004

Dorothy Bruce

Republic of Ireland

In April 2002 Dorothy pioneered to Shannon for a period of two years.

Celtic Days

My two years here are almost over. Having been born in Northern Ireland, the country was already familiar to me and the accents have a kinship too! It also helps to discover that this town where I live – Shannon, Co. Clare – is nicknamed 'little Belfast'! This is because so many refugees came here from Belfast during the worst troubles in the north. Shannon is a new town of housing estates created in the sixties from land reclaimed from River Shannon marshes and influenced by the need for airport staff and workers in the new industrial estates. In common with the Faith, it is in a constant state of growth and change. Since arriving, new motorways have appeared all round the town, after months of using old potholed roads and sudden changes of route to accommodate the road works. The small shopping mall, which is the town centre, is dwarfed by a huge building site intended to become a very large shopping complex.

I have learned many things from the Bahá'ís in Ireland. They have such an alive enthusiasm and such a genuine affection for each other. It is plain to see they enjoy being in each other's company and can really relax and laugh together. This atmosphere may partly be explained by the background of the local Bahá'ís, as most became Bahá'ís about the same time in their teens and twenties when there was a great surge of activity round nearby Limerick in the sixties. Most have married, had families and grown middle-aged together. It is so noticeable how they support each other in illness and crisis and extend it to attending exhibitions of any talented members of the community. In my first year, with a group of Bahá'ís, I attended two art exhibitions of works by two Bahá'í artists and watched a talented young Bahá'í pianist and a singing group perform at a religious unity concert presented by non-Bahá'ís in Ennis.

The process of working on the study books has also found an enthusiastic response. A comment in *New Day* (*Ré'Nua*), the Irish newsletter, describes this: 'The acceptance of study circles in Ireland has been amazing and is preparing the Irish Bahá'í community for what is to come.' I have found these group meetings a most enjoyable event among the Irish Bahá'ís!

In connection with the enjoyment of each other's company, I have met up with Bahá'ís from other areas who joined us on picnic outings to local sites of interest or the seaside and the beautiful, haunting Burren area of north Clare. We have also met socially to visit local caves and to attend a fortnightly film night in a Bahá'í home, these films chosen for their message or uplifting theme. Then there are many opportunities to support devotionals and meetings in nearby areas.

One special outing I must mention was a joint pilgrimage to a very remote peninsula in south Clare where an English pioneer, Stan Wrout, is buried. Sadly, he drowned while bathing, soon after arriving in this country. The sea washed his body up on the shore after several days. The place was a remote settlement called Kilbaha. The day we were there was fresh and sunny and his resting place very peaceful. In a short time we all had tidied the area of the grave and said some prayers. Our cluster area here was named, by choice, 'Stan Wrout cluster', in his memory. I was new at the time they chose it and, not knowing the story, was totally confused at why they all wanted this odd title!

Two special bounties were given to me while I was here. First was my luck in finding a really good flat at reasonable rent. I expected only to afford to board or share a place and the agent we saw said there was nothing at the price I could afford. As we left, something made me say, 'Do you think I might be lucky?' She responded, 'Wait, I think there is a place but you may not like it as the owner wants to use a room and share the bathroom.' On viewing, this was no problem, as this room was off the small hall and my living room door was my 'front' door. Within two days of arriving, I had a place to stay! My landlord has proved to be very thoughtful and helpful and only comes in occasionally. This flat has offered the community another place to meet! It has now been rented by another Bahá'í, a long-time pioneer from Wales, Gillian Phillips.

The second bounty was the gift of three tapes from the Irish National Assembly to the Local Assemblies, which we were able to copy for each person. These are treasures, as they are collections of talks given at Waterford summer schools by Adib Taherzadeh. The Irish Bahá'ís feel especially close to Adib because of their long connections with him and he is quoted and remembered often here, wherever Bahá'ís meet together. I am especially touched to have this as I declared as a Bahá'í at a fireside when I first met Adib, who was the speaker for the evening. My declaration was delayed by the hostess so that he would have the excitement of hearing about a new Bahá'í!

141
July 2004
Sarah Munro
Faroe Islands

Should they attempt to conceal His light on the continent, He will assur-
edly rear His head in the midmost heart of the ocean, and raising His
voice, proclaim: 'I am the life-giver of the world!'[26]

Bahá'u'lláh

With these words of Bahá'u'lláh and the promises of the Guardian and
Universal House of Justice about the significance of teaching the Faith in the
islands of the North Sea forefront in my mind, I undertook a three-month
short-term pioneering move to the Faroe Islands from January to March of
this year. I had gone there in June last year travel teaching and fallen in love
with the people of the islands, the Bahá'í community and the landscape – so
much so that, on my return, I sent out 16 letters begging any school to give
me a job! Having secured one for ten weeks in a town of five thousand called
Klaksvik, I was off . . .

The local Bahá'í community instantly welcomed me and allowed me to
stay at the National Centre in the main town of Torshavn at the weekends so
I could join in activities going on there. As I was paying for accommodation
in Klaksvik too, this considerably cut down costs.

Meeting people to introduce to the Faith was not difficult. I immediately
struck up friendships with the teachers at the school, some of my students and
friends of the local Bahá'ís. I was regularly invited to visit these new friends
in their homes and had many opportunities to talk about the Faith. They all
received Bahá'í literature in the Faroese language too. Determined to system-
atically teach the Faith to my open-minded and receptive students, I also set
up a weekly English discussion evening, where I would of course choose the
topic along the lines of the teachings, such as global citizenship, marriage,
prayer, art and spirit, etc., generally using the words of 'Abdu'l-Bahá. Four
students came regularly, and even though none of them expressed a desire
to know more about the Faith directly, the fact they kept coming back for
more was a testament to their interest! It was clear I was introducing ideas to
them they had never considered. This is an exciting bounty of teaching. One
student even came to the Naw-Rúz event at the National Bahá'í Centre.

After the session on prayer (when seven students came!), I suggested holding a regular prayer meeting, which one of them agreed to. He is a strong
Christian and it is lovely to know that a regular multi-faith devotional gath-

ering has been held at the school, even though it was just the two of us. He was very attracted to the Bahá'í prayers and said, 'I find it amazing that even though you're a different religion from me, we can still sit and pray together. Even many Christians of a different sect would not do this!' Unfortunately, he's right, and there exist people in the Faroes (a very strongly Protestant society) who allow their religion to affect their social and political ties. Same old story!

Another way I felt I could offer service to the community was through the arts. The Fiftieth Anniversary Committee asked another pioneer (who has experience directing community theatre in the United States) and me to create a short drama evoking the spirit of the Knight of Bahá'u'lláh for the Faroes, Eskil Ljungberg. After intensive weekly rehearsals, we created a 20 minute piece which was successfully performed at the Naw-Rúz celebration. Eskil, a Bahá'í from Sweden, arrived in the Faroes in 1953 at the age of 67 and died there aged 99. His life of dedicated and sacrificial service is an inspiration to all.

One of the highlights of my short service was a fantastic opportunity to proclaim the Faith through the media. A newspaper journalist contacted me after hearing me speak on the radio and asked for an interview 'to discuss the Bahá'í Faith'. I was thrilled! It resulted in a double-page centre spread in one of the two weekend newspapers on the islands. The Faith was constantly referred to very favourably and this generated a lot of interest among the local people. A very clear answer to ardent prayers!

Now I am home, I am determined to encourage other Bahá'ís to travel to this wonderful country, where I found the people receptive to the teachings and easy to associate with, and the landscape among the most beautiful I have ever seen. If you're planning a holiday soon please consider a teaching trip there to assist the consecrated band of pioneers already serving in the Faroes.

There are areas which cry out for pioneers and travelling teachers; the mind turns, for example, to the work among the Sami and other people of the arctic and sub-arctic areas . . . We contemplate the significance of teaching the Faith in the islands of the Mediterranean, the Atlantic and the North Sea . . .

The Universal House of Justice[27]

142
October 2004
Fiona Young
Gibraltar

Fiona (Beint) and her husband, Peter, have enjoyed living on the Rock of Gibraltar.

I have just returned from Gibraltar where my husband Peter and I have spent just under two years working in law firms on the beautiful rock. It is a wonderful place.

The Bahá'í community is like a loving family that takes everyone under its protective wing and ensures that all are made to feel welcome. There are many highlights of our time there but there is one that sticks in my memory the most (and is the most recent event). It all began in July when my brother Payam Beint and my cousin Na'im Cortazzi came to visit Peter and me. In return for their 'keep' I asked Payam and Na'im to put on a concert of their recently produced CD which is a selection of prayers and Hidden Words put to beautiful music. They performed on a warm summer evening on the terrace of our house and about 20 friends attended. Everyone was mesmerized by the incredible music. The following day a close friend of the Bahá'ís of Gibraltar finally took her opportunity to officially declare her belief in Bahá'u'lláh.

The Spiritual Assembly of Gibraltar was prompted to invite Payam and Na'im back for another visit. This time we booked the beautiful and historic Garrison Library in the centre of Gibraltar and were audacious in sending out invitations and press releases. An article concerning the concert was printed in the Gibraltar *Chronicle* on the day before the concert and the Gibraltar Broadcasting Corporation advertised the event on television and radio. The concert was performed in the garden of the Garrison Library and we decorated the patio with hundreds of twinkling lights and candles. The spirit of participation amongst the Bahá'ís was utterly overwhelming. The children swept the patio clean, cleaned the garden chairs, set tablecloths on the tables and helped prepare flower arrangements to decorate the performance area. One friend organized the sound system, another set up the chairs, another set out food and refreshments. Everyone was involved and the spirit of cooperation and deep love infiltrated the surroundings of the Garrison Library and created an incredible atmosphere of love and peace. As dusk fell the candles were lit and the people began to arrive. We expected 30. At least 50 came, the majority of whom were our friends, colleagues and enquirers. The performance was incredible. A glowing report of the event was printed in the *Chronicle*. It read as follows:

A balmy night, and hundreds of tiny candles and twinkling lights set the scene perfectly for Rowshan's second performance in Gibraltar, last Friday evening. Payam Beint and Na'im Cortazzi returned to Gibraltar at the invitation of Gibraltar's Bahá'í Community to perform songs from their debut CD, entitled Rowshan. The exquisite setting of the Garrison Library's garden was the ideal backdrop for the ethereal sounds created by Rowshan and the audience were suitably captivated by the combination of the beautiful sound created by the skilful guitarists and their entrancing vocal harmonies. Payam and Na'im's accomplished performance of songs inspired by the Bahá'í writings not only thrilled the ears, but also uplifted the hearts of all those present. Rowshan also treated the audience to a glimpse of things to come, with the more up beat, but no less alluring 'Wildseed' (not on their current CD). As the last note faded, it was clear from the applause that Rowshan will be gladly welcomed back to Gibraltar in the not too distant future.

That concert was a fitting end to our time in Gibraltar, although, as one Bahá'í in Gibraltar told me, Gibraltar is just like the song 'Hotel California' by The Eagles: 'You can check out any time you like but you can never leave.' I trust that, God willing, I will have many more trips to the beautiful Rock in future.

143
January 2005
Dale and Helen Cameron Rutstein
Philippines

Helen and Dale and their three children have lived in many countries for UNICEF, which they have combined with service to the Faith. Helen's husband Dale has written the following.

Dear *Pioneer Post*,
I hope your editorial policies can be stretched to allow an American – spouse of Helen (Cameron) Rutstein – to enter into the pages of your journal! I have, after all, spent many years in amazement over details of your regular correspondents: vegetable shopping in Tanzania, leaky plumbing in Russia, study circles in Bangkok and sub-zero deserts in Mongolia. I am quite possibly one of your most avid non-British readers, having followed your pages from my various places of residence: Papua New Guinea, Pakistan, Israel, Albania, Italy and now the Philippines.

My wife Helen (daughter of former London fireside-holders Earl and Audrey Cameron) and I recently returned to our present home in the Philippines from a US holiday, where, among other highlights, we spent two enchanting days in Manhattan on the sidelines of Earl Cameron's latest cinematic turn as the president of fictional African republic Matobo, in Sydney Pollack's latest movie *The Interpreter*. The film also features two well-known film actors, Nicole Kidman and Sean Penn. Earl entertained us with stories from the set of this diplomatic thriller, including a blow by blow account of the big scene where he delivers his main speech from the actual podium of the UN General Assembly, the hall full of extras representing every UN member state, while Nicole and Sean frantically search for his would-be assassin. Thrilling stuff.

Your readers may be especially excited to know that during one idle moment on the set of *The Interpreter* Nicole Kidman and Earl were chatting and his associations with the Solomon Islands as a pioneer came up in conversation. Nicole apparently was fascinated as to how a Bermudan-born, London-based actor would ever find his way to Honiara, and Earl was left with no other way to explain it than pioneering for the Cause of God. This was Nicole Kidman's first ever exposure to the word Bahá'í! (She was fascinated to hear that there was a Bahá'í House of Worship in her hometown of Sydney.)

We are currently living in the Philippines in the vast metropolis of Manila. We moved here from Albania and Italy in January 2003 when I took up a new UNICEF posting as chief of communication. We are finally adjusted to life here in this sprawling Asian city of somewhere between ten and twelve million people. It's been quite a task.

I am still pursuing my career interest of the past several years: looking for ways to use broadcast television in the developing world to bring about social change. My latest project involves Philippines youth producing their own weekly TV magazine which airs on three national networks including Nickelodeon.

Helen is an overtime mom and a part-time relocation expert for Crown Relocations, Manila. She is setting up a new service for Crown's corporate clients who need expert advice about settling in families to overseas postings. Helen may well be more qualified than many others for such a post, having performed the miracle of raising three happy kids in nomadic conditions. Helen is also an unofficial advocate of enhanced cross-cultural understanding at the International School, Manila, where our three kids are currently enrolled. She manages to exert her own brand of community-building with a smile and a laugh.

That's all for now. We offer a standing invitation to our hospitality to anyone arriving at our Manila door holding a copy of the UK *Pioneer Post*.

144
January 2005
Negin and Nima Anvar
Grenada

Negin's parents, Izzat and Shirin Ghaemmaghami, left Swansea 25 years ago with their two daughters to pioneer to Grenada. Since then their daughter Negin married Nima and they have two children.

First, we want to thank everyone sooo much for the kind thoughts and prayers. For those of you who don't know what we're talking about – on 7 September Grenada had THE worst hurricane in its history. Probably one of the worst hurricanes of all time in the world – Hurricane Ivan (category 4). Grenada had not been hit by a hurricane since 1955 and that was a category 3.

Grenada has very seldom suffered hurricanes, the reason being that we are too far south. Well, not this time! The damage was devastating throughout the island (90 per cent of homes were damaged or destroyed). Both our business and home got hit hard and it will take a long time to get things back to normal – one much worse than the other. But we thank God that we are alive and healthy. Many had it much worse.

The hurricane lasted for 12 hours (from 2:30 p.m. until 2:00 a.m.) and was the scariest event of our lives. I was alone with the kids and spent the entire night in the bathroom. The kids were terrified and I tried my hardest to keep a brave front for their sakes. We prayed and sang Bahá'í songs all night long (except when we'd collapse from exhaustion). I had to lean heavily against the door to prevent it from crashing open. Nima was at our (business) hotel and we lost all forms of communication from the very beginning of the hurricane. We didn't see each other until the next morning. Nima was so worried that we were dead.

The looting had already started by the time we left our home in the morning to go to our other hotel. It was a dreadful sight to see. How low can people get? And not for food but for non-essentials – DVDs, CDs, snorkelling equipment (for people who don't even swim) – you name it. We NEVER thought that it would be this bad. No one did. The looting and crime was actually worse than the hurricane itself. Things seem to have begun to settle down now.

We didn't have electricity and water for a long time afterwards. We washed ourselves and did our laundry in the sea. We would actually laugh about it. What else can you do?

The kids and I, Negin, left Grenada through the US Consulate a week after the hurricane. Nima stayed. My parents were out of the country and missed the whole event, since they had left for vacation a few days before we were hit. We returned home mid-October, having spent one month in the United States and Trinidad with friends and family. We are delighted to be back together again in Grenada. We thank God for everything.

With my dad, Izzat Ghaemmaghami, we are now working to get things up and running again. All of our staff are alive. Most have lost their roofs and some have lost their entire house. Some are staying with us and others have managed to get back on their feet. The situation here is stabilizing but there are still random incidents of lawlessness. The water supply is now much better but there are still times where we have no running water. The food situation is good with plenty of frozen chicken and beef but we are still missing green vegetables and fruit.

145

January 2005

Sandra Cooles

Dominica

Sandra and Philip have been pioneers in the Caribbean island of Dominica since 1982.

A couple of years ago, after having done the delegate elections in one particular isolated area of the island, I noticed that there was one solitary name, Veronica, on the list from La Plaine, a village down a dead end road. Wondering who on earth this extremely isolated Bahá'í could be, I decided to find out.

After driving for what seemed like forever, down roads that make even the Swiss hairpin bends seem straight, I came to La Plaine and started my search. A woman hanging out hundreds of red shirts (must have been a football team!) said what amazed me beyond belief. She told me she didn't know Veronica but she did know of a Bahá'í. Now this was truly unbelievable! A person, who to my knowledge had never been visited, was known in this village as a Bahá'í! My interest increased. Off I went again. A group of men were just 'liming' (doing nothing) under a mango tree so I asked them. A one-eyed Rasta said he knew Veronica and would take me to her house. When we arrived, there she was, a large, beautiful, Carib Indian woman, sitting on an upturned bucket on the uneven mud floor of her rusted, galvanized, cooking out-house, with a huge bucket of washing between her knees.

She was obviously very busy and had a sick child leaning against her knee while she worked but she smiled welcomingly and invited me to join them. I introduced myself and, finding another bucket, sat down. After all the normal pleasantries, we got down to business! I told her I was a Bahá'í and why I had come. Immediately she gave an enormous smile and said she too was a Bahá'í but no one had visited her for a long, long time; it actually transpired that it was over 15 years! After a very pleasant chat and promises to return, I was killed with curiosity about who had taught her the Faith. She told me that she had become a Bahá'í in Giraudel, another village much closer to town. Now Giraudel is in an area that I had visited, so I looked at her with great interest but got not a flicker of recognition, so decided that a travel teacher must have taught her the Faith. I asked her to describe the person. She said that her teacher had been white and had little white children with her. I said that I had three little children and they were the only white children I knew of, but, taking a closer look at her, that I had definitely never visited anyone who looked like her. She looked at me, very appraisingly, and also decided that she did not know me. Eventually I asked where she had lived in Giraudel. Imagine our disbelief when we worked out that I knew and often visited Ma Barty, the relative whose home she had lived in for a month. We laughed and talked more and then, suddenly, I remembered when Ma Barty had become a Bahá'í that there was a young, slim, pretty but very silent Carib girl standing against the wall. She had seemed interested in what I was saying so I asked her would she like to be a Bahá'í as well. I had never seen the girl again because shortly after that she left and Ma Barty died. Well you can imagine our delight. We hugged and laughed and hugged once more. Our laughter brought the neighbours, who of course all had to be told that we had been friends for over 15 years and had just found each other again.

Straight away Veronica started to actively teach in her village. She held children's classes and firesides and even had Feasts with her family. She was elected onto the National Spiritual Assembly, and though it was hard to get to meetings, she never missed one, leaving her five children with friends or relatives.

Why am I telling you this story? Out there, in every country in the world, there are people like Veronica, who even though no one has visited them, are still Bahá'ís. We must never give up on them, we must never lose hope. Every single effort we make will be rewarded, we just need to pray for the strength to keep going.

146
January 2005
Michele Wilburn
Zakynthos, Greece

*Michele pioneered from Hampstead, London, to the Ionian island of
Zakynthos in 2004.*

We had enjoyed the wonderful hospitality of the Greek people on several previous holidays, so when Greece was elected as a priority goal for travel teachers
a few years ago during the Three Year Plan, my daughter Romani and I were
excited to adopt Greece as our personal travelling teaching goal. We travelled
several times to Greece over the next couple of years, mainly to the islands.

At the end of the summer in 2002, with a few days on our hands, the only
last minute plane tickets to Greece within our budget were to Zakynthos. This
presented a new adventure to an island in an area of Greece as yet unknown
to us. Romani and I have always been adventurous travellers, preferring not
to book accommodation in advance. We decided that when we arrived at
the airport in Zakynthos we would say a prayer and ask three people what
part of the island they thought we should head off to. Guided to Vasilikos,
we discovered a remote, unspoilt, southern area of the island, which has now
become home for us.

The powers of divine guidance never cease to delight me, when with
hindsight I recall the steps that have led me to this wonderful pioneer post.
Zakynthos is a beautiful island, a floating paradise, the southernmost of the
Ionian islands and third largest in area and population. An island full of contrast: the greater part is covered by low, pine-covered mountains, alternating
with fertile planes; to the northeast and south there are some of the loveliest
beaches in Greece, while to the west, along spectacular rocky coasts, marine
caves have been formed which provide great tourist attractions.

The climate is mild and Mediterranean, with a lot of rain and sunlight,
creating an ideal location for abundant agricultural produce, the cultivation
of olives and citrus fruit, and entrepreneurial activity, mainly in the tourist
sector. The Zakynthos environment has become an object of international
interest because the loggerhead turtle *Caretta caretta*, an endangered species
protected by international conventions and by Greek legislation, lays its eggs
in the southernmost shores, where I now live.

Having travelled to Zakynthos a few times within the space of a year, we
decided this was the pioneering post for us. This beautiful island, with so
much to offer the Cause of Bahá'u'lláh in Greece, has so totally captured our

hearts and blessed our lives. Last year we spent five summer months living in a tent, cooking on an outdoor fire, working for free in the most popular beach resort on the island, getting to know a wide range of Zakynthian people, coming to understand their culture and providing the opportunity to assess how best to develop a Bahá'í teaching plan. We made many friends and came to understand that with a population of 35,000 locals, there are two distinct seasons to life here. The summer months are dominated by a tourist invasion and activities, an abundant nightlife and a challenge for the locals to make as much money as possible to keep their business thriving and to see them through the winter months. In contrast, from 31 October until 1 May, life returns to normal for the locals, with harvesting the olives, a quiet family-orientated social life and the opportunity for deeper communication.

Last October I was blessed with a few days in the Holy Land, praying at the shrines, where my intentions for pioneering to Zakynthos were confirmed. Over the winter I set about restructuring my business activities so that my income would be dependant on my on-line shop. I also had to set about recovering from an accident, which left me unable to walk and with a serious back problem.

In May 2004 I arrived in Zakynthos with a suitcase of essentials and rented a tiny but affordable studio in the home of an elderly local couple, who have become wonderful friends. The simple things I miss the most, such as no washing machine, only one hot plate to cook on, no transport for the 14 km journey into town to purchase good food – simple challenges, yet all blessings in disguise.

The WorldSmart youth leadership programme provides a fantastic opportunity for youth between the ages of 18 and 29 to travel together in three continents for 20 weeks, applying the principles of consultation for planning and problem-solving, staying with different host families each week, embarking on service-orientated community projects in each location, not to forget providing a wonderful opportunity to share the Faith.

So while Romani spent a gap year travelling with the WorldSmart youth leadership programme, over the summer I deepened friendships with the locals and enjoyed filming a Zakynthian dance and singing project, involving over one hundred local residents. I am currently pursuing business and Bahá'í teaching plans simultaneously, with the development of a new holistic mind, body and spirit exercise and lifestyle regime, with the dual potential for international workshop programmes, while also serving the local community and providing me with an opportunity to develop Bahá'í teaching activities. Between September and December I filmed over 120 disks of footage in glorious outdoor Zakynthian locations for a series of holistic DVD programmes.

I was offered a fantastic home for the winter by a local family and have moved from my small studio into a mansion, right by the sea, which reminds me of Bahjí, with huge white balconies. Now my firesides are truly beginning, with a roaring fire every evening, burning olive wood, and a blessed spot to invite friends to learn about the Faith. Aware of my plans, the family have invited me to develop cultural and workshop programmes from here; let's see!

147
April 2005
Pippa Cookson
Macedonia

Pippa Cookson is from England but spent 14 years living in Belfast, Northern Ireland. She pioneered to Macedonia in November 2003.

Since August of last year I have been living in an old house in the old town of Ohrid. It has a real personality, not like the raw new concrete flats I was staying in before. Ohrid has a population of about 50,000 – many of whom turn out on fine days on the Charshiya (the pedestrian central street) so I usually meet one or two people I know. They also walk the wide promenade along the edge of the very beautiful lake when it's sunny.

I'm learning Macedonian. I had a head start with the (Cyrillic) alphabet because I once learned Russian. I can't yet understand the spoken language well, though I can struggle to speak it if I have to.

The old town of Ohrid is wonderfully picturesque, stacked higgledy-piggledy on the fairly steep hill below Tsar Samoil's fortress. The roads are flagged and just wide enough for single-lane traffic – which doesn't deter local drivers! Round the old town there was a wall, a lot of which still exists. My house is about a hundred yards from the lower gate, the tower on one side of which is well preserved. I live opposite two small churches, St Nikola and St Bogorodica ('Mother of God'), which were used as hospitals and for quarantine when Ohrid was still the walled city. I think they make the house feel spiritual and they are a pleasant component of the view, made of beige stone, with terracotta roofs.

Recently I was eagerly anticipating the visit of two previous pioneers to Ohrid. The day they arrived I got the quilts and sleeping bags out of the cold back room to air and distributed them around my bedroom, which was awash with sunshine. I didn't think about the snow still blanketing the roof – also basking in the sunshine! When I went into the room later there was a round dark patch on one sleeping bag and the other was a sideways target, as the old roof was leaking! There was soon a 'potty orchestra' of drips into various containers!

At sundown it froze and so did my visitors, used to central heating! And when they opened out the bed-settee, they failed to hook the two parts together so they spent a very uncomfortable night! Next day the temperature rose with the result that the snow on the shady side of the house melted and the drips were in my visitors' bedroom instead – and on the landing too, for good measure.

I hoped our run of bad luck was over the following day. I took my electric heater down to the living room and plugged it in – it spat fire at me and disabled the two cooker sockets! So I managed without it and plugged the cooker in elsewhere. In the evening my luck turned. A young Bahá'í came by. He bought for me a room aerial, which he fitted to the elderly TV, and adjusted it, transforming the viewing. Then he tested the fire, which was OK, and improvised a fuse to put the cooker sockets back into action. Oh, the joys of pioneering!

I have to say that the weekend wasn't unalleviated gloom – we had lots of fun and positive experiences and we didn't allow the leaking roof to dampen our spirits!

148
April 2005
Richard Poole
Angola

Richard is a veteran pioneer of Sudan, Tanzania, Barbados, St Lucia, Ecuador, Guinea and Uganda.

A short while ago the editor of *Pioneer Post* asked me if I would list for her the dates and the places to which I had pioneered. I duly did my calculations and replied, noting that I had pioneered fairly continuously in half a dozen countries in Africa and the Americas since 1978, whereupon Thelma kindly wrote back pointing out that pioneering is the 'prince of all goodly deeds'. I had not heard it described as such and was a little bit surprised to hear it now, not least because it had never occurred to me that there was anything particularly noble or distinguished about it, at least not the way that I had done it. To be perfectly frank, I had stepped from one relatively well-paid job with a humanitarian agency to another, arriving at each new location to find a house and a car, and competent and willing staff, waiting for me. Having always had a bent for adventure, even from my earliest days, it all seemed heaven-sent and

I grasped each new opportunity that came along with both hands and a heart filled with gratitude.

There was no sacrifice on my part, quite the reverse in fact; a greater sacrifice would have been to have stayed at home. Indeed, I felt that I had discovered what many missionaries must have discovered in recent years, namely, that working in a mission in Malawi or Zambia, for example, is infinitely easier and more pleasant than working in inner-city Manchester or London. To be honest, I felt somewhat envious of those Bahá'ís who in earlier days had been what I would consider to be 'true pioneers', those men and women of all ages who simply took off with no prospect of a job in sight, not knowing what the next day was going to bring. To be fair to myself, I cannot say that their desire to serve the Faith was necessarily any greater than mine, but I did, and still do feel that their willingness to depend exclusively on God reflects a degree of courage and faith that I personally have not had to prove, and I suspect that the spiritual benefits may have been commensurately greater as a result. Under such circumstances as these, I would be inclined to agree that pioneering is 'the prince of all goodly deeds'.

A curious phenomenon that I have noted with each new posting has been the similarity between the condition of the job that I was taking on and the condition of the local Bahá'í community. If the one was fledgling and small, the other tended to be the same; if the one was fraught with schism and difficulty, the other was likewise; if the one was well established and healthy, so too was the other. And this has continued to the present time here in Angola, where the country is just recovering from 27 years of civil war and 13 years of anti-colonial war before that.

The Faith arrived in Angola in 1953 but never managed to gain the firm foothold that it did in other sub-Saharan African countries. For many years the Angola community was administered from Zimbabwe until forming its own National Spiritual Assembly in 1992. At the present time the Bahá'í community is trying to regroup after many years of being unable to function properly as a result of the dislocation caused by the war. Like many of their fellow countrymen and women, the Angolan Bahá'ís, along with recently arrived refugees from the Democratic Republic of the Congo, are suffering considerable financial hardship, as well as the hardship that accrues from having health and education services in disarray. A good many of the Bahá'ís, again like their fellow countrymen and women, have been traumatized by their war experiences but this you can usually only guess at because they are not subjects that many are willing to discuss. But the potential of the Bahá'í community, like that of this vastly oil-rich, mineral-rich country, is enormous. Like virtually any country in sub-Saharan Africa, the people are receptive to the word of

God, their hearts are open and they listen without prejudice, and under such conditions the future can only be bright. And the two are, of course, interconnected because no society can aspire to lasting material prosperity without a solid spiritual foundation. As ever, I feel privileged to be here, attempting to re-build both the country and the Bahá'í community from the ground up, except that I can't help wondering where all those years have gone!

149
July 2005
Susan Kouchek-zadeh
Guinea-Conakry, West Africa

Susan and Shidan have been long-term pioneers in West Africa since 1966 when they arrived in Sierra Leone. In 1975 they pioneered to Guinea-Conakry, where they have stayed on more or less until the present time. Now finally they are packing up to leave their pioneering post.

Well, this is probably my last chance to contribute to *Pioneer Post* as a genuine pioneer. By the end of this month we shall be home in the UK for good, or bad, or until we decide to go somewhere else. So cheeky of me to say we shall be home when half of us, Shidan, has not been 'home' in 50 years. And besides somewhere in the writings it does say that it is better to be homeless!

We left Guinea over three years ago but were back within six months – rather embarrassing in view of the goodbye party and gifts and testimonials – so this time we intend to sneak out quietly.

These last three years have been spent in comparative luxury; we've been living in an apartment block which has a small swimming pool. I swim every day and sometimes again in the evening with Shidan. Today we were attended by a posse of inquisitive, scruffy-looking, young vultures on the surrounding rooftops.

As Shidan has been trying to reduce his work load lately we travelled a lot in 2004, visiting Santa Cruz, California, where my sister lives (we attended a 19 Day Feast at the Bosch School and the Declaration of the Báb at the very swish Los Angeles Bahá'í Centre) and then we spent Christmas in Santa Cruz, Bolivia, with our elder daughter Vadiay, who works (very long hours I have to say) at the Bahá'í University of Nur.

Guinea is currently blessed with three wonderful pioneers from the Congo who are doing great work . . . and they can sing like angels too! One of them has settled in the back of beyond . . . a thousand km from the capital . . . in the area where most of our Bahá'ís live and has set about transforming our permanent institute there and the surrounding communities. This year we didn't go to the National Convention which is usually held in that area (part of the 'sneak out quietly' policy) but heard that it ran like clockwork with meals served right on time – not an easy feat when you're cooking in the open on wood fires and have no kitchen.

So I've just typed my last Local Assembly *Ordre de Jour* (Agenda) for Conakry and am just tidying up my last National Treasurer's report and after 40 years in West Africa we shall soon be facing the rigours of Europe.

150
July 2005
Brian O'Toole
Guyana

Brian and Pam have been pioneers in Guyana for the past 26 years. They run the School of Nations, a 650-student school, and are to open a Bahá'i-inspired university in September 2005. The University will offer courses from London University.

We have now been in Guyana for 26 years. We came very close to leaving a few times in the past few years. We felt exhausted, that whatever contribution we were able to make had been given and it was time to 'move on'. As I have travelled over the years I have seen that same pattern in the lives of so many pioneers – the feeling that years had been invested and seemingly limited 'results' gained. We 'know' that we should be as the wind and blow regardless of results, but for most of us the daily challenges weigh heavily.

Both my wife and I serve as Auxiliary Board members here and we were fortunate to be able to consult openly with our liaison Counsellor Rebequa Murphy, with no fear of being judged. She suggested to us that there were still many services that could be rendered to Guyana and that we should persevere. And thank God that we did – not least for what it has done for our own spirits and sense of direction and purpose.

I have read the pages of *Pioneer Post* for many years now. Often I find the letters inspiring, being humbled by what families are offering to bring the healing messages to despairing peoples in some of the very difficult corners of the world.

At other times however the letters are more complex and reflect deep frustrations and a sense of anomie, of not being quite sure of the direction of our lives. For many pioneers who have remained 'in post' for many years – and there are growing numbers of them – there may be a danger that we become settlers and lose our pioneer spirit as we battle the same challenges of daily survival facing those around us. For many of us there is a need to reconnect, to think back to the spirit that motivated us to leave family and home for other lands. The mid-life crisis seems very real as I meet devoted pioneers in many countries. Some were the dynamos of emerging communities and some seem to have lost that pioneering spark and are now asking questions that would not have concerned them before.

Guyana has been a fascinating home for us. It allowed us to raise two boys. Like other parents we feel proud of the paths they are now following. And we are very thankful for the values they learned in this land, which was not always easy in their formative years. We have witnessed large numbers coming into the Faith – on records seven per cent of the population have declared their belief in Bahá'u'lláh. Now literally thousands of them are in New York and Toronto. Others are scattered in every corner of the planet. Few are still to be easily found in Guyana. Despite the exodus, the respect for the Faith permeates the whole country. But we were also witness to the challenges of a 'past-tense identity', where we constantly refer to the way things were in the past – the meetings with three hundred persons each night, the children's classes with children of all backgrounds, the youth gatherings that inspired so many. Our challenge now is to move on – to learn from the experience of the past, celebrate the victories but to learn new approaches and develop and embrace a new vision. But for so many of us it seems that was not to be an easy process. Thankfully in Guyana the present and future tenses have returned to our conversations and there is a depth and passion about the community that is creating a new dynamism and a new culture within the Bahá'í community. These are still early days, we are only beginning to emerge out of the half light, the hibernation of many years, but there is a growing sense of excitement about the Bahá'í community now.

The development arena has always proved very receptive in Guyana. We have a very well respected Bahá'í-inspired NGO, Varqa Foundation, that has worked in the field of development for about 15 years. We have a literacy programme, 'On the Wings of Words', which has touched the lives of more than ten thousand youth and children and which has offered the key of being able to read, to conquer the word, which previously only confused them.

Varqa also pioneered a health partnership with the Amerindians in the Rupununi region on the border with Brazil. This seven year programme worked with the entire population of this region. Varqa is now in the process of re-establishing the project with the arrival back in Guyana of dear

Dr Aidun, a surgeon from Canada who served the project with nobility for many years. A number of years ago I was on a visit to the region to support the project. We travelled many hours in a jeep to a workshop on creating a vision. I spoke with the young health worker sitting next to me in the jeep and asked her if she knew what the Bahá'í Faith represented. She said no but she 'loved it'.

Recently Varqa Foundation was asked by the First Lady to undertake a major programme on behalf of the International Labour Organization to work with child labourers. We were very reluctant to take it on. We knew nothing about child labour, we felt we did not have the human resources and we were fearful of the bureaucracy and demands of organizations like the International Labour Organization. But Varqa took on the project. A visit was made to the project a few weeks ago by the First Lady and the ILO representative in the Caribbean – 31 youths were crammed into an old dilapidated building learning about mechanics. They sat there, different races, many in poverty, ranging in age from 11 to 17 years. Not one of them is attending school. They now speak about being given a new chance and being a little hopeful for the first time in their lives. The ILO rep said it is one of the best programmes he is working with in the region.

Some years ago Varqa began a youth leadership programme called Youth Can Move the World (YCMTW). Over the years we have benefited from annual consultations at the World Centre with members of OSED. To date more than a thousand youth have completed the training. This year OSED challenged us to develop a new vision. The challenge was to take 75 youth (from a variety of religious backgrounds, but few Bahá'ís) through the full sequence of Ruhi books. It all sounded so easy and logical when formulating the plan in the inspiring surrounds of the OSED offices in Haifa. On the plane going home, however, the idea appeared more outlandish than audacious.

Now six months later we are about to embark on a two month intensive YCMTW campaign – already more than 60 youths have asked to attend the full course. The intensive campaign will entail studying the issues facing youth all over the world, completing books 2 to 6 (they have done book 1 already), using the arts to communicate the messages from the special themes and the Ruhi books, and sports. The campaign has the potential to transform the community – already we are seeing signs of what the gathering of momentum means as a new spirit inspires our consultations, as we move beyond the things that often irritated us about one another in the past and as we see the potential drawing closer. Already a team of 13 university youth from Edmonton, Canada, are here for the summer to help with this programme. Not one of them is a Bahá'í but they are full of idealism and a desire to be of service.

About ten years ago my wife Pam and I opened School of Nations in Guyana, an all-age private Bahá'í-inspired school. Now there are 650 full-time students (representing 22 nationalities) and three hundred adults who pursue University of Cambridge International Diplomas in the evenings. As of September 2005 we are to start offering University of London undergraduate and postgraduate degrees through our newly created 'Nations University'. There will be over 60 courses to choose from – we are thinking at present of offering degrees in business, law, economics and development.

The School of Nations has recently opened a small branch in one of the rural areas, Essequibo Coast, which is emerging as one of our promising clusters. A wonderful Ethiopian pioneer family manage the school. They were assisted this past year by two Canadian short-term pioneers. The school is a not-for-profit venture and has played a very valuable role in developing the Bahá'í identity in this region. We may open similar units in other parts of the country.

151

October 2005

Lois and David Lambert

Mongolia

Lois and David pioneered to Mongolia in 1992 and are still there 13 years on. Both currently serve on the National Spiritual Assembly. Lois has sent this wonderful story about one of their study circles.

The Story of a Study Circle in Mongolia

The story of our present study circle/family group began when our landlady, Altantseteg (Adi), noticed that there were often many pairs of shoes left outside our door. One Sunday evening she knocked at our door to find out what was going on. At that time there were four different level study circles happening at the same time. We introduced her to each group and showed her the material we were studying. She became very excited and asked if she and her family could participate. She was very eager that the youth in her family should study this material and, although Adi herself never had the time to come in the next few weeks, three of her young nieces began to study Ruhi 1. Soon after this, Adi went to Singapore to study English and we put her in touch with Rose Ong, who used to be the Counsellor responsible for Mongolia in the early days of the Faith here, from 1991 to 1996. By the time Adi returned to Mongolia, she was a radiant and dynamic Bahá'í and was eager for all her family to study Ruhi.

Adi's family is huge and extraordinary. Her father is the protocol officer of Mongolia's president and is at the president's side wherever he goes, whether home or abroad. Her aunties, brothers, sisters and cousins include Mongolia's top heart surgeon, one of the only four female members of parliament, the president of one of Mongolia's most successful and fast growing banks – the only female director of a bank in Mongolia – and the director of the Judicial Monitoring Committee of the Government of Mongolia. Adi herself works for the Mongolian parliament as a human resources officer. We began a new study circle with nine members of her family and several other friends who had become interested during a recent teaching campaign. We decided to have a team of three facilitators, so that the study circle could operate both in English and Mongolian and would be able to continue on a regular basis, even though one or two of the facilitators were sometimes unable to attend because of institutional duties.

One by one each of the participants in the study circle became a Bahá'í, nine of whom were members of the same family. In total 14 friends declared their faith in Bahá'u'lláh during the study of Ruhi 1. We linked our study circle to other core activities, in particular to regular devotional gatherings. People would regularly bring their friends and, on two occasions, also brought the taxi drivers who drove them to the devotional gathering. Those who came to the devotional gatherings were invited to join other Ruhi 1 study circles and there have been a number of other groups who have studied Ruhi 1 and are now studying Ruhi 2. The original group is just finishing Ruhi 3 and will soon be starting a children's study circle in the area. Ruhi 4 will be starting shortly. The youth are participating in junior youth groups.

We link our studies with practice. We celebrated the completion of Ruhi 1 with singing and dancing, shared food and photographs, and the next day our study circle's first teaching campaign began. It was to be an 'Aunties and Husbands' teaching campaign, to teach all the members of their family. It began with a celebration at the home of the grandmother of the family, whose children, grandchildren and great-grandchildren all helped to prepare a delicious and sumptuous spread for us all. There were about 30 family members present and after the meal all those who had taken part in the study circle shared what they had been learning. First there was a devotional, with many sung and chanted prayers, with most of the family joining in.

Afterwards there were dances and dramas prepared by the junior youth group, songs sung by the children, and stories and teachings narrated by members of the study circle. It was a truly joyous occasion and at the end of the afternoon the grandmother and the aunties gathered around to ask questions and hear more stories. The grandmother spoke of her pleasure and pride in seeing that her children and her children's children were learning such beautiful things, and this was echoed many times by her daughters, the aunties.

The men of the family were present and clearly enjoyed the event. Kaliuna's husband Ganzorig, the heart surgeon, prepared a delicious curry for us but the men seemed to be more shy of becoming involved. So the 'husbands' part of the campaign continued with daily prayers that the husbands would be drawn closer. In the last few weeks Ganzorig has become the first adult man in the family to declare his faith in Bahá'u'lláh.

Each member of the study circle is choosing several people – family, friends, teachers – to nurture and help progress towards acceptance of Bahá'u'lláh. Visiting families to study deepening themes with them is ongoing and after completing Ruhi 3 a children's class will be established. The youth are translating stories from published English children's books into Mongolian for the *Mongolia Bahá'í Medee* (News).

Most of the group is actively involved in teaching. There are many stories to tell. Here are just two.

One of the youngest members of the group, Khulan, who is 14, spoke to her teacher, Bayermaa, about the Faith in front of her whole class and later invited her to the Birthday of Bahá'u'lláh. She came, bought a number of books and soon became a Bahá'í. She participated in an intensive study of Ruhi 1, joined our original group for the study of Ruhi 2 and is now studying Ruhi 3 with the rest of the group. This teacher taught her mother, who is now attending devotional gatherings at our home and studying Ruhi 1. Four members of the original study circle/family group joined Khulan last week to visit Bayerma's mother and one of her friends to share deepening themes.

Bahá'u'lláh tells us that one prayer has the power to transform a whole city. Adi has seen for herself the power of prayer at the Mongolian parliament building where she works in the cabinet secretariat. She shares a room with her boss, who used to come to work at about 10:30–11:00 a.m. and whose usual manner towards his subordinates was very distant. After Adi became a Bahá'í it became her practice to read prayers in the morning at her desk. Her boss came in a couple of times to find her involved with her prayers. When he asked her what she was reading, she showed him her prayer book. After a while she noticed that he began to come in earlier in the mornings and would sit there while she said her prayers. Then one day he said to her, 'I used not to enjoy being in this office, but now I am much happier. I feel better about my work and about my life. I think it is the prayers you are reading.'

Often we wish that we were not so busy with our studies or our work so that we could serve the Faith more. But in reality our busy professional lives, or our university and school days, are not obstacles but opportunities to teach the Faith to the waiting masses, hungry for the bread of the spirit. The members of our study circle are determined to make the most of those opportunities.

152
October 2005
Jean Reynard
Tanzania

Jean is a frequent visitor to Tanzania, having lived there for 30 years from 1959 until 1989.

I went to Tanzania for the first time in 1959 and from the moment I stepped off the plane I fell in love with Dar es Salaam, then the capital city. It was hot and humid but the roads leading into the town were lined with beautiful acacia trees (giving the name Acacia Avenue to the main street) spreading a canopy of colour overhead as you walked or drove into town. I originally thought of staying for a few months but stayed for 31 years. I give thanks every day of my life for the wonderful opportunity I had to live in this very beautiful country and for some of the wonderful people I met during my years there. In 1979 I became a Bahá'í in Dar es Salaam.

I came to the United Kingdom in 1991 as my two sons had to finish their education in Britain and it wasn't until last year that I had an opportunity to return to Tanzania after an absence of 14 years. I was met at Dar es Salaam airport by the secretary of the National Spiritual Assembly who has been a friend for 25 years and he took me to his home where I was a guest for a few weeks until I found accommodation 22 km from town in an area called Bahari Beach.

The house was situated just a few minutes' walk from the Indian Ocean and had a very large garden with many trees, including the neem tree which, it is claimed, can cure 40 different illnesses. Benezet, who works as a cook for a Bahá'í-owned restaurant in town, his wife Esther (both born into Bahá'í families) and their five children moved into the property with me and for two weeks a young Tanzanian who is still waiting for a place at the university joined us and we started to discuss how to put a teaching programme in place. I hired a night watchman and Frank – the student – started to talk about the Faith with him and three times a week we had a devotional to which we invited him.

As I was so far from town, and my house was three miles from the nearest bus stop, I had to buy a car. There were always several bicycle taxis waiting at the bus stop to ferry people to their various homes but I felt that maybe I am past the age when I can comfortably sit on the back of a bicycle and be pedalled home! It was a secondhand car and the nicest thing about it was the air conditioning – it was getting to be very hot in December. It was also very useful for taking Esther, Benezet and the children into the Bahá'í Centre on Sundays and, occasionally, for a drive to a nearby hotel for a 'soda'. They always sat very quietly and upright in the car with big eyes and the three year old told me very seriously, 'My daddy is going to get a car like this soon.'

Driving into town is an experience not to be missed if you are thinking of taking up rally driving. It is hair-raising. The traffic on Dar roads is simply incredible, mainly because there are so many private buses, known locally as dalla dallas (from 'dollar-dollar' as it used to be a dollar a ride) and the drivers of these vehicles know nothing about signals, hand or otherwise. They pull in and out picking up passengers and give you a cheery thumbs up sign if you manage to stop in time to let them go. There are also many lorries lumbering to and from town, loaded with sand or cement blocks, always with several people hanging half on and half off, cyclists and handcarts and we all wobbled our way through the enormous potholes and, if you can believe, speed humps!

When the rain started at the end of November the road became a series of lakes and the breakdowns became more frequent. There were several times when I couldn't reach home and had to stay with friends in town. And often when I did reach home there was a Lake Victoria across the road leading to my house and I had to call on a local doctor friend with a four wheel drive to pull me through. But through all this the bus drivers, the dalla dalla drivers, the pullers of handcarts and the cyclists have an exuberance and enthusiasm which is a joy to experience. Although stuck in traffic many, many times, I never ever felt the stress that I feel constantly in London. There was so much entertainment going on all around, laughter, spontaneous dancing, vendors selling just about everything with such good humour, that it was often difficult to resist them. When the rain stopped and the roads dried up there appeared even more potholes to be avoided and if, as often happened I couldn't avoid them or hit them by accident, there was a horrible grating and crashing sound from somewhere underneath my car!

Dar es Salaam has changed tremendously in the 14 years since I left and, as far as I am concerned, not always for the better! There are several large luxury hotels selling the same chocolate croissants, Danish pastries, sausage rolls that are now available throughout the universe it seems. It was a pleasure to take some local Bahá'í friends into one of these places just to visit the very luxurious toilets. I think the taps were gold plated!

There are frequent electricity cuts and water is a huge problem. For the expatriates and the more well-off, water is available at a price, transported by lorry to fill up huge tanks in their gardens. But the majority of people have to purchase water from street vendors who fill up their plastic bottles. Alternatively, as I often witnessed, they dig up the roads to find a pipe running to someone's house and just cut it to fill their tins and bottles. But people mostly remain good humoured, hospitable and colourful in all their adversity.

In my own house I rarely had the luxury of water coming from the taps and mostly I had to wash with bucket and jug. Many times I arrived at the Bahá'í Centre to find that there was no electricity and therefore no computer working. On one occasion there was no petrol for four days in any petrol station in and around Dar es Salaam and people were sending text messages to each other whenever there was a rumour of petrol being found somewhere.

The Bahá'í community is wonderful and especially the youth. The Bahá'í Centre is mainly run by the youth. They clean, cook, take care of the garden and spend two hours every day studying the Ruhi books. Mr Akida, a Bahá'í of many, many years, has just finished translating the Kitáb-i-Íqán into Swahili. There are many Bahá'í writings that still have to be translated and I managed to get Anna, the daughter of the late President Nyerere, to make a start on the Kitáb-i-Aqdas, which she did beautifully.

An American Bahá'í has started a children's orphanage and has employed six Bahá'ís to help her. There is a fast food restaurant in town, owned by non-local Bahá'ís. A few of the Bahá'í youth have been trained and employed there in various capacities but employment is a problem, especially for the youth who have studied at Ruaha School, maybe up to O or A level. As students they tend to have expectations, which, of course, cannot be realized as there is little opportunity even for further education. It was thought-provoking for me to meet a young man who had studied at Ruaha School with my son, Aly. Aly completed his PhD last year and this young man is struggling to live, working for approximately £30 a month.

I can't finish this account without mentioning Prosper Nduke. Prosper is now 74 and has been pioneering in a village just outside Bukoba since 1979. I met up with him in Dar es Salaam where he had come for his son's wedding. It had taken 30 hours by bus for him to arrive in Dar es Salaam but that didn't stop him from enthusiastically telling me about the primary school he has built himself in his village and where he takes in all school-age children in his village and from beyond. His son told me, 'It is an embarrassment to travel anywhere with my father because all he ever does is look around trying to find someone – anyone – he feels would be receptive to the Faith, and then he can spend his journey teaching. That's when he is really happy!'

I left Tanzania in January after spending four months there. For most of my life I have felt that my real education only began when I went to live in Tanzania and I feel so privileged and enormously grateful to have been able to spend a large part of my life in such a beautiful country and with such beautiful people. Thank you Tanzania.

153
October 2005
Jimmy McGilligan by Tom Wilmot
India

Jimmy, originally from Coleraine, Northern Ireland, is married to Janak from India. Together they run the Barli Development Institute for Rural Women in Indore. Below is a write-up about him by Tom Wilmot, a British volunteer to the Institute who worked directly with Jimmy.

An Irishman in Indore

In English on one side and in Hindi on the other, 'James R. McGilligan, Manager' reads the business card of a man whose Irish name is as singular in Indore as the man himself. Indore is an industrial and relatively unremarkable city in the heart of the central Indian state of Madhya Pradesh, and is home to the NGO in which I spent my five-month volunteer placement. Jimmy, as he prefers to be known, is the manager of the 'Barli Development Institute for Rural Women', although he also holds the official title of Indore's 'Unofficial Correspondent to the British High Commission'. One wonders, on first acquaintance, what has led him to this unconventional position. What brings a self-employed land reclamation engineer and industrial contractor thousands of miles from Northern Ireland to a development institute for rural women in deepest India?

India. That notoriously penetrating cocktail of a nation, colourfully resplendent but spiked with vibrant life and starkest death, infused with an ethereal spirituality; a tonic of insidious chaos to the western consciousness. India, with a sort of organic vitality all of its own.

The heady effects of coming to live and work in India for over 15 years should not be underestimated. A thick skin may be useful but will never allow anyone to really live a fulfilled life in this wondrous land, as Jimmy has done. You need adaptability, understanding, a sense of humour and a strong character, as well as a sense of perspective and critique. Add belief in yourself and faith in your philosophy to your packing list and you might just survive. My point is that for any of his volunteers spending time in India, Jimmy is certainly someone to learn from.

If you ask him how he came to be here, he will tell you that's a good question but involves a long story. The reasons for the paths of all our lives are difficult to fathom at the best of times. In Jimmy's case many would claim that destiny had a big part to play, although Jimmy himself tends to lean more towards the 'well, it all just sort of happened like that' attitude. In any case, one senses that his new life has certainly brought him enviable happiness and fulfilment.

Brought up in a farming family in rural Northern Ireland, Jimmy started his own business after getting one of his toes cut off in an agricultural accident at the age of 16. With typical enterprise and enthusiasm, he used the £500 compensation he received at the time to buy his first digger and built up his business from these humble beginnings, taking contracts in various areas of agriculture and industry, gaining most experience in land reclamation.

Whilst running his own business more or less singlehanded, he was an active member of the community in which he lived and he still tells remarkable stories from those days, from mountain climbing to rally car navigation. The business of land reclamation and agriculture provided a rewarding and stimulating occupation, as it would for any ambitious young man, and Jimmy enjoyed his work immensely.

One volunteer proposed that his friends and family at home must think Jimmy has a wonderfully exotic life, having left this all behind for a new start in India of all places. 'Actually, they think I'm crazy', Jimmy responded.

However, his experiences in his field of work combined with a critical and conscientious mind also gave him an appreciation of everything that was wrong with how certain things were done in countries like the UK. Things he witnessed and experienced – the countless gallons of milk poured into the sea and the wildlife havens colonized by the creeping advance of overstretched intensive agriculture are just some of the examples he cites. The squandering of precious resources and the lack of ethical responsibility over which environmentalists so lament, and which Jimmy witnessed first hand, became part of his reason to divert his skills to a better cause. It was not a sudden change of heart or some sort of life-changing revelation. It was a rational formulation of opinion based on experience and conscience. Even at this time Jimmy never dreamed he would come to work in India, let alone get married and settle there.

Jimmy first came to India as a volunteer in 1986 to work on reclamation of saline soil in Gwalior, to the north of Indore. He met his wife-to-be, Janak, who had founded a vocational education institute for rural and tribal women grounded in the principles of the Bahá'í Faith, of which Jimmy had been a follower for several years. They were married in 1988, an unorthodox match in this conservative quarter of central India but an apt and happy one. The two complement one another marvellously and perhaps this is part of the secret of how the institute has gone from strength to strength ever since. Now renamed the Barli Development Institute for Rural Women, the large campus on the outskirts of Indore accommodates over 80 trainees (for six months at a time) and a dedicated staff of employees and volunteers. The trainees are taught vocational skills, health, literacy and personal development during their time here, and the curriculum is constantly monitored, updated and improved. There are countless success stories from the institute's graduates but this story is concerned with that of its manager.

The institute had not previously taken on male volunteers until two short-term volunteers came over the summer followed by myself for nearly six months. So we were something of an experiment. As the trainees at Barli generally come from remote rural and tribal areas, from very traditional cultures and backgrounds, it is important that the institute can guarantee a safe and comfortable environment within a large, rapidly modernizing city like Indore. Therefore it was felt that it would be inappropriate for male volunteers, especially foreigners, to be part of the girls' training. However, Jimmy's interest and subsequent enthusiastic work in solar energy has given the institute a whole new dimension and now a potential opportunity for volunteers of both sexes to get involved with the Barli success story. He has become a pioneer of solar cooking, with an ambition to bring the techniques and facilities to the people who need them most.

In many rural areas across India, indeed throughout much of the developing world, the use of wood as fuel is becoming increasingly unsustainable and problematic. Aside from the obvious environmental damage, firewood is ever more expensive and scarce, and wood smoke causes serious respiratory problems, particularly for young children. Collecting the wood is a major chore, often a task performed exclusively by women and children. This aspect links neatly with the main goal of the Barli Development Institute: the empowerment of young women through education and training. Jimmy's work to promote solar cooking is another integral aspect of development in the areas the Barli trainees come from.

In recent years Jimmy has been working on the manufacture of huge community solar cookers. The technology involves a ten square metre parabolic reflective dish that focuses the heat of the sun to a point where temperatures up to 1000 degrees Celsius can be generated. The institute now has three of these solar cookers and almost all of the food is cooked in this way.

Jimmy's enthusiasm for solar cooking technology has led to many success-ful ventures elsewhere. Most recently he and his staff have installed the largest solar kitchen in Madhya Pradesh, at a school in the tribal area of Jhabua. The installation has to be seen to be believed. Five beautifully shining dishes lined up staring directly at the sun and towering over a low building housing five cooking places at five blistering focal points where five outsize pans of various descriptions are used to cook for the school's seven hundred or so children.

More such ambitious projects will doubtless follow but also there is always more work to be done within Barli itself. For example, building enterprise con-stantly generates a surplus of work for Jimmy and his employees. During my stay I witnessed and helped with the latest installation. Designed by Jimmy, it is a large multi-purpose hall to be used for various teaching purposes as well as providing an excellent venue for the many functions held at the institute. I have observed with interest the catalogue of battles that Jimmy has fought with contractors and labourers in order to get the building built to his stand-ards in the way he wants it done, and in a reasonable time. It is very interesting to learn from his dealings with the bewildering multitude of people who are involved with the building. He knows how to handle the situation through his experiences of both disasters and successes in the past. While the contractors are prepared to go to great lengths to get away with doing as little as possible as cheaply as possible, Jimmy is constantly campaigning vigorously for higher quality and fewer imperfections. Herein lies the source of the various conflicts.

There was the battle with the Bengali plastering boys who realigned a window frame to match their crooked brick design on the external wall. There were the labourers fitting the windows who worked into the small hours fixing the mosquito grills in time for the visit of the trainees' families. There was the painter who spent several long hours diligently applying expensive paint on top of a thick coating of rust. Long debates and elaborate deceptions over obtaining a good quality of electrical wire. The list goes on. Such constant problems require enormous patience and tenacity.

Amongst other challenges he has had to rise to in India, learning to communicate in Hindi was perhaps one of the most essential. Not one for structured formal education, Jimmy has simply picked up Hindi by the absorption method. He is modest about his language skills and jokes that he has been here for 15 years and still can't speak the language. The joke being that he makes this claim in Hindi!

Jimmy naturally relates well to people and has had a keen mind for learn-ing new things all his life. I'm sure that to a native speaker Jimmy's Hindi is far from perfect but one is constantly impressed and entertained by his joking with the trainees, chatting with visitors, coordinating his employees and, when necessary, berating hapless contractors or labourers when they try to cheat him. The two employees who work mostly with Jimmy on the solar cookers have enormous respect for and devotion to their employer. During my time as a volunteer I observed the impressive level of understanding in this relationship. There was a very real sense of cooperation and good humour, resulting in a rewarding work ethic.

What struck me most about Jimmy's unconventional occupation was his dedication to the cause and firm belief in the philosophy of the institute. It was not something he generally spoke about but I was reminded of it whenever he explained to interested parties the importance of what the institute is doing, and with a sincerity devoid of any obsequious vanity. With his outspoken manner I can easily imagine Jimmy explaining to Osama Bin Laden himself how important it is for women to be educated and empowered in any society, about how women are the first educators of their children and why their status should never be seen as secondary to that of men.

My experience of working with and getting to know Jimmy has certainly been a memorable one. I hope after reading this you don't think that he is crazy, for there are great things afoot at Barli and I would recommend any volunteer to get involved.

154
January 2006
Phillip and Ann Hinton
Australia
Portals to Malaysia

A 40-year friendship between two Sydney Bahá'í families recently produced an unexpected outcome. Phillip and Ann Hinton met Ho-San Leong at Stratford-on-Avon in England in 1966.

Says Phillip:

We'd been married about a year. I was in my first year with the Royal Shakespeare Company and we were isolated Bahá'ís, busy with career, setting up home, etc., so it was refreshing to meet this young Malaysian Bahá'í whom Ann had met at the Frankfurt Temple dedication in 1964. We kept in touch and have always been close to Ho-San, his wife Mariette and their children. The Leongs saw my one-man play 'Portals to Freedom' about Howard Colby Ives, a disciple of 'Abdu'l-Bahá, and Ho-San suggested I take it to Malaysia.

It seemed an impossible dream until Joan Sinnathamby, Mariette's sister who lives with her husband Sinna in Kuala Lumpur, visited Sydney. Mariette arranged a meeting and soon there came an invitation from the National Assemblies of Singapore and Malaysia to make a three-week tour. I was amazed how quickly it all happened, and actually, I was uneasy about it. Singapore would have the right theatres for my play – but Malaysia? And would they have the lighting to make it work? I've performed 'Portals' all over the world but even in America where you'd imagine such things are commonplace, it was often chaotic finding the technical support to do the play properly. Would the audiences have sufficient English? I needn't have worried – the Malaysians were an inspiration! Firstly, the tour had the solid backing of the two National Assemblies – very important. Joan and Sinna basically took a month off from work and devoted themselves full time to booking theatres, forming support teams from the Local Spiritual Assemblies sponsoring the tour, marketing the play to the Bahá'ís, printing programmes, tickets and posters. (They even sent a short CD extract of the recording of the play to each community to be played at the 19 Day Feast!) They visited each venue before we arrived and checked all the requirements – it was brilliant.

Singapore: Two packed houses on the Friday and Saturday nights in a beautiful studio theatre, the Actor's Den. Singapore was arranged mainly by Chew Sin Yang, former Australian National Assembly member. Everything fell into place like magic. Perth Bahá'í David Lucas, living in Singapore, is an accomplished theatre lighting designer who helped with 'Portals' in Perth a few years ago, so he designed and operated the lights and came with us as far as Kuala Lumpur. We'd also decided to try a 'question and answer' session after each performance – me on stage fielding questions from the audience. It worked well, particularly in Singapore and KL, where people have good English.

Ann and I also held the first of five planned 'workshops'. With advice from professional storyteller Donna Jacobs Sife, we devised a programme in which we led groups of about 25 plus on a journey of discovery – to the point where they became effective storytellers. By the end of a session our nervous participants were finding their creative selves – fairly bouncing off the walls!

Malaysia: On Sunday morning, the Hintons, Sinnathambys and David, in our red tour van, drove across the causeway to our first Malaysian venue, Johur Baru. A few technical hitches but all overcome through David's resourcefulness and goodwill.

Malacca was next and another successful night, with another almost full house, a good percentage of the audience 'community of interest'. There were even a few Muslim guests. A couple approached me in the foyer after the show and posed some keen questions. 'How do Bahá'ís pray?'

The old port of Malacca is fascinating, with its 350 year old Buddhist temple and its antique shops and restaurants. Only two days there, so it's on our list for a revisit!

On to Kuala Lumpur and a packed schedule – four performances and two 'workshops' in six days. At times exhausting, but dear Joan and Sinna were our 'fortress'. A great little 200 plus theatre – and excellent audiences. Shopping and sightseeing, then to the north – Ipoh and Penang. Mostly Tamil background Bahá'ís, so there was a brief pre-show chat in Tamil. Some of these dear friends had travelled two hours by bus. Over three weeks 'Portals' played to about two thousand people, 25 per cent of them 'community of interest'.

What a marvellous adventure! When you travel as Bahá'ís, the doors open to so many new experiences, insights and, above all, friends. Malaysian Bahá'ís are exemplary in their commitment to the Bahá'í Cause. There, and in Singapore, they get on with the work of the Faith with such joy and good grace. I was able to serve briefly as an artist and Ann shared her experiences as an educator.

This was a new experience for the Malaysian and Singapore Bahá'ís – their first 'arts' tour and, in their culture, quite a bold venture. But our offering was truly valued and no effort was spared in taking care of our every need – everywhere there were helping hands! The hospitality was overwhelming. Malaysians expect you to do as they do – eat, round the clock! Of course, the food is delicious, so we gave in! How can we ever forget the generosity and warmth of these precious Bahá'í friends?

155

January 2006

Joe and Atieh Donnelly

Bulgaria

Joe and Atieh pioneered with their two children to Bulgaria ten years ago from Ireland and settled in Plovdiv. Since then lots of changes have occurred both in their lives and in the Bulgarian community.

O ye close and dear friends of 'Abdu'l-Bahá!
In the Orient scatter perfumes,
And shed splendours on the West.
Carry light unto the Bulgar,
And the Slav with life invest.

'Abdu'l-Bahá, 1893[28]

In August 2005 we celebrated ten years pioneering in Bulgaria. In some ways it seems such a long time ago, August 1995, when we arrived with 16 pieces of luggage and two words of Bulgarian – '*Leke Nosht*' (Goodnight!) and '*Zdravei*' (Hello!). Bulgaria of course has changed, the Bahá'í community has too, and we have changed as well. Have the changes been for the better?

We would have to say a resounding 'Yes'! The structure of the Bahá'í community has changed enormously with the advent of the Five Year Plan and the 'cluster culture' but the needs and the goals of the Faith are clearer now with the emphasis on the three core activities – study circles, devotional gatherings and children's classes. For the first time ever, the international Bahá'í community seems to be on the same 'wavelength' as regards teaching and proclamation. There is no doubt that if Bahá'í communities focus on one goal, the 'acceleration of entry by troops', great advances for the Faith are, and will be, achieved.

The institute process has developed very rapidly in Bulgaria, and Sofia cluster at this time is the focus of intense and sustained teaching and consolidation. A 'mini' IPG (intensive programme of growth) was launched in June of this year and with four new Bahá'ís. These 'new creations' include a radiant 98 year old woman who had been looked after by a Bahá'í lady. On hearing some passages read to her from *Paris Talks* and some Bahá'í prayers, she declared her faith in Bahá'u'lláh. Another lady who called at our apartment and had attended one devotional meeting nine months previously, taking some Bahá'í prayers and leaflets with her which she had been reading, said, 'I want to become a Bahá'í!' A policewoman who had started a sequence of Ruhi courses came with her Bahá'í friend to a 19 Day Feast. On being told lovingly that she had to be a Bahá'í to attend Feast, she promptly said, 'I am a Bahá'í' and signed a declaration card straight away! Another new Bahá'í, who declared at the Bahá'í Centre in Sofia, wanted to know how much she should pay to Ḥuqúqu'lláh! Our community of interest is now in excess of 20 souls and things are looking good!

In addition, we are making rapid progress in the area of children's classes and this can only be complementary to other activities already happening in a cluster. Two Bahá'í families have returned from overseas, bringing with them a total of five children, and this has greatly reinforced and enriched the activities in Bahá'í children's classes in Bulgaria.

Quite a lot of change has occurred to our family during this period too. Neysan, our son, after graduating from Townshend International School, decided to live in Macedonia for his year of service. Melody, our daughter, also a graduate of Townshend, was nine years old when she first came to Bulgaria. After several months of service in Swindon, UK, she returned to Bulgaria to complete a year of service working with two travel teachers from Perth, Australia, as an interpreter and children's class teacher.

Joe is currently teaching his twenty-first semester (ten and a half years) at the local university and Atieh divides her time between housework and the Faith, with housework coming a bad second!

One of the great bounties of living in a Bahá'í community with few resources is that you have the opportunity to serve in areas like pioneering, Ḥuqúqu'lláh, the training institute, etc. In other words, every Bahá'í wears several 'insignia'.

The Bulgarian economy has moved on a bit in ten years. There are now new opportunities for business-minded people or, if you like, entrepreneurs! The number of motorcars has trebled in the past three years and the building industry is going through a boom. Property values have soared. So prospective pioneers take note! Of course Bulgaria is hoping to become a member of the European Union in January 2007 and there is a hectic rush to align the laws of the country with the ever demanding standards from within the European Community.

156
January 2006
Sylvia Miley
Chile

Sylvia, from Southport, Lancashire, recently visited Chile on holiday. She relates the following 'teaching' incident.

I was standing looking at an active volcano near Puerto Varas in Chile. Earlier I prayed hard for an opportunity to teach 19 people – if nothing else, just the word 'Bahá'í' would do.

I thought to myself how many of us stand and wait for the opportunity and then when it comes we gush with enthusiasm, pouring out the heat of joy and melting the hearts. If only . . .

Normally when travelling I call into the tourist offices and ask if there is a Bahá'í community in that town. Some interesting responses have come over the years but at Puerto Varas, in this very Spanish-speaking town, it was closed. So I asked our local tour guide the question.

'Is there a Bahá'í community in this town?' He digested my English slowly and then said, 'I have not heard that word since I was 13 years old.' A small volcano erupted in me and as we were moving on for tea and cakes, he was busy mustering the rest of the tourists, so I asked if I could sit with him.

We sat together, two smiling faces – more than that, two beaming faces –

linked by a word. All the guide could remember were two words, 'Abdu'l-Bahá and Alláh-u-Abhá! We savoured these words instead of the cake and he told me he was a Bahá'í for three weeks as his friend was a Bahá'í. He used to go to meetings where he enjoyed the prayers and at school, when the teacher asked what religion the pupils were, he said he was a Bahá'í. The teacher told his mother and he got told off. Summer came and the Bahá'í child did not return to the school.

We got back into the coach. He picked up the microphone and said, 'I have been having a most interesting conversation with one of your tourists who is a Bahá'í and I haven't heard that word since I was 13 years old.' Nineteen tourists heard the word which I had been whispering for a few days and no one had asked me any questions. But the story doesn't end there!

At the next stop, Punta Arenas, our English tour guide told our new local tour guide, Jaime, about the Bahá'í in the tour and he said, 'I have not met a Bahá'í since I was eight years old. My teacher called Miss Williams and a boy called Fariborz were Bahá'ís and all I learned was that Bahá'ís do not kill. But,' he added, 'they are going to build a temple here in Chile!'

I was introduced to Jaime and once again the joy poured out of me and I gained such enthusiasm and courage as I asked him if I could take the message to one of the waiters, a beautiful gracious black boy from Peru. A time was arranged and through translation I delivered the most precious gift in a way I have never done before. I gave them some small prayer cards and showed them the picture of the temple to be built in Santiago. The other tourists remained impassive – but then the heat of volcanoes doesn't affect everyone; only the noise and the roar. Maybe another time, another place.

157
April 2006
Karen and Tim Shrimpton
Returning to the United Kingdom

Knowing how difficult it often is for returning pioneers to settle back home, I asked Karen to write something on this very challenging subject. Ed.

Eighteen months ago we returned to the UK after living in developing countries for eight years. Having been asked to write something for *Pioneer Post* about what life is like for a returning pioneer, it is only now that I feel I can write something that doesn't sound too negative.

It has been more difficult settling back into English life than I ever imagined it would be. We spent two years in the Philippines, four years in Uganda and two years in Bangladesh. We had planned to stay in Bangladesh longer but owing to serious health problems, we made the difficult decision to return to the United Kingdom. We were both in need of time for recuperation and regeneration without having to think about boiling and filtering the water, bleaching fruit and vegetables and wading through several inches of contaminated water to get to school.

Our major apprehension in coming back to a small market town in Norfolk (where we had a house) was how our children Jasmine and Kenny would fit in. We adopted them in Uganda and they had never spent more than a few weeks at a time in the UK. On some of those visits to Norfolk they had experienced racial prejudice from other children in public parks and playgrounds. Rural Norfolk is extremely non-multicultural. However, our fears were allayed in the first few weeks, when we enrolled Kenny on a Norwich City Football in the Community course (he is passionate about football) and he was voted 'Player's player of the week' by the other children in the team. Jasmine and Kenny were the only two black faces to be seen out of about three hundred children, but not an unkind word was spoken the entire week. Once they started school at our local primary school, they made friends quickly and are well liked in the town.

However, for Tim and me and our 18 year old son Robbie, things have not been so easy. Robbie started an A level course at a college in Norwich and was disappointed at the narrow-minded thinking of most of the young people. Many of their lives were focused entirely around drugs and alcohol or, alternatively, cars, hairstyles and the latest fashions. Living in developing countries, there had always been young people interested in philosophy and religion, and even if his friends did partake of drugs and alcohol, they were still able to have deep discussions and play music, etc. After a year of seeing Rob getting more and more depressed, Tim and I finally agreed to let him give up his education (which was very difficult, as we are both teachers) and embark on a period of service.

Although we were given the advice to think of being back in Norfolk as a 'new' posting, it has been very difficult coming back to the same house in the same town where very little has changed. We have many acquaintances in the town but very few people we can call real friends. We tried not to have too many expectations but there were people whom we thought would be pleased to see us back and friends that we were looking forward to spending time with. However, we soon realized that people are very busy with their own lives and comfortable with the way things are. Although we contacted people when we first came back, not many have made an effort to get together. We felt the need to be nurtured but no one seemed to realize that – not friends, family or even the Bahá'ís. We couldn't get on with anything because everything seemed too overwhelming and we just didn't know where to start. Having said that, we are now gradually meeting new people and beginning to meet more people we can relate to. We have recently made contact with several people locally who have expressed an interest in the Faith and have also started holding children's classes for our children and several of their non-Bahá'í friends.

Of course, in many ways it has been a wonderful time for us since being back in England. We have been able to drink water from the tap, eat fresh wholesome food (we've really enjoyed cooking our own food again and knowing exactly what we are eating), breathe clean air and concentrate on getting fit and healthy. Picking blackberries in the autumn and walking in the countryside without being stared at have been joyful experiences for us.

However, there's no doubt about it, we have experienced major 'culture shock' on returning to the UK – probably more so than we did in going to either Asia or Africa. One of the biggest difficulties has been the amount of choice in absolutely everything from brands of toothpaste and soap, to telephone companies, cell phone networks, Internet providers and even gas and electricity suppliers. For eight years we had very little choice and just made do with whatever happened to be in the shops or markets. It is only in the last couple of years that we even had a supermarket open and it certainly wasn't anything like the scale of Sainsbury's or Tesco. The first few times I went into one of these huge stores after returning to England, I had to turn around and walk out again. It was simply too much to cope with. We are now used to it again and enjoy the ease of shopping and being able to get whatever we want whenever we want. It is frighteningly easy to get caught up in this materialistic world and yet we know that the majority of the world's peoples are struggling to feed and clothe themselves. Here, we feel like little fish in a big ocean, whereas overseas as pioneers we were like big fish in a small pond. It is a huge responsibility but at the same time it is very exciting and invigorating though not easy.

We are certainly not feeling totally settled in England and we are currently in the process of exploring job opportunities in other parts of the world. We pray for guidance and hope to serve Bahá'u'lláh in whatever capacity we can wherever we are.

In closing I would just like to say I think the most helpful thing for returning pioneers is to be in touch with other recently returned pioneers. This support network is vitally important for a healthy state of mind.

158
April 2006
Richard Poole
Rwanda

Richard is a veteran pioneer of Sudan, Tanzania, Barbados, St Lucia, Ecuador, Guinea and Uganda. He moved to Rwanda in September 2005.

A Pioneer's Growing Pains

I find it intriguing to reflect sometimes upon the circumstances that can beset pioneers in the early days of their pioneering. One might expect, so the reasoning might go, that God, through His Supreme Manifestation, Bahá'u'lláh, would be so delighted that someone has chosen to rise up in His name and serve His Cause that He would remove every obstacle from his path and smooth the way ahead, perhaps even rolling out a red carpet in his honour, pioneering, after all, being 'the prince of all goodly deeds'.[29] This, however, seldom seems to be the case; in fact, if anything, the opposite seems more likely to occur.

A rapid review of the fortunes of pioneers that I have known both in Africa and Latin America, and also in Europe, shows that the new arrivals are not infrequently beset by a surprisingly diverse range of problems. These problems might include, for example, falling foul of debilitating sickness and insanitary living conditions, encountering tedious and tiresome obstacles in looking for a job and getting your papers sorted out, as well as such minor frustrations as finding a snake inside your house, being unceremoniously robbed or having your carefully planned and packed luggage containing your entire life-support system mysteriously not arrive. Indeed, in certain cases, a number of stout-hearted pioneers have been so sorely tested that they have been obliged to pull up stakes and move on somewhere else, and probably been left wondering what the whole thing was all about. In fact, this type of initiation seems to be something of a norm rather than an exception, to the point that one might be forgiven for wondering whose side God is actually on.

And it can come as quite a shock, as I know from personal experience. The nice orderly life that you left behind at home has suddenly and unexpectedly come to an abrupt end and you find yourself scratching your head in the midst of tests so severe that you wonder if you are going to survive. Of course, you will and you do, and the wisdom of it will later become apparent, but you will never be quite the same again, and this, I presume, is the object of the exercise. The decision to pioneer is an opportunity for growth and, as we all know, God, since time immemorial, has sent suffering to His loved ones as a means of fostering their advancement. Still, it is impossible to deny that one occasionally finds oneself asking something akin to what Topol asked himself when he sang, 'If I were a Rich Man' in *Fiddler on the Roof,* namely, 'Would it spoil some vast eternal plan if I were a wealthy man?' Might He not, for instance, bend the rules for me just this once and give me a nice easy landing, the smooth entrance into my new life that I was expecting, and perhaps feel I deserve?

Of course such an eventuality is always a possibility, so it should never be ruled out entirely. And we do know, as 'Abdu'l-Bahá has assured us, that no one will ever be tested beyond his limits, so there is really nothing to get too concerned about. And so the conclusion I have arrived at is that God might well be thinking something like this: 'OK, so you want to pioneer; well, let's find out just how serious you really are!' I suspect that in the end it is all about growth and finding out just what our limits actually are. Painful stuff, invariably, but few of us if any, I should imagine, come the finish, would have wished it any other way.

159

July 2006

Gill and Fuad Ta'eed

From Papua New Guinea to Tasmania

Gill and Fuad were pioneers in Papua New Guinea for 20 years before moving to Tasmania.

After reading Karen Shrimpton's letter (April 2006) about their experience of leaving a pioneering post and returning to the United Kingdom, I am moved to write and tell you our story.

Fuad and I left Papua New Guinea in January 2003 exactly 20 years and five days after moving there from UK in January 1983. We had always believed that leaving would be difficult, and we resisted it as long as we could, but finally we had no choice as Fuad no longer had a job there. Fortunately for us we had permanent residency in Australia and we were able to move on to a new country that had all those modern conveniences of the developed world that Karen talks about and which we appreciated so much after the difficulties of living in Port Moresby where we constantly had to be on the alert because of the breakdown there of law and order and the constant and very real threat to one's personal safety. However it was not a return to UK: rather it was an onward move to a new country and a new community. I think that this was the thing that has helped us and which I want to recommend to other returning pioneers.

278

I know that many others may not be able to make an onward move but they can look to see where their services will be most useful in whatever community they go to. When we left Papua New Guinea we made the decision to try to go somewhere in Australia where they needed pioneers. So rather than move to Sydney where our two oldest sons Vahid and Collis were living, we moved to Tasmania, which is one of the two home-front pioneering goals in this country. Many people asked us what on earth we were going to do in Tasmania – surely we would have more opportunity of finding a job in Sydney or Brisbane? But by going to Tasmania we moved to a small community which welcomed us with open arms – literally. The community we had decided to move to sent two people to the airport to meet us on arrival to make sure that we were not tempted away to another area! We have been very blessed here. I have been able to start a completely new career after many years of not working in an income-earning capacity because of our desire that one of us devote all their time and energy to serving the Faith in our pioneering post. I know that if we had moved to a big city this opportunity would not have come my way. Fuad was able to do some consultancy work for three years which took him back to Papua New Guinea about every two months and that eased his transition into this country. Now he too has a full-time job. But the biggest joy has been serving the Faith in a new place and getting fully involved in the institute process and the Five Year Plan. In Papua New Guinea we had been very busy serving the Faith but most of the time we were in the background serving in the National Office and doing administrative work.

When we left PNG only our youngest son Anis (out of four children) was still living at home with us and at first it was very difficult for him. He was born in Papua New Guinea and it was very hard to leave all his friends and come and live in a very different environment at the age of 15. Here again I think we were blessed to be in a small community with a lot of active youth who have now become his closest friends. In 2004 our daughter, Corinne, who had left Papua New Guinea for a youth year of service at the Bahá'í World Centre, also chose to come back and live with us and study here in Tasmania rather than in one of Australia's larger universities where she had been accepted before leaving for Israel. They are both happy here now and are actively serving the Faith.

So all is well with us and I think what I wanted to say is that we, like all pioneers, had found joy and fulfilment in serving the Faith in our pioneering post and were really worried that this had all come to an end when we left – and in a sense it did. But there is so much opportunity to serve this beloved Faith of ours everywhere in the world and we were blessed to find a new field of service, new challenges and new joys in a different environment. This is what I want to recommend to others and if anyone is able to come and join us here in Tasmania we will be the first ones to welcome them at the airport!

160
July 2006
Dave Menham
Nepal

Visit to the Abha School in the Mountain Kingdom of Nepal: A Personal Account

I arrived at Kathmandu's Tribhuvan International Airport in February. Once through customs I jumped into the 1973 Nissan taxi and we bounced our way along the rutted roads, dodging oncoming traffic, sacred cows and pedestrians. I struggled for a few minutes before I could fasten the homemade seatbelt but finally succeeded. We were heading for 'the petrol pump' where I was to meet Dirgha Vikram Shah, the director of the teaching institute who was also to be my Nepalese host. Then the taxi rattled on towards his home before Buddha, the taxi driver, sped off to pick up another fare. I had come as a volunteer to assist in the development of the Abha Community School in the far eastern corner of Nepal.

The Abha School is situated some 500 km east of Kathmandu in the Morang district (one of 75 such districts in Nepal), one of the most densely populated regions outside the capital. Although I had been invited to fly to Biratnagar, the nearest city to the school, with a population of 166,000 people, I chose to travel by bus instead in order to keep my costs as low as possible and to endure things as a Nepalese would have to endure them. After breakfast we took our luggage and walked out to the area of town where we would be taking the first bus ride. Another Bahá'í joined us and so we became a party of three. After a little negotiation Dirgha found us a suitable minibus and we crammed ourselves in alongside another 12 passengers. This was a nine-seater minibus but somehow we all managed to get ourselves installed. The luggage was strapped onto the roof and off we went. The journey was to last for around six to seven hours and would be constantly interrupted with passengers climbing in and out as we drove towards our final destination which seemed to lie so far ahead of us.

We stopped quite frequently at various checkpoints that had been set up along the route manned by Nepalese soldiers and stopped yet again to pay the toll charges for each section of the road that we travelled along. We also made a number of welcome coffee-cum-toilet stops (not that there was any coffee for sale) en route. We finally arrived in Narayanghat, our intermediate overnight stop, at about 3:00 p.m. We then took a rickshaw ride to the hotel where we were to spend the night. The temperature in this part of the country was a few degrees higher than in Kathmandu, so we took a rest from our journey in our hotel rooms before we went out for a meal at a local restaurant which had a very colonial feel to it. After our meal we took to our beds and retired early. Unfortunately for us, a coach party had booked into the hotel the same night and were there to celebrate a Hindu wedding. Their all-night-long celebrations were an unfortunate addition to a long, tiring and rather uncomfortable bus ride! Somehow I managed to get some sleep before we got ourselves up and ready for the second leg of the journey to Sisabani village still a few hundred kilometres away. This time, however, the bus was a little larger and a bit more comfortable. The bus boys who rode on the side of the bus kept me amused as they hung precariously to the side of the bus as we travelled, jumping on and off to pay local toll charges from time to time and to help people on and off the bus with their luggage and various packages which ranged from anything from a bag of rice to a TV set.

We finally arrived in Khanar after several stops en route, which included the now familiar checkpoints. We rode in a rickshaw to Sisabani and to the house of the Nepalese family where we would all be staying. Just before we arrived at the house, and being a keen cyclist, I asked if I could ride the rickshaw (with all our luggage still on board) but was unable to pedal it more than a couple of metres. Unsurprisingly the rickshaw driver found this very amusing!

Sisabani gives you the impression that you have been cast back in time, maybe some five hundred years or more. The handcrafted houses with their wonderful straw roofs, mud walls and bamboo structures contribute to this illusion. The natural grasslands – fields filled with hand-tended crops and grass-covered avenues with their tall palm trees – create an extra dimension to your experience. Added to this, the totally unspoilt agricultural vista of out-standing beauty with its oxen, pigs, chickens and goats seems to stretch back timelessly over the centuries, a somewhat mystical utopia well out of reach of most modern Europeans. Nevertheless, electricity has found its way into the village and has brought a little extra comfort even if the cables which bring it are supported by bamboo rather than metal or heavy wooden structures as in the West.

Having adjusted myself to my new surroundings I could now focus more fully on the reason for my visit. I wanted to see if there was any way I could assist this well-established educational project embracing 169 children. What I at first perceived to be some kind of youth training camp appeared in fact to be something far more wonderful and awe-inspiring as each day unfolded. Here are village children in a remote area of the countryside whose parents are subsistence farmers with small plots of land scratching out a day to day existence. Most of these parents were illiterate before they became enrolled in the expanding literacy project that is taking place on a daily basis in the village and were totally impoverished before they became members of the expanding number of community banks.

Their children from an early age are in the wicker-walled classrooms, simultaneously learning to speak English while also learning in English all the main subjects recommended by the government agencies, which include an introduction to computer studies – at the same time they must also become literate and numerate in Nepalese.

In addition they are receiving a bi-lingual education while learning values and virtues to such an extent that their enthusiasm for life simply shines out of their souls like the flames of strongly lit candles. A far cry from most well equipped and modern schools in the West where boredom and unrest are the order of the day and language skills are rejected for more easily obtainable results in subjects such as Religious Education, an RE, I may add that seems devoid of spirituality.

There is no electricity in the majority of these simple classrooms with their mud floors, wicker walls and suspended blackboards. A lack of audio-visual aids does not prevent the native Nepalese teachers from generating a power-house of learning. Sometimes classes start as the sun begins to rise but each child radiates enough energy to light a thousand stars as they swing into place on the hard wooden benches. Even 19th century classrooms would seem well equipped compared with these flimsy six rooms packed with between 20 to 30 children busily reading out loud or chanting what they have learned. Rote learning is now despised in the West but here a kind of spiritually charged enthusiasm overrides everything else to make it more than possible for the simplest approach to become the most effective learning tool without the back-up of any visible form of technology whatsoever. The three Rs practised here are relationships, respect and rigorous learning.

So here I am standing side by side with the school principal wondering how all these immaculately dressed children could possibly keep themselves and their clothes so clean without one washing machine in the whole village. The answer is startlingly simple – devotion to cleanliness. The spirit of self sacrifice on the part of the teachers is overwhelming as they could be earning more money if they were to work in a government school. However, they prefer the atmosphere of the Abha School which, after all, is government approved but also a place where consultation and cooperation are paramount and where the whole community has been involved in the planning, purchase and development of the school from day one; all achieved initially without any foreign financial help whatsoever.

At present there are children attending the school from pre-primary level up to grade 6. From grade 7 onwards the children have to make the journey from the village across to Biratnagar, a town that has little to offer in terms of natural beauty or fresh clean air. There are plans to expand the school up into the higher grades, but to make it all economically viable the school will have to be enlarged, the classrooms upgraded and hostel accommodation provided in order to attract children to move from the town to the village.

At some later stage an agricultural college is also envisaged by the school board. This could help the local economy to flourish and bring new sources of income to the local inhabitants. The land occupied by the school, however, would have to be enlarged at least four-fold in order to accommodate such changes. The rural setting of the village is certainly an ideal location for a school that could lead the way in pioneering a new and greener form of education. All this I have no doubt will be achieved through the unswerving devotion of the Nepalese Bahá'í community and will bring great benefits to the cause of education as originally envisaged by 'Abdul-Bahá where the physical, intellectual and spiritual dimensions of human existence can find their true balance and harmony expressed quite simply through the 'Art of Divine Living'.

161
July 2006
David Renwick Grant
From Scotland to Haifa

Pilgrims walk – don't they?

It was a nutty idea to start with, I suppose, especially as there was no way I would have time to do it. But the image of pilgrims of old making arduous journeys to reach their goal was strong in my mind, when finally my invitation for a nine-day pilgrimage arrived. I determined that I should walk at least part of the way from Scotland to Haifa, taking an overland route for the rest of the way.

On 2 July, greatly helped by the Galloway friends, I made a token start, walking from St Ninian's Cave to Whithorn, where Christianity was first brought to Scotland about 400 AD. The serious walking began next day when I headed off into the Border Hills south of Moffat.

A week later I reached Hadrian's Wall near Lanercost Priory, where Edward

I had stayed on his way to hammer the Scots. It had rained earlier and I had had a taste of being soaked but now it was baking hot. The view was magnificent, the wall fascinating but trudging up and down the rolling hills with a 50lb pack (and still very unfit) was sweet torture.

On to Burnlaw to say hello to Gary and Rosie Villiers-Stuart, where I arrived, unplanned, just in time to take part in the Earthing the Spirit festival. If I needed a stiff dose of spiritual uplift, the next ten days provided it, together with a variety of wonderful workshops and marvellous music. At the close I was driven south by Steve Day, staying with his family before hitching across England to Harwich and the Netherlands ferry.

Friends greeted me in Rotterdam, where I stayed a night before walking most of the way to Nijmegen, not far from the Bahá'í-owned conference centre of De Poort, where I joined the Dutch summer school. Fellow-participants Maryam Manteghi and Jasenko Nuhi, from Bosnia, lifted me all the way to Langenhain, Germany.

This was my first visit to any House of Worship and I was both awe-struck and ecstatic. I offered a few days of service and spent several happy days dead-heading roses and other flowers with gardener Gisela von Brunn. The staff was kindness personified and if I had not had a journey to make, I might have been gardening there yet!

Bahá'u'lláh was, as ever, watching over me. At a filling station just east of Frankfurt I asked a Turkish lorry driver for a lift – and was taken all the way to the Austrian-Italian border. Being dropped at 1:30 a.m. was something of a test, however! Nevertheless I made it, to old friends in Dravograd, Slovenia, by the end of the day. This was where my family and I had spent many months during our horse-drawn travels (see my book *The Seven Year Hitch* for that story). After a few days, a lorry lift down to Croatia was arranged for me. And there I almost stuck.

I intended to hitch to Sofia, where I had arranged to help with preparations for the Bulgarian summer school. But not a glimmer of a lift could I raise, and not liking the look of some of the people roaming about, I took to a hotel for the night. Next day was as bad and I began to wish I had gone on to Sarajevo with the Slovenian lorry. Eventually I accepted a lift to Osijek and from there took a bus, via the still war-damaged town of Vukovar, to Belgrade. A sleeper to Sofia cost only £22 equivalent, so I booked one and went in search of something to eat.

An American pioneer to Bulgaria for nine years, Bertha Petruski met me at the station next morning. Besides helping prepare papers for the school, I saw something of the city and the surrounding country, thanks to Bertha. Then Mr Afshin, the main speaker, arrived and we all travelled to Plovdiv, where the school was held. There was a good mix of nationalities at it, from Albania to Ireland, including Knight of Bahá'u'lláh to Moldova Anne-Marie Krueger.

A walk in the hills beckoned as soon as the school finished. I took a train 25 km south and then hiked sweatily upwards. It was cooler at three thousand feet and I had a delicious five days plodding through woods and meadows and enjoying the peace, the birds and my own company.

It took four lifts, after returning to the plains, to reach Edirne. The first was in a rattle-trap Russian UAZ pickup going to small farms collecting milk for delivery to a central tank. The last was with three young Turks returning from holiday. They took me to the door of the Saray Hotel, where I had booked a room.

The lovely gardens at the 'Izzat Áqá house captivated me. It was a privilege to be able to work for a few hours in the garden. In a different way, the newly-restored Riḍá Big house gave me a tremendous sense of peace and spirituality, as well as being very emotional, especially when saying prayers in the room that had been Mírzá Mihdí's bedroom. The young caretakers at the new pilgrim house, Tahireh and Fikrat Karaçay, made me most welcome. The gorgeous Süleymaniye mosque, where Bahá'u'lláh used to pray, was another attraction in this pleasant, bustling town.

Any Bahá'í's visit to Turkey should include Istanbul, if only to visit the house at Fatih. The original house was destroyed by fire and earthquake but the present one is a haven of peace, where the caretaker Miss Vekil welcomes you. I went upstairs to pray in the main room and was overwhelmed to find that in a frame on one wall is a coat of 'Abdu'l-Bahá, while displayed in a glass cabinet are a ring, handkerchief and lock of hair that belonged to the Blessed Beauty. No one had mentioned these and, once again, I found my eyes watering.

I took a ferry from Istanbul to Bandirma, then walked for four hot, perspiring days before taking a bus from Yenice to Çanakkale, then a short ferry trip to the Gallipoli Peninsula. In 1915 my father had fought here with the 4th/5th Royal Scots, so this was a personal pilgrimage. It was a bonus knowing Bahá'u'lláh, too, had been here. Returning to Çanakkale, I took a long bus ride south to dispel the terrible sadness of that blood-soaked, deathly Peninsula. A visit to Ephesus and a tranquil mosque in Selçuk ('May I say my prayers in your mosque?' I asked the Imam. 'Of course. It's all the same God,' he replied), followed by three days' walking (feeling more liquid than solid) did that. Reaching Bodrum I embarked for the Dodecanese island of Leros, where, in the waters around the island, my half-brother's submarine, HMS Trooper, still lies somewhere, having been lost with all hands in October 1943.

There were two ways to reach Haifa other than by air. One was overland via Syria and Jordan but that route was long and of uncertain duration.

First I had to check out possibilities on Cyprus. Back in Bodrum I caught a 16-hour night bus to Mersin and the port of Tasucu. Afterwards I realized we had passed through Konya, where Rumi had lived. No time for regrets about not stopping there, though, as a high-speed catamaran whisked me across to Girne in the Turkish Republic of Northern Cyprus (TRNC), from where a short bus trip took me into Nicosia.

After a disjointed first day I was 'rescued' by Frank Kennedy and accommodated in his still-unfinished flat, an act of kindness I cannot sufficiently thank him for. Adjoining the flat is his Euro Learning Centre, the computer and English language school, which provides a living for this doughty Irish pioneer. The TRNC is not recognized by any nation save Turkey, which makes some aspects of life awkward. However a five-minute walk takes one to the Greek Cypriot side, so one has the best of two worlds. But there is no unity in the diversity between Turkish and Greek Cypriots and it will take some time yet to undo this Gordian Knot.

I was able to carry out quite a lot of service in both the north and south Nicosia Bahá'í Centres. Most of this was cleaning and tidying around the outside, removing a fallen tree, hacking back bamboo and fierce encounters with beautiful bougainvillaea, which is jaggier than barbed wire, but included some tiling and minor joinery in the north.

I reluctantly accepted that a sea voyage to Haifa was, disappointingly, not going to be practical. The cheapest option was to fly to Tel Aviv, returning via Cyprus and thence a charter to the UK. In the end it didn't matter, I was going on pilgrimage!

Suddenly it was 23 October. Mount Carmel, here I come!

162
January 2007
Angela and Robert Tidswell
Bulgaria

Angela and Robert Tidswell pioneered to the little village of Ossenovo, near Varna on the Black Sea, in December 2003.

Before the summer school which took place in Balchik, close to the summer palace of Queen Marie of Romania, in the summer of 2006, I received a phone call from a journalist asking me questions about the summer school. For example, how many people were expected to attend and from which countries? I said that I would write something up and email it to her later that day. Fortunately Bertha Petruski, a Bahá'í then living in Sofia but now back in the United States after nine years as a pioneer here, was working with me on the registrations for the summer school. Together we wrote up a short piece for the journalist responding to her request but added that 'The summer school is a time for learning more about the Bahá'í Faith and its teachings, and also about how to achieve peace in the world. Peace is the main aim of the Bahá'í community, as well as unity in diversity.'

One day during the week of the summer school I received a phone call from a lady who told me her name was Valentina. Unfortunately I couldn't understand the rest of the conversation as my knowledge of the Bulgarian language was very limited. It turned out that Valentina had telephoned the hotel where the summer school was taking place and so it was fortunate that I could hand her call over to a Bahá'í friend, just passing through the reception area at the time, who spoke Bulgarian.

It transpired that Valentina and her husband Sezgin had read the article about the Faith, which mentioned my name, and had somehow managed to obtain my phone number. They said that they had been searching for the answer to religion and when they read the article they just knew from the few short lines that this was it! And they became Bahá'ís there and then! After the summer school ended some Bahá'í friends visited them on their way home and left with them some books and some music. More recently some of us Bahá'ís from Ossenovo and some friends from Varna made the trip to see them in their home town of Tervel.

They are a delightful family, poor in all save God. Sezgin has a severe problem which means he must lie down for 22 out of 24 hours of the day. When we arrived, there he was, wearing a Bahá'í T-shirt with a Bahá'í symbol on it, the Greatest Name was above his bed on the wall and during our prayer time together he played music from the World Congress. He and his wife Valentina are in their mid thirties and their daughter Norsel is eight years old, a lovely child, quite mature and very well behaved. Although they are a happy family it is obvious that their material circumstances are dire. Another little miracle!

163
April 2007
Brian O'Toole
Guyana
School of Nations, Guyana

Establishment of Rural Bahá'í Schools

We established School of Nations in the capital in Guyana almost 11 years ago. It started, in part, because of our frustrations with the 'best' school in the country that our two boys were attending. I had the opportunity to visit a Bahá'í-inspired school in Lomé, Togo, and was moved by what one Bahá'í couple had managed to achieve there.

School of Nations is now recognized as one of the outstanding schools in Guyana. The school has more than 650 students from all corners of Guyana and from 30 other countries. Nations is the school of choice for a number of the diplomatic missions here. We are also able to offer about 30 full-time or part-time scholarships, including some to native Amerindian children from deep in the interior of the country on the Brazilian border.

We are now embarking on an exciting extension development programme of School of Nations. By September 2007 we plan to open five rural Bahá'í schools in various parts of Guyana, in our priority clusters. These schools will, of course, be open to persons of all backgrounds. To ensure as broad a cross section of students as possible at these rural schools, the fees will be kept to a minimum – no more than US$20 per month per child. These schools will begin with classes from Prep A to Primary 4. In later years a nursery department and secondary classes will be added.

Our goal is to offer a programme of academic excellence within a clear moral framework. As with other Bahá'í-inspired schools in other parts of the world, we believe that the spiritual life of our students is a key element in their overall development. The students at Nations will learn the essential truths of the world's major religions including Christianity, Islam, Hinduism and the Bahá'í Faith. We will stress the formation of a positive world view, respect for the belief of others and the development of moral capabilities.

We believe in the innate nobility of humanity. In all our schools we ensure that the innate worth of all individuals is recognized and that their full potential is realized through mutual respect and cooperation.

164
April 2007
Anna and Robert Kinghorn
The North Calotte, Finnish Lapland

Anna (from the Isle of Wight) and Robert Kinghorn (Northampton) have been pioneers in Finland since 1975. Presently they live in Rovaniemi, the regional capital of Finnish Lapland.

We would like to share with you the lovely experience we had when we went to the tenth anniversary celebrations of the Bahá'í Centre for the North Calotte in Inari, Northern Finnish Lapland, which coincided with the Birthday of Bahá'u'lláh. But first, I think it would be good to share with you what and where the North Calotte is.

The area under the Bahá'í Council for the North Calotte covers the Arctic regions of Norway, Sweden and Finland, and until recently it included the Kola Peninsula in northwest Russia. It now falls under the auspices of the National Spiritual Assembly of the Bahá'ís of Finland. The Council, which has members from all three countries, is responsible for the teaching and direct administration of the region. While naturally the aim is to reach out to everyone living in the area, special consideration is given to the Sámi, the indigenous people of this area. The region also has a Training Institute Board and there are study circles ongoing in several localities; in fact, two of the youth in the circle in Rovaniemi became Bahá'ís recently.

The region has four clusters: two in Norwegian Lapland and one each in Swedish and Finnish Lapland. That means that our cluster alone covers an area of about 150,000 sq km! At the moment there are three groups, one in each country, that are close to becoming Spiritual Assemblies and smaller communities and individual believers dotted about throughout the region. Here in Finnish Lapland we have communities in Inari (the heart of Sámi culture in Finnish Lapland) and Rovaniemi.

This is a wonderful part of the world and the believers are actively working to establish the Cause of God in the region. Distances are long, winters are harsh, vehicles break down but the friends keep going.

The tenth anniversary of the Bahá'í Centre was attended by Counsellor Hannu Olkkonen, representatives from the National Assemblies of Norway, Sweden and Finland, the Regional Council, the Training Institute Board and Bahá'ís and their friends from all three countries.

It is always wonderful to see everyone, maybe especially as we are all so scattered. There were prayers in all the languages of the region, songs and wonderful music, some of it composed especially for the occasion. The Counsellor and the National Assembly representatives gave their loving greetings and encouragement, and we watched a little presentation of these past ten years of the Centre. Over the years it has housed many a study circle, tutor refresher weekend, children's class, devotional, holy day, Feast and Council and Training Institute meeting. It always feels like coming home when we walk through the door. Local people and organizations also use the Centre for their meetings, which makes it a real centre for the community at large.

The Universal House of Justice has always taken a keen interest in this cooperation between countries, reaching out to the Sámi and the activities here on the fringes of Europe. I would like to end with a short excerpt from a message from the Universal House of Justice sent for the occasion of the Centre's inauguration:

> The inauguration of a Bahá'í Centre in Inari, in the heart of the homeland of the Sámi peoples is an event of great significance for the advancement of the Cause of Bahá'u'lláh in the Arctic regions. This centre is, at one and the same time, the Ḥaẓíratu'l-Quds of the Bahá'ís of Inari and a centre for the study and activities of the Faith throughout a region which spreads across four countries from the Atlantic Ocean in the west to the White Sea in the east, involving the active collaboration of four National Spiritual Assemblies.[30]

165
April 2007
Danielle Pee
India

Danielle (from Camberley in Surrey) is spending six months studying in Lucknow, India.

I have always been brought up to believe that the role of education is to mine out the gems that are latent within each and every one of us. This belief was reinforced as I started to read the works of philosophers, great thinkers and spiritual messengers who assert that it is only through education that mankind can benefit, stating that knowledge is as wings to our life and a ladder for our ascent. But what type of education are they talking about? In most western countries, at least, we have a near one hundred per cent literacy rate, gender parity within education, relatively high employment rates and a good economic position in the global market. Despite these successes, these countries are still plagued by unquestioned social norms of gender, age, race and class inequality. These inequalities remain the accepted status quo of our society, and despite the high educational attainment of western populations, these social ills don't seem to get challenged by the average person. Coupled with increasing cases of depression, self-esteem issues and violence within these societies, surely it's about time we start asking some important questions about our education system. The most significant question that comes to mind is: what is so wrong about our education system that it fails to help us recognize our nobility as human beings and so inadequately prepares us to develop our capacities to become seekers of truth and agents for social transformation?

This is the question I asked myself four years ago when for the first time I consciously experienced the meaning of gender inequality. I was applying for my Master's, something I was told at school I would never in my wildest dreams be able to achieve. This is where my journey began and my exploration of education originated. The Bahá'í writings provide a beautiful vision of what education should be. Such education would allow individuals to recognize their inherent oneness while celebrating their diversity, cultivate in children an understanding of their nobility, develop the faculties of critical thinking, empower children to serve humanity in actions that are conducive to social change and encourages the school to be a social space for lifelong learning, the hub of community activity, celebration and exploration.

In this journey I will be spending the next couple of years exploring cutting edge alternative educational models around the world to see how this vision can be made into a reality. My first stop has been the Foundation for the Advancement of Science (FAS). The Foundation is a Bahá'í-inspired educational organization committed to developing education appropriate to the needs of a world in transition. It works very closely with FUNDAEC based in South and Central America, which has won many awards for best practice as an educational model for social change. Based in Lucknow, India, the Foundation works with peoples from rural communities and encourages them to take ownership of their educational endeavours.

Since being in India I have worked closely with my boss on developing a holistic science curriculum and holistic teacher training programme. Most of my time is spent in consultation with the parents, children, community and teachers. It is through these consultations and reflections on the Bahá'í writings that the curriculum is modified and prepared for its next batch of field testing. In all, the field testing will continue for the next ten years through a continuous process of study, planning, action, reflection and change until it no longer becomes necessary to make drastic modifications. However, it will continue to review the process after the ten year period. This is because the Foundation's mind set is one that believes that we are all part of an ever-advancing civilization and to meet the requirements of such a civilization we inevitably need an ever-advancing education system. The learning mode the NGO is engaged with ensures that there is no such thing as failure but simply learning opportunities for growth. The grassroots nature means that such a project is sustainable and the ownership is with the community. FAS has been offered hundreds of thousands of pounds from donor agencies all around the world, which it has rejected for the simple reason that if anything were to ever happen to FAS, these schools need to be in a position to sustain themselves. There are so many cases in India of humanitarian agencies that have gone into areas and provided educational, medical and nutritional services, only to leave after a couple of years when such an area is no longer deemed by the 'experts' as a priority. An examination taken after ten years or so with an unbiased eye will show that actually these people have not benefited in the long run and in some cases suffered more as a consequence. These people are poor, not stupid. They don't need charitable money. They have the answers and with their capacities developed can create their own bright futures.

So this is my journey so far and I am loving every moment! It's exciting, interesting and frustrating. It keeps me awake at night and wakes me up early in the morning! There are so many ways of education out there to tap potential, unleash creativity, encourage participants to be conscious subjects of their own growth and help facilitate them to become agents for social change in the advancement of civilization.

166

April 2007
Massoud Derakhshani
Botswana

Massoud and Mojgan have been pioneers in Gaborone, Botswana, for the past ten years. Previous to that they were pioneers in Swaziland for 17 years.

At the end of every educational year, which for us in the southern hemisphere is early December, we celebrate a wonderful gathering called 'Teacher Recognition Ceremony'. All Bahá'í students nominate a much loved teacher. The organizing committee invites the teacher to the event along with their head teacher and, in addition, a representative from the Ministry of Education. The students with their parents, friends and family, and members of the Bahá'í community come to the National Bahá'í Centre for the award-giving celebration.

The programme begins with some prayers and continues with Bahá'í readings about the station of teachers in the Bahá'í Faith. The Master of Ceremony welcomes everyone and says many appreciative things to the teachers on behalf of their students. The representative of the Ministry of Education says a few words and this is followed with the presentation of awards to the teachers from their students. With the award is included a quotation about the station of teachers.

It is a ceremony full of love and appreciation for the teachers by the students – all the more appreciated because such love and kindness is given out at the time of the student-teacher encounter rather than at some later time when each has parted company from the other. Some singing completes the award ceremony before some closing prayers. Finally all are invited to have refreshments at an informal gathering with the Bahá'í community.

167
July 2007
Will Rankin
Slovakia

In August 2005 Will Rankin moved from the county of Devon in the UK to Devin, a village just outside Bratislava in Slovakia, to do a year of youth service. He decided to stay longer and is still there. He now intends to stay for as long as he is useful.

Many of you will have heard the Chinese curse 'May you live in interesting times'. Well things have been pretty interesting over here in Slovakia of late but I would not say that we've been cursed, far from it.

The law in Slovakia stated that to be recognized as a religion a group must obtain twenty thousand signatures in support. This is extremely difficult in this staunchly Catholic and conservative country. The Slovak government, however, decided that this was far too easy and decided to change the law so that a group would need twenty thousand *members* to be recognized as a religion, a change that would make it all but impossible for the Bahá'í Faith, or indeed any other religion, to be recognized for many years to come.

When I heard of the proposed change I must admit to being a bit downhearted. There was no way our tiny community could possibly collect that many signatures before the law was toughened. We had a month . . . if we were lucky. The law, even as it stood, seemed designed to make it hard for us. Most people don't like to be stopped in the street by someone with a clipboard. Then we had to explain who the Bahá'ís were. People were suspicious that we wanted to try to get them to sign a declaration card there and then – we had been the victims of misinformation in the press. If we managed to explain who we were and what we wanted we then, by law, had to ask for their signature, full name, address, post/zip code and national identity number. Obviously this was quite a lot for a stranger on the street to ask for and required a lot of trust.

Then the news came that the Universal House of Justice had contacted our National Spiritual Assembly encouraging us to press forward for recognition and stating that the World Centre would be praying for us. How can you respond to a message like that?

It was like an electric shock passing through Bratislava. Day and night Bahá'ís were pounding the streets, standing around bus stations, airports and university halls. This was in February when it gets chilly in this part of the world. It was cold for me (coming from Devon in England) but my real admiration goes out to the year of service Bahá'ís who hit the frozen streets fresh from an Australian summer. That is true dedication.

The community worked hard. People took time off work. People were up early to catch people on their way to work, people were out past midnight catching late-night travellers at the airport. Some local Bahá'í revealed an indescribable capacity for leadership and sacrifice, urging the rest of us on. The signatures rolled in.

There are innumerable stories. From my own experience I'll mention just a few:

An individual Mormon I approached to sign took a petition sheet to his church and got his congregation to sign.

I approached one man and asked him to sign, only to find he was collecting signatures for the 'Church of Humanism'. We decided it was fair play and our groups traded signatures, then sat down together for a rather surreal coffee break/metaphysical debate.

I asked a Hari Krishna Temple Master if his group could sign the petition. He regretfully told me that he had a policy of not signing any petition so as to ensure neutrality, though he assured me that he would pray for us – a position I appreciated. As soon as I left the building I was met by a group of his acolytes who had overheard what I said and who all wanted to sign so long as their master didn't find out.

Help also came in ways I could not have hoped for. The most amazing people came to help collect signatures – from the Czech Republic, Poland,

Austria, the UK and all over Europe. These people were literally blessings. I really don't know how to express my thanks to these Bahá'ís. They not only collected unbelievable numbers of signatures thanks to their zeal and charm, they also brought with them a fresh energy that kept the rest of us going. With only a week to go we had collected an immense number of signatures – around 16,000, if my memory serves me right. Yet we were warned that at least a third would be invalid. To be safe we needed another ten thousand, in a week. By the end of a week we had nearly 29,000. In the cold, on the streets, in a nation that is avowedly Catholic.

Before we started it was said that it would take a miracle to collect enough signatures. I stand by that statement. It took a miracle – and that is what can happen when Bahá'ís are united.

Since that time we have received the confirmation that we have been recognized. The petition has sparked a big boost in interest, with the result that we are all very busy. I myself am involved in two circles of Book 1 and a weekly fireside as a direct result of the petition. The community is united as never before and plans are being drawn up for another 'big push' over the summer. I can't speak for the whole community here but I think I would sum up my experience of the last few months as exhausted, enthused, blessed.

168
July 2007
Stephi Clash
Corfu, Greece

Wesley and Stephi Clash moved to the island of Corfu in 1993 with their 11 year old daughter Giselle. They were relatively new Bahá'ís from Shepway in Kent. Wesley works as a deep sea diver and is thought to hold the world record for teaching the Faith in 140 metres of water in the Arabian Gulf, sitting in a rather small diving bell with his diving partner (captive audience)! Stephi is a painter, mainly in watercolours, of their lovely island.

This August we will have been in our pioneer post on the island of Corfu for 14 years and we're not moving! In fact, so immovable are we that we even have a grave plot in the local cemetery . . . with sea views! But now for something completely different:

From the two Bahá'ís who arrived in 1993, we are now five Bahá'ís and I know many of you out there will be thinking thoughts like 'entry by trickles' but you have to know that here it's not that easy to teach . . . which is why

Bahá'u'lláh gave us a nudge towards this lovely land of Greece as we are tenacious, re. the grave plot.

There is a lovely story of a dedicated pioneer to the island of Rhodes in Greece who was beginning to feel dismayed at the lack of results from teaching in Greece. He felt he wanted to go somewhere in the third world where souls were just leaping to embrace the Faith. Well, this good man had a dream where he was walking in the dry moat of the crusader's castle in Rhodes and he saw 'Abdu'l-Bahá with a spade struggling to dig the earth. 'Abdu'l-Bahá called out to this believer, 'Come and help me dig. Don't you know the ground is very hard here?' This was all the answer the believer needed for him to stay in his pioneer post.

Looking back over the years I remember hosting events with our tiny resources and manpower with little result but which exhausted us in the process and made us feel as if we were somehow conning our friends and contacts into attending Bahá'í gatherings. Now it is all so simple as we have the study circle and core activities which are an amazing way to invite people to join us in activities. Also, we are so excited about the study circle that it is with genuine enthusiasm and joy that we invite people to tranquillity zones or devotionals or simply to that most Bahá'í of activities . . . to talk. We have now managed to get one of our number to complete the whole series of Ruhi books, which is great because before we had to rely on the goodness of others to take time out from their busy lives to come to Corfu and facilitate our group. This obviously led to a lack of momentum in our study circle. This member is now becoming quite a 'Ruhi junkie' and has just got back from the book 5 junior youth animator's course in Athens and is full of enthusiasm to tackle the real need of our kids.

Corfu is a safe place for kids as family ties are very strong and children are seen as belonging to everyone where safety conditions and love are concerned. That doesn't mean to say that the not so nice aspects of materialism, narcotics and bad media images are not taking hold here and this is why the need is so strong for our kids to know where they can help themselves and the world to be better for all.

In April we celebrated Greek Easter which is the biggest festival in the Greek calendar and follows the whole gamut of sorrow at the crucifixion to the sheer joy of the resurrection. I remember one Easter some years back when we held a youth teaching workshop in our house and all of us trooped into the village square with lit candles on the Saturday night. At midnight the priest cries, 'Christ is risen!' and the answer is, 'Truly He is risen'. One of the Bahá'ís turned to me saying, 'And we really believe it!' Since then, for me, Easter has always been such a confirmation of Bahá'u'lláh's mission and a reminder of what we're here to do. It always pleases our neighbours to see us attending Greek festivities and that helps us to teach them.

For the last 12 years we have been renovating our two hundred year old village house and we now have space enough to put up our dear friends and open our home for Bahá'í workshops, schools or whatever Bahá'u'lláh sends. This has been a dream for all those years and I guess many of you out there will be thinking, 'Wow, they do everything there slowly', but the reason is that my darling husband, Wesley, works off-shore in the oil industry and loves to do the renovation work himself. He's upstairs as I write, ripping old planks off the balcony. So life ticks on here and I am still amazed by the beauty of this place and the blessings we have had in our pioneer post . . . both those we welcomed and those we endured! I sometimes miss the excitement and support of a large community such as we had in UK but as Bahá'ís it's good to be flexible and learn skills like self-motivation, organization and a sense of humour . . . and, of course, the Concourse on High is just waiting in serried ranks to rush to our aid.

169

July 2007

Rosie Smith

Zambia

Youth Service

Rosie Smith (Cornwall) is at the Banani School in Zambia. Here she writes about a camping trip into the bush (South Luangwa National Park) taken during the spring school holiday.

Muli bwanji friends!

We caught the 6:00 a.m. coach to Chipata from Lusaka early one Sunday morning. After eight hours careering along a narrow, windy, tarred road through the bush, we arrived in Chipata. Then we booked a minibus to drive us the additional four hours to Flatdogs (apparently that used to be the local term for crocodiles) campsite on the border of South Luangwa National Park. The driver was flying over the narrow dirt roads like his life depended on it, and as dark was falling we had to navigate a treacherous stretch of the trail where the annual floods had eroded the track really badly, leaving deep trenches on either side of the road. That was scary and we were all holding our breath! After what seemed like an eternity and some very sore backsides, we took the turning for Flatdogs down a raised dirt road with scrub land beneath us either side. A sudden shout from someone, 'That's a big cow – oh! An ELEPHANT!!!' and there were three elephants shuffling around in the bright moonlight – magic!

We checked in and a lady showed us where we could pitch our tents. The whole site was full of soft river sand, great heaps of it everywhere, left by the high floods of a few months ago, which made it difficult to walk anywhere at a reasonable speed. She showed us to a site with a little concrete table that had a power point, a lamp and a sink with running bore water, saying we could pitch our tents up on the platforms in the trees if we wanted to – 'It is nice to be off the ground when the hippos come through!'

We climbed up into the trees and managed to put up our four-man tent for five people on the rickety platform with no railings about four metres off the ground. Vital tent poles were missing but we improvised with string and shoelaces and our tent was pretty tree-worthy. We got down and started getting the food out to cook dinner (we were supposed to keep our food in a store house 100 metres away so we didn't get pestered by baboons) when a park guide came over with his flashlight:

'Are you cooking dinner?' We replied that we hadn't started yet.

'Then I have to disturb you. The elephants are headed this way. Do you have any vegetables?'

'Um . . . we have oranges and apples!'

'They love fruit! They will come and take all your food, so I suggest you put it all up in one tree and retreat to the other.'

Then we were frantically packing up our food, crying, 'The elephants are coming, the elephants are coming!' We did as the guide asked and watched from the apparent safety of our tree as mother and baby elephants came crashing through the undergrowth, stripping the leaves off everything and flattening bushes and shrubs everywhere. They were right there, a few metres away, while we were shining our torches on them. Hunger eventually drove us down and over to the food tree, where we sat and ate cold beans and dry bread and noticed a massive bull elephant in the bush next to us. We were quite glad that he hadn't noticed us running across from tree to tree a few minutes earlier.

That night we didn't sleep much, cramped in our hot sweaty tent on hard wooden boards. My friend and I spent most of the night with our heads poking out of the tent, watching for elephants (you can hear them trumpeting to each other and crashing through bushes), plus the hippos which kept us awake with their constant grunting – it sounded like they were laughing at us! At one point we even heard a lion roar.

At 6 a.m. we went for a game drive. It was awesome – from our open car we saw everything we hoped to see: hippos, zebras, antelopes (impalas and pukus), lions, elephants, eagles, a giraffe, water buffalo, a monitor lizard . . . We got incredibly close to the lions – we could have touched them if we had stretched out our arms – and we got right next to a hippo in the bush which I thought was going to charge us. Our driver was a bit cheeky, as he kept taking us off road to get ridiculously close to these animals, despite the fact that it's illegal to go off-road in such parks. Staring into a lion's eyes, it's easy to forget that it's wild and would definitely go for you were it not nap-time. It was really good; we pulled back into camp about 10 a.m.

We visited a local batik factory in a nearby town and it was amazing to see the artists at work. They used flour and water instead of wax (they squeezed it on using old ketchup bottles), and they created beautiful designs in seconds, without any plans or drawings to help them. It was a big, open-air, jungly place, with African music blasting out from big speakers, and baboons with sky blue bottoms clambering over the corrugated rooftops. It appeared to be a really nice place for the local villagers to work in.

That night we saw no elephants, so we just laughed ourselves silly telling jokes around the fire, with cocoa and frankfurters. I slept in the tent right next to the edge of the platform, which was really uncomfortable and a bit scary, as I'd wake up with my leg dangling over the edge. It was scary if you had to use the bathroom in the night, climbing down the ladder, listening for any beasties, checking around with your flashlight, then legging it over the massive piles of sand to the bathroom (we'd be walking quite calmly, then we'd hear a hippo grunt near by and bolt the last couple of yards, terrifying but hilarious to watch us stumble over the deep, uneven sand).

In the morning we got up at 5:00 to pack and our minibus came to pick us up as agreed at 6 a.m. We needed to get the coach in Chipata around 10:00 (but buses never leave on time in Zambia, usually a couple of hours after scheduled time is a good guess) and we started off fine, but then the driver stopped in Mfuwe to 'pick up the conductor'. After some minutes we got out to see what was going on and they were changing the tyre!

'Why didn't you do this yesterday, when you were waiting around for us with nothing to do?' we demanded to know. Eventually we got on the road again but, despite our insistence that we had booked the whole minibus to ourselves and no other passengers should be picked up, the driver constantly stopped to chat and crammed about eight extra people in, most of them in the tiny space between the seat and the door. Considering there were already 11 of us in there with at least ten big backpacks, this was not comfortable. Our protests were ignored. Obviously to the driver, a minibus with empty seats was a terrible waste!

Driving over the badly eroded stretch of track was scary as we were really tipping over. We were taken a different route through the back roads of Chipata (to avoid police checks) and somehow we got to the bus station by 10:30. We jumped on a battered old coach that was just leaving for Lusaka and scored the back seats, which were more comfortable. We thought we were making good time until we stopped for what we assumed was a rest break at a shop in the next town. It turned out the coach needed repairs but the drivers didn't tell anyone this when people were boarding because that would be a waste of seats! We then had to wait a couple of hours outside an Indian grocery store with nothing but fruit cordial, old biscuits and cheap and cheerful *chitenges* (broad cloth material) for sale, which promptly closed, obviously not wanting to make any money from the thirsty, hungry passengers sitting on its doorstep!

Finally the coach was fixed and we got back to Lusaka eight hours later that evening, only to find no buses that could take us home. Eventually we decided it would be better to find a minibus or taxi to take us back to Banani School. Some guys actually appeared with a minibus so, overjoyed, we all piled in and set off. Luckily at that time of night there weren't many people on the road for the driver to pick up. But at the police stop on the way we got pulled over as it turned out that no minibuses were allowed on that road at night. After paying a hefty fine to some Zambian policewomen, we were on our way again and at long last found ourselves back at Banani to be greeted by our favourite feral kitten, Marmite. It was an awesome holiday.

170
July 2007
Parvin Morrissey
India

Parvin Morrissey and Moira Johnstone from Tillicoultry, Clackmannanshire, spent the Easter holidays volunteering at the Barli Development Institute for Rural Women in Central India. Parvin has written this account of their trip.

News of Jimmy McGilligan

We left Scotland one sunny morning at the end of March to spend our Easter holidays at the Barli Development Institute for Rural Women. Although Barli is an independent charity, the teachings of Bahá'u'lláh provide the inspiration for the work that they do there. Jimmy and Janak McGilligan who run the

Institute met us off the plane and looked after us during our stay. Jimmy, who is originally from Northern Ireland, has been a pioneer in India for over 20 years during which time he has warmly embraced the peoples and culture of his pioneer post. His ability to turn his hand to almost anything is a key factor in the success of the project.

Every six months, 80 young women, most of whom have had no formal education, are accepted into the Institute for a period of residential training. Each cohort is taught basic literacy, numeracy, health and nutrition. In addition they are taught skills such as sewing or dyeing which will help them earn a living when they go back to their villages. This is where Moira and I came in. Moira is a tailoress and showed the girls how to improve their sewing techniques, whereas my job was to teach them some first aid skills.

Throughout our stay I was struck by the way in which the methodology of the core activities was being used to educate the women. With 80 students in a class, it is not possible for one trainer to give them individual attention, so the more advanced students are 'fast tracked' through the curriculum and then act as facilitators for a small group of their fellow students. In this way the study circle method is used to make the most of the human resources available to the Institute. In addition, about a third of the girls are Bahá'ís and they had their own study circles using the animators' materials.

Although much of the emphasis at Barli is on gaining practical skills, these are always underpinned by strong spiritual principles. Above all else, the women are encouraged to develop virtues such as honesty, assertiveness, service, compassion and tolerance. Each session starts with a heavenly chorus of prayers sung by the women.

Another important theme at Barli is sustainability and caring for the environment. With the help of the women, Jimmy farms a large piece of land at the back of the campus and as a result, Barli is almost self-sufficient in food production. All the sewage water collected on campus is treated and recycled to irrigate the crops. Impressive though these achievements are, the thing that Barli is becoming world famous for is its solar cookers. Jimmy has adapted an original design to create simple solar dishes. Sunlight bounces off the shiny surface and is focussed on a small area where a pot can be placed. An ingenious mechanism made from old bicycle chains slowly rotates the dish as the sun moves across the sky. Where previously firewood had to be collected for fuel, all the cooking on campus is now done using these dishes. Jimmy is regularly asked to give papers on the solar cookers at conferences and his advice is sought out by academics and NGOs alike.

In keeping with the Universal House of Justice's emphasis on sustainability and systematization, Barli's connection with the women does not end when they finish their training and return to their villages; rather, they are 'accompanied' by the Institute. Jimmy and Janak keep in touch with them via a newsletter and three outreach centres. With Jimmy's help, several graduates of the Institute have set up solar cookers in their villages and the skills they have learned at the Institute benefit their whole community.

The trip was a fantastic experience for both of us. Despite its challenges, Barli is a wonderful example of how the Bahá'í teachings will transform the world and bring about the betterment of human society. The enterprise is built on the loving sacrifice of Jimmy and Janak, their staff and the many volunteers who give service at Barli every year.

171
July 2007
Jane Helbo
Denmark

Jane (Sadler) left Cumbria to pioneer to Poland in January 1993. In April 2000 she married Ole Helbo and since then her home has been in Denmark.

Our really big challenge this year has been water! It started with storms at the end of October, when the sea water was forced into the Kattegat and Lille Bælt straits. This gave extra water in the fjord and, when the water in the fjord tried to ebb out, caused a storm flood of about two metres over the normal level here in Vejle! For us it meant that during the afternoon of 1 November our garden was flooded to over ankle depth. Ole rang the council to get sandbags to hold the water out of the cellar but was told that the technical department was closed! One and a half hours later we just had to watch as the cellar filled up with one metre of river water.

All in all we got off lightly. My musical instrument repair workshop escaped with only water under the floor, not in the workshop itself. With instruments and thousands of small spare parts it could have been a catastrophe. After three weeks of humming dehumidifiers the cellar and the space under the workshop were dry and smelled sweeter. Our freezer survived its swim but not the (nearly new) washing machine.

In January the water came again from another source – the river was so swollen with rain that it burst its banks! This time we were ready with sandbags but in fact we were the only house in the area that didn't suffer. Ole took some great pictures of the streets in the centre of Vejle that resembled Venice – but with stranded cars instead of gondolas!

When it comes to 'the water of life', our Bahá'í activities have changed nature during the year. Since January 2001 we have held regular devotional meetings open to all, sometimes in rented venues, other times in the local library or community centre or in the little Bahá'í Centre (old shop premises!) in the ground floor of our house. We are now focusing our energies on holding devotional evenings in our own flat on the last Thursday in the month. We have a group of regulars attending and expect it to develop as people begin to bring their friends. We also look forward to offering our improved house as a venue for study days or weekends now that we have the room for it and, in fact, are starting a book 1 group with two seekers after the summer break. Our old Persian tenant, Jalal Mohammadi Dahaj, succumbed to old age and moved back to Copenhagen in April to live with his daughter but left us a priceless legacy of six Persian families which he had attracted to the Faith over the five years he lived in Vejle. Taking the opportunity of a visiting Persian Bahá'í from Canada, we were able to invite all these people to a 'Farsi fireside' at the end of May. This turned into the most animated evening one could have wished for. The travel teacher was bombarded with relevant questions. Of course we didn't understand a word but provided dinner, tea and refreshments and enjoyed the wonderful atmosphere! What we can say is that our friendships with these people deepened because of that evening. As to further participation in the processes of cluster development, a few of the Bahá'ís from our area (Jutland, west Denmark) are involved at the national level in supporting the priority cluster over in the Copenhagen area which is a B cluster and needs to reach A status.

172
July 2007
Iman Fadaei
Nepal

Iman (Gloucestershire) spent the first six months of his youth year of service of 2006/07 in the Faroe Islands. From early March his second six months were spent serving the Faith in Nepal. The following extract is from his online blog.

Waking up at 3:30 in the morning was surprisingly easy, probably due to my anxiety at the thought of the bus trip to Biratnagar, a major city in the south of Nepal in an area known as the Terai. A few of the Bahá'ís in Kathmandu were telling me that the bus drivers often drink heavily on the journey and that as a result there have been many accidents. My only other information about buses in Nepal was that if a pedestrian is injured due to a vehicle, the driver will attempt to finish off the job and kill the victim because it costs less to pay the death money than the upkeep of an injured person.

The Bahá'í National Spiritual Assembly of Nepal had proposed this visit for the main purpose of providing a service for the local people of Biratnagar – Bahá'í and non-Bahá'í alike; I was to teach English at the Bahá'í Centre there. In addition, I could visit the villages in this cluster (Morang and Sunsari) to experience the exciting activities going on there and perhaps give some Ruhi refreshers, if required. This was the cluster shown in 'Building Momentum' and mentioned in *Reflections on Growth*, so I was pretty excited to see what was happening.

So 4:00 a.m. found me on a battered, dirty bus with metal bars in most of the windows and Hindu ornaments everywhere, producing a rather claustrophobic atmosphere. Being much taller than any of the Nepalese people, my legs were also a little longer than theirs, which meant that my knees were also rather battered by the end of the 13 hour journey. However, it was not nearly as bad as I had been told. The worst part of the journey was getting used to the VERY fast and VERY dangerous driving. The bus sped round tight hilly corners overlooking sheer drops of often more than three hundred metres, and though the speed in itself was scary enough, the bus would overtake everything in its path, often missing an oncoming vehicle by less than a metre – and this was just normal driving for them.

For the first half of the journey, the landscape was seen from a winding round angle, through lush green hills overlooking hundreds of paddy fields and clay and bamboo huts. We stopped every few hours for food and toilet breaks. Breakfast was fried Nepalese bread (a sort of round ring, like a big, thin donut, which can't be healthy) and water and bananas. I stocked up on biscuits and water at the first break so always had sufficient provisions – an increasingly essential necessity as we drew into the hot, flat south lands, the Terai. We reached a bus station after 12 hours and changed buses to one heading for Biratnagar – the landscape becoming more urban.

Biratnagar is the second largest city in Nepal and appears to be a one-road city. It is built around this main road but has spread and the smaller towns around it now join into the hundreds of villages in which most of the people live. Biratnagar is less polluted than Kathmandu but more dusty and MUCH MUCH hotter. I drink about four litres of water every day, sometimes more. From the bus station to the Bahá'í Centre, I took a rickshaw, the local taxi, with my friend Raju. The Bahá'í Centre in Biratnagar has large grounds in which are many fruit trees, such as mulberry, mango and banana. The building itself is a large square construction with two floors, although the top floor is incomplete and not in use. The caretaker has a little house next to the main building in which he lives with his wife, young baby and sister-in-law. There are two toilets of the hole-in-the ground variety, which are a luxury here – in the villages it is open toilet, i.e. anywhere you like. I found sleeping a little difficult owing to the heat and mosquitoes but much better after moving my bed underneath the fan.

In the morning I had breakfast at 'Ratnar' Hotel – everything has so much spice in it! With Raju and Dipesh, another Bahá'í living in Biratnagar at the moment, we attended the cluster meeting in a village called Tollu Sucachara which was a 20-minute bus ride followed by a 30-minute walk through increasingly rural villages. There were representatives from many of the villages in the cluster, an equal number of men and women. It was nice to see how the equality between men and women is so clear with the Bahá'ís in a country where gender equality is a long, long way away. The meeting was very similar to our own cluster meetings in Gloucestershire! The successes of the last plan were shown and the new plan, drawn up by the Area Teaching Committee, was discussed and amended with everyone else. I shared a few things, mainly about the Ruhi process, and sang a few book 5 songs we translated into Nepali in Kathmandu – these went down very well!

The next day many of the students-to-be came to say hello. We sang some songs and I tried (spectacularly unsuccessfully) to make pancakes with the local pots, to the amusement of the students. It was a great day and we all went out and they helped me to buy some provisions – watermelon, bananas, eggs, milk, flour, water, biscuits, bread, etc. I prepared some more of my English course and Raju went to get it printed but there was a bunt (strike) the next day and no shops were open so we didn't have the materials for the first day.

After the first lesson I did a little litter-picking and tidying of a pile of loose bricks in the centre grounds as a starting point for my mini-project to improve the grounds. People in Nepal just throw their rubbish on the floor – I haven't seen one bin yet. The sewage/dirty water from the houses goes down into specially constructed waterways along the side of the streets. Then some people come and dredge the solid material in these water ways and dump it on the side of the road. It dries and then someone else comes and puts it on the local open area (where kids play and cows graze).

With Dipesh and Raju, I was able to give an animator refresher session for some of the Bahá'ís in a town called Canal. It was held at another Bahá'í-inspired school, called the New Era School. It has a beautiful bamboo construction over which a tree grows, forming a natural roofed area. The refresher session was great and I taught them a few book 5 songs, in Nepali and English, a few games which we really enjoyed and an art activity – painting and making a presentation frame for it, including a quote from *Breezes of Confirmation*. It was the first time some of them had ever painted and they were enthusiastic to be able to offer it to their junior youth (there are 125 junior youth at the New Era School, some 30 of them Bahá'ís).

Nepal is one of the poorest countries in the world, with a large proportion of the population living below the poverty line. This is more clear in Biratnagar than in Kathmandu. Most of the children wear tattered clothes and they eat almost only rice because it's so cheap. Most children in the city go to school, the exceptions being the children of the lowest castes who help their parents with their dirty, manual work. In the villages a lower proportion of children go to school.

Iman went on to spend several months serving in both Biratnagar, where he worked with local Bahá'ís to establish children's classes, assist with junior youth activities and teach the Faith, and Kathmandu, where he assisted the Training Institute to train and encourage cluster coordinators and local Bahá'ís to develop their use of the practice elements and artistic activities in study circles.

173
October 2007
Layli Foroudi
Guyana

Layli (16) from Chippenham, Wiltshire, and her friend Bonnie Smith (15) from Cornwall were volunteers in Guyana. Here Layli writes about the exciting times they experienced.

For six weeks in July and August I lived in Guyana and took part in the Youth Can Move the World teaching project. This was almost a homecoming for me, as I spent three years of my childhood in Guyana with my parents who pioneered there in the mid 1990s.

Guyana, on the Atlantic coast of South America, is next to Venezuela, Surinam and Brazil. It is a former British colony and so it has more links with the Caribbean countries than the rest of South America. It is a country with lush tropical forests, vast savannahs and a very long and muddy coastline, where almost all the population live. Guyana is a land of many large rivers and creeks. The largest river, Essequibo, is so wide that it takes almost 30 minutes to cross it in a speed boat! I travelled to Guyana with another youth volunteer, Bonnie Smith from Cornwall. After a long 24-hour journey, owing to a lengthy stay in Barbados airport and a series of delays, Bonnie and I entered the country.

The programme Youth Can Move the World was organized by the Bahá'í community of Guyana and the Varqa Foundation, a Bahá'í-inspired foundation for social and economic development initiatives. This programme was open to everyone and the majority of the attendees were non-Bahá'ís.

On arrival we stayed at School of the Nations in Georgetown, the capital of Guyana. School of the Nations is a Bahá'í-inspired school founded by two UK Bahá'í pioneers in Guyana, Pam and Brian O'Toole, who made their school building available for the programme.

The daily routine was Ruhi in the morning followed by a social issues workshop, followed by lunch. Lunch was chicken and rice every single day. After lunch we had more Ruhi and then an arts workshop. We had free time in the afternoon when we could play sports, swim, socialize, go to the market or the sea wall OR, for the enthusiastic ones, do extra Ruhi. After free time we would eat dinner – which was chicken and rice EVERY NIGHT. It's lucky I like chicken and rice. After dinner we would have either Ruhi, reflection or free time, depending on what day it was.

The programme went extremely well, although we faced difficulties at the start. Ruhi was excellent for introducing and informing people about the Faith and helping to motivate the youth to render service among their communities. It was quite amazing to see non-Bahá'ís also tutoring! The social issues were at first done by an organization called Help & Shelter, which conducted workshops about abuse. After that the youth took charge and organized them. I did one on drugs and alcohol with a Canadian Bahá'í, Jon Kiai. There were other workshops such as HIV/AIDS, global prosperity, marriage and relationships, equality, etc.

The Canadian dance theatre group, Wildfire, were with us in Georgetown. They ran the arts workshops and we also were able to enjoy their incredible performance! The arts workshops were an inspiration! I took part in the dance workshop and the visual arts workshop, both of which were really enjoyable. We had fun activities in the evening, such as the talent show which was hilarious and enjoyable – a huge majority of the participants took part!

The programme in Georgetown lasted for three weeks. At the end of the three weeks everyone was sad to leave and the goodbyes were emotionally draining. The programme was very successful and the great thing was it was a programme for youth, enjoyed by youth and run by youth. The task force consisted of three Guyanese youth – Louisa, Rosheni and Lall – who made a great effort and faced and triumphed many tests in order to keep the programme running smoothly. Volunteers from abroad were plenteous; there were two boys from Haiti; a couple from Utah; a man from California; two men from Canada; and the whole of Wildfire, plus myself and Bonnie of course.

At the weekends the various youth would go back to their communities and do some kind of service in their communities and with their friends and families. Bonnie and I had been visiting the West Coast Demerara community and stayed at the Bahá'í Centre with a lovely couple called Uncle Moeen and Aunty Sabra. We started a local youth group there which was a huge success and continues to run and grow every week. Roger, a local youth who was heavily involved in the group, said, 'You should have been here yesterday, we had to start using the benches as there weren't enough chairs!'

After the Georgetown intensive programme had finished we spent nine days in West Coast building up the youth group and holding firesides, storytelling evenings, unity feasts and children's classes. At the end of the nine days we felt so at home and had grown so close to all the youth that it was very hard to say goodbye. It wasn't hard, however, to say goodbye to the mosquito nets that we had to use there as for some reason the mosquitoes there were particularly vicious . . . I do hate mosquito nets.

We travelled from West Coast Demerara to the Essequibo region of Guyana. Our journey involved travelling in a speed boat to cross the mighty Essequibo River. Speed boats are used as public transport and carry about a dozen people sitting in a long wooden boat with a very powerful outboard engine. The ride was incredibly enjoyable, even if I did get soaked. In fact it complemented the high temperatures.

As we got off the boat we were attacked by a swarm of taxi drivers all saying, 'Good price' or 'I'm your captain' or 'Whe-yo-wan-go?' We found a good taxi and drove along the pothole-ridden roads to a white gate which opened onto a long grassy drive leading to a big house: Club Nations. Club Nations belongs to School of the Nations and is extremely comfortable – we got beds, toilet seats AND not chicken and rice every mealtime!

My favourite part of the house is the balcony at the back which looks out onto the beach and the Atlantic Ocean. The water looks almost blue in the morning (it is really brown and muddy all the time). We had a very comfortable two-week Youth Can Move the World programme with the same sort of things happening, except we had to do all the social issues and arts workshops ourselves, so Bonnie and I ran the music workshop and I ran a social issue workshop on chastity with a Canadian Bahá'í, Shawn.

The Essequibo intensive programme was very different from the one in Georgetown as it was smaller but it was nice and 'homely' and people got to know each other well. In the evenings we sang folk songs, played games and laughed a lot.

A highlight of this intensive was once again the talent show. Always hilarious. Always full of talent. Always full of show. Always full of fun. The end of the intensive was, as always, hard but everyone was happy as the two weeks had been so successful (although occasionally we could not shower owing to lack of water on the top floor which was unfortunately the girls' floor). Four days later, after consuming a large amount of roti, going on market traipsing trips and on minibus rides (the bus rides were memorable), Bonnie and I were back on the plane flying home to England. On the drive to the airport I felt incredibly sad to leave as I really did feel like I lived there. The Guyanese are so open and friendly and I am going to miss them so much.

174
October 2007
Maureen Sier
Visit to Samoa

Maureen (Aberdeen) and her family were UK pioneers in Samoa from 1997 to 2002. Since then she has made four return visits – her last visit coinciding with the passing of the Malietoa of Samoa.

On Wednesday, 16 May, after his passing, the body of His Highness the Malietoa, Head of State of independent Samoa, was brought from the Liga Liga funeral parlour to his family home at Fa'atoia. The distance covered was about three miles and people lined the roads. The final half mile of road ran from Lelata Bahá'í Centre to the gate of his humble home.

In the blazing sun for over an hour the Bahá'ís stood waiting for the remains of the first reigning monarch to recognize Bahá'u'lláh to pass. Most stood in respectful silence, some chatted quietly, occasionally everyone would gently sing a Samoan Bahá'í prayer. In the distance shouting and gunshots could be heard – getting louder and louder as the funeral procession approached. Walking slowly and with dignity in full Tongan regalia were members of the Tongan royal family, related through marriage to His Highness. Samoan police in sun-dazzled white uniforms fronted the solemn procession as it swung round the bend. The hearse passed, followed by a cavalcade of cars holding family members and dignitaries from around the world. Again Bahá'ís gently chanted prayers.

The most moving moment for me came as the daughter of His Highness, Princess Toa Tosi Malietoa, rolled down her window to wave at her fellow

Bahá'ís, calling out 'Alláh-u-Abhá, Alláh-u-Abhá', a smile of recognition on her face.

Then from behind the cars almost a hundred Samoan warriors dressed in black lava lavas, with painted bodies and red bandanas and wielding guns, machetes and axes leapt towards the crowds, firing their guns, smashing at poles with their axes, thrashing at bushes with their machetes and yelling at the crowds to move out of the way. The change of tempo was so dramatic it was exhilarating. These warriors were the Manu Samoa – men chosen from ten villages around Samoa as the king's protectors. From the bushes beside me an old man, too old to join the procession earlier, emerged and joined his fellow warriors for the last stretch of the journey. This powerful demonstration of loyalty to the highest chief was a re-enactment of earlier times when such a death brought mayhem to the land.

That evening the Bahá'ís joined hundreds of others from various churches in an evening vigil of prayer and song and in the morning the body of the Malietoa was brought to outside the government building to allow 24 hours to pay respects before the official state funeral on Friday and his final interment in the tomb of his ancestors.

Perhaps of most significance was that the devotional events of this historic week began on the Sunday immediately following his death with a beautiful Bahá'í service in his honour at the Bahá'í Temple and they ended exactly a week later with a memorial service again at the Temple. Both services were packed with Bahá'ís and their friends, local dignitaries and representatives from overseas. I was honoured, on behalf of the Bahá'ís of Scotland, to assist in the preparation of the programme for the first Temple service and was asked to read at that same service a beautiful quote about the journey of the soul after death. During the state funeral Bahá'í representatives were permitted to say the prayer for the dead – assisting his precious soul on its eternal journey. Media coverage of the passing proclaimed loud and clear the Bahá'í message and that the Head of State of Samoa was a Bahá'í. The Samoan community around the world and the international Bahá'í community mourn the loss of this wonderful man.

175
October 2007
Gemma Enolengila
Tanzania

Gemma and her husband Lesikar are involved in the Aang Serian (House of Peace) Community Secondary School in Arusha, Tanzania. The following is a note of some significant dates of exciting activity taken from her journal in 2007.

9 July

Today at the holy day celebration, Tipilit, one of our newest Bahá'ís, sang a version of 'Look at me, follow me' that he had made up in the Maa language, with such emotion that Kiza Punda (one of our long-standing believers who originally came to Arusha from Lake Victoria as a home front pioneer) announced jokingly that he was giving up his job and moving to the Maasai village of Eluwai!

22 July

Eight Maasai warriors came along to the Unity Feast in the end, sadly not including Lesikar as he had to drive some volunteers out to the bush, nor Tipilit as he had an important meeting in the village. They made a striking picture, sitting on the bench together – seven of them wearing robes and full jewellery, the other in a shirt and trousers – and before long they all launched into an enthusiastic performance of a traditional Maasai spiritual song. It went on so long that none of us who had been in the book 7 study circle could keep a straight face, as when we were discussing the arts I had told the others how much Maasai warriors loved to sing and said that they would have to keep the singing to the end in their study circles, otherwise they would end up singing all day and would never do any studying! We did eventually manage to start the official programme of prayers, readings and a brief introduction to the Faith, which they seemed to find very moving, and they were especially impressed by the fact that some of the Bahá'í prayers and a few short extracts from the holy writings had been translated into Maa. A handful of other non-Bahá'ís came as well, including Kephas, the school gardener and environmental studies teacher who had been so interested in the pictures of the holy shrines and gardens (although unfortunately he was late and missed most of the programme).

23 July

This morning we started our first Ruhi 1 study circle (Swahili) with four of the warriors from the Unity Feast, two others who had just come along to hang out with their friends and then decided to join in, and Mura, an older man who has been coming to our devotional meetings. I had been trying to contact him all week to ask if he wanted to come to the study circle but hadn't managed to get through to him on the phone. Amazingly he turned up to drop off a book just as we were about to start. It was quite an uphill struggle to get through the material, as Mura didn't have his glasses with him, two of the six warriors were hardly literate at all, one could read but couldn't write and another knew how to write a little bit but could barely read! It took two hours just to get to the end of the first page but there was a wonderful spirit of encouragement and fun, and the looks on some of their faces when they started to understand the holy writings made it all worthwhile. Hopefully tomorrow they will get into the rhythm of it a bit and make faster progress.

25 July

The study circle was amazing today – we had three new people (including Ngariapusi) and two of them didn't speak much Swahili, so Tipilit was translating between Swahili and Maa and also coming up with examples and stories to explain some of the points so that everyone could relate to them. He is a fantastic teacher and has a real rapport with the other group members. I wish there was a way that we could both drop everything else and just do a block course for the entire Ruhi programme so that he could get straight out to the villages and start tutoring – but I know the *Mto wa Mbu* plan will probably be better for everyone – hmmm – detachment needed! Of course everything will happen in its own time, I am just impatient to see all that love and energy channelled into a systematic training process and the unlocking of dozens of hearts. Towards the end of the session he said something that almost moved me to tears – that he has been through so much struggle and hardship in his life, travelling all over East Africa, and has tried all sorts of different churches, Lutheran and Catholic and even a mosque, but now at last God has led him to a beautiful garden where he can stay forever.

31 July

The atmosphere changed today when we decided to go round the whole circle and ask individual members to say whatever was in their heart. Some of them shared their own stories about the power of prayer, like this one from Ashimo:

I remember a drought that went on for so long that we thought God must have died. There was no water anywhere, even the springs and the water-holes dried up. We really believed that we were finished and we were in tears. Then the women prayed together and that night the rains came in a huge torrent. By the morning it was only drizzle and those whose houses were not leaky didn't even believe that it had rained at all until they looked out of their front doors and saw the mud. That day God showed us that we should never stop trusting in Him.

Several of them had been inspired by the quotation 'Intone, O My servant, the verses of God . . .'[31] and talked about how society could be changed if people sang only the verses of God and other things that are positive and uplifting. They realized that some of the traditional songs praising war, raiding and robbery have a damaging effect on their community.

Others spoke about the Bahá'í Faith itself and why they were so attracted to it. Mako, one of the newcomers I almost threw out yesterday, said that it reminded him of the ancient Maasai stories of the days when people lived together in peace and harmony, before the war and raiding began. Like Tipilit, he said he had been to several churches in his life but had never come across one quite like this, where there are no priests or pastors and the believers are actually encouraged to study and understand the writings for themselves instead of just dozing off during the sermon.

176

January 2008

Billy and Christine Lee

Botswana

Billy and Chris (originally from Burnley) have been pioneers in Africa for 34 years.

When Christine and I offered to pioneer to Africa at National Teaching Conference in 1973 we had no idea that 34 years later we would still be on this continent. At the time we were living in Chester, having been home front pioneers for a year.

Our initial post was in Zambia, which was full of confirmations from the very start. The National Spiritual Assembly of Zambia was thrilled when I told them that my new employer in Lusaka, the capital, was transferring me to Ndola in the Copperbelt region of Zambia, where we were instantly able to reactivate the Bahá'ís we were able to locate.

They enquired as to my new postal address in Ndola – wait for it – PO Box 1844.

With two infants and a new challenge we arrived in Ndola in October 1974 after witnessing the country's ten years of independence celebrations in Lusaka in the company of many wonderful Persian pioneers who were mostly employed in government posts. Our large house in Ndola became a halfway point for travel teachers and visitors to the northern regions of the country. Many of the friends visiting called it the Bahá'í Hotel.

During our time on the Copperbelt we established close friendships with Jessie and Eric Manton – Eric had moved to Northern Rhodesia in 1962 with a young son and met his wife, Jessie, there. Their stories of the old days were magical!! We also met up with Val Rhind with whom Christine had been on a youth trip to Berlin many years earlier. Our two families eventually joined forces again in later years in Gaborone, Botswana.

We quickly reformed the lapsed Local Spiritual Assembly in Ndola and most gatherings were initially held in our home, usually over a weekend as most of the local believers found it easier then to travel in from the suburbs. Feasts and holy days had great attendance of up to 30 and all gatherings were conducted in Bemba, the regional language of the Copperbelt. Christine was elected onto the Local Spiritual Assembly but I was spared – little did I realize what was to be in store for me some years later! Eventually our young children attended a private nursery school and soon revelled in the lovely climate and the many house visitors. The National Assembly requested that I take over the maintenance of the Bahá'í Land Rover, which was quite old but fairly reliable for teaching trips into the bush areas. Unfortunately, it kept snapping half shafts and I was kept very busy with simple repairs. There are many precious memories and one bounty of being the only pioneers in a town was when Hand of the Cause Dr Muhájir came to stay with us en route from Lubumbashi in Zaire to Lusaka.

Although our time in Zambia was only 27 months, we will always remember the wonderful Bahá'í community, especially the many Persian pioneers who had arrived in the country often in the most difficult circumstances.

In 1977 I was offered the opportunity to relocate with the same employer to Botswana, and after discussing the situation with the Pioneer Committee in Nairobi, Kenya, we were advised that we would also be fulfilling a British pioneer goal in Botswana. Off we went!!

I arrived in May 1977 ahead of the family and soon settled into, then, a very small community in what was the most stable country at the time in Africa. The country was quickly developing on all fronts and I was very fortunate to be extremely busy with new engineering projects and to have both children enrolled in an English medium primary school. Our daughter, Abigail, who still lives here in Gaborone, will be enrolling her second child, David, in the very same primary school in January next year!

There were mostly American pioneer couples in Botswana at the time and soon Persian friends arrived to help with the work. Travelling was often very difficult, as there were not a lot of tar roads constructed throughout the country at the time. A 4x4 vehicle was virtually essential. A common problem with Batswana is that they often have three places of residence – first where they work in formal employment, second where they tend their cattle or farm and finally their home village where they were born! It is a full-time job for the National Office to keep tabs on the movements of the believers and also to maintain accurate data and statistics.

I was elected onto the Gaborone Local Spiritual Assembly at Riḍván 1978 and have been a member ever since. The Baháʼí community in Gaborone has swelled over the years and we now have many pioneer families who have established themselves in the local business world and are well known, especially in the construction and education sectors. The Baháʼí Faith enjoys a considerably high profile and many of the community are well known to the leaders of the country. Botswana has also been blessed to have witnessed a Continental Counsellor being appointed from our community – Lally Warren, whose parents were the first Batswana to embrace the Faith, in 1954.

Hand of the Cause John Robarts was the first Baháʼí to teach the Faith in Botswana, undertaking teaching trips into the country from Mafeking, South Africa, where he lived with his family. In those days Botswana was known as the Bechuanaland Protectorate and was administered from Mafeking by the colonial government. Botswana became independent in 1966 and the Faith celebrated its fiftieth jubilee in December 2004. The main celebration took place at the new national Baháʼí Centre, which was designed and constructed completely by Baháʼí-owned and managed companies.

Greater Gaborone is now an A cluster with three Baháʼí properties throughout the city where regular activities are held. At present 13 children's classes are held weekly and some of them have attendance solely of children from non-Baháʼí families. Christine teaches a class of 9 to 11 year olds and I assist with Ruhi book 1. There are numerous firesides and study classes but we are still endeavouring to increase the number of devotional meetings and home visits. The community is always reminded that being an A cluster leaves no time to rest on our laurels!

There is no doubt that the Faith has been recognized in the field of education because the Baháʼí Faith is included in the national secondary school curriculum and it is not uncommon for teachers-in-training to visit the

National Bahá'í Centre for information packs. Many speakers from our Bahá'í community are invited to address students on moral values as part of the civic and community studies programme, and numerous NGOs regularly contact the Bahá'í Public Relations Office for involvement in seminars and work-shops, the programme content of which would be of interest to the Faith.

The recent situation in neighbouring Zimbabwe has seen many immi-grants enter the country and many new declarants have come from this group.

Junior youth are increasing their involvement in all aspects of Bahá'í community life including hosting 19 Day Feasts, teaching children's classes, helping as Ruhi book tutors and animators and involvement in the core activi-ties. They also possess many musical talents and add lots of entertainment to our gatherings.

Gaborone has its own share of problems, which is no different from other large Bahá'í communities throughout the world. It is no secret that there are too many pioneer families living in the capital. The Gaborone LSA attempts to constantly vary the administrative content at 19 Day Feasts in order to stimu-late, encourage and at the same time educate, particularly the new believers, on fundamentals such as Huqúqu'lláh, the Bahá'í Fund, burial law, the wedding laws, chastity, on non-involvement in politics, etc. Many firesides regularly take place with good attendance and a very interesting range of topics.

The urbanization of Botswana has brought with it the same problems of apathy, peer pressure and a materialistic outlook as is evident in western cultures, and the Faith continues to respond to these challenges with the con-tinued guidance from the Universal House of Justice and the assistance from our dearly loved Counsellor Enos Makhele.

Botswana is essentially a Christian country and has established a morals-based culture which is being threatened by the modern world. The Bahá'í community has earned true respect for its principles and manner of tolerance in dealing with other religious organizations and continues to grow steadily and hopefully will attain all the targets within this plan.

177
April 2008
Peter Smith
Thailand

Peter Smith, originally from Bristol, has resided in Bangkok since 1985.

As to my sojourn in Bangkok, I am reminded of the famous comment by

Arthur J. Outreach III who fell off the top of one of Chicago's highest sky-scrapers and on passing the 22nd floor on his way down was heard to remark, 'Well. So far, so good!'

Bangkok has changed over this past almost quarter century. As indeed have I. When we first came here I felt I was melting in the heat and humidity. I would wake in a pool of sweat. Now I wear a jacket in our winter and the time before last when I was in England (in April) spent three days in what felt like near-hypothermia, shivering despite wearing every single item of clothing I could find. Other than that, I have become a Bangkokian. One relative informs me that my body language is now Asian rather than western, and my Thai friends ask me whether I am half-Japanese or Chinese. My knowledge of and sympathy for Buddhism and Buddhist perspectives has greatly increased. There are days when all my conversations are in (my not very good) Thai rather than English.

This past eight years or so public transport in Bangkok has greatly improved (I am an acknowledged master on Bangkok buses). Regretfully, I therefore no longer have that bracing, early morning experience of hanging onto the outside of a bus with the breeze in my hair as we whiz past street furniture with inches to spare – one of the most invigorating ways I have come across of waking up. Again, it is years since I have been dragged along the road by a bus, or damaged my knee, shin or ankle, or broken a toe trying to board a bus (traditionally, Bangkok buses didn't really stop but sort of semi-slowed down a few lanes out in the traffic to allow would-be passengers a chance to get on whilst others were trying to get off – ideally one leapt accurately but sometimes one did not). With a new overhead railway, I can sometimes miss the traffic jams altogether (my personal best in the 'old days' was an epic seven and a half hour bus journey home one night, but that was years ago).

The past few years the floods have been relatively mild. The very first year we were here we had flood water inside the house to a depth of about 18 inches and it was interesting to see fish swimming around one's toes without having to leave home. Several years with heavy floods, it was fun to walk along the side of the road with water up to one's knees and feel the water flowing like a powerful river when one tried to cross over the street. The presence of unseen removed manhole covers beneath the dirty waters was an added excitement.

Walking around the city is still fun. There are areas that are distinctly dangerous at night, but for a man at least, Bangkok is probably much safer than the average English town when the pubs are closing. Although Thailand has one of the highest murder rates in the world (double that in the US), most violence here is personal (business dealings, romantic or political problems) and not random. The real dangers are from tripping on broken sections of pavement – basically, the whole city – or from getting some projecting board or rod in the face because you're looking down at the pavement to find a safe footing. Sometimes motorcyclists ride on the pavements – sensibly to avoid the traffic on the road – which can be a little annoying for pedestrians, but often the pavements are so chock-a-block with food vendors that both motor-cyclists and pedestrians have to use the road (if you know where to look you can buy tasty street food any hour of the day or night). Late at night there are sometimes illegal motorcycle races on the main roads, youthful racers lying flat on their machines for extra speed. The death rate is quite high.

Crossing the road in traffic is generally easy if you know how. Soon after I first came here I was able to terrify a couple of visiting members of the NSA by the simple expedient of leading them across the road whilst cars and motorbikes whizzed around us. I thought the situation more amusing than they did. On the other hand, my Thai wife's son (now a novice monk) was knocked over on a zebra crossing by a motorbike a few years ago and lost his spleen, so the danger is real.

I still don't like mosquitoes and termites. The night-time mosquitoes are more annoying and can keep one awake for hours with their buzzing but Bangkok is not malarial and it is the daytime 'mossies' that are more dangerous here – presumably, along with almost all other Bangkokians, I have probably had a mild dose of mosquito-borne dengue fever at some time (severe cases are more noticeable if they lead to death). Termites are interesting in that they can turn masses of papers and books into an unrecognizable mulch – much recommended for all those old papers you had always intended to sort but never had time to attend to. The ants in food provide extra protein, of course, and the occasional cockroach in your shoe when you leave for work at five o'clock in the morning again provides a stimulus in the process of waking up. The house lizards chasing each other up the walls and across the ceiling with romantic or cannibalistic intent can provide entertainment, as can the neighbours who play loud music late at night (one of our teachers lived in an apartment block where the security guards used to have night-time karaoke competitions on their two-way radios; another – who no longer works for us – would sometimes fire his air rifle at noisy revellers below).

I just turned 60 but there is no retirement option for me (apart from vertical swimming in the Gulf of Thailand, of course)! This is partly because I don't have any money but it's also because I need to have an annually-renewed work permit in order to stay here and I really don't fancy trying to live in a cardboard box on the street side back in Lancaster or wherever (here many poor people of necessity sleep on the pavement or in shop doorways).

I forgot to mention the fried insects!! These are readily available on some street stalls – water bugs, wormy things and, naturally, grasshoppers (I tried one of those once but it had been badly cooked and was rather oily). Nowadays these are fairly safe, as the bugs are produced commercially, but when I was first here, there were stories of people dying from eating grasshoppers which had themselves died from DDT poisoning (we don't have much enforcement of those wimpy safety regulations that annoy people so much in England).

Bangkok is a wonderful city for food. Leaving aside the Iranian restaurant that recently put me in hospital on a drip for three days with severe food poisoning, we have lots of (unsurprisingly) really good Thai restaurants, in addition to excellent Arab, Mexican, Indian, Italian, Vietnamese and Chinese food – not to mention the masses of Japanese and Korean food places (the wonderful Ethiopian restaurant that used to be here has now closed, alas, so I can no longer get enjera, pancake-like bread). Many of these are relatively inexpensive even for us locals, and as with most people here, I eat out as often as in. We used to have a Thai restaurant that was apparently the largest eatery in the world – the waiters all wore traditional Thai dress but with the addition of roller-skates to bring you your food quicker.

I work at what is obviously the best ('cos I helped set it up), English-medium university colleges in Thailand. We now have over two thousand students, including two hundred or so in the social science programme that I head. Building this up has been a lot of work and there is still much to do but we have reason to be reasonably satisfied. I have former students who are now doing post-graduate study at places like LSE, SOAS and Harvard, so we must be doing something right.

I have been unable to serve on any Bahá'í Assemblies or committees since coming to Bangkok. This is partly because five or six hours a day on Bangkok buses and a 4:30 a.m. rising time leaves one rather tired, but it's also because I have tried to devote the few spare energies I have available to writing – a somewhat solitary pursuit. This has been difficult – undoubtedly remaining in England would have been much better from this standpoint but I have managed to produce seven books on the Faith here, including the recently published Cambridge *Introduction to the Bahá'í Faith*. I take the view that as the Faith becomes better known, there will be more interest in it at colleges and universities and therefore a demand for accounts of the Faith that are academic in nature.

Death is always present here. Funerals are major social occasions, and sadly, I have attended several of my own students' funerals over the years – primarily due to disease and road accidents. Our former gatekeeper's adult son was shot by a hot-tempered neighbour a few years back for making too much noise – the blood stain was visible at the gate for weeks after. The murderer fled the scene and I don't think any attempt was ever made to catch him – he was well-connected and the dead man wasn't. Ditto the brother of one of the maids. Some of my students tell me horrific stories of murders and disappearances in their families.

On one of the local radio stations where I can normally listen to hip-hop music (young at heart!), there is a weekly Buddhist half hour on Sunday mornings in which two monks discuss Buddhist teachings in broken English. Apart from the broken English, it has often struck me that this would be a very good format for Bahá'í radio broadcasts. Because the discussion is informal and natural, it lacks the rather stilted style that sometimes characterizes monologues.

Two Buddhist teachings that always seem very relevant here are 'un-satisfactoriness' (*dukkha*, normally translated as 'suffering') and impermanence.

178
January 2009
Charlie Pierce
Vanuatu

Charlie and Barbara Pierce have been pioneers in Vanuatu in the South Pacific since 1971.

Letter from Vanuatu

After repeated annual requests to 'write something about pioneer life in Vanuatu', I've finally managed to find a window of opportunity – a space between completing all NSA correspondence from our last meeting and starting on the minutes – and can put down a few thoughts about what it means to be serving Bahá'u'lláh in a remote tropical island.

Well, of course, it's really the same as serving the Faith anywhere, particularly in these days of clusters, core activities, reflection meetings, 'Anna's presentation' and constant activity. I suppose that one difference is the high receptivity of the local population. Another is that when you move to another country for pioneer service you are freer from old world obligations and family pressures and can devote more of your time to the Cause. Also, in a small island nation like Vanuatu, everyone knows you are a Bahá'í and your life is transparent.

Vanuatu is a Y-shaped archipelago of 80-odd volcanic islands stretching for about 800 km in the southwest Pacific. It is famous for having the most accessible volcano in the world (Mount Yasur on the island of Tanna), for the remarkable land-diving ceremony on the island of Pentecost (the inspiration for 'bungee jumping'), for having the world's only joint Anglo-French colonial government between 1906 and 1980, and for being, according to the UK's New Economics Foundation, the 'happiest place on the planet'. It has just two towns and a population of some 220,000, of whom 98 per cent are indigenous people of Melanesian origin, known as ni-Vanuatu. Its economy is based upon subsistence agriculture, exports of copra, cacao, coffee, kava and beef, and on tourism.

The Bahá'í Faith has been here since 1953 when Knight of Bahá'u'lláh Bertha Dobbins, a schoolteacher from Australia, first set foot in Port Vila. Today, almost three per cent of the population are Bahá'ís, three of our 18 clusters are functioning at A level and one of our islands, Tanna, is aiming to become the world's first 'Bahá'í island'.

I've been here since March 1971, when I came to take over the running of Nur Bahá'í School in Port Vila. Although born and bred in the United Kingdom, I became a Bahá'í in Australia while on a round the world adventure and shortly afterwards offered to fulfil an Australian pioneer goal in what was then the New Hebrides. At the end of 1971 Nur School had to close for economic reasons and I returned to Perth, Western Australia, to get married to Barbara. We came back to the New Hebrides on our honeymoon and have been here ever since! I found a new job working for the condominium government as a statistician, then later went back into teaching, first in the country's main English-medium secondary school, and since 1999, as a lecturer at the Vanuatu Institute of Teacher Education – where I am still employed. Barbara worked as a primary school teacher for many years but has now retired from full-time employment and assists as a supply teacher when needed. We live on the edge of the capital city of Port Vila on the island of Efate, which is about the same size as the Isle of Wight but has just sixty thousand people.

Our two sons, Daniel and Sam, were born and grew up here. We took them with us when going on teaching visits to villages in the outer islands, and in keeping with 'Abdu'l-Bahá's advice, they became accustomed to hardship from an early age. Both are now living and working in Australia. Daniel had a five-year spell as a pioneer in Tahiti, also in the South Pacific, but returned to Adelaide in 2004. As I write this, he and his wife and infant daughter are again back in Tahiti: this time his trip is funded by the firm of consultant engineers for whom he works, as they needed a French-speaker for a new project in French Polynesia – so Daniel and his family have three days for work and six for visiting the friends and helping with Bahá'í activities.

So now, having lived here for so long, we are well integrated into island life. We have seen the New Hebrides become Vanuatu and lived through 28 years of independence. We have been involved in the education of thousands of young people, many of whom have risen to the highest levels in the public and private sectors. We have seen the Bahá'í community grow from tens of believers living on just three islands to thousands of believers living on 20. We participated in the establishment of the National Spiritual Assembly and have been deeply involved in the education of the friends – ranging from learning together on Assemblies to facilitating deepening classes and study circles.

There are three official languages in the country – English, French and Bislama – but it is the latter that everyone uses. It's a form of pidgin English that also incorporates words from French and indigenous tongues, and is easy to learn. It's our main method of communication in the Bahá'í community – the language for teaching the Faith and for institute courses – and because it has such a limited vocabulary, this means that we are forced to explain difficult concepts in a manner that everyone can understand. Perhaps for this reason we have a relatively high percentage of believers who have completed the full sequence of Ruhi courses – even some who cannot read or write!

There are so many exciting things happening in our Bahá'í community. At a national level, we have good relations with the government. In fact our National Spiritual Assembly has an ongoing programme of inviting national leaders to come and consult with the Assembly at one of its regular meetings in the National Ḥaẓíratu'l-Quds: in the past year visitors include the Prime Minister, the Deputy Prime Minister, Attorney-General, and Director-Generals of both Education and the Prime Minister's Office. We have regular Bahá'í programmes on national radio and television. The Rowhani Bahá'í School, on the island of Santo, is becoming well known for its emphasis on character training and academic excellence. At cluster level, all three A clusters have in the past few months achieved record numbers of enrolments and many of the new believers are being instantly absorbed into the institute process. And the junior youth programme here is gradually taking root in the wider community, with real potential to transform the whole of Vanuatu society.

On a personal level, things are always hectic, the more so since our cluster (Efate) started operating at A level three years ago. As well as having a full-time job, I do part-time lecturing at the local university extension centre, write school textbooks and am a chief examiner at Year 12 level for the South Pacific Board of Educational Assessment, based in Fiji. I have been secretary of the NSA for most of the period since its inception in 1977 and am involved in the demanding work of translating documents and sacred writings into Bislama. Each week Barbara and I facilitate three study circles – a group of experienced believers, old and young, who are doing book 7; a group of new believers doing book 1; and a group of my students at the Teachers' College (mostly non-Bahá'ís) who are doing books 1 and 2. Each weekend we help with youth gatherings, deepenings, children's classes and junior youth groups in Port Vila and a nearby village. In the current cycle (no. 9), we formed a teaching team with five new believers, and although the expansion phase has now finished, the momentum and joy that was created means that our team continues to run fortnightly firesides. As new enrolments come, so the size of our teaching team increases!

Of course, there are challenges of living here. In this tropical environment, where the constant heat, rainfall and humidity cause even the fence posts to grow into trees, small cuts become festering sores and diseases such as malaria and hepatitis are endemic. We have regular cyclones and earthquakes. Our home has been broken into over 12 times in the last nine years. Things happen according to 'island time' and this can mean long-delayed meeting times and other frustrations. Inter-island travel is unreasonably expensive. And we are a long way away from our children and grandchildren!

But in reality, these things pale when compared with the joys of being in a community where friendliness is the norm and where it is so easy to speak about the Faith to others. As you walk along the street, you smile and greet everyone, and very often you will already know them. Everywhere you go, you come across fellow Bahá'ís and address them with 'Alláh-u-Abhá'! Our Bahá'í community thrives on music and singing: almost everyone can sing in tune and harmonize, and all our meetings, study circles and firesides feature choral versions of prayers and sacred writings that truly warm the heart. For lovers of sea and sand, you have the Pacific Ocean on your doorstep – literally for us, since our house is just one hundred metres from the breaking waves. You are in a largely unspoilt rural environment where most people live in villages, traditional customs are still strong, you are surrounded by greenery and all your food is organic. And at the same time, you can have access to the latest technology – the Internet, satellite television, mobile phones. The latter are revolutionizing our Bahá'í communications. Members of cluster agencies can now ring each other from remote villages and mountain tops to organize and stimulate activities, and teaching teams can quickly arrange alternative venues if a particular home is no longer available.

I suppose that for most of the time we do not think of ourselves as 'pioneers'. We are just Bahá'ís living here and trying to do what all Bahá'ís are trying to do everywhere – live the life, teach the Cause, fight one's own spiritual battles. But it is such a privilege to be here in this wonderful country, with its beautiful people and verdant landscapes.

179
January 2009
Jo Harding
Greece

*Jo, from Cardiff, arrived at her pioneering post in Athens on 21 April
1991.*

News from Athens

My last contribution to *Pioneer Post* was about nine years ago. So it's time for
an update! Back then there were no clusters and fewer study circles, and an
IPG was a sort of science fiction. I am in my eighteenth year in Athens now
and our tiny community is aspiring to be an A cluster; thanks to all those Ruhi
books and an astonishing enthusiasm for growth, we do at last seem to have
some signs that things are moving.

The average Greek soul is very deeply bonded to the Greek Orthodox faith,
so we are seeking other communities of interest. There is a very big community of black folks around our Bahá'í Centre and another of Turkish speaking
from northern Greece, mainly of Islamic background, who are much more
open to the idea of a new spiritual identity. So we have had seven declarations
in this area in six months, after using that wonder-tool, 'Anna's Presentation',
with these groups.

I guess Bahá'u'lláh has plans for me to carry on here for a while yet as I
am blessed with good health. Doing yoga and meditating every day help to
maintain it. Not least being happy and grateful!

I am in my eighty-fifth year, and 'playing for extra time' – which means, as
ever, that I have a wish to get a goal or two!! . . . to be part of an A cluster, to
keep my door wide open for whoever comes to explore their spiritual selves.
Since we are so few (just 12 in Central Athens at this time) we need, and get,
some wonderful souls from outside to help us, and I greatly enjoy having
them to stay in my home. Their presence and their contributions are inspiring, and joyful. Monday firesides are still going strong – we started them in
1994 and they are a place where friendships are formed and people can be
found to join a study circle or attend a devotional.

In between all the above I find some time to paint and belong to a small art
group run by a local Bahá'í – another good vehicle for sharing the Faith across
the table with the paintbrush in hand.

One of the compensations for the fewness of numbers here in Greece is
the fact that we really are one family – knowing each other well, enjoying a
friendship and intimacy with each other, a feeling of closeness and tender

connection though some of us live far away. We pass on some of this at our Bahá'í summer schools, which are pure delight for all who attend. Sun, sea, and spirit. Come and try it!!

180
January 2009
Helen Smith
Lithuania

Helen, from Guernsey, has been a pioneer in Lithuania since 1989.

In Lithuania there was a great upsurge in the proclamation and teaching work during the summer months of 2008. Spearheaded by our able Auxiliary Board member, aided by a resource person from Kazakhstan and supported by a small band of committed and enthusiastic believers, they planned a project to take the town of Klaipeda by storm. This small group of Lithuanian friends, joined by a believer from Estonia, three from Latvia and a group of youth from Canada, set about preparing themselves for a week of hard work. The planning included not only the system to be used in teaching the local people, but the accommodation, the food and how to deal with language problems. The whole group worked as one to find the solutions so that the day-to-day activities would run as smoothly as possible. Prayers, deepening and roleplay on 'Anna's Presentation' were carried out to a timetable adhered to by everyone and not taken lightly. This was serious business.

The group divided into small units and targeted the local housing apartment blocks, the parks and even the beach. Seekers and contacts were invited to join in devotional and study circle meetings. This precious band of believers worked from morn till night, always with joy and enthusiasm. The youth from Canada had a particularly difficult time because of the language but they soldiered on, never complaining.

There were a few registrations in Klaipeda and the local friends, helped by the pioneers in that area, have been doing their best to maintain contact with these new believers and seekers, encouraging them to join study circles and devotional meetings.

After saying goodbye to the friends from Estonia and Latvia the local believers moved their activities to Vilnius. Vilnius is a bit more active as a community so there was more local support for the project. Again they prayed, involving the whole country in prayers, deepened in the writings and went out into the streets and apartment blocks. Because the local group members were in their home territory they were able to visit their neighbours and friends, invite the children to children's classes, invite the parents to observe the children's classes, target the youth and junior youth. No group of friends could have worked with more devotion to the Cause of God. There were regular reflection meetings, devotional meetings and study circles, and all were welcome to join.

There were a few registrations and the local believers continue with the core activities while two friends have made it their special responsibility to pay particular attention to the junior youth and older youth in their area.

Not content with these several weeks of planning and action, the group moved to Daugavpils in Latvia where the Latvian friends who had joined the Klaipeda project lived. Again they set about their planning, praying and deepening, and went out to teach the Faith. There were more registrations.

At this time our precious youth from Canada had to return home. Each and every one was a valuable asset during the project. They may not have been able to speak the language but their dedication, support, knowledge and love made up for any other shortfalls.

The next step was Tartu in Estonia. Tartu is a university town, and although it was still holiday time, there were more than enough people around to hear about the Faith. The local friends in Estonia are diligently working at the core activities with the new believers, seekers, contacts and friends.

It was an exhausting summer but the buzz from the constant activity, prayers, fun and, of course, teaching the Faith more than compensated for any feelings of tiredness.

181

April 2009
Eric Hellicar
Cyprus

Eric and Margaret pioneered from Durham to Nicosia in 1969. This is an extract from Eric's personal diary about the Istanbul Conference, first published in the Newsletter of the Bahá'ís of Cyprus, March 2009.

Istanbul Regional Conference

How mundane airports can make any city. There we were, arriving in the 'Great City' of Istanbul, gateway between East and West, ancient city of Byzantium, famed for the Ayia Sophia of Constantinople, once the capital of the Ottoman Empire and seat of the Caliphate – and it looked just like any other airport. We glimpsed the usual modern sprawl as we raced along the huge highways, with the taxi driver proud to be doing 150 km/hr. Occasional glimpses of minarets stroking the skies above imposing new mosques – which the driver named 'old' because they were from 50 years before! Then we arrived at our conference centre in the midst of a private university that looked like a collection of towering blocks of flats, with luxurious central heating and conference rooms like executive halls – not a sign of student life anywhere, not a whisper of adolescent rebellion!

But then the faces. We were suddenly surrounded by a hubbub of welcome and eager questions. Youth everywhere to answer all our queries with a smile; people bubbling with happiness and helpfulness. Hunting for roommates from Albania, meeting up with old friends from school in the Czech Republic, meeting new ones from all over Turkey: a foretaste of why we were there.

The next morning we gathered, stuffed with institutional breakfast (I loved it, reminder of boarding school days!), and nine hundred of us grew quiet while God was praised in Turkish tongue and traditional Turkish music. Expectantly we listened to the Supreme Body who had called us together, as they had in 40 other cities around our world, and we began to feel united. Praise for the great strides forward in the host country, for the obedience to the divine call in Albania and our enthusiasm in Cyprus. We heard our Lesley (Habibi) read the message and felt proud, as we would later when Maria intoned a prayer in Greek, and even later when Amir and Zafir, two of our youth, spoke so confidently of our plans in Cyprus – but these were soon submerged by our awareness that we were linked with a throbbing world community of Bahá'ís, as varied as the flowers of our planet!

Then we heard from the representative of the Universal House of Justice. International Teaching Centre Counsellor Stephen Birkland spoke with a friendliness and narrative touch that both comforted and delighted, without ever diminishing the dignity of the message he bore. He told us stories from the early days, and from last week, which made our moments together part of the whole magnificent marching history from the first revelation of Bahá'u'lláh to the coming day of the Most Great Peace. Gathered in that Great City where Bahá'u'lláh had revealed the word of God, we dared to grasp that we were part of the people of the world who were charged with working for the new civilization of mankind, for world peace – once the kings and rulers had ignored or rejected His summons. We were helping to spread that world-healing unity, ready to conquer every prejudice that stood in its way! He reminded us of the source of our faith, and that the best way we could now teach was through the latest methods given to us.

Then I had to speak of the situation and learning in Cyprus – hastily rephrasing the NSA's agreed points to fit into the spirit that we now felt. The main points we made, and we managed to share some of our new enthusiasm, but what I felt was the amazing love with which everyone, from Cyprus, from Turkey and Albania, from the World Centre, felt for everything we had to offer. How proud we felt to be able to share our latest experiences of teaching in Famagusta and Nicosia and welcoming the wonderful souls who had responded to it. Fifty of us were there, including all nine members of the NSA, four members of the Institute Board and, most important of all, 28 friends from the priority cluster that will soon blossom into our IPG – intensive programme of growth.

Next we wended our way towards various rooms to study key letters from the Universal House of Justice. Thirty-three of us squeezed into a room with 15 chairs. How much easier it is to see new things in these vibrant letters when people from many countries consult on them. We were left with a plea to study the amazing fourth paragraph of the 20 October 2008 letter – and suggested dividing it into separate verses of 'this great prayer'.

Lunch and rain, with every Cypriot exclaiming, 'I hope it's raining in Cyprus too!' Mashed potatoes and meat, plus another plate of macaroni – they were obviously used to feeding hungry students!

Then the second representative of the Universal House of Justice, Counsellor Ayman Rouhani, reminded us of the fundamentals of the Five Year Plan and the core activities, before bringing on a number of friends who spoke of different ways in which their clusters had broken down barriers and experienced great results, some through individual pioneering into run-down areas, Zafir from Cyprus speaking of how such understanding and enthusiasm could come to youth from the Ruhi courses, while others stressed united action and thrilling children's classes. It was an amazing combination of inspiration from the World Centre and response from the individual Bahá'ís.

In the evening we had a dazzling mixture of traditional music, classical music, happy youth banging out modern stuff, some excellent mime, troops of happy African swingers (which set some children running around the stage in joy), some lengthy folk songs (very reminiscent of our Cyprus folk songs) and a vigorous group of Turkish dancers who proved that they can dance longer and louder, and with more costume changes, than anyone else!

Sunday morning, more rain, more eggs and salad, more happy conversation – listening to Angeliki, our first ever Greek Cypriot Bahá'í, in the midst of Istanbul. Memorable. Then the Counsellors in Turkey, so well known to us in Cyprus, Fevziye Baki and Ilhan Sezgin, gave us our marching orders, in the kindest and most exciting way possible. We then split into consultation groups, the Cyprus priority cluster staying in the main hall as we were so many – 60 of us altogether. Patiently we worked through translation with our Counsellor Nadia guiding us. It wasn't easy to consider carefully everyone's views, with some wanting to hurry and start our IPG at Riḍván (as many other clusters decided at the conference), others feeling July was more practical – no one interested in our old goal of Riḍván 2010 or the more recent one of September 2009. The decision was for July at the moment, with a hint from Counsellor Birkland that we might yet reconsider it in favour of Riḍván!

We knew we had a lot to do to be ready but we also knew that if we waited until we felt completely prepared we might find ourselves years behind the rest of the world! When it came to the practical goals that every individual offered it was easier, and a great crowd of promises were scribbled down. Already we have heard of meetings at which those promises are being put into practice. The friends in the south were very eager to offer lots of help. The Counsellor stressed that it must really be the Baháʼís in the cluster itself who must adopt any new goals. A hurried lunch, a desperate rush to the book stall, photos with babies, abandoning plans for trips round the city, and we began the final session. All so short and quick – a glimpse of the speed at which we must now begin to work.

Further beautiful stories, so inspiring, helping us realize how real the promises of divine assistance are. Announcements of plans, cluster by cluster. Confidence that the report to the Supreme Body would be heart-warming and joyful – and that was that. Taxis, mundane airports (except for the lucky ones who went on to Edirne and the holy House of Baháʼuʼlláh from which those Tablets announcing the Most Great Peace were disseminated) and back to try and tell others of the incredible feeling of confidence we had gained. For two days we had forgotten all about the petty confusions of international financial crises and the political disharmonies of the world – we had only cared about the Faith, each other and the future of mankind. It was great. We, Albania, Turkey and Cyprus, will never be the same again.

The Conference had closed with Counsellor Ilhan Sezgin singing his victory song, written one night when a Local Spiritual Assembly had been formed and now sung all round Turkey and Cyprus: 'Heidi, Heidi, Heidi', which seems to mean 'Let's go, go forward, now!'

Final Thought
Davey Vincent
April 2009

People may not be aware of how much *Pioneer Post* has meant to so many pioneers. I'm sure I speak for many in saying that there were times *Pioneer Post* simply changed the way we were living. There must be many pioneers like me, who eagerly opened and rushed through *Pioneer Post* then went back and read it all through again.

As much as I loved being a pioneer, I know there were times when it was hard to stay at my post, especially when I was quite isolated and went for long periods without seeing any other pioneers or old friends but really wanting to. I want you to know that *Pioneer Post* was immensely encouraging to me so many times, reminding me of our oneness and connectedness and I'm very grateful for all those regular breaths of inspiration and moving reminders of the joy of service.

Snippets

Biographical Information about Contributors to
Stories from Pioneer Post

Farid Afnan

Farid was born in London in 1964 to a German mother and Persian father.
He was raised in a Bahá'í family and has been married to Mercedes, a Spanish
Bahá'í, for 20 years. They have three children: Yasmin, Alex and Marco. In
1994 Farid and Mercedes spent a short period in the Solomon Islands before
returning to England at the end of the year. Farid currently runs a small architectural practice in London. He is chairman of his local Bahá'í community
and also of the properties working group which oversees the maintenance of
Bahá'í properties in the United Kingdom.

Mojgan Agahi (von Duering)

Mojgan was born and brought up in a Bahá'í family in Tehran. She became
a Bahá'í the day after her sixteenth birthday. In 1986 she moved from Iran to
Leicester where she studied English for a year. She then moved to Northern
Ireland where her brother lived, settling first in Ballymena and then in
Newtonabbey, and enrolled at the University of Ulster where she studied bio-
chemical sciences. After graduating she worked for a while and then realized
she needed more challenges in her life. In the spring of 1995 Mojgan pioneered to Macedonia where she taught English to adults and at the same time
tried to establish a Bahá'í community. She suffered lots of ups and downs in
Macedonia. Owing to the country's political instability, she had to leave after
one year as she could not extend her visa. Since she was able to speak a little
German, she decided to try her luck next in Germany (1996). She married
Bodo von Duering in 2001 and they live in the small town of Holzkirchen
on the outskirts of Munich. They have two children, Adrian Shayan (7) and
Kian Valerian (4).

Greg Akehurst-Moore

Greg was born in Eastbourne, Sussex, in 1956. When he was two he emigrated with his parents and older brother to the suburbs of Los Angeles, where
they lived until he was 12. In 1969 his father passed away, and Greg and his
family returned to northwest England, settling in Southport. In 1974 he met
Tom Fox, a young Bahá'í and school classmate who introduced him to the

Bahá'í teachings. Attendance at public meetings and firesides in Southport led Greg to embrace the Cause in 1976. He pioneered to Queensferry in North Wales to open that area to the Faith in 1979. After that he continued to pioneer to various places on the home front until he moved to Haifa in 1993 to serve in the Office of Social and Economic Development at the World Centre. Serving there for two years and 9 months, he returned to the UK before moving to the Czech Republic in 1997 to serve for five months at the Townshend International School. In 1998 he returned to the Czech Republic to teach at Townshend School. He has since worked at local language schools and now teaches at Townshend and at South Bohemia University.

Negin and Nima Anvar

Negin and Nima were both born in Iran. Negin's family Ghaemmaghami pioneered to Wales in the early 1970s when she was four years old. Later, when she was 13, they pioneered to Grenada. Negin attended university in the United States where she met Nima. As a couple they pioneered to Grenada in 1997 and love raising their two children there. Negin and Nima continue to serve in various ways – mostly with youth and junior youth. They served as editors of 'Bahá'í Parenting', a bi-monthly e-magazine, for several years. They also published the book *Bahá'í Parenting Perspectives* (George Ronald, 2006). They own and manage a small hotel.

Sammi Anwar Nagaratnam

Sammi was born in the Middle East to Bahá'í parents and sent to a convent boarding school in London with her older sister when she was five and her sister was 12. Although very young, there was always the consciousness of being a Bahá'í and the protection that came from it. The few prayers she knew by heart sustained her for the three years they lived there. At the age of 14 a mystical experience confirmed her total belief in Bahá'u'lláh. As well as being part of a pioneer family in the Middle East, Sammi has lived in Thailand for many years with her family and one year in Fiji with her husband. Right now they are living in southern Thailand working at a university, offering what service they can.

Wendy Ayoub Lind

Wendy was born in North London, a stone's throw from where the Guardian's resting place is now. At age 21 Wendy emigrated to the United States and settled near Chicago, within walking distance of the House of Worship. She even worked for an employment agency on Michigan Avenue for a short time and had as one of her accounts the Bahá'í Publishing Trust. Wendy believes

Bahá'u'lláh had His eye on her because two years later, as a showgirl in Las Vegas, she heard about the Faith and immediately became a Bahá'í! Her life changed drastically . . . Within a year she was married and went home front pioneering from Las Vegas to Las Vegas South and from that community began her life as an overseas pioneer. When the Universal House of Justice was elected, in 1963, and called for pioneers, Wendy and her family went to the Bahamas. Business took them to England and to the Netherlands. After some years back in America, in 1979 Wendy pioneered to Denmark and from there to Greenland for 17 years. Wendy says she has had a blessed life, has met some wonderful people and has been able to serve many institutions of the Faith in five countries, plus having the bounty of several trips to the Holy Land. She presently serves at Desert Rose Bahá'í Institute in Arizona.

Shohreh Azarkadeh

Shohreh was born into a Bahá'í family in Tehran and as a child loved saying prayers. When she was about 14, her family moved to the UK where Shohreh found herself becoming a confused and rebellious adolescent. She moved away from home, and from the Faith too, until, after much pain and suffering in her early twenties, through prayer she found herself connected to the Faith again. This time she found satisfaction through teaching, travel teaching and pioneering. She went to eastern Europe, the West Indies, Hackney (London) and Africa. She also experienced confusion in her career. After changing career four times, she found her calling in psychotherapy and counselling. She particularly loves working with adolescents and young adults, as this is what she needed in her youth. She currently lives in Wellingborough, Northamptonshire, with her six year old daughter, enjoying the core activities and wondering, 'Where next?'

Neda Azemian (Heath)

Neda was born in Tehran. Her mother's family converted from Islam during the time of the Báb and her father is from a half-Muslim/half-Bahá'í background. During the 1979 Iranian revolution toddler Neda and most of her family were on a long summer holiday in the UK. By 1980, life for Bahá'ís in Iran had become dangerous and the formerly comfortable middle-class family had become penniless refugees. They made Wales their new home and the Bartlett family there had the most formative impact on Neda, lovingly guiding her to investigate the Faith independently and not accept it just because she was born into it. Whilst at secondary school Neda decided to learn Russian and prepare for a year of service in Russia. However, in 1994 Russia was no longer her first choice and she went to Poland instead. It turned out that her year in Poland served as a heaven-sent transition from childhood to adulthood. In Poland Neda learned that 'home' is not a geographical place – 'home' resides in the bonds of love between family and old and new friends wherever we go and is immune to the lapse of time and physical distance. Neda remains grateful for the weird and wonderful twists and turns of destiny that have led her to be happily married and settled in London.

Thelma and Ron Batchelor

Thelma was born and brought up in Surrey. She first heard of the Faith in Montreal from Terry Smith and became a Bahá'í in San Francisco in 1964 at her first fireside. She met Ron, a Londoner from Pimlico, at an international youth summer school in Berlin in 1965. They were married in 1970 and shortly afterwards pioneered to the Solomon Islands. Ron declared in the Shrine of the Báb en route to their pioneering post. Their son, Simon, was born in Honiara in 1972. On their return to England in 1973 they settled in Leatherhead, Surrey, and two years later their daughter, Suzanne, was born. In 1976 they pioneered to Kathmandu, Nepal, where they remained for many happy years until 1985. Since then they have continued to live in Leatherhead and have tried to serve the Faith to the best of their joint abilities. Thelma's prime interest for most of the years since they returned from pioneering, apart from being a very keen tennis player, has been in service to international pioneering – thus the newsletter *Pioneer Post UK*, which was initiated in 1988 and has been gathering momentum ever since.

Joy Behi

Joy was born in Carmel, California, and became a Bahá'í in Guam, Pacific Ocean, almost 30 years later. She has always been a pioneer . . . of sorts. The family moved from Micronesia to India, from India to the UK . . . and Wales. Then after visiting it for short, and longer, periods of time, in 1994 Joy pioneered to Poland. She has six children living as Bahá'ís in six different parts of the world – England, Wales, Los Angeles, near Carmel in California, Poland and somewhere at sea on the Pacific Ocean – and one son in the Abhá Kingdom. She also has 19 grandchildren dotted around the world and one great grandchild, God willing, to be born in the spring of 2010. Joy served on the National Spiritual Assembly of Poland for nine years and was appointed an Auxiliary Board member for Protection (in Poland) three years ago. She is presently living in Warsaw where they are working on establishing an intensive programme of growth by the end of this Plan. Joy's daughter and son-in-law and two grandchildren are also important participants on the team of teachers and lovers of Bahá'u'lláh in Poland.

Fiona Beint (Young)

Fiona was born into a Bahá'í family in Northampton and spent her childhood and youth playing an active part in local and national Bahá'í events. In her early teens Fiona developed an interest in writing and performing music and developed this interest with her close school friend, Victoria Leith (née Howarth). In 1993 Fiona made her lifelong dream a reality by travelling with Vicky on a youth year of service to the Kingdom of Swaziland in southern Africa. They spent the year working in the Bahá'í primary school and also took every opportunity to sing! On returning to the UK Fiona continued to serve the Faith, as a member of the National Youth Committee, as an assistant and as a Local Spiritual Assembly member. She studied law at university, qualifying as a solicitor in 2000. In 2003, together with her husband Peter, she pioneered to Gibraltar. Fiona and Peter currently live in Gibraltar with their two children, Dylan and Shadi.

Robin Bell

Robin was born in Leeds, in God's Own County of Yorkshire (as it is known to the locals!). In his early years he spent much of his time at the local church, becoming St Barnabas' head choirboy, and in his late teens seriously considered becoming one of the clergy. However, he eventually chose the next best thing – a career in advertising! His work took him to Manchester and while spending years trying to sell things to people that they didn't really need (!) he found something that everybody needed and, with the help of his friend Martin Perry, he became a Bahá'í in 1996. Three years later, on hearing that a friend was 'Africa-bound', he thought about serving overseas. The UK Pioneering Committee introduced him to a country he'd barely heard of – and he was soon travelling (for days!) to the other side of the planet to a place called the Marshall Islands. He served for three years assisting the NSA secretary and Counsellor Betra Majmeto and also helped organize the country's pan-Pacific 'Ocean of Light' gathering in June 2000. Robin returned to the UK in 2003. The following year he married Carmen, Manchester's year of service volunteer from Bolivia, and they now live with their daughter in Salford, Greater Manchester.

Sylvia Schulman Benatar

Sylvia was born in Bulawayo, Southern Rhodesia (now Zimbabwe), although her parents, of Jewish background, were living in the Belgian Congo. Her mother went to Bulawayo when Sylvia was due to be born so she would be born British and not Belgian! After eight years in the Congo Sylvia lived in London for four years with her mother and brothers. It was the Great Depression and her father called them back to Africa in 1936 where he was general manager of the hotels on the Copperbelt in Northern Rhodesia (now Zambia). Sylvia studied music in Cape Town at the South African College of Music. In 1948 she moved to Salisbury, Rhodesia, where she met and married 'Sue' (Salvator) Benatar. Sylvia's career as a concert pianist took a backseat for about five years but she returned to the piano in 1953. The following year she and 'Sue' met Knights of Bahá'u'lláh Kenneth and Roberta Christian but after the Christians left Salisbury the Benatars were taught the Faith by Lawrence Hautz. They became Bahá'ís just before Riḍván 1955, the first 'white' people to do so in the Federation of Rhodesia and Nyasaland. In 1963 they moved with their two children, Mark and Odette, to England just prior to the first World Congress held at the Albert Hall, where 'Sue' was one of the official photographers. For a short while they lived in London, then eight years in Cambridge followed by five years in Bedford and 18 months in Luton – all home front pioneering posts. Sylvia continued with her career as a pianist at the same time. At the end of 1977 they pioneered to Cape Town where 'Sue' passed away in 1995. In early 1997 Sylvia was asked to serve as office manager at the National Bahá'í Centre in Johannesburg where she remained until late 2006. She is now a home front pioneer in Swellendam in the Western Cape Province, still involved with music performances and teaching, and working hard with the four pioneers to launch their intensive programme of growth by Riḍván 2010.

Nasrin Boroumand

Nasrin was born into a Bahá'í family in Iran in 1948. Her first pioneer move was with her parents to Susa prior to the passing of the Guardian. In 1969 Nasrin pioneered to India where she was greatly encouraged by Hand of the Cause Dr Muhájir in her several moves around the sub-continent. After she married Douglas Fawbush, a pioneer from America, they moved to Patna, the capital of Bihar state. After 20 years of pioneering in India and being involved in mass enrolment in Jaipur, the capital of Rajasthan (where virtually every district, town and village had thousands of new believers and hundreds of Local Assemblies), Nasrin was witness to two hundred believers – tribal and local, all self-supporting – attending the dedication of the Mother Temple of the sub-continent in 1996. Nasrin eventually moved to London and then Scotland and a had spell in the islands of the North Sea. From Britain she pioneered to Baku, Azerbaijan, then to Tbilisi, Georgia. For three years until December 2005 she was active in the teaching field in Kingston, Jamaica. Nasrin then moved to the United States and now resides with her son, Lee

Fawbush, and his Malagasy wife and child in Antananarivo, Madagascar, in the Indian Ocean.

Charles Boyle

Born in Aberystwyth, Wales, Charles grew up in Henley-on-Thames where he, his twin brother Richard and a dozen others became Bahá'ís one night in 1971. Shortly after completing a degree in architecture, in 1981 he pioneered to the Solomon Islands, living there for 13 years and travelling extensively throughout the Pacific, notably attending the dedication of the House of Worship in Samoa. In 1994 he moved to Queensland, Australia, to undertake doctoral studies in tropical architecture and went on to spend three years in Papua New Guinea. He now lives in Perth, Australia, with his wife Sholeh whom he first met on that memorable night in Henley. Charles's father believed in God but thought that religion was a bad thing; his mother did not believe that God existed but thought that religion was beneficial. Charles inherited the better parts of his parents' views.

Dorothy Bruce

Dorothy became a Bahá'í at the age of 24 in 1957 in Bangor, Northern Ireland, through Winnie Whelan and Billy Glass and through reading the book *Bahá'í Revelation*. The LSA of Bangor was formed that year and she became its secretary and a delegate to the National Convention. She also served on the Northern Ireland Teaching Committee. She enjoyed meeting Bahá'í friends such as Lady Hornell, Charles Macdonald and Adib Taherzadeh. From 1960 Dorothy worked in Hamilton, Scotland. She next moved to Glasgow for three months in order to secure the Local Spiritual Assembly. In 1966 Dorothy married Robert Bruce in Bangor. They continued to live in Scotland but in 1971 they moved to Lympstone, Devon. They met the Herbert family who became Bahá'ís and in 1981 Dorothy's husband became a Bahá'í. They spent many happy years together in Devon. Robert died in 1997 and Dorothy spent the millennium year in Alice Springs, Australia. There the Bahá'í community had expanded with many Aboriginal Bahá'ís. In 2002 she pioneered to Shannon, Ireland, for two years. At present Dorothy tutors Ruhi books in the Exmouth area.

Stephanie Christopherson

Stephanie was born in 1976 to Bahá'í parents Kari-Anna and Oliver Christopherson. She grew up in Stevenage, Hertfordshire, with her older sister Pippa and brother Robin and became a Bahá'í when she was 15. She attended Bishop Grosseteste University College Lincoln where she did Christian studies but later switched to psychology at the University of Westminster in London. Stephanie gradually lost her sight in her later teenage years and was provided with her first guide dog when she was 22. She currently teaches A-Level Psychology at North Hertfordshire College to classes of 16 to 18 year olds. Stephanie is now working on her Master's in evolutional psychology. The three months she spent at the Barli Development Institute for Rural Women in India in 1995 was a special highlight of her life.

Wesley and Stephanie Clash

Wesley, a Welsh valley boy with a gypsy spirit, is a born adventurer with a strongly fixed belief in hard work, determination and the Bahá'í Faith. Stephi is a gentle complement to Wes and their daughter Gissy's wilder natures but an enthusiastic organizer who loves filling the house for Bahá'í events. Through their pioneering efforts they have met and navigated the ups and downs of marriage and child-raising. They have experienced poverty but pushed on to build a secure future on the island of Corfu. In 2009 they opened a gallery to show their artwork after discovering and consolidating artistic talents. They have been overwhelmed by blessings and abundance in all spheres of life and are truly grateful to Janet Defremont and Bella and Jagdish Saminaden for giving them the wondrous gift of faith. For Stephi and Wesley pioneering has turned out to be a long-term, life-long vocation and they've realized that integrating into a community and their acceptance of that community with all its idiosyncrasies is a way to promulgate the Faith of Bahá'u'lláh. Sometimes the apparent lack of progress in teaching is in actual fact the mortar that puts the Faith together. They feel that sometimes this apparent lack of progress can be attributed to their own ego but in reality the magic of the influence of Bahá'u'lláh is constantly working through them as pioneers.

Debbie Conkerton (Tibbey)

Debbie grew up in Hull in East Yorkshire, and was raised in a Church of England family with her parents and two older brothers. She first encountered the Bahá'í Faith at the age of 17, while studying A-Level general studies. It all made complete sense, except for the existence of God . . . that took a year of questioning and prayer until she realized that it was her own limited understanding of God (old man on white cloud, à la William Blake) that stood in the way. Debbie declared not long before her nineteenth birthday. She took a degree in drama and art, followed by a teaching certificate in primary education. This took her to Liverpool where she also served for the first time on a Local Spiritual Assembly. From 1990 to 1993 Debbie answered a pioneering call to run the first Bahá'í primary school in Mbabane, Swaziland (starting with 18 children and building by a class every year). Typhoid fever brought her back to England but the school continues to thrive and currently accommodates children from five to 15 years old. Debbie now lives in Dorset with her husband and two sons and is the deputy head of a village first school.

Pippa Cookson

Pippa was born in 1936 in a small village in Wiltshire. She married and lived near St Helens, her husband's job taking them to Geelong, Australia, where they lived happily from 1962 to 1969. Pippa did a year's research on wool before producing three sons. Returning to England, Pippa taught in a small Quaker boarding school in Oxfordshire. In 1988 she and her husband separated and Pippa moved to Northern Ireland, as her Quaker belief had made her very interested in peace. The Belfast Bahá'ís used the Quaker meeting house for meetings, so she got to know them. She regularly went to firesides and declared after a year. She had met Philip Hainsworth, and when she read about a project in his name that required pioneers and travel teachers for the Balkan countries, she went for a month to Macedonia. She soon decided that she would be more use there than in Belfast. In 2003 Pippa moved first to Bitola and then to Ohrid, where she thought she was set to spend the rest of her days. However, at New Year 2008 she was sent out of the country by the police under a new law (three months in, three months out) for foreigners on tourist visas. Pippa decided to spend her three months out in Pogradec, a town in Albania at the other end of Lake Ohrid where she now has lots of friends.

Sandra and Philip Cooles

Born in Northern Ireland and raised in England, Sandra learned of the Faith in 1974 and declared at the Irish summer school in 1976. Philip declared in 1978 (they met at a public meeting) and they were married in 1979. They became home front pioneers to Kincardine, Aberdeenshire, where their first child was born in 1980 and their second in 1982. Before the birth of their second child they prayed that their plans to pioneer overseas would materialize; 30 minutes after giving birth the call came for them to leave for Dominica! They arrived on an island recovering from a major hurricane. Their food was beans, rice, flour and sugar; accommodation was derelict, and the police were putting down a Rasta uprising against foreigners! As a hospital doctor, Philip was repeatedly asked to stay by the government. Their third daughter was born in Dominica in 1984 on half a bed – the ants had the other half! In order to put down roots they built a house and became citizens. Sandra's time is now taken up with teaching the Faith, study circles, children's classes and visiting

Bahá'ís. Philip continues with his medical work and the Sunday devotional meetings.

Na'im Cortazzi

Na'im Cortazzi grew up in Leicester in a Bahá'í family. At the age of 19 he travelled by land to Belarus and taught the Faith in the cities of Minsk, Vitipsk, Grodno and Brest from November 1993 to August 1994. He returned to Belarus a year later at the request of the UK National Spiritual Assembly to observe the election of the first National Assembly of Belarus. Na'im served on the LSA of Nottingham in 1996/7 while attending university and was awarded an honours degree in contemporary arts. He was awarded a Prince's Trust grant in 1998 and built a recording studio where many notable artists have worked with him. Na'im currently resides in Leicester but travels widely around the world as a musician and rock sound engineer for artists such as Beverley Knight, The Fun Lovin' Criminals, Happy Mondays, New Beautiful South and Bahá'í musician Conrad Lambert (Merz). With his cousin Payam, Na'im produces and performs in the much-loved Bahá'í music group Rowshan, whose music set to the Hidden Words of Bahá'u'lláh inspires devotionals across the land.

Janet and Ned Cundall

Janet was born in 1954 in Glasgow, emigrated to Canada aged three, went to school in Winnipeg and graduated from university with a BSc in integrated sciences. Through encouragement from Dr Richard St Barbe Baker, a Bahá'í known as 'the man of the trees', she earned a MSc in forestry at Oxford. Janet became a Bahá'í at William and Judith Hatcher's home in Quebec and on arrival in Cameroon to do research in social forestry was taken into the loving arms of Dr Mehdi and Ursula Samandari. Edward (Ned) was born in 1951 and spent his early childhood in Nigeria. He went to school in Harrogate and took a BSc in genetics at Edinburgh and a PhD in agricultural botany at Aberystwyth. Ned did research on oil-palms in Cameroon from 1981 to 1986, and there met Janet, a social forester. They married a year later. Their children, Alan and Alicia, were born during their next overseas posting in Papua New Guinea (1986–90) where Janet, the Mills family and local believers taught Ned the Bahá'í Faith. Their next posting was in Africa again, near Mtwara in Tanzania (1990–4). Janet worked as a consultant for the Bahá'í Office of the Environment at the UN and was very active in local communities while Ned bred cashew trees. From 1994 Ned worked in Scotland where Janet obtained a Montessori Early Childhood Education certificate and a MSc in education for sustainable development from Edinburgh University.

In 1999 Janet taught biology at the Maxwell International Bahá'í School and worked with the Maxwell Community Service Institute while Alan and Alicia started high school.

Adrian Davis

Adrian Davis was born and educated in Cheltenham. He has a twin brother and younger sister, as well as an elder half-brother and half-sister (one of his nephews, Darren Howell, is also a Bahá'í). He first took a degree in philosophy at Warwick University and then studied at Exeter University to qualify as a teacher, by now contemplating a spiritual vocation as an Anglican priest. However, while at Warwick he met Shirin Razavi (Tahzib) and it was her humble introduction of the Bahá'í Faith combined with the powerful impact of the new revelation as 'a modern and scientific religion' that sowed the seeds of a life-changing transformation. Adrian first taught in Ealing, London, (1988–90) and it was here that he became a Bahá'í. He then went to teach at New Era in India (1990–2), followed by service at the School of the Nations in Macau (1992–4). He gained his Master's in education at Hong Kong University (1996), specializing in the psychology of learning and teaching. He has been teaching at Macau Polytechnic since 1998 and is now teaching English to social work students. Adrian married Sandy Chan in 1997 and they have three children: Julia (7), Jonathan (3) and Rosabella (3 months).

Nichola Davis

Nichola was born in Madras, India, in 1947 where her father had his own architect's practice and was knighted by the Pope for his services to the Catholic Church. In 1956 the family relocated to England and Nichola received a Catholic education. In 1969 she embarked on her nomadic life by accepting a job in Ottawa, Canada. After ten years and an unsuccessful marriage, she worked as a consultant for the World Bank in DC. Here Nichola first met a Bahá'í who gave her the impression that all Bahá'ís were good company, interested in addressing the serious issues plaguing society and actively involved in community development. In 1983 Nichola was selected as an IT consultant by the Singapore government. With the goal of meeting interesting Singaporeans, Nichola looked up and phoned the Bahá'í Centre and began attending weekly firesides. Although she was looking for a change in her life, becoming a Bahá'í seemed much too big a change. It took a whole year before she finally declared in July 1984. Her family accepted the decision gracefully and her older sister too became a Bahá'í a year later. Nichola spent seven years at the Bahá'í World Centre (1986–93). She has pioneered in Vietnam, Mongolia, India, Indonesia and Myanmar and is currently in Thailand.

Massoud and Mojgan Derakhshani

Massoud was born in Tehran. One evening at a youth summer school a Counsellor addressed the youth, saying: 'Just imagine, the body of the world is dying in front of you, and you are the only Mullá Ḥusayn. What will you do? Let the world die, or arise and save it by going pioneering?' Shaken by these words, Massoud and some other youth formed a team and short-term pioneered to one of the villages close to Tehran. When he was about to finish his university studies, he began to look for a Bahá'í whose wish also was to pioneer and who would accompany him to Africa. In 1977 Massoud married Mojgan Sabet and the following year, after Massoud graduated from the Faculty of Art and Architecture, they were on their way to Africa. The outbreak of the revolution in Iran caused them to temporarily change their direction and they arrived in the UK. In this way they became UK pioneers to Africa. They settled in Swaziland where they remained for nearly 18 years and where their son Sabá and daughter Navá were born. In 1997 they moved to Botswana. Mojgan has worked with USAID and SADC and Massoud has his own architectural firm. They say that activities in Africa are endless!

Joe and Atieh Donnelly

Joe grew up in Kilkenny in the southeast of Ireland and comes from a long line of Catholics (95 per cent of people in the Irish Republic are of Catholic background). He first heard of the Faith in Kilkenny in 1977 and became a Bahá'í after attending summer school that year. By then his parents had passed away but his sister, a staunch Catholic, has never reconciled herself to his conversion. Atieh was born in Tehran. She is a twin and one of the youngest of seven children. Her childhood and youth were spent in the bosom of the Faith in Tehran. One vivid memory she has is of the family home being right beside the house where Ṭáhirih, disciple of the Báb, had hidden in an underground tunnel – a place which Bahá'ís liked to visit. At the age of 20 she pioneered to Tenerife, Canary Islands, for seven years. In 1982 she and Joe met each other at the Irish summer school. They married and for a time lived in Ireland. In 1995 when their children Neysan and Melody were 11 and 9 years old respectively, they decided to pioneer to Bulgaria and for almost 13 years lived in Plovdiv, close to the Turkish border and the town of Edirne. In 2007 they returned to live in Kilkenny, Ireland, where the experience of teaching abroad is proving to be of great value.

Ann Dymond

Ann was born in December 1928. She had an on–off education until the war started in 1939 and she attended Brentwood County High School in Essex. During the Easter holiday of her last year at school she visited her aunt, Helen Spaull, in Bournemouth. There she met and studied the Bahá'í Faith with Elsie Cranmer and after three weeks declared as a Bahá'í. Ann left school at 16 and did various jobs before joining the WRAF in 1949. Two years later she married Ronald Dymond, also in the RAF. After a couple of overseas tours (to Singapore and Bahrain) they bought a house in Didcot, Oxfordshire, where their family of three children grew up. Ann made contact with Jim and Dori Talbot in Reading and for the next 20 years she served on the Local Spiritual Assembly of South Oxfordshire. Ann's husband died in 1988 and the next year Ann did a world tour, meeting Bahá'ís in Hawaii, Western Samoa, New Zealand, Tasmania, Australia, Hong Kong, Canada and Alaska! During the Holy Year (1992) Ann pioneered to Gibraltar, returning to the UK in 1999. Nowadays Ann is a Ruhi book facilitator and makes annual visits to Gibraltar to maintain contact with all the friends she knows and loves there.

Gemma Enolengila

Gemma, an only child, grew up in Bursledon, near Southampton, and became a Bahá'í in June 1996 while in the first year of a biochemistry degree at Oxford. In 2003 she married Lesikar Olengila, a Tanzanian Maasai. They have two daughters, Lucia and Suzanna. Since 2003 they have been living in northern Tanzania. Gemma started playing an active role in the Bahá'í community in the summer of 2007 when she completed books 2, 4, 6 and 7 of the Ruhi sequence in an intensive six-week block course to become one of the first four tutors in the Arusha region. In addition to tutoring Ruhi courses, Gemma enjoys direct teaching among receptive populations in Tanzania and developing new teaching materials – especially songs. With Lesikar she has been working to establish a secondary school and other educational projects in Maasai villages. Over the years she has dabbled in all sorts of things including ecotourism, traditional medicine research, writing, campaigning against female genital mutilation, and managing a hotel – some more successful than others. Gemma still lives in Arusha but plans to return to the UK in September 2010 to train as a teacher.

Iman Fadaei

Iman was born in London but grew up in Hampshire and then in Stroud, Gloucestershire. He was born into an active Bahá'í family and was thus subjected to relentless love and support in all things, particularly those activities which were of service to the wider community. At school he was an active sportsman and enjoyed lessons on a number of instruments, finally settling on the saxophone which was itself, much to the dismay of his mother, replaced by the guitar. Iman undertook six months of his year of service in the Faroe Islands before serving the remainder in Nepal. He has since returned to the Faroe Islands twice in pursuance of the goals of the Five Year Plan. Iman has served on various national Bahá'í committees and on his university's Bahá'í Society and has represented the Faith at the local and national levels. He is now studying law at university in London and graduates this year with some doubts as to the attraction of a career in this field.

Kathy and Hamid Farabi

Hamid met Kathy in 1972 and they married in Birmingham in 1977. One year later, when Hamid had completed his PhD, they set off to pioneer to Trinidad and Tobago. Hamid had a job teaching chemical engineering at the University of the West Indies but Kathy had no work permit and experienced tremendous culture shock during the first year. They have three children, Ruhiyyih (born 1980), Anisa (born 1982) and Samandar (born 1987). From 1980 to the present day Hamid has served as a member of the National Spiritual Assembly of Trinidad and Tobago, first as vice chairman, then chairman and then as secretary. From 1985 to 1997 he served as a member of the Inter-Religious Organization of Trinidad and Tobago, and as its president from 1991 to 1994. This afforded numerous opportunities for teaching prominent people and for media work. Hamid has also served on many Bahá'í committees and made several travel teaching trips. Kathy also has served on several Bahá'í committees and was an Auxiliary Board member from 1991 to 1996. She became the first coordinator of the Ruhi institute in Trinidad and Tobago. At present Kathy teaches art in a primary school and also produces paintings inspired by the Bahá'í writings. Hamid and Kathy continue to be involved in the teaching activities in Trinidad and Tobago and in tutoring institute courses.

Judy Finlay

Judy was born in Edinburgh, not to a Bahá'í family but to parents who had a belief in God and a faith that accepted all religions, though they themselves followed one and were members of the Church of Scotland. Judy became a Bahá'í on the Isle of Skye in November 1993, having been introduced to it by friends. In 2003 she took a year out from her job as an occupational therapist on the island. Her parents had passed on and her children had left home so she was able to make the move away. Judy spent six months at Burnlaw in Northumberland helping with all the numerous Bahá'í activities hosted there and she became particularly interested in the youth activities. The six months there were split in two, on either side of her trip to the Marshall Islands where she spent six months helping the Bahá'í community create radio programmes. Since returning to Scotland she has continued to live on Skye, trying to serve the Faith by helping with study circles and devotionals and serving on a summer school committee, but the yearning for travel is always there.

Janet Fleming (Rose)

Janet became a Bahá'í in Fiji in the mid-1980s. She grew up in Epsom, England, studied modern languages at Edinburgh University and subsequently became a professional librarian. She went to Fiji in 1983 with Voluntary Service Overseas to work in a community library on the small island of Ovalau. After Fiji she undertook another two-year term with VSO and went to work in the National Library of the Maldives. Later she had the bounty of serving for six years in the library at the Bahá'í World Centre in Haifa. Her experiences of island life in Fiji and the Maldives later inspired her to make a travel teaching trip to the Faroe Islands. She is now married to Andrew Rose and lives in St Albans, Hertfordshire (but still manages to fit in visits to exciting islands now and then!).

Layli Foroudi

Layli was born in Bath. In 1994 she moved to South America when her parents pioneered to Guyana. Their next move was to Dubai. Returning to England in 2001, Layli lived and studied in Chippenham, Wiltshire, until the age of 18. At the present time she is doing a year of service in Toulouse, France, where she is helping to start up and sustain children's classes and junior youth groups as well as training up animators and teachers for the classes. She loves working with people towards something positive, whether organizing a football tournament for little kids, writing music together, painting or sharing prayers. Layli loves bonding with people and communities. She loves exploring new perspectives and cultures! She loves truthfulness. She does not like cabbage!

Payam and Shirin Foroudi

Shirin was brought up in Sarawak, Malaysia, where her parents are pioneering. She came to the UK in 1976 for schooling and then studied medicine at Liverpool University. Payam also arrived in Liverpool to study engineering and after their marriage in 1986 they tried to pioneer. However, this did not materialize until 1993 when they were able to move to Guyana with their three year old daughter, Layli, and their four month old son, Naysan. They lived in Guyana for three and a half years where they were able to work while loving being part of the Bahá'í community and being involved in their many activities. Lian, their third child, was born in 1996. In 1997 they reluctantly left Guyana but had the opportunity to move to Dubai in the United Arab Emirates where they lived for just over three years. While a very different situation to Guyana, nevertheless there were many opportunities to serve the Bahá'í, and wider, community. Shirin, Payam and their three children returned to the UK in 2000 and settled in Chippenham, Wiltshire. In different ways they are all trying to serve the UK Bahá'í community and are happy to be playing their little part in a mighty spiritual enterprise.

Jeremy Fox

Jeremy was born in Falmouth in 1941, spent his childhood in Cornwall and attended Sherborne, a British public school. During his first year studying languages in Downing College, Cambridge, he became the first Cambridge student to become a Bahá'í, having learned of the Faith from Ian Semple, who was the first at Oxford. Jeremy married his first wife, Denise, in Cambridge. In 1963 they moved to Swansea where Jeremy did teacher training in order to pioneer there (Swansea's first Local Spiritual Assembly was formed at the start of the Nine Year Plan). Jeremy and Denise then pioneered to Tobermory, Mull, from 1968 to 1980. In 1980 they pioneered to the Basque region of France where Denise passed away in 1996. Jeremy and Denise had three children: Nickie (who died of cancer in 2007), Jago (who died in 1968 aged two and is buried near the Guardian's resting place in London) and Rhiannon, now living on Skye. Jeremy returned to live in Scotland in 2000 and married his second wife, Carolyn, in 2000. Jeremy has travel taught extensively, including in French-speaking Africa, more recently with Carolyn with her viola. Jeremy is the author of *Letter to the Christians* published in French in 1995 and in English in 2004. Jeremy and Carolyn now live in Stirling.

Sylvia Girling

Sylvia was born in Birmingham in 1939. The war greatly influenced her young life at that time. As a child she attended many different Christian Sunday schools and began to wonder at the religious divisions. She was married at 20 and had two daughters, one now living in Australia and the other in England. Sylvia met the Faith in 1979 while working in a MEB shop. She sold a washing machine to a lady who gave her a book about the Bahá'í Faith. She was struck immediately by the magnitude of Bahá'u'lláh's words and became the first Bahá'í in Bridgnorth, Shropshire. In 1990 she visited Poland. She fell in love with the young people there who had had a difficult early life but had emerged all the stronger for it. She soon pioneered to Poland and served on their National Youth Committee. In 1997 Sylvia moved over the border to Slovakia as the youth there needed support. In 2000 she left for Australia to help her daughter with her first grandchild. From there she has made frequent trips to Thailand to support the hill tribe youth, part of a Bahá'í project. She says that to have received so much love from so many young people has been a great privilege.

David Renwick Grant

David was born and grew up in Edinburgh, against a Presbyterian background. Subsequently, he obtained a MA at Aberdeen, and later a MSc in ecology at Edinburgh. He has worked as a jackaroo in Australia, for the Nature Conservancy (now Scottish Natural Heritage), as a crofter and prawn creel fisherman on Skye and as part of a film crew on Orkney. He travelled around the world by horse and caravan *en famille* with his (ex-) wife and three (now grown-up) children, and became a Bahá'í in Mongolia in 1996. In 2000 he kayaked from Sweden to the Black Sea, following a Viking route via the rivers Daugava/Western Dvina, Ulla, Berezina and Dneiper and visiting local Bahá'í communities. David went on pilgrimage in 2005, walking part of the way and covering the rest by hitching, bus, train and ferry. En route he carried out five days' service at the European Temple in Frankfurt and spent a month at the two Bahá'í Centres in Cyprus. In 2008 he travel taught for a few weeks in Solent. Since then he has been involved with core activities in Angus, where he lives, and in Dundee and, more recently, has spent ten days travel teaching on Shetland.

Rita Green

Rita has been a Bahá'í for over 40 years, first meeting the Faith in Burnley, Lancashire in 1967. She home front pioneered to Oakham in Rutland in 1971 with Derek and Sima Cockshut to form a group with John and Vera Long. There she took up her first teaching post in a small village school outside Oakham. It was in Oakham that she experienced mass teaching with over one hundred declared Bahá'ís by 1973. Sadly, most of those lovely souls were not to remain as active Bahá'ís. In 1974 she married and had two children. For the next 30 years Rita taught in various Leicestershire schools, including a special unit for itinerant children. When her own children were independent, Rita decided to volunteer her skills abroad with VSO. For the next five to six years she worked in many developing countries helping to develop primary education. She is now retired and back in Melton Mowbray, assisting the A cluster of Leicester in its teaching activities.

Michael Hainsworth

Michael was born into a Bahá'í family, in Leeds, Yorkshire, in 1968 and grew up with the Faith all around him. In 1988 Michael went on tour with Conrad Lambert to southern Africa, capturing Bahá'í-inspired music, which led to the Dairai Dairai compilation. In 1989 he served at the Bahá'í World Centre for one and a half years. During the 1990s Michael embarked on further trips with Conrad which included performing at the New York World Congress in 1992 and later in Kazakhstan. They toured with a second Bahá'í-inspired music group within the gypsy community in Spain and Michael was European tour manager for the first Bahá'í Malawian music group to come to the UK on an extensive teaching trip in 1991. Most recently Michael has returned from two years short-term pioneering in Moscow, Russia, with his wife Olga and daughter Anastasia.

Philip and Lois Hainsworth

Philip was born in Bradford, Yorkshire, on 27 July 1919 and left school before his fourteenth birthday to work in a worsted mill. He became a Bahá'í in 1938 and immediately began to teach the Faith, resulting in the formation of the Bradford Assembly. He was 'called up' into the army after the outbreak of war in 1939 and registered as a 'conscientious objector', which entailed attending a tribunal. The Guardian was so impressed with the result of the tribunal – the first time the Bahá'í Faith was mentioned in a British court – that he published a summary in two editions of *Bahá'í World*. Philip served in the North Africa and Italian campaigns and afterwards was commissioned. His services in many spheres of Bahá'í activity, including 44 years on two National Assemblies, the hours spent with the Guardian, his pioneering services and the opening of Uganda to the Faith in 1951, are detailed in his autobiography, *Looking Back in Wonder*. He died on 16 December 2001.

Lois was born in Nottinghamshire in 1927. Music and writing have been the foci of her life – she studied singing in Vienna for three years. She became a Bahá'í in June 1956, met Philip on 8 September, married him on 29 September and returned with him to Uganda a week later. There she served as secretary to the committees dealing with the Temple in Uganda and worked for the equality of women. When Lois and Philip returned to England in 1966, she took up her work with women's organizations, serving in several capacities at the national level. In 2003 she was awarded an MBE for her services to women. The greatest joy for both Philip and Lois has been the services to the Faith of their three children, Richard, Zarin and Michael (two of whom are NSA members in Russia and the UK), and the growing contributions of their grandchildren, Arwyn, Reissa, Melissa, Iman, Anisa, Erfan and Iqan – and now their eighth, Anastasia.

Richard and Corinne Hainsworth

Corinne was born in Caerphilly, South Wales, and was one year old when her father became a Bahá'í, followed three years later by her mother. Richard's earliest memories are of Uganda and of his parents, Philip and Lois, as pioneers and members of committees and institutions. Even on leaving Africa their discussion revolved around which UK pioneer post to settle in. A world map with red spots for Bahá'í communities inspired Richard while a youth to pioneer to the greatest expanse of white, the USSR. Corinne, who took a degree in music at Cardiff University, met Richard at a youth school in Llangollen just after he returned from six months travel teaching around Africa. They married in 1978, Richard studying at Birmingham University and Corinne teaching music. Weekends were spent travel teaching with the music group Fire and Snow. Corinne and Richard arrived as pioneers in Moscow in June 1982. When Communism collapsed they were able actively to teach the Faith. Starting in 1989, they witnessed the growth of the Moscow and Russian community. In seven years the region once known as the USSR went from no LSAs to 15 NSAs, Richard serving on each of the NSAs covering Russia. Corinne has served on several national committees, the Institute Board and the Regional Council and for many years has been assistant to the National Treasurer. They have two daughters, Reissa and Melissa, now in the UK, and a son, Arwyn, who lives in Japan with his wife Kayoko and son Ray.

Jo Harding

Born in Ely in 1924, Jo was the eighth child in the family of the local doctor. Her parents had met in India serving as missionaries, so she was brought up as a Christian. Her parents were devout people but Jo gave up on religion in her late teens. She married a South Wales coal miner, joining a sturdy working class family in Cardiff. They were communists for a while, and when that proved to be a betrayal of their own values, they left politics behind and peacefully raised four children. Jo's husband died when her youngest child was two and she became a working single mum. Learning to meditate brought her through these difficult times and awakened her to spirituality. Later she moved to Canterbury in Kent, and met Annie and Tony McCarthy, who taught her the Faith. When her youngest was an adult, Jo pioneered to Greece, arriving on 21 April 1991 and finding herself forthwith on the LSA of Athens. She is still in her post there 18 years later, remaining active at the age of 85. She finds contacts through teaching people to meditate and has had weekly firesides for the past 15 years. Jo loves Greece dearly and hopes to be useful there for some years more.

Nina Harvey

Nina was born in 1953 in Colombia, South America. Her family immigrated to Canada in 1965. A near death experience at the age of four led her indirectly to finding Bahá'u'lláh. In 1971, after seeing the word 'Bahá'í' on John Kendall's album of Seals and Crofts, she accepted the Faith. Between 1971 and 1982 she was married and had a daughter, Zia, and a son, Bayan. From 1983 to 1989 she trained as a nurse, remarried, had a son, Aaron, and moved to the UK. Blessed with another daughter, Roshan, in 1991, she suffered a heart attack which decided her to serve the Faith overseas. Receiving direct guidance from the House of Justice in 1995, her family pioneered to Panama to serve as caretakers at the Mashriqu'l-Adhkár atop Cerro Sonsonate (Singing Hill). Following directions from the National Spiritual Assembly, Nina initiated classes based on the Virtues Project. In 1997 she helped plan and implement the twenty-fifth anniversary of the House of Worship. At the same time she joyfully sang in the choir and helped welcome hundreds of guests to the Temple. From 1998 to 2001 she worked with native Guaymi people on the island of Bocas del Toro (Isla Colon). After a brief stint working at the British Embassy, for personal reasons Nina returned to the UK in 2002 with her two youngest children. She is active with the core activities in her little hamlet in Norfolk.

Jane Helbo

Jane was born into a church-going Church of England family in London in 1954. When she was very young her father's engineering work took the family to Turkey and Switzerland, so she was used to other cultures and languages. From the age of eight she was brought up in Cumbria. Jane did teacher training in Bromley, Kent, and worked as a teacher for eight years. She then retrained as a woodwind and brass instrument repairer following a crisis where she needed to find answers to life's purpose. She met the Faith when she began playing in a folk dance band in Cumbria and declared in 1984 at the Irish summer school. Jane was the first Bahá'í in her family, although her sister Rachel had met a Bahá'í at university some years earlier and declared a few years after Jane. In 1986 Jane pioneered to Northern Ireland for several months; to Lincolnshire and Nottinghamshire from 1986 to 1989 and then back home to Allerdale in Cumbria. In January 1993 Jane pioneered to Poland. There she served as National Secretary for three years and later as Auxiliary Board member. In April 2000 she married Ole Helbo and moved to Denmark, where she is currently serving as National Secretary.

Eric and Margaret Hellicar

Eric and Margaret Hellicar pioneered to Cyprus in December 1969 and have been very happy living there with their six children (now six grandchildren as well) ever since. Margaret comes from Edinburgh, which is where Eric met her and the Faith in 1960. Eric was born in Salisbury and as a clergyman's son had lived in many vicarages around the south of England. Eric and Margaret first pioneered to Durham and then left for Cyprus, where they both took up teaching. They have just retired after 40 years and live in a delightful old mud-brick house in the village of Pera – with nine of the family in homes in the same place. Eric is now writing a book about finding the Faith and their experiences in the island. The Bahá'í community is now a thriving one, despite the division of the island. From a few believers, the community has grown to establish its National Spiritual Assembly in 1978, living through some difficult but exciting times. The community started its first intensive programme of growth in 2009, in the north; they hope the south will have its own soon. To them living in Cyprus, the family, teaching, running children's classes (mainly for the grandchildren), running parenting courses, working within the Bahá'í community – it's all one.

Phillip and Ann Hinton

Phillip was born in war-time Britain and grew up in Cape Town, South Africa, where his parents emigrated in 1947. In 1961, through a distinguished Bahá'í pioneer, Lowell Johnson, Phillip became a Bahá'í, the first male youth of 'white' background to accept the Faith in South Africa. The same year Phillip decided on the stage as a career path and in 1963 made his way to London to pursue his profession and to attend the first World Congress of the Bahá'í Faith. Later that year, in a West End musical, he met a young dancer, Ann Constant, whom he married in 1965. In 1974, on their second Bahá'í pilgrimage, they were encouraged by Universal House of Justice member David Hofman and Hand of the Cause Paul Haney, to move as pioneers to Australia, which they did later that year with their two sons, Sean and Simon. They settled in Sydney, where a third son, Benjamin, was born in 1977. In Australia Phillip has continued his acting career and has served the Bahá'í community by presenting the Faith on national radio and through his 'one man play' on the life of Howard Colby Ives, *Portals to Freedom*, which has played to audiences in several different countries. The Hintons are now basking in the joy of their six grandchildren.

Vicky Howarth (Leith)

Vicky grew up in Northampton with her parents and four brothers. She met Fiona Beint (Young) when she was 11 and learned about the Bahá'í Faith through going to firesides and chatting late at night with her. She accepted Bahá'u'lláh as the latest Manifestation of God at about the age of 12 but declared publicly when she was 16. Vicky pioneered to Swaziland in October 1993 and returned back to the UK in July 1994. She then started her degree in teaching. Vicky is mother to daughter Maya Olivia and wife of Tom – they still live in Northampton. As well as being a full-time mother, Vicky also writes articles and books on positive and healthy living and songs to uplift the heart!

Mahin Humphrey

Mahin was born in Iran, arriving in England in 1954 as a youth pioneer during the Ten Year Crusade. Amongst some of her closest friends at that time were the Hofmans and the Semples. In 1957 Mahin helped form the first Local Spiritual Assembly in Portsmouth. In 1959 she pioneered to Cambridge where several youth accepted the Faith. In those days there were few Bahá'ís in the UK and everyone who could would pioneer! In 1961 Mahin married Ray Humphrey and they had two sons, Vahid and Abbas. In 1984 they were invited to serve at the Bahá'í World Centre where one of Mahin's tasks was to work with Rúḥíyyih Khánum restoring the interior display in the Mansion of Bahjí. Their home was the Master's Tea House. In 1988 they pioneered to Taiwan to help with mass teaching and deepening. In 1992 Mahin decided to go travel teaching to as many countries as possible, especially with doors opening in eastern Europe. She visited lots of countries, met some most wonderful people, suffered some physical deprivations and was spiritually very happy. Mahin is particularly grateful to her family and friends around the world for all the support and love they have given her. She packs a pair of comfortable shoes and a light bag and off she goes! As Ray says, 'she takes all sorts of risks but lands on her feet safely!'

Karen Jamshidi

Karen was born into a Bahá'í family and lived in Omagh, Northern Ireland, for 19 years. She then volunteered to do a year of service in Saipan, Mariana Islands. She worked in a Montessori school during her service and this has guided her decisions ever since. She then attended university in Edinburgh and studied psychology for four years. At this point she realized that education was without a doubt one of the most important and significant services she could give to humanity. As a consequence she went to Toronto, Canada, for a year to train to be a Montessori directress. She worked as a Montessori directress in Toronto and now lives in London, England, where she is head directress of a new Montessori school.

Tanya Jones

Tanya was born in a small town in North Wales, where she came across and embraced the Faith as a young teenager. After finishing school, she thought that she would like to dedicate a year to the Faith and decided to do a year of service. Poland was the country where she felt her abilities could be of most use. After her year was over she moved to Nottingham and was very active in every aspect of the Faith, serving on the LSA and becoming very involved in the institute programme, facilitating many books and animating junior youth groups. There she also carved out a career in sound engineering, later becoming a lecturer on the subject until July 2009, when she decided to pioneer to Greece. She is currently trying to build a life and serve the Faith in the city of Thessaloniki, northern Greece.

Arthur Kendall

Arthur was born and raised in Goole, Yorkshire – so long ago, he says, that he was ten and a bit before sweets came off ration. Money was short. At the age of 14 he 'went halves' with his brother raising two pounds ten shillings to buy a secondhand bike which had no tyres so they rode on the rims! You could hear them for miles. He declared at age 40 at Riḍván 1979 after attending firesides in Solihull, West Midlands. Arthur and his two sisters, Vivien Crook and Christine Deihim, who declared in the early sixties, are the only surviving members of a family of eight children and the only ones to accept the Faith. On taking 'selective voluntary severance' from National Power in 1992, Arthur pioneered to Estonia for almost six months then visited the Temple in Chicago and attended the World Congress in New York. During the mid-nineties he chauffeured minibuses of young Bahá'ís to the Czech Republic and southern Portugal and in 1999 attended a teaching project in Poland. He now lives in Braintree, north Essex, where he enjoys playing the piano to an audience of one if the cat goes out.

Ramin and Rozita Khalilian

Ramin was born in Doha, Qatar, in October 1960 to pioneering parents. After some years his family returned to Tehran but when Ramin was 17 years old his parents sent him to Cambridge to further his studies. Two years later he was joined by his sister Rose and within a few months his parents followed, after the

Iranian revolution in 1979. Ramin and Rose both graduated from university, Ramin in electronics engineering and Rose in architecture. Rose married Kit Leung, a Chinese from Hong Kong – a country they pioneered to, followed one year later by their parents Houshang and Homa Khalilian (currently living in the northern territories). Rose, Kit and their two children, Shirin and Olinga, now live in Macau. Ramin married Rozita Shirmohammad from Barcelona and just after the birth of their first child, Carmel, they decided in November 1991 to pioneer to Gibraltar. Their first boy, Kian, was born in 1995 and then Kourosh in 1997. Ramin works for Gibraltar Broadcasting Corporation and Rozita works in the accounts department of Sapphire Networks. The first Spiritual Assembly of Gibraltar was established at Riḍván 1995 and there is currently a very active and vibrant Bahá'í community in Gibraltar with adults, children, junior youth and youth all engaged in the core activities.

Gohar Khosravi (Beint)

Gohar was born in 1975 to Marion and Beman Khosravi and grew up in Belfast. In 1986 she attended the inauguration of the Bahá'í Lotus Temple in Delhi and returned in 1994 to offer a year of service in the Barli Development Institute for Rural Women Indore. The Institute works with women from the surrounding villages to train them in basic life skills such as health and hygiene, growing fruit and vegetables and riding a bicycle. She continued to travel and in 2007 volunteered as an optometrist in Tibet, offering eye care to the nomadic population. Gohar married Payam Beint in 1999 and now works as a hospital optometrist and cares for their daughter Laila.

Anna and Robert Kinghorn

Robert was born in Edinburgh and moved abroad with his family to Peterborough, England, when he was a small boy. Anna grew up in England, Ethiopia and Hong Kong. They became Bahá'ís as young adults – Robert was one of the 40 youth who enrolled in Peterborough back in 1971 and Anna became a Bahá'í at a public meeting in Rugby in 1974 on the evening they met. They married on the Isle of Wight and pioneered three weeks later to Finland in November 1975. They have lived in various communities and as isolated believers, including 12 years in Lapland, which is part of the North Calotte. Robert served on the National Child Education Committee in the UK and on the National Child Education Committee and National Pioneer Committee in Finland. He currently serves as editor of *Icebreaker*, the newsletter of the Bahá'í Council of the North Calotte. Anna has served as assistant to the Auxiliary Board and as a Board member. They have both served on Local Spiritual Assemblies and were actively involved in activities in the North

Calotte. They moved to Turku, southwest Finland, in the summer of 2009 to be near two of their four children.

Jody Koomen

Jody grew up in South Oxfordshire where he attended an international school. He was brought up as a Bahá'í but feels that he only recognized Bahá'u'lláh as a particularly powerful Soul when he was 17. It was then that he decided to try to follow His teachings and felt enamoured by His energy. When Jody finished school he decided to offer his services in a school run by Bahá'ís in Swaziland. He returned home after eight months and started university. Currently he is living in rural Northumberland with his wife Gemma and baby daughter Maya.

Susan and Shidan Kouchek-zadeh

Susan was born in Bournemouth in 1942 to socialist/agnostic parents and became a Bahá'í while still in secondary school. After obtaining an honours degree in sociology from Leeds University in 1963, she married Shidan Kouchek-zadeh. Shidan, who is a fourth generation Bahá'í on his mother's side with a Muslim background and second generation on his father's side with Zoroastrian origins, came to the UK at the age of 15 and graduated as a civil engineer from the University of Manchester (UMIST). Susan worked as a child care officer for Manchester City Council until 1966 when they pioneered to Sierra Leone in West Africa where at that time there were no Bahá'ís. In 1975 Sierra Leone formed its first National Spiritual Assembly and Susan and Shidan pioneered to neighbouring Guinea where they remained for 30 years, retiring back to Bournemouth in 2005. Shidan was always able to find engineering work to support them and Susan did a variety of teaching jobs ranging from kindergarten to teacher training college. They have two daughters, Vadiay, who is at present pioneering in La Guardia, Bolivia; and Vafa, who is living and working in Australia.

Vafa Kouchek-zadeh (Otia)

Vafa grew up in Guinea-Conakry (West Africa) in a Bahá'í family, with her parents Susan and Shidan Kouchek-zadeh and her elder sister Vadiay. When she was 18 she returned to England to study at the University of Exeter. Having qualified as a secondary school mathematics teacher, she served at the School of Nations, Brasilia, Brazil, for half a year after her short trip to Russia. She worked at St Peter's School in Bournemouth for a few years and then pioneered for two years to the Czech Republic where she worked at the Townshend International School. Vafa then had the bounty of serving for a year and a half at the Pilgrimage Reception Centre of the Bahá'í World Centre where she met her husband Azah Otia from Cameroon. They now live next door to the Mother Temple of Australasia and have the fortune to be working for the national secretariat of the National Spiritual Assembly of the Bahá'ís of Australia. Vafa is currently serving on the Area Teaching Committee of the Sydney North Shore Cluster and as an assistant to the Auxiliary Board member. So far Vafa says that her life has just been one long series of blessings and of encounters with the most wonderful and inspiring people.

Amelia Lake

Amelia Ashwell Lake was born into a Bahá'í family and spent her childhood and young adult years within the warmth of the Northern Ireland Bahá'í community. Before taking up her place at university Amelia spent seven months of her 'gap year' in India but also spent time in Indonesia where her grandparents pioneered from Iran (with their very young family) in the 1950s in response to the call of the Guardian. Amelia's grandfather, Dr Fazlullah Astani, passed away in January 2003. However, her grandmother remains in her pioneer post in western Sumatra and is a constant source of inspiration! While Amelia has travelled extensively, the time in India with her close friends Gohar and Stephanie remains a pivotal life experience. Amelia is married, lives in North Yorkshire now and works as a senior lecturer in food and nutrition, with a research focus on improving the nutrition and health of young adults.

Conrad Lambert

Conrad's great-grandmother became a follower of the Bahá'í Faith in San Francisco in 1911. Conrad served as a gardener at the Bahá'í World Centre in 1987. At the age of 19 he made the first of five annual trips to Africa to record folk and popular music in 12 different countries for various projects supported by the Bahá'í World Centre's Office of Social and Economic Development and British cultural organizations. Concurrent to his African trips Conrad joined the South American folk group El Viento Canta for eight months, touring Europe, Africa, the former Soviet Union and Asia. He is still involved in music work and currently lives in Bern, Switzerland.

Lois and David Lambert

Lois was born in 1940, a third generation Bahá'í. Her grandmother, Louisa Charlot Ginman, became a Bahá'í in San Francisco in 1911, and her mother, Alma Gregory, was a Bahá'í child and youth during the early years of the growth of the Faith in the USA and the British Isles. Before moving to China in 1989 Lois toured internationally as performer, maker and musician in cele-

Ron Batchelor

Thelma Batchelor

Janak & Jimmy McGilligan

Greg Akehurst-Moore

Shirin Youssefian Maanian

Massoud & Mojgan Derakhshani

Karen & Tim Shrimpton

Susan Kouchek-zadeh with daughters Vadiay & Vafa

Carol Spencer

Rosie Smith

Jeremy & Denise Fox

Ann Dymond

Helen Smith

Bayán, Manijeh, David, & Holly Smith

Pam & Brian O'Toole

Joy Behi

Michele Wilburn

Shohreh Azarkadeh

Charlie & Barbara Pierce

Richard Poole

Philip Hainsworth

Lois Hainsworth

Vicky Howarth & Fiona Beint *Joseph & Atieh Donnelly* *Stephanie & Wesley Clash*

Tahereh & Silan Nadarajah *Lois Lambert*

Adrian Davis & family *David & Gayle Rutstein & family* *Irene & Falai-Riva Taafaki*

Gohar Khosravi & Stephanie Christopherson *Rozita & Ramin Khalilian* *Gillian Phillips*

Sandra Cooles

Marie & Eddie Whiteside & daughter Kerry

David Renwick Grant

Sarah Munro (left) *dressed as Martha Root*

Nima Anvar & family

Alan & Marion Pollitt

Guita Youssefian

Mojgan Agahi

bratory theatre and served on the Arts Council of Great Britain Drama Panel. Since moving to Mongolia in 1992 Lois has served both as Auxiliary Board member and as a member of the National Spiritual Assembly of Mongolia. She is a consultant with United Nations agencies UNICEF and UNDP and has been named State Honoured Citizen by the Mongolian government for her services to moral education. David became a Bahá'í in 1974. Before leaving the UK David lectured in drama and the expressive arts at Bretton Hall, University of Leeds. In Mongolia he served with the Voluntary Service Overseas for 13 years. He was Director of the National Teacher Training Project for the Ministry of Education and Soros Foundation and has trained teachers at the University of Humanities and the National University of Mongolia. In 2003 he was awarded the MBE by Her Majesty the Queen for services to the development of English language teaching in Mongolia. He has served on the National Spiritual Assembly of Mongolia since 1995 and serves as Deputy of the Regional Board of Trustees for Ḥuqúqu'lláh for Mongolia and Russia. Lois and David have three children, Zoe, Conrad and Richard, and two granddaughters, Tilly and Nubia.

Heather Lansing (Halford)

Heather was born in the United States of America into a Bahá'í family in the late 1960s. The whole family moved to Kendal in the United Kingdom in 1976. From an early age Heather had always wanted to live in Africa. In 1989 she went to Botswana as a youth to participate in one of the summer Star Projects just before completing her degree in education. Little did she know that she would later return to live, marry and have two children there! As life has its twists and turns, she first found herself living in Venezuela for two years from 1995 to 1997. After those two years she was offered a teaching position in Botswana. She spent nine years there, ended up running an 'events' business in partnership with another Bahá'í and was able to put on functions for the Bahá'í community. Since returning to England with her husband Brett and two daughters Lauren and Nicole, she is near completing a four-year degree level study in homeopathy. Currently Heather is one of two Bahá'ís living in Salisbury where a fortnightly study circle is run.

Billy and Christine Lee

Christine, née Whiteley, from Barnoldswick in Lancashire, became a Bahá'í in 1964. William was raised in Liverpool and declared there in 1969. They married in Skipton in 1970 and lived in Liverpool for a short time before pioneering to Chester. After the birth of two children, Jason and Abigail, they pioneered to Zambia in 1974 and then in 1977 relocated to Botswana, where they still reside. Both overseas posts filled pioneer goals of the National Spiritual Assembly of the United Kingdom at that time. In Zambia, after a two month stay in Lusaka, they moved to Ndola and assisted in re-establishing the Local Spiritual Assembly there. They experienced the wonderful bounty of hosting the late Hand of the Cause Dr Raḥmatu'lláh Muhájir as a house guest during late 1976. William is a consulting engineer by profession and has been fortunate to have been involved in the designs for the National Bahá'í Centre in Gaborone, Botswana. He has served continuously on the Gaborone Spiritual Assembly since 1978. Christine is an active Ruhi book tutor and a children's class teacher for many years. Their daughter, Abigail, is married with three children and lives close by in Gaborone. Jason is married with three children and lives in Camberley, Surrey. Their third child, Thomas, born in Johannesburg in 1986, is working in England.

John Lester and Barbara Stanley-Hunt

John was born in Buckhurst Hill, Essex, and became a Bahá'í in 1968 while living in Worcester. He left for New Zealand soon after. He pioneered to Hastings in the North Island, becoming a member of the first Spiritual Assembly in 1970. A year later he moved to Christchurch to serve on its first LSA, also the first to be formed in the South Island. There he became the first Bahá'í travel teacher to the Chatham Islands, answering a call from Hand of the Cause Dr Muhájir, and twice visited Niue Island. Barbara Stanley-Hunt was born in Takapuna, New Zealand, where she learned of the Faith in 1964 from the sister of a Danish Bahá'í. During the 1970s she, too, visited the Chathams and spent four years in the Solomon Islands where, by using the local markets, she could live on one pound a day. She supported pioneers in Gizo, Western Solomons, and was assistant to the Auxiliary Board member in Malaita, Eastern Solomons. In Honiara she worked with Knight of Baha'u'lláh Gertrude Blum. Once, desperate for water, she prayed and it rained just the amount she needed. Barbara and John married in 1983. Having revisited the Chathams, they visited the Solomons in 1985 when Barbara was able to assist a New Zealand pioneer in the birth of her third child in a small village six miles away from any medical assistance. John and Barbara moved to England to the London Borough of Havering in 1988.

Simin and Bruce Liggitt

Simin was born in Iran and arrived in the UK at the age of 13. Bruce was born in Zimbabwe and grew up in Zambia and Malawi. They were married in 1994 in Oakham, where Simin was working at the Bahá'í Publishing Trust. After a couple of years in Oakham they travelled and lived in South Africa and

Zambia for about six years. Three years in Zambia were spent at the Masetlha Institute and Banani International School where Simin was financial controller and Bruce developed a sustainable agriculture programme. Their daughter, Tajalli, was born in 1998. They returned to the UK in 2003 and are now settled in Ely, Cambridgeshire where Simin has recently changed careers and is working as a mathematics teacher and Bruce is working for an international conservation NGO. They have served on a number of Bahá'í institutions.

Colette and Vessal Maani

Colette was born in Canada and left at age six months when her parents returned to Northern Ireland. Then they immigrated to Australia until Irish homesickness called them back once again. It was while studying at the University of Ulster that Colette first encountered the Bahá'í Faith. The university canteen was open after hours one evening and she asked someone why and it turned out they had kept it open for the Bahá'í youth as it was the time of the fast and they only ate after sunset. They seemed such a happy group and it was so weird in that university 'anything goes' environment that so many were taking spirituality so seriously. Colette became a Bahá'í the same week she graduated – it felt right. She finished her PhD in physics, had three sons and was working in research when in 1994 she and her husband Vessal both decided to resign from their jobs and pioneer to a goal area abroad. They ended up on the Greek island of Rhodes and lived there for almost ten years. It was tough for the family but there was also laughter and the joy of wonderful loving Bahá'ís. Such love builds bonds that cross continents and barriers of age or culture.

Fleur Mazloum (Kennedy)

Fleur was born in York into a Bahá'í family. Through most of her childhood there were no other children or youth in her community, apart from her older brother, but she gained many Bahá'í friends from attending regular summer and Easter schools as well as youth camps. At 19 years old she took a gap year to dedicate herself to a year of service and went to Thailand where she was lucky to be around many young and active Bahá'ís. When Fleur arrived back in the UK she continued her studies and gained a Master's in social work. Fleur has now returned to her home town of York where she is currently a member of the LSA, is a busy mum to her three young children and continues to work as a social worker with young people.

Peter McAlpine

Peter is Scottish by birth. When he left university he felt that living in the UK was not for him. Not only did he have an unfulfilled desire to travel more, but he also wanted to look for another country to live in. So, he left his first job and went travelling around the Caribbean, South America and Central America for over a year. While in Dominica, Peter met Dr Ta'eed, a Bahá'í pioneer who introduced him to the Faith – not that his mother hadn't tried to do so for years! When he reached St Vincent he accepted the Faith. Peter's choices of where to live were reduced to Chile and Thailand. He chose Thailand, moved there in 1984 and found a job teaching English at Songkhla Teachers College. He has lived in different parts of Thailand since then and now lives in Bangkok with his wife, Klooay, and two adult children from his previous marriage, Jasmine and Jason. Peter says he is never satisfied with what he has done for the Faith but knows exactly how he is going to leave a legacy for the Faith in Thailand, once he has raised the money to move up north – by selling bio-fertilizer. One of his goals is to be a source of inspiration and guidance for youth, and that is essentially what he wants to be remembered for when he departs this world at the age of 85!

Mike and Mahin McCandless

Mike grew up in Walla Walla, Washington, USA. He participated in the first Bahá'í children's class there. Its most notable achievement was to send a small contribution to Shoghi Effendi, for which they received a priceless personal acknowledgement in return. Mike graduated from Antioch College and in 1979 obtained a Master's degree from the School of Public Health at the University of North Carolina. He headed off to the Navajo Indian Reservation in Arizona, where he managed a satellite health clinic and later worked as a health planning officer for the Navajo Tribal Government. Mahin was born in Dargaz, Iran, and spent most of her childhood and youth in Mashhad, nurtured by a dynamic and loving Bahá'í community. After completing secondary school Mahin moved to Tehran, got a job in a bank and studied banking science. At the tender age of 26 she became head of the personnel office – a remarkable achievement for a woman, and especially for a Bahá'í woman in a Muslim country. From the age of 19 she has taught Bahá'í children's classes. She was a pioneer in Nantes, France, for nine years. Upon arrival she spoke no French but within a short time she obtained a post-Master's civil law degree from Nantes University. Mike and Mahin met at the Bahá'í World Centre where they served for 12 and nine years respectively. In 1995 they moved to Hastings and in 2002 pioneered to Kourou, French Guiana, purchasing the English Institute from an American Bahá'í family who needed to return to the US. They currently operate the Institute and serve on the Spiritual Assembly of the Bahá'ís of French Guiana.

Jimmy and Janak McGilligan

James (Jimmy) grew up in a Protestant family near the village of Garvagh, Northern Ireland, and in 1984 was the first Orangeman to accept the Faith. He pioneered to India in response to a call from the Bahá'í World Centre in 1986 to reclaim 72 acres of saline marshes of land at Rabbani School near Gwalior. His voluntary service started at the Bahá'í House of Worship in Delhi during its dedication ceremony. He successfully completed his mission at Rabbani school and was commended for his services by the Bahá'í World Centre. On 16 October 1988 he met Janak Palta, the director of the Bahá'í Vocational Institute For Rural Women in Indore (now known as Barli Development Institute for Rural Women) and they were married a month later. Jimmy moved to Indore and was appointed the Institute manager where he has very many responsibilities (maintenance, infrastructure, development, gardens, food production, information technology, audiovisual, environmental education, development and transfer of solar technologies). In November 2008 he was awarded the OBE by Her Majesty the Queen for 'his services to social causes and the use of alternative energy in rural communities in India'. Janak Palta McGilligan was born in Jalandhar (Punjab), grew up in Chandigarh in a very Hindu family and embraced the Faith in 1980. She home front pioneered from Chandigarh at the request of the NSA of the Bahá'ís of India to establish the Institute in Indore in 1985. Now the Institute is at the centre of this couple's world – it is their home and their work, their passion and the purpose of their life. Janak has been granted several awards for her work and in March 2008 was honoured with the Rajmata Vijaraje Sindhia Social Service Award conferred by the Madhya Pradesh government, Bhopal.

Dave Menham

Dave grew up in Newcastle upon Tyne where he incidentally at a later date became a Bahá'í after attending a weekend school in St Andrews in 1973. Since then he has pioneered to a number of different locations both at home and abroad until finally he married while living as an isolated believer in Berwick upon Tweed. After his marriage to his Hungarian wife Zsuzsa and a brief stay in Newcastle, he eventually moved to West Yorkshire and attended the Bradford School of Peace Studies. In 1991 together with his wife and two young daughters he moved to Austria and lived there for 14 years. Zsuzsa and Dave returned to the UK in 2005 with their daughter Joanna and are now members of the Dronfield Bahá'í community. Their other daughter, Dawn, continues to live and study in Austria.

Sylvia Miley

Sylvia was born in 1939 and has lived in Southport all her life. Her brother David Hopper became a Bahá'í at university but her parents were firm in their Christian faith. After Sylvia married in 1962 she found this was also the case with her in-laws. It was hard for the family to realize her independent search for truth. Her search took nine years and ended when she eventually embraced the Cause of Bahá'u'lláh in 1969. When she became a Bahá'í she had two small children and was not allowed to tell anyone about her new-found Faith. She continued to attend church and, indeed, took her children to other churches and places of worship. Over the years, and after the children left home, she used to teach the faith, or rather pepper her conversation with the word 'Bahá'í', especially when her husband was out of earshot. Holidays have now become her focus for teaching and she likes to travel and share jewels of wisdom whenever and wherever she can. For 15 years, until recently, Sylvia served on the UK Year of Service Desk, being privileged to advise and assist about one thousand youth in their efforts to serve.

Corinna Mills

Corinna was born in Iran to a Persian mother and British father, both Bahá'ís, but returned to England to grow up in the Lake District, her father's homeland. In 1976, at the age of eight, Corinna went to live in beautiful Portugal (near Lisbon), where the family resided for about 14 years. She returned to the UK for final years of schooling and university in Northern Ireland, where she studied dentistry. After finishing her studies she went to work in Manchester and North Wales for over two years, then packed up and went for two months to Albania and a month of study in Landegg, Switzerland. There she met her husband, Jalal Mills, from Papua New Guinea, and for the past 12 years they have lived in that amazing country. They have two children, a boy Thornton and a girl Amelia, and now reside in Brisbane, Australia, for the sake of the children's schooling. Corinna's husband, Jalal, still comes and goes between the two countries and they all regularly go back to PNG as their work is still there.

Hooman Momen

Hooman was born in Iran and his family moved to the United Kingdom when he was three years old. He had all his education in England: primary in Bournemouth, secondary in Taunton, undergraduate in London and postgraduate in Liverpool. In 1970 during his gap year between school and university he visited the Bahá'í community in Guyana and other countries in South America. He married Monireh Obbadi in Haifa in 1975. After obtaining his PhD in parasitology from the Liverpool School of Tropical Medicine, he moved to Rio de Janeiro in 1977. There he worked for the Oswaldo Cruz Research Institute of the Ministry of Health for 24 years. In 2001 he was hired by the World Health Organization (WHO), and moved to Switzerland. He is currently the coordinator of WHO Press and resides in Nyon, Switzerland, with his wife and one son, Saam. His other son, Taam, is married and lives near Peterborough. He has been a member and an officer of the Local Spiritual Assemblies of Liverpool, Rio de Janeiro and Nyon. He was also a manager of the Bahá'í Publishing Trust of Brazil.

Parvin Morrissey

Parvin was born into a Bahá'í family and grew up on the outskirts of London. She studied in Liverpool and then moved to Scotland after her marriage to Pat. The couple pioneered to Scotland's 'wee county', Clackmannanshire, in 1981, where Parvin's two sons, Sean and Matthew, were born and raised. Parvin and Pat remained in the area until 2007 when they moved into the nearby city of Stirling. Parvin is a lecturer in biology and is currently working as a curriculum quality leader at a large college of further education in central Scotland. In 1995 she became secretary of the Bahá'í Committee for Scotland which later became the Bahá'í Council for Scotland. Apart from a five year appointment to the Auxiliary Board for Protection, she has served continually on this body as secretary, chairperson and now treasurer. She loves to travel and visit Bahá'í projects around the world.

Sarah Munro

Sarah was born in Derry, Northern Ireland, into a Bahá'í family. Although as a child Sarah attended Bahá'í 'Sunday school' and learned about the Faith's basic teachings and spent six months serving at the Bahá'í Primary School in Swaziland at the age of 18, it was not until she went to serve at the Indian Lotus Temple at the age of 21 that she began to read for herself, learned and fully accepted the Faith. Explaining the Faith's teachings to the visitors that came to the Temple really helped her a lot in that process. Since then she has trained as a teacher of English and drama and as a performer. Inspired by stories from the history of the Faith, she has written and performed quite a number of short dramas and travelled to different Bahá'í communities around the world to perform them as well as offering other services to those communities. Sarah has visited Iceland, Faroes, Cyprus, Belgium, Hong Kong and East Asia.

Silan and Tahereh Nadarajah

Silan is from Malaysia and accepted the Bahá'í Faith in 1965. Tahereh is from Iran (her mother's family came from Yazd and were Bahá'ís from the time of 'Abdu'l-Bahá). They first met in Kenya when, separately, each of them pioneered there in 1972 in order to assist with the achievement of the Nine Year Plan goals in Africa. Both lived in the UK from 1973 to 1978 and were married in 1974. Tahereh completed her Master's in metallurgy at Sheffield University and Silan his professional examinations for chartered accountancy. In 1978 they pioneered to Papua New Guinea for 11 years. Since then they have lived in Mongolia for six years, in Kosovo for two years, in Timor Leste for two years, in Syria for one year and in Lebanon for three years. Silan worked initially for the United Nations and later for the International Monetary Fund. In all these countries, Tahereh was actively involved with non-governmental organizations and undertook assignments for the UN and other international organizations. Both have been active members of the Bahá'í community in whichever countries they have lived. They have four children (Nura, Hujjat, Taraz and Rayhan) and now live in Australia, where they have been naturalized.

Tish Oakwood

Tish grew up in London, discarded her non-religious 'Judaic' heritage at the age of 14, had a dream at the age of 19 that began her spiritual questing, and travelled extensively overseas for seven years from that time, leaving the UK with £60 in her pocket and searching for a truth which she eventually found in Wales nine years later when she bumped into a couple of Bahá'í travel teachers. She has lived in England, Israel, Finland, Greece, the Netherlands, Spain, the Canary Islands, Wales and the Caribbean. She pioneered in north Wales for six years and in the British Virgin Islands for three and currently lives in England. She has served on various Local Spiritual Assemblies, been an assistant to the Auxiliary Board, a delegate, was briefly a National Spiritual Assembly member in the British Virgin Islands, and spent several happy years on the overseas pioneering committee in the UK. She loves to write and to sing – and to travel.

Brian and Pamela O'Toole

Brian and Pamela O'Toole pioneered from the UK to Guyana over 30 years ago in 1979 – they are still there. Pam met the Faith in Glasgow shortly before pioneering. Brian was born into a Bahá'í family with his mother coming from Iran. Pam currently serves as the secretary of the NSA and Brian is one of the Auxiliary Board members for the country. They have established a one thousand student School of Nations in Guyana that serves students from nursery to university. They have developed the Varqa Foundation – a Bahá'í-inspired NGO that has been operating in Guyana for almost 25 years and which has attracted funding from the European Union, the government of Luxembourg, UNICEF, ILO, the World Bank, IADB, Save the Children and the embassies of Germany and the UK. They have two sons who were born and raised in Guyana. Both are married to devoted Bahá'ís. Liam, the elder, serves at the Bahá'í World Centre as one of the coordinators. Cairan is presently working for UNICEF in Guyana. Guyana has been very good to the O'Toole family.

Melissa Parsons

Melissa was born in Oban, Scotland, to Bahá'í pioneering parents. She grew up in Kirkcudbright, Dumfries and Galloway where she attended high school. In 1995 she went on an inspirational youth teaching project to the Faroe Islands. In 1996 she undertook a year of service to a community project in Manitoba, Canada, with another youth from north Wales, which included working on a literacy project with indigenous Cree people. In 1997 she started a degree in social anthropology with development at Edinburgh University. She took a year out (2000–1) to combine field work, service, work and travel in Latin America. This is where she spent several months in Talamanca, Costa Rica, with the Bribri indigenous people and in affiliation with a Bahá'í social and economic development project. She graduated in the summer of 2002 and started working on a European funded employment and skills project in north Wales. She has worked in community and economic development in the voluntary and public sectors in north Wales and the northwest of England since then and is now living near Chester.

Danielle Pee

Danielle was brought up in Surrey. In 2004 she was part of a group of 19 youth from around Europe who were invited to participate in a FUNDAEC course entitled 'Intellectual Preparation for Social Action'. Inspired by the ideas presented by FUNDAEC on education and development, upon her return to the UK Danielle enrolled in a Master's degree course in education and international development. This gave her the opportunity to learn more about mainstream education and FUNDAEC, a cutting edge Bahá'í-inspired NGO. She then spent the next three years learning about a practical approach to curriculum development and community capacity building by working in various Bahá'í-inspired programmes of a similar nature in India, Honduras and East Asia. Currently Danielle is doing a PhD based on what she has learned over the past couple of years.

Gillian Phillips

Gillian was brought up in the small sleepy market town of Narberth in the heart of Pembrokeshire in west Wales. Her life has been full of departures since she became a Bahá'í in 1964 in Romford, Essex, at the beginning of the Nine Year Plan. Ten years after she declared, her mother also became a Bahá'í. Gillian's first pioneer move was to Chester in 1966, then to southern Ireland in 1968, making her way to Limerick where during the next few years many youth entered the Faith. Pioneering was the priority for these youth and they made up the LSAs in the south that were the basis of the National Spiritual Assembly of Ireland formed in 1972. Gillian moved to eight towns, eventually returning to live in the Limerick area of Co. Clare. Nursing has been her career and for the past seven years she has spent the longest period of her life in one place, at the Limerick General Hospital. She plans to retire soon and hopes to continue putting all her energy into the Ruhi books and direct teaching.

Charlie Pierce

Charlie was born in Nottingham during World War Two. His family were practising members of the Church of England. A graduate of Bristol University, Charlie began teaching in a comprehensive school in Bristol and, after a couple of years, he decided to travel the world! He joined an expedition travelling overland to Nepal and on to Thailand, Malaysia and Australia. After coming into contact with all the major religions and realizing the essential unity of them all, he came across the Bahá'í Faith in Malaysia. Much later, he declared in Sydney in 1968. At a conference in Adelaide in 1970 he offered to pioneer to anywhere in the Pacific and was directed to what was then the New Hebrides (now Vanuatu). He arrived in Port Vila in March 1971 to take over the running of Nur Bahá'í School from the original pioneer to the New Hebrides, Bertha Dobbins. Later that year he married Barbara in Perth, Australia. Weeks afterwards they returned to Port Vila on their honeymoon and are still there. They have raised two sons – Daniel and Sam – both of whom now live in Australia. Charlie served on the National Spiritual Assembly of the South West Pacific from 1974 to 1977, and since then on the National Spiritual Assembly of Vanuatu. In addition to Bahá'í administrative service, he does a lot of translation of the holy writings and other Bahá'í materials from English and French into Bislama.

Marion and Alan Pollitt

Marion became a Bahá'í in Burnley in 1963, thanks to the late Abbas and Shomais Afnan, and Alan became a Bahá'í in 1966. Between them they have two sons and two daughters and, in addition, wonderful grandchildren. They both served on the LSA of Burnley until their move to The Gambia in 1997. After a visit to The Gambia at Easter 1993 they decided to pioneer there when they realized it was an unfilled UK goal. In addition, since the official language of The Gambia is English, it meant that Marion would be able to teach in school if necessary. They moved in April 1997 and stayed for almost six years. Marion and Alan can honestly say they would not change that experience for the world. It still gives them opportunities to teach here in the UK when meeting people of African origin. From pioneering, they learned so much about the people of West Africa, their traditions, culture and beliefs, but they learned even more about themselves. They are currently living in West Yorkshire and serving on the LSA of Calderdale. They serve as members of the Office of International Pioneering and Travel Teaching. Marion also serves as a Representative for the Board of Ḥuqúqu'lláh and as the Cluster Institute Coordinator for West Yorkshire.

Richard Poole

Richard became a Baháʼí at three o'clock in the morning on 14 July 1975 in the city of Liverpool without knowing anything about the Faith! An Iranian student who happened to be living in the same house at the time, a certain Hooman Momen, had lent him a book, *The Reality of Man*, a compilation of excerpts from the writings of Baháʼuʼlláh and ʻAbdul-Bahá. It had been lying by his bedside for seven months unopened. Richard read just one line, 'This evening I wish to speak to you concerning the meaning of sacrifice'[32] and that was it! He did not know who Baháʼuʼlláh was or anything about Baháʼí belief, just that he was a Baháʼí. For the record Richard is the first Baháʼí in a family that hails from Bristol. He first pioneered to Sudan in January 1978 and has been pioneering pretty much ever since, the countries being Tanzania, Barbados, St Lucia, Ecuador, Guinea, Angola, Uganda, Rwanda and now, finally, back where he started all those years ago, in Sudan. Specific services have included being chairman of the NSA of Sudan 1980–1; a member of the Discourse on Science, Religion and Development, Kampala, Uganda 2001–3; and a member of various Local Assemblies and committees when called upon to do so.

Mihan and Dariush Ram (Gabriel)

Mihan was born in Tehran and at the age of 16 married Dariush Ram. Both were third generation Baháʼís. They had three children: Vafa, Nava and Guita. For many years they served in Iran as confirmed teachers for official firesides and youth classes. In the 1970s Mihan was invited by the Counsellor Dr

Masih Farhangi (later martyred) to travel around Iran, after special training, to promote the importance of teaching the Faith. In 1977 Mihan and her children Vafa and Guita (already studying in London) and later Dariush resided in Elstree, helping to form the first LSA of Hertsmere. In 1985 Mihan and Dariush pioneered to Montevideo, Uruguay, which was a pioneering goal of the United Kingdom. Their arrival coincided with the preparation for the Year of Peace in 1986. They expended all their time and effort helping to erect the Time Capsule in the central plaza of Montevideo to be opened in 50 years' time. Mihan was able to obtain unprecedented publicity for the Faith owing to her very successful contacts with the media and with prominent people in general. In 1991 she founded a branch of the International Tree Foundation in Uruguay. This gave her the opportunity to proclaim and distribute a considerable amount of Bahá'í material amongst dignitaries. She is currently trying to persuade bookshops to display and sell Bahá'í books to the public.

Will Rankin

William Rankin was born in Plymouth, Devon. Though not brought up in any particular religion, William was always interested in spiritual topics, which is why he started a Master's in applied (Christian) theology. It was during his studies that he came across the Kitáb-i-Aqdas and the Kitáb-i-Íqán, which he read and promptly became a believer in Bahá'u'lláh. He then decided that he had better find some Bahá'ís. After successfully making contact with the Plymouth Bahá'í community, William left his theology studies as he found the answer to every essay question was 'See 'Abdu'l-Bahá'! In August 2005 William moved from Devon (UK county) to Devin (a village) just outside Bratislava in Slovakia to do a year of service. After meeting the wonderful Bahá'í community there he decided to stay longer. This was a good move as in his second year in Slovakia he met a lovely young lady who was also doing her year of service, and to whom he later proposed. As of the time of writing, both he and his bride to be, Nava, are still living in Slovakia and are both happy to be members of the Slovak Bahá'í community.

Jean Reynard

Jean was born in Portsmouth, Hampshire, but spent the war years living in Lancaster, returning to Portsmouth in 1947. In 1959 she travelled to Tanganyika, then a UN Trust territory administered by Britain. She still remembers alighting from the small plane in Dar es Salaam airport and feeling the blast of heat that greeted her arrival. Dar es Salaam in those days was a small and very pretty town with acacia trees lining many of the roads, amazing flowers and bougainvillea everywhere, and women dressed in colourful garments. She fell in love with the place immediately and, given the opportunity of work, decided to stay. In 1979, living on the outskirts of town in what was then a village, a 'white' man passed by carrying a small child. Jean was intrigued to come across another white person. They made friends as he lived nearby, and regular visits occurred between him and Jean's family during the next few months. He was an American Bahá'í pioneer and was her first contact with the Bahá'í Faith. The visits and discussions that followed were intoxicating and within a few months she 'declared', followed by her then husband and later her teenage daughter. She remained in Tanzania until 1989. Nowadays she makes regular visits. She says the one constant in her life has been the Faith and the wonderful Bahá'ís she has met. That day in 1979 was truly the day when a beautiful jewel was offered to her and, in accepting, her life has been enriched in so many ways.

Audrie Reynolds

Audrie was born in 1924 at Burton-on-Trent. She heard of the Faith at a meeting given by Marion Hofman while she was teaching in Birmingham. She declared as a Bahá'í in 1953 to Anna Kunz in Zurich, Switzerland. In 1954 she pioneered to Chester. In 1963 at the World Congress in London Audrie met Johnathan Reynolds from the US. and they were married in July. They went to live on the Standing Rock Sioux Indian Reservation, North Dakota. From then on they were involved in all the Indian teaching activities. In 1971 they moved to New Mexico and were a part of the Crownpoint Navajo Assembly area. They were members of the Navajo Teaching Committee and visited many Navajo families, helping with the formation of Assemblies. In 1978 they moved to the Eskimo village Unalakleet, Alaska, during the High Endeavours teaching effort, and then south to Juneau. From there they made many flights piloted by Bahá'í Sid Korn along the Yukon River. In 1991 they pioneered to Petropavlovsk-Kamchatsky, Russia, where an Assembly was formed that year. They visited the Yakutz Spiritual Gathering of native tribes and helped with the Kamchatka Spiritual Gathering in 1995. They returned to live in Douglas, Alaska, in 2009.

Valerie Rhind

Born in Cardiff in October 1944, Valerie was the first Bahá'í child to be born in Wales – to Rose Jones, who served on the first Local Spiritual Assembly of Cardiff, and to Matthew Oswald Jones, who died in 1947. In 1951 the family moved to Chiswick, London. Valerie started studying the Faith when she was 14 and declared as a Bahá'í in 1961 when she was 16. She home front pioneered to Bedford in 1966 and a year later studied geography at Sussex

University. In January 1969 she went on pilgrimage where David Hofman suggested that she pioneer to Zambia. Upon graduation that year she moved to Kafue, Zambia, to work as a primary school teacher. She met and married Islay Mackenzie Rhind, a distiller/brewer, in 1972 and they relocated to Kitwe, Zambia. Their first son, Matthew, was born in 1974; their second son, Eion Taher, was born and died in 1977; and their third son, Alasdair, was born in 1978. They have lived in eight countries in Africa including Botswana (where they stayed for 18 years until Islay joined the Coca-Cola Company), Zimbabwe, Tanzania, Nigeria, Angola and South Africa. They are currently back in Nigeria again and will welcome all who wish to visit!

Janet Rowlands

Janet was born in Ecclesfield, Yorkshire, and moved to Northumberland when she was ten. In her teens she attended the Methodist Church and was a Sunday school teacher. Janet was introduced to the Bahá'í Faith after meeting Rosie and Gary Villiers-Stuart at a Natural Childbirth Trust meeting at their home Burnlaw in Northumberland. She became a Bahá'í in 1984 after listening to a talk given by Lou Turner at Mary Jameson's house in Newcastle. Janet became an LSA member in the very active Allendale community where great use was made of the performing arts at unity feasts, children's classes, holy days and other fun occasions. In 1989 Janet moved to southern Ireland with her son, where she remained for eight years. She started children's classes with Annie Wise in Limerick and organized a two to three monthly slot 'Thought for the Day' on Clare FM Radio with junior youth reading writings from Bahá'u'lláh and 'Abdu'l-Bahá. In 1997 Janet pioneered to Malta for a year. These days she lives in Northumberland and cares for her mother. Janet still feels that she hasn't done enough for the Faith and needs to do more – her feet are still itchy!!

Dale and Helen Cameron Rutstein

Helen and Dale were brought up in Bahá'í families on opposite sides of the Atlantic: Helen in the UK and Dale in the US. Helen's parents have Christian Bermudian and Russian Jewish heritage and Dale is a fourth generation Bahá'í on his mother's side with Russian Jewish roots through his father. They met at the Bahá'í World Centre in 1985 while Helen was serving there and Dale was a three day visitor. After one dinner together, just before sunset on the third and final day of his Haifa visit, Dale wrote Helen a note admitting that he had an interest in getting to know her better with a view to marriage. Helen was attracted by the simple and direct approach in matters of the heart and six months later they married in Amherst, Massachusetts. After Dale completed a Master's in education in 1987 with a focus on educational media for the developing world, they went to visit Helen's parents, who were pioneering in the Solomon Islands, and applied for jobs in Papua New Guinea, where Dale began his career in UNICEF. Their three children were born while they lived in Papua New Guinea. They have since lived and worked in PNG, Pakistan, Israel, Albania, Italy, Philippines and currently China. They have brought up their three children in seven different countries – excluding the US and UK. Kalan and Siria are now at college in the US and their youngest daughter, Sophie, attends an international high school in Beijing. Dale and Helen feel immensely blessed to have befriended people in remote villages and in urban centres all over the world.

Gayle and David Rutstein

David was born in Tulsa, Oklahoma, and raised as a Bahá'í. He is a fourth generation Bahá'í. His grandfather Curtis Kelsey served 'Abdu'l-Bahá and Shoghi Effendi in Haifa. He grew up in various locations within the USA and finally moved to Amherst, Massachusetts. Gayle was born in Glen Ridge, New Jersey, and raised as a Bahá'í from the age of six when her mother, Mary Hardy, became a Bahá'í in Switzerland. After living in Switzerland for five years, they moved first to Canterbury and then to Henley-on-Thames in England for 12 years. Gayle moved to the USA in 1977 to study. She met David in April 1980 at a Bahá'í youth conference and they were married in August 1980. They have three children – Jared 26, Lauren 24 and Evan 23. In 1987 they pioneered to Micronesia. David worked as a family physician and Gayle home schooled their three small children. They returned to live in Silver Spring, Maryland, in 2000 where David is an Assistant Surgeon General of the USA. Both Gayle and David serve on the Local Spiritual Assembly and Gayle is a Representative for Ḥuqúqu'lláh.

Karen and Tim Shrimpton

Karen was born in Chicago and spent most of her childhood in Denver, Colorado. She moved with her family to England as a teenager and discovered the Bahá'í Faith while training to be a teacher in Liverpool. She declared at the age of 20 and served on her first Local Spiritual Assembly at the age of 21 in St Helens, Lancashire. Karen lived in several communities in England with her first husband Tom Fox before pioneering with their two children, Esme and Robert, and her second husband Tim Shrimpton to the Philippines in 1996. Subsequently they spent four years in Uganda where they adopted two beautiful souls, Jasmine and Kenny. Later Karen and Tim spent two years in Bangladesh and since 2006 have been living in East Asia. Karen has had the bounty of serving on external affairs committees and national children's education committees and participating in Ruhi study circles in four different countries.

Maureen and Nick Sier

Maureen grew up in Elgin in the northeast of Scotland and became a Bahá'í in 1976 at the age of 17. In 1978 she went to Malawi in Africa for a few months to see if she could be of service to the Bahá'ís there and ended up typing a book, *The New Garden*, in the local language. Maureen met her husband Nick that year and they were married in 1980. By 1987 she was mum to four children – Ben, Sonya, Zoe and Tom. In 1990 Maureen decided to go to university. This led her to do research in Samoa in 1995 and finally to move there with the family in 1997 to do her PhD and to work at the National University of Samoa. The family lived briefly in the village of Fa'atoia, then three years in the village of Puipaa and for almost two years in the town of Apia. They love Samoa and try to return there on an annual basis to visit friends and to be of service. Since returning to the UK in 2002 for family reasons Maureen has worked in interfaith development for a charity called the Scottish Inter-Faith Council and also for the Scottish government. She currently represents the Bahá'í community on the European Women of Faith Network.

Barbara Smith

Barbara spent her childhood in Wiltshire and her husband Terry was brought up in Bristol. Two years after they married in 1953 they immigrated to the Montreal area of Canada, and a couple of years later they moved out of the city to Beloeil in the province of Quebec. They both became Bahá'ís in 1961–2 and made up the LSA of Beloeil. It was a wonderfully united and happy LSA and the guidance and love that Barbara and Terry received from those Bahá'ís helped to make them strong in their early years in the Faith. Those lovely people were Bill and Priscilla Waugh, Mrs Ellen DeMille, John and Moira Pollitt, and David and Pam Fairchild. In 1966 Barbara and Terry left Canada and returned to England, settling in Chippenham, Wiltshire. Terry was an enthusiastic teacher of the Faith and passed away in 1983 in St Austell, Cornwall, where he and Barbara had settled two years earlier. Barbara continues to live in St Austell and for a number of years has been involved with interfaith activities in Cornwall.

(I would like to take the opportunity here to convey a thousand 'thank you's to the Smith family and, in particular to Terry, who first told me about the Bahá'í Faith in Montreal - Thelma Batchelor.)

Cymbeline Smith-Rowshan

Cymbeline was born in Sussex in the early seventies. She grew up in England, Zimbabwe and Mauritius. She learned about the Bahá'í Faith from her mother and enjoyed the diverse events the Bahá'í community held wherever she was in the world. She was drawn to the arts and spent her teenage years performing with Bahá'í groups around Europe. Cymbeline became a Bahá'í when she was 15 and has realized that that was only the beginning of her learning about life, the universe and everything! Her fascination with how we, as human beings, find meaning in our lives has taken her from having an acting career, to co-founding an all-female production company, FiddleHeadFern Productions, finishing her Master's degree in clinical psychology and starting her clinical practice! Cymbeline now lives in Los Angeles where she is raising her toddlers, twin boys, the biggest blessing in her life, with her husband Kamal.

David and Manijeh Smith

David and Manijeh met the day Manijeh became a Bahá'í in 1987 and were married in 1989 at the end of her year of service in Liverpool, with Manijeh joining David in his home front pioneering post in Leatherhead. Manijeh heard about the Faith while at school in England through the Khalilian family (at present, pioneers in Hong Kong and Gibraltar). David's parents became Bahá'ís in Montreal in 1960 when David was three years old. As a result of his dear friend Roxana Djalili persisting in inviting him to Bahá'í activities, he met friends like Peyman Sabeti, who encouraged him to read the Kitáb-i-Íqán, which changed his whole life. He served as secretary of the National Youth Committee and was on the organizing committee of both the Manchester Youth Conference and Peace Moves in Sheffield. With two small children, Bayan (born 1991) and Holly (born 1993), David and Manijeh pioneered to Zambia in 1994 without knowing where it was or what it was like! After consulting a map and a few amazing exemplary souls, the greatest adventure of their lives began when they arrived at the Banani International School. They learned what marriage was really about, they learned reliance on prayer and that the *only* source of succour and protection is Bahá'u'lláh. David had the bounty of serving on the National Spiritual Assembly for nine years and was privileged to attend the International Convention in 1998. Manijeh served on the National Teaching Committee and worked as secretary to the Continental Counsellor resident in Zambia. They arrived back in the UK in 2005 and live in Penzance, Cornwall.

Helen Smith

Helen (née Wilson) was born in Bellshill, Scotland, and later moved to England and Wales to complete her SRN and SCM studies. Always a champion for prisoners of conscience, she was an active member of Amnesty International as well as other organizations including Greenpeace and CND. During her time in Cardiff she became involved with the Evangelical movement, taking part not only in meetings and crusades but also in soup runs around the Cardiff dockland area. In 1971 she moved to Guernsey where she was employed as a midwife at the local hospital at which she worked until her marriage in 1974. Helen went to a Bahá'í public meeting after reading an article about the plight of the Bahá'ís in Iran at the beginning of the Iranian revolution and accepted the Faith of Bahá'u'lláh a few weeks later. In 1989 she pioneered to Lithuania, then part of the Soviet Union, where she remains until the present day.

Peter Smith

Peter Smith became a Bahá'í in Bristol in 1964 and was an active member of the British Bahá'í community for many years. He is one of the pioneers of the modern academic study of the Bahá'í Faith and has published several books on the Faith intended for a university audience – including most recently *An Introduction to the Bahá'í Faith* for Cambridge University Press. He also spent time in Africa in 1969 as one of the first generation of youth volunteers sent out from the UK in what has now become the year of service projects. He and his family moved to Thailand in 1985.

Rosie Smith

Rosie was born in 1987, the eldest of four children, and grew up in the quiet village of Connor Downs, Cornwall, not far from St Ives. The Smiths are a music-making, music-loving family. When she was 11 years old, Rosie moved with her family to Penticton, British Columbia, for a year. There they spent much of their time travel teaching on the Alaskan Highway and singing prayers together in the back of their pickup truck. Back in England a few years later, Rosie officially declared her faith in Bahá'u'lláh at the age of 15. In 2006, after she finished college, she left Cornwall at age 18 to do a year of service at Banani International Secondary School in Zambia. This service involved teaching a small class of students at the local primary school during the day and living in a dormitory of 28 teenage girls for whom she was immediately responsible at night. Currently Rosie is in her final year at the University of Manchester and very much involved in the local Bahá'í community.

Carol Spencer

Carol Spencer was born in Middlesex but did most of her growing up in North Yorkshire. She was raised in a practising Christian (Methodist) family and does not remember questioning the existence of God, though she questioned just about everything else. Leaving home at 18, Carol worked in Germany and the Lake District of the UK before going to university to study agricultural and environmental science. Meeting evangelical Christians there only served to deepen her conviction that God was accepting of people of different faiths. She moved to Wales, where she worked as a volunteer helping learning disabled adults gain agricultural and social skills, and she met, worked and talked with Bahá'ís. Eventually she decided to accept the daily challenge of being a Bahá'í. Carol went on to train as an occupational therapist (OT). She spent three years (1997–2000) with the VSO in Palawan, in the Philippines, helping to train local health workers in rehabilitation skills, while being an active member of the Bahá'í community. Carol has been involved in teaching Bahá'í children's classes and acted as director of the Thomas Breakwell School Northeast for three years. She continues to work as an OT and to raise her adopted son.

Irene Taafaki

Irene and Falai-Riva Taafaki have been living in the Marshall Islands in the central Pacific since November 1994. Born in Cardiff, Irene and her sister Val Rhind are the daughters of Rose Jones, the first Bahá'í to reside in Wales. Trained as a teacher in the UK, Irene pioneered to the Gilbert and Ellice Islands in 1971, where she met and married Falai-Riva, who is from Tuvalu. After spending ten years (1975–85) serving at the New Era School, India, the family moved to the United Sates where both she and Falai-Riva earned their doctorates from the University of Massachusetts. Irene has written books and articles for children, teachers and parents, including *Thoughts: Education for Peace and One World*, published by George Ronald. While in the US she served on the National Bahá'í Education Task Force, which developed the US Core Curriculum, its teacher training programme and co-authored *Foundations for a Spiritual Education*. In the Marshall Islands she developed the Moral Education curriculum for the Majuro schools and co-authored books and articles on aspects of Marshallese culture. Irene is currently the Director of the University of the South Pacific Campus. She and Falai-Riva have three children – Munirih, Jane and Justen – and four grandchildren.

Gill and Fuad Ta'eed

Gill was born into a family of dockworkers from the heart of Liverpool, the city famous for 'pop' music and, although she never met him, is quite closely related to Ringo Starr, the drummer for the Beatles. She became a Bahá'í at the age of 19 while studying psychology in Bangor, North Wales, after being taken to a fireside by John Netherwood. John had learned about the Faith from her husband Fuad, so she and Fuad had a spiritual connection before they met in 1972. They married the next year and always wanted to serve the Faith together and ultimately to pioneer overseas. After serving as home front pioneers in West Lothian, Scotland, and then in Doncaster, Yorkshire, they lived for a year in Birmingham while Fuad completed his Master's degree to increase the chances of finding a post overseas. In 1983 when their children, Vahid and Collis, were five and three, they left for Papua New Guinea, where they had the joy of serving the Faith for 20 years. In 2003 they arrived in Tasmania not knowing what the future would hold. They have been truly blessed in every way. Despite a gap of 30 years Gill has been able to work as a clinical psychologist and Fuad has continued to work in his profession while also having the bounty of being appointed, by the Universal House of Justice, as a resource person for Papua New Guinea. Every day they are thankful for having the bounty of serving the Five Year Plan and watching the growth of the Faith in this beautiful island.

Angela and Robert Tidswell

Angela and Rob were born and grew up in Thurrock, Essex, attending the same school, although they didn't know each other at that point. They met in 1966 when Angela was 14 and Rob 16, marrying in 1969. They declared together in 1977, helping to form the first Local Spiritual Assembly of Thurrock in 1979, serving as its secretary and chairman. Other members included Angela's mother Ivy and sisters Lorna and Sheila. Angela and Rob were taught the Faith by Kaff and Tony Conroy, Lois and Philip Hainsworth, Hugh McKinley, Angela's sister Lorna, and many others. In 1982 Angela and Rob pioneered to Rochford, Essex, to open it to the Faith. They later pioneered to Colchester to bring it back to Assembly status after a two year lapse. There they served on the LSA until they pioneered to Bulgaria in 2003, where they currently reside. They have four children who have all embraced the Faith: Alison born in 1970, Daniel in 1973, Elisa in 1981 and they later adopted Amy, born in 1987. The Faith rapidly spread throughout Angela's family and at the time of her mother's passing in 1993 there were a total of 22 believers. For 11 years Angela served the Faith at the Ḥaẓíratu'l-Quds in London as a secretary/personal assistant.

Anisa Turner (Barrett)

Anisa was born in Bangor, north Wales, and spent her early years in Colwyn Bay, Southport and Shrewsbury with her mother and grandmother (Zoë and Lou Turner). She caught the travel bug early after accompanying her folks on various Bahá'í teaching trips and pioneer moves. By the time she was five she had travelled with Lou and Zoë to Kenya, Uganda, Tanzania, Australia and Vanuatu. She was delighted to be able to return to the Pacific islands as part of her youth year of service in 1997, spending six months in Tonga. On her return from Tonga she moved to London to study at university. Anisa has a degree in social anthropology and development studies from SOAS (University of London). She moved to Edinburgh in 2002 and met her husband while working in university administration. She feels blessed to live in the beautiful city of Edinburgh with her husband and her young son. As a full-time mum her days are now filled with baking, colouring, playing trains and cars and cleaning felt-pen off the furniture! She hopes someday to continue her travels, starting with the Western Isles of Scotland!

Davey Vincent

Davey was born in Scotland but later went 'home', as he says, to Africa. He found the Faith at 16, having had a conversation with the father of a school friend – an atheist who decided to take him to a fireside at the home of his boss (Nuri Sabet in Motherwell). As a student Davey's focus was on teaching children and junior youth at different events around the UK. During his time at university he took a year off to travel teach and home front pioneer in Berwickshire during the final push of the first Five Year Plan, and then went back to finish his degree. In 1981 he pioneered to St Vincent, Windward Islands, before returning in 1984 to the UK with an adopted son in need of schooling. For the next five years he served on different LSAs and committees in the UK until at last, in 1989, he was enabled to pioneer to Mozambique, where he remained for the next ten years. Next he moved briefly to Malawi before pioneering to South Africa. In 2007 he returned to the UK for an intended short stay but remained longer, partly owing to some health concerns. Although returning to social work in Brighton, he has kept his house in South Africa, hoping to go home again to the place he loves so much.

Margaret and Bob Watkins

Margaret was born in 1928. As a young child she was evacuated to Wales during the war. She married her husband, Robert (Bob), in 1964 and their son, Paul, was born in 1965. Margaret became a Bahá'í on 12 November

1965 and Bob accepted the Faith shortly afterwards in Haifa following the 1968 Palermo Conference. They were active members of Bahá'í communities in London and Reading and later in Totnes, Devon, where they opened The New Era health food restaurant which doubled as a Bahá'í meeting venue. In 1985 they left the UK to serve at the Bahá'í World Centre, Margaret serving as building manager for the Seat of the Universal House of Justice and Bob in a supervisory role within the maintenance department. After a stint back in the UK, Bob and Margaret pioneered in 1990 to Belgrade in the former Yugoslavia. Despite the upheavals in the country they stayed in their post for four years and oversaw the first translations and publishing of the Bahá'í writings into Serbo-Croat. In his final years Bob was a devoted member of the (UK) Venues Committee. He passed away in 2007 aged 80. Margaret continued as an active member of the South Hams community in Devon until suffering a severe stroke in 2008 and is currently residing in a nursing home in West London.

Marie and Eddie Whiteside

Eddie and Marie grew up in Northern Ireland where they became Bahá'ís in 1968. Following their marriage in 1969 they pioneered to Ghana, West Africa, then a British priority goal. Eddie was elected to the first National Spiritual Assembly of Ghana in 1970 and served as its treasurer. During this time they had the bounty of meeting Hands of the Cause Rúḥíyyih Khánum, Enoch Olinga, Dr Muhájir and Mr Khazeh. They left Ghana reluctantly in 1971 on the advice of Rúḥíyyih Khánum, owing to illness, and returned to Northern Ireland. Their next overseas pioneering post was to the Falkland Islands in 1988. They were accompanied by their younger daughter Kerry, aged eight. The family served there for six years before returning in 1994 to Newtownards, Northern Ireland. As well as serving on various Local Spiritual Assemblies, their present one being Newtownards, both have served as assistants to Board members. Eddie has been serving on the Bahá'í Council for Northern Ireland since it became an elected body. They also act as tutors for the Ruhi institute courses. They have two grown up daughters, Jenni and Kerry, and two grandchildren.

Michele Wilburn

Born and raised in New Zealand and Fiji, Michele initially trained as a school teacher in New Zealand, majoring in physical education and the arts. She became a Bahá'í in New Zealand in 1978, following a series of dreams. She travelled extensively before settling in London to raise her daughter Romani, while developing a career in production and publishing. In 1993 her book

Starbound, encompassing health, fitness and lifestyle planning, was published. Having been actively involved in the UK Bahá'í community, Michele adopted Greece as her personal teaching goal. She pioneered to the Ionian Greek island of Zakynthos in 2004 where she has remained while her daughter completed her studies in history at Cambridge. Michele continues to operate her health and fitness businesses with online Internet shops in four continents. In Zakynthos she has developed Energyia Holistic holidays, which are attended by guests from all over the world during the Greek tourist season from May to November. With her daughter she now also films, presents and produces DVD productions, weddings and corporate documentaries. Their work in these fields has provided a perfect opportunity for Michele and Romani to introduce the Faith to the people of the island. Embracing the core of Greek island life, including the arts and music, has enabled them to become thoroughly acquainted with the traditions, religion and soul of the Zakynthian people, who are increasingly open and ready for the message of Bahá'u'lláh.

Tom Wilmot

Tom grew up in sleepy Suffolk on the east coast of England, and it was really a series of chance events and decisions that led him to work with Jimmy McGilligan at the Barli Institute in India. Tom studied science at the University of Bath and it was there that he signed up as a volunteer through a UK-based development education charity called Development in Action. He learned a huge amount during his time at the Barli Institute, from an Indian, a Bahá'í and simply a human perspective. This was Tom's first experience of the Bahá'í Faith and he has stayed in touch with the community ever since. Last year he got married to Kirsty, who also volunteered with Development in Action in southern India. They travelled around India for their honeymoon and visited both their places of work, a perfect opportunity to catch up with what was going on at Barli. Tom has huge respect for the love and dedication he discovered there and can only hope that he has managed to employ some of this in his career as a teacher back in Suffolk, where he now teaches science in a secondary school.

Andrew Wilson

Andrew grew up in Wales and the Caribbean. He always had a great love for the Faith and looked forward with excitement to his fifteenth birthday when he could declare. As a child he taught the Faith to three people who became Bahá'ís. He is now married and lives in the UK.

Guita and Shahob Youssefian

Shahob and Guita were both born in Tehran to third generation Bahá'ís. Shahob's family moved to London at the time of the World Congress in 1963. One day in Iran, Guita, who was only 13, listened to an inspiring talk by Counsellor Dr Masih Farhangi (since martyred). He spoke about the importance and bounties of pioneering. When he finished he asked for those in the huge audience who wanted to pioneer to raise their hands. Being very young and sitting in the front row, Guita felt her hand shooting up but she refrained from doing so. However, in her eagerness to see how many adults were moved to pioneer, she turned expectantly to look behind her but, much to her surprise and regret, not a single hand was raised. That is when she pledged to herself to pioneer as soon as she was able to make an independent decision. In the 1970s Guita and her family moved to the UK and became pioneers in Elstree, Hertfordshire. After Guita and Shahob were married in 1984 they decided to apply only for jobs in countries that the International Teaching Centre designated as international pioneering posts. When Shahob completed his PhD in 1986, he applied for posts in many developing countries and Guita constantly prayed that they would be guided to a place where Bahá'u'lláh would be their only supporter. That is how they ended up in Akita, in northern Japan, three days before Naw-Rúz 1987. Their two children, Shafa and Adora, were born in Akita and the city's first LSA was formed at Riḍván in the Holy Year, 1992. They have now served as pioneers in Japan for 23 years.

Shirin Youssefian Maanian

Shirin was born and raised in a Bahá'í family in England. In 1991 she pioneered to Romania where she lived for three years and met her husband Socrates. This led to her next pioneering post, Athens, Greece, where she has been living since 1994. Her mother and sister are pioneers in South Africa and her brother is a pioneer in Japan. Her services to the Faith have included membership on the European Bahá'í Youth Council and the National Spiritual Assemblies of Romania and Greece, and as external affairs officer in Greece. Her professional work as an actress has produced theatre covering themes such as race relations, human rights abuse and the treatment of women in Iran. In 2004 and 2005 Shirin internationally toured a one-woman play about the life of Ṭáhirih, *Pure*, written by Annabel Knight, and was invited to perform it at the United Nations headquarters in New York. She is a founding member of the music group SKY which in 2007 released the CD *A Cycle of Divine Love Songs*, a collection of Bahá'í writings set to original music and sung a cappella. SKY is currently performing live concerts around Europe.

Bibliography

'Abdu'l-Bahá. *Selections from the Writings of 'Abdu'l-Bahá.* Haifa: Bahá'í World Centre, 1978.
— *Tablets of the Divine Plan.* Wilmette, IL: Bahá'í Publishing Trust, 1993.

Bahá'u'lláh. *Gleanings from the Writings of Bahá'u'lláh.* Wilmette, IL: Bahá'í Publishing Trust, 1983.

Grant, David R. *The Seven Year Hitch: A Family Odyssey.* London: Simon & Schuster, 1999; Pocketbooks (pb), 2000.
— *Spirit of the Vikings: A Journey in the Kayak Bahá'í Viking.* Long Riders Guild Press, 2008.

Lights of Guidance: A Bahá'í Reference File. Compiled by Helen Hornby. New Delhi: Bahá'í Publishing Trust, 5th ed. 1997.

Momen, Moojan. 'Bahá'í Faith in the United Kingdom'. UK Bahá'í Heritage Site. http://users.whsmithnet.co.uk/ispalin/heritage/ukhist.htm.

Nabíl-i-A'zam. *The Dawn-Breakers: Nabíl's Narrative of the Early Days of the Bahá'í Revelation.* Wilmette, IL: Bahá'í Publishing Trust, 1970.

Quickeners of Mankind: Pioneering in a World Community. Wilmette, IL: Bahá'í Publishing Trust, 1998.

Rabbaní, Rúhíyyih. *A Manual for Pioneers.* New Delhi: Bahá'í Publishing Trust, 1974.

The Reality of Man. Wilmette, IL: Bahá'í Publishing Trust, 1962.

Shoghi Effendi. *The Promised Day is Come.* Wilmette, IL: Bahá'í Publishing Trust, rev. ed. 1980.
— *The Unfolding Destiny of the British Bahá'í Community: The Messages of the Guardian of the Bahá'í Faith to the Bahá'ís of the British Isles.* London: Bahá'í Publishing Trust, 1981.
— *The World Order of Bahá'u'lláh.* Wilmette, IL: Bahá'í Publishing Trust, 1991.

The Universal House of Justice. Letter to the Bahá'ís of Albania, Riḍván 1992.
— Letter to the Followers of Bahá'u'lláh in Europe, Riḍván 153 (1996).
— Letter to a National Spiritual Assembly, 30 March 1971.
— Letter to the Participants at the Arctic Teaching Conference and the Inauguration of the Lapland Bahá'í Centre in Inari, 1 November 1996.
— Message Addressed to the Continental Boards of Counsellors, 27 December 2005.

References

1. Hand of the Cause of God John Robarts, from an address at The Gathering, Batterwood, Ontario, Canada, 3 August 1980, in *Quickeners of Mankind*, pp. 102–3.
2. Shoghi Effendi, *Unfolding Destiny*, p. 385.
3. ibid. p. 384.
4. The Universal House of Justice, Message addressed to the Continental Boards of Counsellors, 27 December 2005.
5. ibid.
6. 'Abdu'l-Bahá, *Tablets of the Divine Plan*, pp. 41–2.
7. Shoghi Effendi, *Unfolding Destiny*, p. v.
8. Bahá'u'lláh, *Gleanings*, p. 334.
9. From a letter of the Universal House of Justice to a National Spiritual Assembly, 30 March 1971.
10. From a letter of the Universal House of Justice to all National Spiritual Assemblies, 5 June 1966, in *Lights of Guidance*, no. 1957, p. 579.
11. Rabbaní, *Manual for Pioneers*, p. vii.
12. ibid. p. 86.
13. Shoghi Effendi, *Unfolding Destiny*, p. 243.
14. ibid. pp. 251–2.
15. Momen, 'Bahá'í Faith in the United Kingdom', UK Bahá'í Heritage Site, http://users.whsmithnet.co.uk/ispalin/heritage/ukhist.htm.
16. From a letter written on behalf of Shoghi Effendi to the National Spiritual Assembly of the British Isles, *Unfolding Destiny*, p. 305.
17. See, for example, ibid. p. 306.
18. From a letter of Shoghi Effendi to the National Spiritual Assembly of the British Isles, ibid. pp. 310–11.
19. ibid. pp. 369–70.
20. Momen, 'Bahá'í Faith in the United Kingdom', UK Bahá'í Heritage Site, http://users.whsmithnet.co.uk/ispalin/heritage/ukhist.htm.
21. The Universal House of Justice, Letter to the Bahá'ís of Albania, Riḍván 1992.
22. Shoghi Effendi, *Promised Day is Come*, p. 122.
23. Bahá'u'lláh, *Gleanings*, p. 334.
24. ibid. p. 288.
25. The Báb, quoted in Nabíl, *Dawn-Breakers*, p. 92.
26. Bahá'u'lláh, quoted in Shoghi Effendi, *World Order*, p. 108.
27. The Universal House of Justice, To the Followers of Bahá'u'lláh in Europe, Riḍván 153 (1996).
28. 'Abdu'l-Bahá, *Selections*, p. 270.
29. Bahá'u'lláh, *Gleanings*, p. 334.
30. From a letter of the Universal House of Justice to the Participants at the Arctic Teaching Conference and the Inauguration of the Lapland Bahá'í Centre in Inari, 1 November 1996.
31. Bahá'u'lláh, *Gleanings*, p. 295.
32. 'Abdu'l-Bahá, in *Reality of Man*, p. 47.

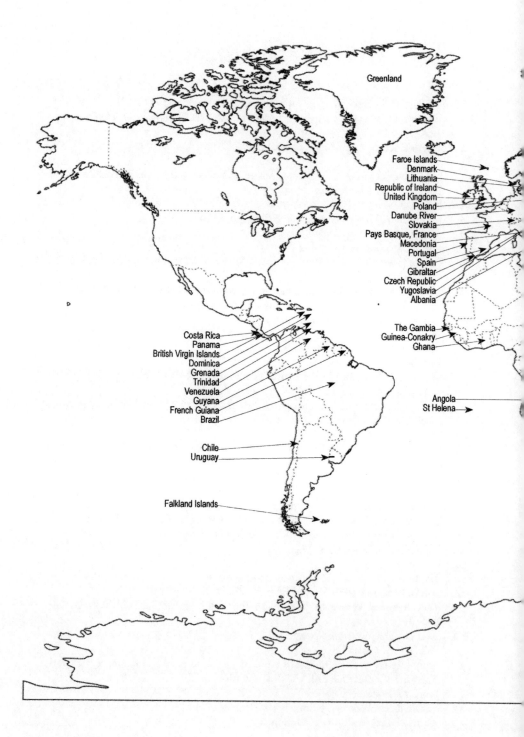

Greenland

Faroe Islands
Denmark
Lithuania
Republic of Ireland
United Kingdom
Poland
Danube River
Slovakia
Pays Basque, France
Macedonia
Portugal
Spain
Gibraltar
Czech Republic
Yugoslavia
Albania

The Gambia
Guinea-Conakry
Ghana

Costa Rica
Panama
British Virgin Islands
Dominica
Grenada
Trinidad
Venezuela
Guyana
French Guiana
Brazil

Angola
St Helena

Chile
Uruguay

Falkland Islands

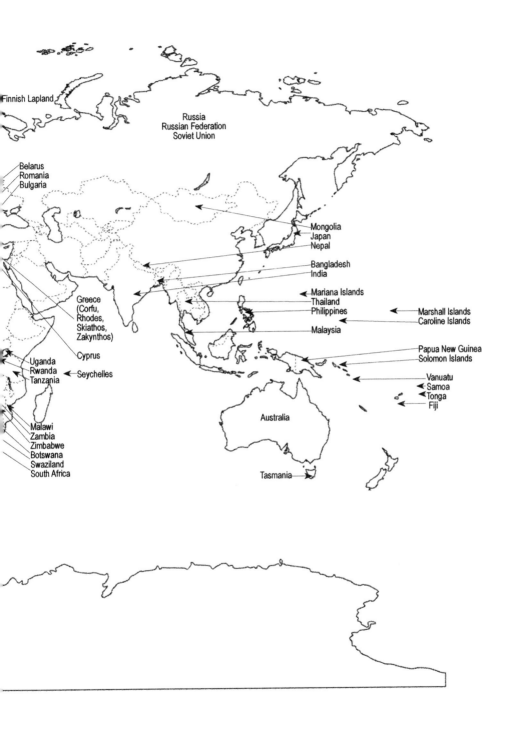

Finnish Lapland

Russia
Russian Federation
Soviet Union

Belarus
Romania
Bulgaria

Mongolia
Japan
Nepal

Bangladesh
India

Greece
(Corfu,
Rhodes,
Skiathos,
Zakynthos)

Mariana Islands
Thailand
Philippines

Marshall Islands
Caroline Islands

Malaysia

Cyprus

Uganda
Rwanda
Tanzania

Seychelles

Papua New Guinea
Solomon Islands

Vanuatu
Samoa
Tonga
Fiji

Australia

Malawi
Zambia
Zimbabwe
Botswana
Swaziland
South Africa

Tasmania